# MANAGING BUSINESS TRAVEL

Improving the
Bottom Line through
Effective Travel Management

# MANAGING BUSINESS TRAVEL

## Improving the Bottom Line through Effective Travel Management

*Darryl Jenkins*

**National Business Travel Association**

**BUSINESS ONE IRWIN**
Homewood, Illinois 60430

This publication is designed to provide accurate and authoritative information in regard to the subject matter covered. It is sold with the understanding that neither the author nor the publisher is engaged in rendering legal, accounting, or other professional service. If legal advice or other expert assistance is required, the services of a competent professional person should be sought.

*From a Declaration of Principles jointly adopted by a Committee of the American Bar Association and a Committee of Publishers.*

Sponsoring editor: Cynthia A. Zigmund
Production manager: Mary Jo Parke
Jacket designer: Renee Kyczek Nordstrom
Designer: Heidi J. Baughman
Compositor: The Wheetley Company, Inc.
Typeface: 11/13 Palatino
Printer: Book Press

**Library of Congress Cataloging-in-Publication Data**

Jenkins, Darryl.
   Managing business travel : improving the bottom line through effective travel management / by Darryl Jenkins.
       p.    cm.
   Includes index.
   ISBN 1-55623-751-0
   1. Business travel—Management.   I. Title.
G156.5.B86J45   1993
658.3'83—dc20                                              92–25685

*Printed in the United States of America*

1  2  3  4  5  6  7  8  9  0  BP  9  8  7  6  5  4  3  2

*This book is dedicated with great affection to my parents
Hazel and Gerald Jenkins (deceased), Arthur Jabaay (who is alive
and well), and to my wife's parents Norma and Wes Kirby.*

# Foreword

By John Hintz, President
*National Business Travel Association*

## WHAT IS TRAVEL MANAGEMENT?

Travel management gives a company the ability to control its third-largest cost. It provides an oversight to control all travel-related expenses: airline usage, hotel usage, rental-car usage, and, as much as possible, meetings, corporate training, and any other operation that involves travel. It may also interlink with other positions in the company—controlling the way purchases are made by adopting a charge-card program; affecting the company's expense-reporting system; and increasing buying power by virtue of being able to identify the volume in all of the relative areas. Armed with this knowledge of volume, you now have a unique ability to direct that volume. Directing that volume simply means applying a controlled travel purchasing program. Controlled purchasing programs, even for relatively small amounts of volume, can be very beneficial to small companies and certainly to large companies.

Where does the travel management role belong in a company? In some companies, travel management is under the financial department; in others, it is an administrative function: in still others, it's identified as a human resource function. But a company that uses its volume and manages its travel for the purpose of saving money is clearly engaged in a financial package and a financial product, and thus, it would seem that the financial area should certainly get involved and should certainly have an incentive for controlling potentially large volumes of outlay.

The average travel manager is, at this point in time, probably undergraded, with less authority than is needed to do the job to the maximum effect. He or she is probably well-educated in practical terms, but may lack a professional travel training. With few exceptions, travel managers tend to be, middle-management supervisors or managers. There are probably several dozen companies that have senior management personnel who have the ability to enter into contracts and to steer volume. And this is something that will grow as the awareness of travel management programs becomes more widespread and as the National Business Travel Association (NBTA) is able to affect the training opportunities for people engaged in this area.

One of the primary programs that NBTA is currently emphasizing is to define what the travel manager does in major companies that have good control. This will help us to establish the credentials for the practitioner that fills that role, and, for companies that don't know exactly what kind of travel management a company their size should have, it will give them a much better idea of what's controllable and at what level it should be controlled. Hopefully, this program will give people an opportunity, through practical training, to grow into the position of travel manager and to perform all of the functions that may or may not have been their responsibility in the past. For example, in many companies the traffic department controls the rental-car program. And yet rental cars are clearly a part of overall T&E, and so the decision-makers may not talk to each other when they decide which rental car should be used. And indeed, traffic departments, by applying traffic practices and procedures, may be missing a lot of benefits that are actually out there, especially covert, or soft dollar, benefits that may accrue to an integrated travel program.

Next, I think we should define our terms: *travel coordinator, travel administrator, travel management supervisor, travel manager.* Many people have the generic working title of travel manager who are nowhere near the management level in their companies. They certainly will have the opportunity, with a little bit more input from NBTA, to work toward management level. Also, in many companies, especially smaller ones, there is only one practitioner in this field. Growth is limited to taking on additional duties in addition to travel responsibilities, or being promoted up and away from travel management responsibilities. Another way to grow, which I think many people have not exercised to the maximum, is to take your experience and go to a larger company, where experience with larger volume will be a definite benefit.

There are a lot of companies out there that have a sizable travel budget and have never done anything to control it. For companies who have never managed travel before, depending on their size, there are some excellent consulting practitioners out there. There are travel management companies or agencies that certainly would be more than happy to advise them on their needs and their possibilities. And there are a lot of practitioners who could be hired as inside experts, if you will, to put together a travel management program. For a company that is starting out, it's important for that responsibility to be given to a management-level person, at least to do the study and the initial investigations as to what's available. New travel managers might contact travel management companies, and perhaps a travel consultant or two, to ask them what they would do it they were given the assignment, and then, by attending a number of industry forums where they could ask questions of real practitioners, develop a basic idea of what level of travel management might fit their operation.

Anybody that is anticipating setting up a travel management program at this point needs to know the ups and downs, the pros and cons, of these programs, and certainly needs to have support from very senior management before even embarking on a program like this. Programs can only survive if you have the approval at the board-of-directors level, otherwise the programs don't have the proper teeth and the ability to move volume that is necessary to really be a travel management program.

There has been a great deal of discussion lately about where the control of travel should reside—within the corporation or with an outside agency. Having an outside agency handle all aspects of a company's travel is an interesting concept, but one that doesn't work. I think the most successful programs are those in which the company hiring the service has in place an overseer (the administrator or manager, whichever level is appropriate to their volume), who works as a liaison with the travel management company and makes sure that the travel management company is applying the will of the company instead of steering volume for personal gain or other incentives from outside sources. I see it very much as evolving into a partnership.

When you leave the travel management function to the travel management company, you have developed an immediate conflict of interest, in that commissions are paid by the suppliers for services provided by the agency. Some of those incentives contain overrides that reward the travel management company for moving volume to a certain vendor, whether or not that vendor is the first choice of the client company. This conflict of interest really prevents travel management companies from serving appropriately in the role of travel manager. Now, for a company with relatively small volume, you may gain a lot by simply directing that volume to a travel management company, and in exchange you could at least be the recipient of travel management reports, which would clearly outline the travel patterns of your company.

In the last year, there has been a great deal of change in the business travel management industry. I think that in the future a manager is going to need an ever-stronger mandate from the company to enter into agreements. These are not contracts per se; they are agreements, because you are not pledging a fixed amount of dollars, but you are pledging to use, because of a price differential, one carrier over another. Due to recent airline pricing initiatives that severely limit the number of prices available, I think that corporate users will have to make a stronger commitment, which may put a company in a penalty situation should it not live up to its side of the bargain. Of course, a commitment to the program will only work if the airlines are willing to hold the price at a fixed value over a specific period of time. A failure to do that, or the introduction of many more fares in a market, will only tend to dilute the volume and the potential buying power.

But over the next few years, I think that travel managers must be aware of their volume. Knowing the full extent of their volume and their travel patterns is the key that will let them enter into negotiated agreements. You can no longer bluff; you can no longer guess. So when you have that responsibility, you are going to have to have a good travel management partner who can provide you with the data, which you will then use to the benefit of your firm.

Over the past ten years, airlines have tried several times to create an artificial value for their product by restricting fares or forming an agreement between carriers to match existing fare levels. The latest attempt, in April of 1992, has still left it unclear whether or not they will succeed this time. This time, the pricing formula was clearly aimed at getting as close to the actual cost of doing business as possible, since carriers who are already in a Chapter 11 situation need a more ready flow of cash than can be generated by a rock-bottom-price war. It is still undetermined how many will fall to this, or whether the corporate travel management community has the ability to divert enough volume to these weaker carriers, at the expense of the major carriers, to make a point that volume buying is still a viable option and that those who have the ability to move that volume are willing to.

Corporate travel managers are going to have to learn to blow their own horn. They are going to have to have the ammunition, much of which is going to have to be supplied by an organization like NBTA, to take to their management, saying, "For a company our size, managing $10 million, this is the structure that most corporations in America use. As you can see by this, this is a person at a certain grade level, it is a person with this kind of knowledge, it is a person with this kind of experience. I clearly fit that model, with the exception that I am undergraded and under-paid according to this scenario. Over the past year, based on the numbers that I have from our travel management company, I have effected X amount of travel, and I have saved X amount of money for the company. I am a team player. I work with all the different people I interface with in the company to the benefit of the firm. And clearly, I am a player who should be recognized for my contributions." A little bit of personal lobbying is definitely appropriate, provided we supply the tools.

Let us consider for a moment who the corporate travel manager is working for. Is it the corporation or the corporate traveler? Clearly both. The travel manager is the advocate of the company. In that he or she needs to make sure that he or she has provided an internal service. Flexibility, getting the people to the site where they can do business, is first and foremost. Selecting the right suppliers, based on the service that they are going to provide to the traveler, is very, very important. And the third area, assuming you have met the first two criteria, is to do that at the most economical cost to the firm. That is the basis of the travel manager's function.

Beyond that, with volume buying in place, the travel manager can affect the overall budgets of many different operations that require travel as part of their work.

You know, justifying your abilities is not hard to do if you have the right tools. I may be in a very enviable position, but I do work in direct line to the chief financial manager. I work for the corporate CFO—chief financial officer. In 1987, I was given a charter that was very, very strong for its time. The charter supported the idea that we will do cooperative buying. Even though I work for a company, a partnership where individual offices have a lot of autonomy, I had a very strong charter from the top. Knowing the culture of your company is very, very important. I knew that even with that very strong charter from the top I would still have to overcome an individual office's ability to opt to do things its own way. So I had to take a strong charter from the top and sell it from the user end up to get concurrence from all the potential users. And what we did was set up a travel-buying cooperative, so that everyone was getting far more out of the collective benefits of the operation than they were giving up individually. It's been a very successful program. But I am also, I think, very privileged and probably very much the exception in that because of the way it was set up by our board of directors, every year I must go back to the board of directors and tell them how we did and what our plans are to fine-tune the program in the future, and give them some idea of the financial benefits of the package. Every year I have had a more successful story to tell; and every year I have come back with a stronger charter than I had before. I think this is particularly beneficial to our operation in a partnership environment. And, to my knowledge, though others have tried it, we are still the most successful partnership travel-buying cooperative in the industry.

## THE ROLE OF NBTA IN TRAINING
## NEW TRAVEL MANAGERS

NBTA is going to take a strong lead in training new people coming into the travel management industry. New managers should attend the NBTA summer conventions because in several sessions during the year, and in several sessions that are provided by other industry practitioners and magazines with NBTA sanction and support, they will have opportunities for networking. ~ membership directory, new managers will find names of p~ their area or their industry that perhaps they would be able to for advice. Certainly the networking factor is paramount.

Secondly, NBTA provides a basic travel managers' qualification course. It is a practitioner's course that covers all of the basic areas of negotiating including the way the different suppliers are set up to market their products; what is negotiable and what is not; and an explanation of how the computer reservation systems work. And that will certainly be a benefit. Being able to attend the national convention is a tremendous opportunity for the first-time attendee. We have special programs that are set up just for first-time attendees—a special lunch, a special welcome, people that will tell them how to use the show to their maximum benefit, people who will sit down and look at the course selections that they have made and tell them whether or not that's what they really need for what they're trying to do, or whether that particular program is too advanced for them. In fact, our entire convention is actually set up so that we can identify the courses that are appropriate for the beginning practitioner. Later on, we have courses that are identified for the very sophisticated and experienced practitioner. These tend to be more like round-table discussions where theory and actual practice can be discussed. But the first-time user definitely gains by being a member of NBTA.

## THE CERTIFIED CORPORATE TRAVEL MANAGER (CCTE)

The designation CCTE is really a professional practitioner acknowledgment, and we need CCTE. We need more recognition for the basic travel managers program, and we need more people to take it and to be recognized. We need more self-study materials that people can study on their own while earning points toward their CCTE. We need to capitalize on the abilities of our people who are well beyond CCTE qualification and honor those people with a fellowship, keeping them active in not only talking to other groups about their own knowledge, but working with automation suppliers and carrier suppliers of all kinds to develop new ways to market products, and new ways to purchase those products that would be acceptable from the corporate standpoint. I think there is plenty of room for all those areas.

# Acknowledgments

The task of writing a book like this is really too much for any one person to do with authority. The most I can claim to have done is gather the thoughts of many people, all of whom have accomplished more than I can ever hope to. The person who helped me the most was my wife Arlene. On more than one night she was up with me until midnight making corrections on my manuscript and offering suggestions. When push comes to shove, there are no people who have known me for a long time who do not realize that there was not much to my life before Arlene. Next in line has to come my editor Cindy Zigmund, who, as I am happy to remind her, turned down my first proposal to do this book. Her patience with me as I wrote this book is greatly appreciated. Writers are not supposed to say nice things about editors and I will not break this tradition, but we all know that good books come about only because there are good editors. In addition to Cindy, I am thankful to all of the swell people at Irwin. Over the past year I have come to have a great deal of respect for their abilities and am looking forward to many more books with them. I would also like to thank my publisher, Beth Bettram, and my public relations advisors Melanie Chionis and Julie Thompson. What can I say about my time with Margaret DeWald, other than "I love you."

At a very early stage in writing this book, Paulette O'Donnell at Delta Airlines introduced me to a number of people who were instrumental in shaping my thoughts about this book. The person who opened the most doors for me was John Hintz, the president of The National Business Travel Association. John's encouragement was monumental, and without his help I would still be out meeting people. John's contribution to the advancement of travel management is without parallel.

The outline that I am using was suggested to me by Michael Hadlow at US Travel. Almost all of the material that is included in the various chapters was obtained from telephone or personal interviews. Unless a specific reference is cited, the material quoted is from interviews. A number of articles are quoted from various trade magazines and they are cited. Laurie Berger and Melissa Abernathy at *Corporate Travel* magazine spent a great deal of time helping me, as did Nadine Godwin at *Travel Weekly*. Scott Bray at *Managing Business Travel* magazine also sent me helpful material. Don Munro, a free-lance writer, also contributed important material to this manuscript.

John Riepe gave me invaluable tips for writing the material in chapter 1. John spent a great deal of time with me and helped me in understanding the travel manager's job. A lot of the material in chapter 1 came from my fifteen years in the industry. I am indebted to individuals such as David Wardell at US Travel, Jeff Hoffman at CTI, and Bob Cross at Aeronomics Incorporated, who are the real automation experts in this industry, for the education they gave me.

Most of the material in chapter 2 was suggested to me by Phil Tedeschi at Reliance Electric. His CCTE thesis was an invaluable source of information. Carol Salcito, who is now working with Harold Seligman at Management Alternatives, and Cathy Armstrong, who is at Fokker Aircraft, also spent a great deal of time helping me with this chapter. Jeff Lang, at Amex Consulting Services, wrote a very complete job description for this book.

I took a great deal of material for chapter 3 from *Corporate Travel* magazine, Runzheimer International, and Amex Consulting Services. The chats I had with Peter Sontag and Walter Freedman about policy were pleasant experiences that I cherish. Another pleasant experience was getting to know Sheila Bender at Colgate Palmolive. Sheila is one of the savviest people I know. Jim Carey, a personal friend, helped me develop material about the average-fare myth. Michael Woodward also gave me a great deal of material about budgets. Charles Roumas at Travel One offered the case on professional sports.

The amount of time Harold Seligman at Management Alternatives spent with me on chapters 4 and 5 is without parallel. I am proud to count Harold as a friend. John Hintz's CCTE thesis formed the basis of a very good case on consolidation. Even though they are attorneys, I have come to respect the work of John Caldwell and Mark Pestronk, who contributed valuable information to this book. Bary Berglund at The Center for Creative Leadership also contributed greatly to my thinking.

During the time period when I was researching the first part of the book, I also had the honor of meeting Norman Sherlock, executive director at the National Business Travel Association; Steve Taylor at Lifeco; Hal Rosenbluth at Rosenbluth Travel; Michael Arrington at Arrington Travel; and Harold Stevens at Stevens Travel Management. They all greatly influenced my thinking.

Nancy Wells at IVI Travel convinced me of the importance of including a chapter on quality. I took great liberties in quoting from *Service America* by Zemke and Albrecht and thank Irwin Publishers for their kind permission to do so. Horst Schultze, president of the Ritz Carlton, became one of my heroes in the industry when I did research on this subject. I also had the pleasure of meeting Rolfe Shellenberger and including material from him. Rolfe, along with Harold Seligman, make up a lot of the wisdom and maturity of this business. Jeff Hoffman's suggestions to include automation factors in the quality chapter were well taken and used.

I felt it important to include meals in the section on vendors and thank Jeff Lang for his assistance. I probably got a little carried away in the airline and hotel chapters on automation, but what the heck. If you do not feel inclined, skip the automation sections and go to the negotiating parts. At the same time, it is important to realize that the automation aspects of this industry shape what we do.

Bill Todd and Ray Hays at Choice Hotels, Jack Ferguson at Guest Quarters, Mike Pusitari at Marriott, Joanne Scaglia and all of the other the nice people at PepsiCo, and Roger Mierisch at Rosenbluth Travel all pitched in to make the chapter on hotels one of the best in the book.

Working with Bonnie Wallsch on meetings was a high point for me. I am looking forward to other work with her. Again I am indebted to Nancy Wells, who took me to task for originally planning to put this chapter later in the book.

Gerry Dee at National Car Rental was very helpful. I have never met anybody who is as good at returning phone calls as Gerry. Susan Carney at Hertz also provided material.

I had no prior experience in charter air before writing this book, so if there are problems with this chapter, blame them on Fred

Gevalet at the Air Charter Guide, Fred Bernard at jet Aviation, and Pete Auger at the Mescon Group.

Randy Petersen and Ken Heldt at Frequent Flyer Services were my godsend in writing the chapter on managing frequent flyer programs. Shelley (Rolfe Shellenberger) also did his usual job of correcting my mistakes and helping me become a better person. I also became acquainted with Cary Marsh at Whirlpool, who helped me with material and editorial suggestions.

The chapter on globalization was a challenge to me. There are so few people who have experience in this area and I was fortunate to meet all of them. Steve Taylor started me out, and Mary Kay Dauria at American International Group filled in the blanks. Along the way, I got to know E. J. Hewitt at Libby Owens Ford, Scott Guerrero at Maritz Travel, and Thornton Clark at Thomas Cook. They all helped to create a good chapter.

I am especially thankful to Jeff Lang for the education he gave me on accounting. Sid Bowman was also helpful in teaching me things that I was not previously aware of. Although I had not met Pam Vance yet, our telephone conversations were helpful.

The last section of the book, dealing with special topics, was a lot of fun to write because I came in contact with some very interesting people. Charles Angelo, Bill Todd at Choice, Vicki Dunn at Northwest Airlines, Curt Reilly at the Official Airline Guide, and many others were very helpful to me in explaining the differences between official and business travel.

I am also in the debt of Kristin Moriarty at The Employee Relocation Council for the hours she spent with me.

The chapter on incentives is entirely the work of Bob Swearingen at Maritz Travel. Besides helping me with the book, Bob now picks out all of my ties for me.

# Contents

# SECTION

# I

O ne of the most important decisions a corporation will make during the 1990s will concern the management of travel. Chapter 1 gives the reader the background about the industry that will be needed to understand the rest of this book and Chapter 2 provides the information you will need to set up your own travel department. Most of the discussion is about automation equipment. Travel is a highly automated industry, and much of what the travel manager is able to do in terms of negotiations flows directly from the information fed through the automation devices. Automation is used in the travel industry to price, promote, and market services.

## Chapter One

# Things You Need to Know About the Travel Industry

A nyone who contemplates a career in travel management must be grounded in the travel industry. As a manager, you have control only when you fully understand the forces around you. During the last ten years, the travel vendors (airlines, hotels, and car-rental companies) had total control over your corporate travel life because they controlled the information. In essence control was taken away from you. Under this scenario, the travel vendors (airlines, hotels, car-rental companies) managed your corporate travel and dictated the terms of trade to your company.

To take control of your corporate travel budget, you must understand the forces that drive the vendors. You will need to know the economics of running an airline, a hotel, and a car-rental company. To approach the vendors intelligently, you must know the rules of the game.

Travel managers have existed in larger corporations since approximately 1968. However, in many small and medium-sized companies, the traveler controlled the purchase decision and travel was not necessarily viewed as a separate or controllable cost item. A company would use multiple travel agencies. There was limited travel data, and the corporation received almost no financial benefits because of its lack of control and knowledge.

In the 1990s, corporate travel managers are growing in numbers and influence. The company now controls the purchase decision. Travel is viewed as more controllable, and corporations are consolidating their use of travel agencies to increase their negotiating power with vendors. Travel data collection and analysis are becoming sophisticated, and most importantly, corporations are reaping significant financial benefits.

Some of the most important issues for the travel manager concern travel automation. If you understand the fundamental relationships between the airlines and Computerized Reservation Systems (CRSs) you will be on your way to understanding the travel industry and how it works. Given the complexity of the airline fare system (as many as 100,000 airline fares are changed daily), only automation will provide you with the tools to manage the huge mass of data.

## TRAVEL AGENCIES

During the last ten years there has been an explosive growth in the number of travel agencies. This growth was spurred on by the deregulation of airlines and the proliferation of airline prices available to consumers. Before deregulation, there was essentially one single price for airline tickets. In addition, travel agencies were kept from bidding on business travel with large corporations because of a low commission schedule. With deregulation this all changed. Airlines adopted a pricing strategy called yield or revenue management.

Under revenue management, consumers are charged according to their willingness to pay (the concept of revenue management will be explained in detail in the chapter on airlines). Businesses are charged more and leisure consumers are charged less. Through the use of ticket restrictions and discounts, airlines have trained consumers, who are very price sensitive, to make their travel plans well in advance of their trip. Business persons, who like flexibility and seldom plan ahead, are forced to take higher prices.

The airlines also change their prices according to how fast the plane is filling up. If too many leisure travelers call a month ahead of time, putting the pinch on the number of seats available for full-fare business customers booking just prior to departure, the airline will shut off the number of discount seats early.

Therefore, the prices of airline seats change constantly and increase as the time of departure gets nearer. Because of the large number of fares, it is no longer practical to publish all of them.

This gave rise to the highly automated Computerized Reservation Systems (CRSs), which are run by the airlines and are the main automation tool of all travel agencies and travel management firms.

With this new complexity in pricing, consumers turned to travel agents to help them with travel planning. According to the Airline Reporting Corporation, at least 80 percent of all airline tickets are now issued by travel agencies.

Another development since deregulation of the airlines is the rise of the mega-agencies. The mega-agencies are the ten largest travel agencies. The emergence of the megas was fueled in part by another development since deregulation: consolidation. Consolidation refers to the concentration of buying power within large corporations through the use of one travel agency. The megas and the large regional agencies operate so differently from the typical travel outlet that they should be referred to as travel management companies. The megas, along with a number of very large regional travel companies, were developed with the explicit purpose of managing business travel. The computer software developed by these firms makes corporate travel management easier.

The distinction between a travel agency and a travel management firm is not a trivial one. The skills that are important in helping a family plan its vacation are vastly different from those needed to successfully manage the business of travel. None of this is meant to speak disparagingly of the overworked and underpaid leisure-travel agents. They are the backbone of the retail business. At the very least it is hoped the business person who reads this book will learn, in addition to the practical aspects of managing travel, to be more polite to the voice on the other end of the telephone.

The main source of revenue for the travel management firms is commissions paid by the airlines. The travel management firm lives and dies with the airlines, which comprise the greatest part of the business. Additional commissions are earned from hotels, car-rental companies, and cruise lines.

The savvy financial officer will quickly learn how important it is to have a corporate travel manager who is separate and apart from the travel management company to guarantee that the corporation's best interests are served.

## A BRIEF OVERVIEW OF TRAVEL AUTOMATION

Travel is among the most automated of all service industries. Research is done using computers; inventories are maintained through computers; documents are produced with computers. In the travel management firm, people think themselves ill-used if they are unable to tie their professional lives to a computer—a machine that many understand only vaguely and do not use to its full potential.

Understanding automation, automated systems, and automation-related operations is the key to moving today's travel and hospitality industry professional into the competitive environment of the 1990s. Automation defines the competitive playing field for the modern travel industry. Those that are less than fully at home with the particular automation practices of the industry are always on the sidelines—unable to effect substantive change in products, management, operations, cost control, or customer relations.

Effectively, the computer illiterate or quasi-illiterate is still playing yesterday's game, in which the old rules said you could ignore computers and still have business as usual. Reliance upon the old rules as a competitive strategy failed. That field is littered with the broken bodies of many once-proud companies—airlines, hotels, and agencies—that were unwilling or unable to make the transition to a computerized world.

The story of the appropriate and timely use of automation is the story of the winners and losers in the travel and hospitality industry over the past several years. This chapter describes the major events, practices, and systems used in the industry today. It describes not only how but why—in a historical and practical sense—things work the way they do. All this information is packaged in a way you can use to keep ahead of automation, and the competition it both enables and drives, in the travel industry.

## DATABASE TECHNOLOGY AND TRAVEL AUTOMATION

The automated systems to be discussed rely on databases—some of the largest and most sophisticated databases in the world.

Imagine an airplane and all of the seats on it. Now multiply this by all of the flights that leave one city in one day. The airline databases need to have an accurate record, down to the seat, of how many people will be on each plane. They must show how much was paid for each ticket and when it was purchased.

Now imagine this same situation for all of the airlines over the entire world for one year. Now include the hotel rooms and rental cars and cruise lines for the same period.

All this information is stored in various databases. You can now begin to have some idea of the challenge of servicing just the reservations portion of the industry.

Having the information is one problem. Being able to access it quickly and easily and use it properly is another. This is the primary reason that the travel industry has become computer-intensive.

There are several strategies for information storage and retrieval. The United States reservation systems use technology that was initially developed 30 years ago. Even though the equipment that now delivers the database is state-of-the-art, the database itself is not.

The largest databases are part of airline reservation systems. These Computerized Reservation Systems (CRSs) have had great impact on the airline industry over the last ten years. Developed as simple, relatively inexpensive internal booking processes, these have evolved into highly sophisticated data management systems vital to market power and competitive success.

On a technological level, airline databases are organized around individual transactions, and consider each transaction to be a discrete element. This contrasts with more-modern database technology, where considerable capability and flexibility can be achieved through a relational approach to data element management.

The increasing automation of activities such as reservations, ticketing, schedule planning, pricing, and distribution is helping airlines to cut costs and improve productivity. Many carriers have installed sophisticated programs to allow fine-tuning of inventory, product mix, and revenue, on what approaches a moment-by-moment basis (yield management).

Industry databases have been constructed for tariff information, schedule statistics, interline billing, and revenue accounting. The information gained from dynamic CRS-based inventory and yield management was instrumental in enabling American Airlines to establish the first frequent flyer program in 1981.

Travel automation is inexorably tied to distribution; the history of one is the history of the other. In an industry so closely tied to computers and the companies that sell them, we can only expect that future operational and commercial developments in all phases of the travel industry will be driven by, or tied into, automation.

The rapid expansion of air travel made the original card-based reservation system impractical. Some of the later attempts at organizing massive numbers of reservations for large and complex daily flight schedules are preserved in the Smithsonian Institution in Washington, D.C. Photographs record how trays full of reservation cards traveled by conveyor belt between reservation operator stations, so that new reservations could be physically added to the trays as they were received. Coordination of this manual process between reservation centers and operational stations also became a problem.

The new computers being developed during these years provided the only hope for a new industry rapidly being buried by paperwork. A development effort was undertaken by IBM, with support from several major airlines of the day, including TWA, PanAm, and American, to create a practical airline reservation environment, using the tools of the day, that could be maintained effectively and that would be cost-effective.

In 1968, American implemented a system called Programmed Reservation System (PARS) on its System 360. (The term *PARS* is used as the name for the system architecture of all CRSs and is also used as a brand name for the CRS owned and operated by TWA and Northwest Airlines.) PARS is the essential foundation and conceptual basis for airline reservation systems. Because these concepts were replicated in later modifications and revisions of the original PARS, there is great similarity among all PARS systems. For the following reasons, these systems are difficult, if not impossible, to change in fundamental ways.

1. *They are expensive to maintain.* Airlines must support large-scale inhouse training programs, not only in the applications that programmers and analysts are responsible for, but in the languages and tools they use. The labor pool,

therefore, tends to be relatively small, outside contractors are rare, and development is focused primarily upon maintenance as opposed to enhancement.

2. *They are cryptic.* Advanced screen management, windowing, and visually directed screen forms were all unheard-of or unproved technologies in the early 1960s. PARS-type systems use strings of application-specific commands and codes that are operationally very efficient but that require extensive operator training to understand and use correctly.

3. *They are architecturally complex.* Particularly when development is done in a central environment, large-scale projects tend to take on a life of their own. Highly rigid applications and supporting programs, taken as a whole, become greater than the sum of their individual parts. A large system is structurally too complicated for any individual to understand thoroughly, meaning that the full implications of many programming or structural changes cannot be anticipated or accurately predicted. Subsequent development must, therefore, be undertaken within the personality of the system, instead of undertaking to modify that personality as might be appropriate. This complex, operationally inflexible systems environment becomes self-perpetuating.

Despite the limitations we recognize today, reservation-based airline automation in the 1960s was the foundation for the modern travel industry. It made the vast international expansion of airlines and the growth of the retail travel agency all possible.

## HOTELS, CAR-RENTAL COMPANIES, AND AIRLINES

The same concepts employed in airline reservation technology were transferred to other travel-related industries, such as hotels and car-rental companies, although the original technology platform was not nearly as pervasive in those industries.

Even today, hotels rely on locally managed, not centrally managed, inventory. The only source for true room-night availability is the individual property. Central reservation offices, operated by a chain, a franchiser, or a representation service, almost always function as communications centers funneling reservation messages between travelers and the individual hotels, not as central reservation databases.

Hotels were thus much slower to develop true central inventory systems than were airlines. This left hotels and hotel groups free to remain unautomated or to develop relatively simple, low-cost solutions for basic needs—a situation that has many properties and chains feeling left behind in the requirements of modern data management and changing customer requirements.

The early hotel systems, such as Western International's (now Westin) WESTRON, inherited a great many airline reservation system concepts and technologies. Other systems, such as Sheraton's Reservatron or Hilton's Hiltron, employed different operational premises but retained much of the airline system technology.

Car companies likewise were using many of the same techniques well into their 1970s development projects. The car-reservation transaction lends itself to processing in an airline-like mode, and most major car vendors maintain central office availability. The commoditization of the car product, which occurred almost immediately after the development of national car-rental firms, meant that more robust systems were seen as unnecessary.

The travel world of the 1970s remained much the same as it had been for years. Then the world was shocked by drastic increases in oil prices. The United States was particularly affected by the Arab oil embargo, which lasted from October 1973 to March 1974. During this period, the airline industry was the most regulated industry in history, and shifting prices to match costs was difficult and time-consuming. Distribution costs were suddenly among the few areas where savings could easily be achieved.

## TRAVEL AGENCY AUTOMATION

The job of the corporate travel manager was never easy. Fares were still regulated and changed relatively infrequently, but the growth of business travel created severe problems. Operationally, travel agents were not set up to handle large numbers of point-to-point business travel reservations. Schedules and fares were still maintained in printed books, and agents used telephones to make reservations directly with the airline that would provide service to the traveler. Further, accounting for these new reservations caused paper overload as the agency's volume increased. Hal Rosenbluth, president of Rosenbluth Travel, located in Philadelphia, remembers that "our first corporate travel center was one room with each agent holding a phone to a client in one hand and one to an airline in the other."

Several airlines held a series of meetings to discuss travel agency automation. These meetings resulted in a joint project called the Multi-Airline-Agency Reservation System (MAARS), which was supposed to extend basic airline reservation technology to travel agencies. The effort moved slowly because the project had to represent the interests of several airlines that considered themselves competitors. It eventually came apart when American Airlines, followed quickly by United Airlines and TWA, announced that they would make their own proprietary automation systems available to the retail trade.

The carriers undertook this new project in decidedly different ways:

1. TWA introduced PARS (its proprietary system by that name) into select agencies within the markets it served.

2. United focused its Apollo sales effort primarily on its own markets, but offered automation initially to the larger travel agencies—the ones handling the majority of business travel reservations.

3. American felt that automation was a new profit opportunity, and that market share was the key to this emerging industry. SABRE automation was offered to almost any agency as soon as the system was operationally and commercially able to support them.

Finally, in 1975, agents started to have access to reservation, file-management, and fare-display technology, albeit in a fairly primitive form by today's standards. This was the most significant single step toward defining today's travel industry.

## CRS RATIONALE

The automated systems used in the travel industry were created both for convenience and necessity. There are also sound reasons to invest in automation. After CRSs were first introduced into travel distribution, it did not take long for these systems to become the most profitable single segment of the airline industry.

The major financial benefits of CRS ownership are:

1. The booking fees they charge other airlines, hotels, and car-rental firms for reservation services.
2. The rent they receive from subscribers for equipment and services.
3. The value of the reservation services they provide to themselves.
4. The incremental bookings/revenues they receive because travel agencies use their CRS.

Ownership gives an airline a number of less-tangible and strategic benefits. Airline managers refer to these as control over their distribution systems.

## THE RESERVATION DATABASE

A CRS reservation database consists of passenger reservations created based on the schedule database and including information to specifically identify the passenger holding the reservation. This is called a Passenger Name Record (PNR). The PNR database is the largest collectively in any CRS. The PNR consists of various fields. Some are required fields, in that the end transaction command cannot be consummated without them; others are optional; others are created by the system programmatically and are not available for operator viewing and/or modification.

An individual PNR is created for each traveler's itinerary. Multipassenger PNRs may also be created for passengers traveling together for the entirety of the reservation. Most business travel agents believe it is best to create PNRs for each individual, rather than multipassenger records, because changes to such records are difficult and often create reservation inconsistencies.

Central to the PNR is the traveler's itinerary, which is constructed principally from schedule and availability data. The itinerary contains reservation data for all services that can be electronically reserved through the CRS, including hotel, car, and rail reservations. These segments are all termed reservation segments.

Other segments can be input into the PNR itinerary field, even though they cannot be reserved through the CRS. This is done to preserve reservation continuity so that all facets of a traveler's itinerary can be electronically recorded and stored in a single database, and also so that the travel agents can initiate accounting transactions through the CRS.

There are other required fields in the PNR:

1. *Name*—Specific formats are used to indicate male and female names, children's names, proper placement of titles, and name groupings.

2. *Telephone contact*—The passenger's home telephone number and office or day telephone numbers are entered, as is the number of the individual making the reservation and the number of the travel agency, if applicable. The telephone contact is electronically transmitted to all nonhost airlines providing services reserved as part of the complete itinerary.

3. *Ticketing*—Indicates the status of tickets issued against reservations held in the PNR. Also used as a control field to control automatic cancellations if tickets are not issued by an agreed date and time.

4. *Received from*—Indicates the name of the person making the reservation. This field is referred to whenever itinerary and certain other changes are made, indicating the source of these changes.

5. *Record locator*—The CRS automatically assigns a unique alpha-numeric identification code to each PNR at "end transaction," when PNR creation is complete.

Other optional fields may be added as indicated:

1. *SSR/OSI messages*—These are reservation elements that cannot be accommodated elsewhere in the PNR and that may require action by airlines involved in providing transportation services comprising the itinerary. Once entered in the PNR, they are transmitted electronically to the airlines to which they are addressed. The CRS operator specifies the addressing of the message and determines whether an SSR or OSI status is warranted.

A Special Service Request (SSR) element requires positive action or acknowledgment by the receiving airline. It is used to request special seating, wheelchair assistance, etc. An Other Service Information (OSI) message is more informational in character and does not require acknowledgment or action. It would be used to advise that two passengers were traveling together, yet were listed in separate PNRs.

2. *Address*—This is included when hotel or car reservations are part of the PNR, so that written confirmations can be mailed. The address is electronically transmitted to all nonair vendors whose services are represented in the PNR.

3. *Remarks*—This is an essentially free-form field where other remarks and information pertaining to the reservation may be recorded and accessed by anyone displaying the PNR. Some travel agencies use the remarks field to record information that will be transmitted electronically to the agency's accounting system. This is done because in a travel agency the CRS workstation functions as a point-of-sale device, whereas an accounting computer terminal does not. The sales or reservations agent is often the only person prepared to enter many of these codes into the system.

Other PNR fields, notably the ticketing field, are also used for accounting and interface data transfer.

## FREQUENT FLYER NUMBER

A different procedure is used in most CRSs for entering frequent flyer numbers applicable to host airlines as opposed to off-line airlines. The host-airline process can involve a special field, as is the case in Apollo and SABRE, while off-line airline numbers frequently use a specifically formatted SSR message.

## SEAT AND MEAL REQUESTS

This process varies considerably by CRS and between host and off-line airlines. A separate field is maintained for CRS host seat requests, and for seat requests for vendors that have established electronic seat and boarding-pass issuance agreements with the CRS. A boarding pass cannot be issued without a specific seat confirmation; most travelers prefer to have boarding passes issued in advance to save time at the airport.

The reservations agent or travel agent can display actual seat maps for host airlines. These are simple, character-driven representations of seats on various aircraft types, as determined by the type of craft to be used for any given flight segment. The seating map indicates smoking and nonsmoking sections. The agent can request any open seat in the reservable categories.

## USING THE PNR

The PNR is updated by reservation agents or travel agents connected to the CRS where it resides. PNRs created in one system are generally not accessible in another. An internal security system limits access to the PNR to (1) reservation terminals of the host airline or airlines for the CRS, (2) travel agent terminals within the same office, and (3) travel agent terminals in other offices, usually branches of the same company, where blanket PNR cross-access has been approved and implemented by the CRS.

The PNR functions as the travel agency's most important transaction database. For this reason it is extremely valuable as a marketing-data source and in support of an accounting database.

## DEREGULATION

October 1978 marked the passage of the Federal Airline Deregulation Act, which changed the industry forever. The National Business Travel Association (NBTA) was one of the leading proponents of deregulation. Whereas competition and pricing had previously been tightly controlled by an agency of the federal government, the Civil Aeronautics Board (CAB), airlines were now free to compete on domestic routes, prices, and commissions almost at will.

Fares entered a period of constant change and turmoil from which they have yet to emerge. The publication of printed tariffs eventually became impractical; all pricing is now managed through CRSs. The official domestic commission rate is 10 percent of the gross ticket price. Override commission is always on top on the official rate and is variable from market to market.

When airlines became free to compete on price, travel agents were also free to do likewise. Widespread discounting to major business travel customers began in the late 1970s and continued through the 1980s. This placed pressure on agencies to become operationally efficient for the first time, as margins were no longer guaranteed or predictable. Since the operation and growth of the travel agency industry was now tied to automation, the clamor began—not for just any automation, but for automation that was well-applied.

## FULL BUSINESS AUTOMATION

Airlines, the predominant suppliers of travel agency automation, modified their strategies from simple facilitation of travel agency reservations through their systems to positioning of those systems as full business systems that met most or all of the agency's transactional needs in a single environment. The gates were open for participation in the CRS by car vendors, hotels, and others. These vendors saw opportunities for expanded distribution through increased reliance on agencies and the new technologies for reaching them. Agency-based bookings for major hotel chains and car-rental vendors reached new highs.

Airline control over travel agencies, particularly by those that provided CRS services, continued to grow. Some positioned themselves as the only legitimate suppliers of travel agency business services, and looked upon agencies using their systems as extensions of their own franchise. Screen bias—the creation of availability and pricing displays that favored certain vendors, for a fee—was expanded, and later prohibited by federal statute. Airline commission payments, usually tied to CRS services, financed price-cutting by large agencies, further increasing their size and their dependence on the airlines.

CRS vendor-airline dominance of the travel agency distribution system increased with breathtaking speed. Within a few years, the competitive positions of American and United, the largest and most aggressive CRS vendor-airlines, had developed to the point that they controlled the tone for most aspects of travel agency distribution in the United States. CRS services became the single largest profit centers for several airlines.

## NEW CRS OPPORTUNITIES

Other carriers, notably Eastern Airlines and Delta Airlines, alarmed at this domination, launched late CRS efforts to protect their own agency markets—SystemOne and Datas II, respectively. With the CRS oligopoly cracked, deep computer price discounting to agencies developed, resulting ultimately in highly restrictive contracts designed to prevent vendor-switching, and even closer relationships between CRS airlines and their agencies.

The next step in the evolution of the CRS as an airline distribution control platform was the movement toward multi-airline CRS ownership and CRS globalization.

In mid-1986, there was a much-publicized effort to launch the NIBS project. NIBS, the Neutral Industry Booking System, was intended to eliminate many of the remaining competitive disadvantages that the "have not" airlines felt they suffered at the hands of the "haves" airlines. This movement was championed by Richard Murray, one of the pioneers of American's SABRE system who, at the time, was head of automation for Continental Airlines.

NIBS was basically a replay of the old MAARS project, in that a group of airlines considered building a system that would meet the needs of all its participants. In fact, trying to meet the needs of all meant that the project met the needs of none. NIBS floundered until the Texas Air Group, owners of Continental, acquired Eastern Airlines, and with it SystemOne. With the driving forces behind it off to pursue a new game, NIBS was finished.

## THE RISE OF THE MULTINATIONAL CRS

One side effect of the NIBS experience was a focus on international intercarrier CRS cooperation. Overseas, the CRS as a distribution tool was much less well-developed. Systems were confined to national markets and varied widely in quality.

Europe in particular was primed for a CRS revolution. The success of the European Community (Common Market) in breaking down intra-European commercial barriers culminated in 1992, when all commercial competitive barriers between the community's members were removed. For airlines, this meant that competitors with stronger CRSs could move into the national markets, where weaker systems rejected a monopoly.

Further, the major US-based CRSs were looking overseas for new markets, now that virtual universal automation of the distribution system had been achieved in the US. All European CRSs were uncompetitive with their more advanced American counterparts, and it was clear that the European Community would not indefinitely protect monopolies.

In 1986 the Association of European Airlines (AEA), a trade group, studied the possibility of forming a European CRS. Again, any cooperative spirit was overruled by business interests, and the effort was divided into two groups:

1. *Galileo.* Galileo is the project initiated primarily by British Airways and Swissair, in partnership with US-based United. It will ultimately replace all national distribution CRSs and marketing relationship maintenance systems for its participants. The partnership agreement between the Galileo participants, including United Airlines, provides that Galileo be much more than a European CRS only, as the partners intend to market the system globally, except for the US, Canada, and Japan (where other initiatives affecting the partners were underway).

2. *Amadeus.* Amadeus was initiated primarily by Air France and Lufthansa. US-based SystemOne was selected as the technology supplier but was not a partner. Although Amadeus is a marketing and technological umbrella for its participants, it was never intended to wholly replace their national CRS activities.

## SYSTEM FOCUS

Airline automation during the 1980s concentrated on competition and market expansion. The most successful initiatives were in intelligent workstations. These projects employed microcomputers as front-ends, which compensated for the rigidity of the PARS-based CRS and allowed the vendors to quickly offer many of the features agency users required without undertaking substantive changes to the central systems. Although begun in 1986 by most CRSs, these projects were yet to be fully developed throughout the user base by 1990, and were still undergoing major development.

## SATELLITE TICKET PRINTERS

A recent development in the technology of ticket printing has made it possible for travel management firms to place ticket printers inside a corporate client's office. The satellite ticket printer (STP) is simply one method of ticket delivery and is not a new form of distribution. It is more convenient for the travel management firm to press a button and deliver the tickets in the client's office than to hire an extra employee to drive the tickets over in a car.

## HOTEL AUTOMATION

Hotel systems were a major area of activity during the 1980s. Central reservation-system projects were undertaken by major multinational chains, among them Sheraton and Hilton, all of which used old and inflexible technology. Attempts at diversification by airline CRSs also led to efforts at building hotel systems, notably by American and United.

The most successful of these projects was American's Confirm system, which ultimately evolved into a joint-system venture by American, Budget Car Rental, Hilton Hotels, and Marriott Hotels. Confirm was to replace the central reservation systems of its hotel and car participants with a system employing much of the same technology that had been used in American's SABRE system, while incorporating more modern technologies where appropriate.

## DISTRIBUTION AND NEW TECHNOLOGY

The efficiency of travel agents as primary distributors was established largely before automation changed the rules of the game. One area under intense study is the increased use of machines to issue tickets. A simple and repetitive task such as issuing a point-to-point airline ticket can easily be done by a machine, just as a customer can withdraw cash from a bank account using an automated teller machine (ATM).

The key is the type of transaction. Basic point-to-point airline tickets, particularly the no-reservation type sold through a money machine, involve solely the collection of money and the issuance of a financial instrument acceptable to the airline.

## YIELD MANAGEMENT

One of the most pervasive issues in hospitality automation continues to be yield management (or revenue management, as it has come to be known). This refers to the techniques used by air carriers to obtain the highest possible mix of full-fare and discount seats to produce the most revenue and the fewest empty seats.

Refining these techniques is a primary objective for most travel service providers. It is important enough to be among the most extensive automation projects now in progress at many major airlines and hotels and at several independent software suppliers to the industry.

Airlines and hotels want to fill as many high-priced seats and rooms as possible. To be successful, these techniques are usually highly automated because they entail difficult and complex calculations, real-time monitoring of sold inventory, and constant updates.

## MARKETING PROGRAM SUPPORT

Airlines have used the information stored in their reservation and yield-management systems for marketing support. One such service is the frequent flyer program. Since their introduction by American Airlines in May 1981, frequent flyer programs have been established by almost every domestic airline, with variations finding their way into hotels, car-rental companies, and cruise lines. Frequent flyer programs were developed to stimulate passenger loyalty and are an area of concern to the corporate travel manager because they can actually cost business customers more money.

The more extensive an airline's network, the greater the likelihood that a passenger will have opportunities to both earn and use mileage credits. Air carriers with complementary credits can and do form partnerships to award and redeem credits, diverting passengers from common airline rivals.

Frequent flyer programs are directed toward the most lucrative segment of airline traffic: the full-fare business traveler. Most of these travelers participate in at least one frequent flyer program. Frequent flyer programs are but one example of how automation has reached into the marketing aspects of the hospitality industry.

## CURRENT TRAVEL MANAGEMENT AUTOMATION

It is quite clear that the airlines ruled travel management for most of the 1980s. Travel management depends on information. With the airlines controlling all of the information, they were able to dictate the terms of trade to the industry. A major change took place in 1986, when for the first time CRSs allowed the creation of "foreign software." Foreign software is any enhancement to the CRS supplied by outside vendors. This was a critical point in the evolution of the CRS because for the first time, it became possible for a corporate travel manager to get information other than what the CRS supplied. Now a corporation can decide its own information needs and satisfy them.

The introduction of foreign, or third-party, software is vital because for the first time, corporations can be equal with the airlines in dictating terms of trade. Previously the advantage was entirely on the side of the airlines. It is not the software itself that is important to the travel manager, but rather the information that is gathered and how it is used. The savvy corporate travel manager knows how to use the information provided by foreign software to negotiate with the various vendors. The travel manager is the key to the entire transaction because he or she will be called upon to sit down with the vendors and hammer out the negotiations.

An example of third-party software is the fare-checker system. According to Mac Beatty, vice president of automation planning at US Travel, "the guess is that an agent probably uses less than 10% of the power of CRS. For example, if an agent wants to check flight availability, there are upwards of 100 different modifications that can be done to fine-tune how you try to find out what a flight is doing. The agent probably uses five of these. The trick with automation is to give the agent tools so they don't have to know 100 procedures and remember to do these things by hand."

One of these third-party software systems is made by Travelmation of Stamford, Connecticut. Travelmation's software runs on their mainframe and is designed to sort through the maze of ticket prices and rules. Before using the service, the corporate client supplies its general policies, such as if the traveler can use nonrefundable tickets, accept early takeoffs and late returns, etc. The employee also enters criteria, such as smoking/nonsmoking, aisle seat, etc., and the computer searches out the options that meet the criteria. After a fare is found, the computer will continue to search CRS files automatically until the ticket is printed. Again, the important key to the transaction is the corporate travel manager, who makes the policies.

Sales material from Travelmation and its competitors claims that such systems will reduce air travel costs by as much as 7 to 14 percent. Unfortunately, many travelers turn these fares down in order to fly on the airline with their favorite frequent flyer program. Automated low-fare search programs have become an important tool for travel managers in today's dynamic travel industry environment. On paper, most of these products look very similar, but it is critical to determine if the product is an integrated component of the travel company's operation or just a marketing tool.

A corporation will reap major benefits if the system is integrated into the travel company's operation. The travel company should be able to demonstrate the following benefits to the travel manager:

1. Ensuring that the lowest fare has been obtained at the time of booking.
2. Securing any lower fares that have become available as a result of airline pricing adjustment.
3. Providing opportunity for the travel manager to take action on exceptions.
4. Identifying opportunities for negotiation of specific fares.

Another important development in third-party vendor software is management information reporting. Management information is one of the developments that allows the travel manager to have information equal to that of the vendors. The management of travel information is considered so important that an entire chapter in this book is devoted to its study.

## PROFILES

Profiles of individual traveler preferences can be stored on a CRS. If this information is stored in the computer along with corporate policies, it helps ensure that travelers are offered those travel options, products, or vendors that adhere to the company's travel policy or an individual's preferences. This is important because refining and enforcing travel policy is a top priority with many travel managers. The travel department must be responsive not only to those policies mandated by management but to the particular preferences of individual travelers as well.

Basically, profiles are designed for the creation of traveler preference records that are used to control the sale of airline tickets, car rentals, and hotel rooms. Generally, profile systems begin to work automatically when the traveler's record is retrieved. The information in the business and personal files may be merged or considered separately. In addition to offering selective availability displays, the system automatically moves all data stored in profiles to the reservation. This should include seat requests, frequent flyer numbers, corporate ID numbers, club numbers, forms of payment, and special service requests.

## THE FUTURE

The principal growth areas for automated systems remain sales distribution and management information, with airlines competing furiously to link travel agencies into their computer networks. Display screens have evolved into micro-systems that give access to information such as schedules, seat selection, fare display and calculation, ticketing, and hotel and car bookings.

The economic stakes are high, with agents producing more than 85 percent of total domestic airline sales revenue.

Airline reservation systems will remain the largest, most automated, and most influential devices in the travel industry. Hotel
reservations, long the technological stepchild of the travel industry, have finally entered a renaissance that promises new benefits
for agents and travelers. Reservations are still often dealt with by
hand, and many of the automated reservation systems are so
archaic or noncompatible that inaccurate bookings and poor inventory records and revenue management are the norm.

This problem has partially been recognized, and hotel reservation
systems are undergoing transition, as both the industry and the
consumer demand more accurate data and wider data availability.

## ISSUES FOR THE 1990s

As corporations adjust to the new economy, the need to have
qualified travel managers as a permanent part of the corporate
structure is becoming more apparent. The employment of managers with basic travel knowledge is one of the last frontiers for
companies in their efforts to get a handle on expenses.

## TRAVEL MANAGEMENT TIPS

- Under revenue management, consumers are charged according to their willingness to pay. Businesses are charged
  more and leisure consumers are charged less.
- Airlines change their prices according to how fast the plane
  fills up.
- A major development since deregulation is the mega-agencies.
- The mega-agencies and large regionals operate so differently from the typical travel agency that they should be
  referred to as travel management companies.
- The savvy financial officer will quickly learn how important
  it is to have a corporate travel manager who is separate and
  apart from the travel management company to guarantee
  that the corporation's best interests and not those of the
  travel management company are served.
- Understanding automation, automated systems, and automation-related operations is the key to moving today's

travel and hospitality industry professional into the competitive environment of the 1990s.

- The same concepts employed in airline reservation technology were transferred to other travel-related industries, such as hotels and car rentals, although the original technology was not nearly as pervasive in those industries.
- The automated systems used in the travel industry were created both for convenience and necessity. There are also sound reasons to invest in automation. After CRSs were first introduced into travel distribution, it did not take long for these systems to become the most profitable single segment of the airline industry.
- A CRS reservation database consists of passenger reservations created based on the schedule database and including information to specifically identify the passenger holding the reservation.
- Widespread discounting to major business travel customers began in the late 1970s and continued through the 1980s. This placed pressure on agencies to become operationally efficient for the first time, as margins were no longer guaranteed or predictable.
- Airlines, the predominant suppliers of travel agency automation, modified their strategies from simple facilitation of travel agency reservations through their systems to positioning of those systems as full business systems that met most or all of the agency's transactional needs in a single environment.
- CRS vendor-airline dominance of the travel agency distribution system increased with breathtaking speed.
- CRS services became the single largest profit centers for several airlines.
- Attempts at diversification by airline CRSs also led to efforts at building hotel systems, notably by American and United.
- One of the most pervasive issues in travel automation continues to be yield management.
- A major change in automation took place in 1986, when for the first time CRSs allowed the creation of "foreign software."
- For the first time, it became possible for a corporate travel manager to get information other than what the CRS supplied.
- The introduction of foreign software is vital because corporations can be equal with the airlines in dictating terms of trade.

## Chapter Two

# Setting up a Travel Management Department

F or most companies, the first step in controlling corporate travel and entertainment costs will be in realizing the need to control all costs. Among corporations, the control of travel falls under many different departments. In some companies, the travel department reports to Finance. Because there are policy issues involved, some companies run travel from the Human Relations department. The travel department at Kodak is located in the Transportation department. And there are many companies that feel that the travel department belongs in Purchasing. But considering that travel and entertainment expenses constitute the third-largest category of corporate expense (following data collection and salaries), the business travel department should report to Finance. The National Business Travel Association conducted a survey three years ago, involving the Fortune 500. It was determined that one of the major failings in getting the most out of a business travel department stemmed from the fact that travel management did not report directly to Finance.

Cary Marsh, director of the business travel center at Whirlpool Corporation, makes this observation: "One of the most important things for a travel manager to have is access to senior management because the effectiveness of a travel manager is largely dependent on having that support." At Whirlpool, the travel center is under the supervision of the executive vice president, chief administrative officer, who reports to the chief executive officer.

## ESTABLISHING A TRAVEL DEPARTMENT

Phil Tedeschi, a senior NBTA member and Manager of Transportation Services at Reliance Electric, a worldwide producer of electric motors with over a billion dollars in annual sales, offers this systematic approach to setting up a corporate travel management department:

I. Recognition of the Need to Control Travel Expenses
II. Management Commitment
   A. What drives it?
   B. What does it lead to?
III. Preliminary Actions
   A. Create a travel decision-making team
   B. Hire a travel manager
   C. Formulate and distribute policy
   D. Form agency and vendor alliances
IV. Data Collection
   A. What are the sources?
   B. What is needed and what is not?
V. Data Management
   A. Turning stacks of paper
VI. Employee Cooperation
   A. Selling the benefits of travel-expense savings
   B. Curbing abuses
VII. Data Verification
   A. Expense-report auditing
   B. Going back to the table
VIII. Program Review
   A. How often?
   B. What changes should be made?
IX. External Interaction
   A. Trade Associations
   B. Trade Press

## RECOGNITION OF THE NEED TO CONTROL TRAVEL EXPENSES

Recognition of the need for controlling travel expenses is an essential first step in managing travel. This recognition may come about in various ways. The president of the company may happen across an article in the paper about managing travel, or members of a finance committee might recommend the adoption of travel policies to the board. The experiences of Cathy Armstrong are fairly typical. Cathy is the travel coordinator at Fokker Aircraft, USA, Inc., located in Alexandria, Virginia. She was the winner of the National Business Travel Association's President's Award in 1990 for an outstanding contribution to the business travel industry.

Cathy had been working as a sales assistant when her boss, the vice president of sales, decided to look into the matter of reducing travel expenses. Cathy had previously helped with travel bookings, so she was chosen to research the matter. Cathy personally did all of the research into implementing a travel policy. For the first two years of her job, she continued to work under the vice president of sales. In 1990, company management decided to put her responsibilities under the direction of the Finance department.

The experience of Helen Britain, director of travel at CRT, a futures and options trading company headquartered in Chicago, Illinois, is similar to Cathy Armstrong's in that the impetus to begin CRT's travel department came from the top. After a partners' meeting, Helen was directed to begin research into the management of travel. These two experiences are similar in that each company decided to control its own travel from within the corporation.

## MANAGEMENT COMMITMENT

Tedeschi argues that mere recognition of the need for travel management does not guarantee that a successful program will result. Top management commitment to and support of the program is vital because travel-expense control and management often runs counter to personal benefits lavished on travelers by airlines, car-rental companies, and hotels. Without a firm resolve by company management to enforce policies and procedures, a corporate travel management agenda can achieve only relative effectiveness. Cathy Armstrong at Fokker, Inc., feels that much of her success is due to the fact that her boss backed her completely.

## PRELIMINARY ACTIONS

In Tedeschi's systematic approach, preliminary actions include creating a travel decision-making team, hiring a travel manager, formulating and distributing policy, and forming agency and vendor relationships. Forming agency and vendor relationships will be discussed in later chapters. Now it is time to discuss the role of the travel decision-making team.

## THE TRAVEL DECISION-MAKING TEAM

The travel decision-making team takes various forms in different companies. United Technologies Corporation (UTC) in Hartford, Connecticut, formed a travel council under the leadership of their travel manager, Carol Salcito, who is also an NBTA officer. The travel council is comprised of participants from each of UTC's various operating divisions. There is a chairperson of the travel council. This job is separate from that of the travel manager. Each division is given the opportunity to buy into the travel program. "Buying into the travel program" is a common phrase in the corporate travel world. It simply means that each division is allowed to decide if it will participate or not.

If a division chose not to buy into the program, Carol Salcito would meet with them periodically to explain how the program was evolving and encourage them to participate. In one case it took Carol five years to "convert" one division. Each year Carol would go back to this division and analyze their travel numbers and show them the advantages of being in the program.

A member of the UTC travel council can be anybody who has anything to do with travel, in either a supervisory or an operating position. The members were chosen by the division presidents. The travel council is comprised of committees that oversee various aspects of UTC's travel, such as vendor relations or management information.

Price Waterhouse, a big-six accounting firm, had an interesting problem setting up their travel department. The firm's management committee (similar to a board of directors) authorized the department in late 1986, following an extensive two-year review of the company's travel-buying practices. Prior to the introduction of this program, each Price Waterhouse office throughout the country procured its own travel. Over 450 travel agencies were used nationwide. Since many offices were small, they were unable to have access to accurate management reporting. Even offices large enough to receive reports were unable to share in volume buying since there was no vehicle for sharing this information within Price Waterhouse.

The problem of consolidating Price Waterhouse's travel under one department was difficult because the company is a partnership of over 900 persons. Each managing partner is free to make his or her own decisions on virtually all matters, including travel. Since little in a partnership is absolutely mandatory, centralizing travel management was particularly challenging. Price Waterhouse's experience shows quite conclusively that even the loosest-knit company can effectively manage its travel.

According to John Hintz, travel manager at Price Waterhouse and current president of the NBTA, a travel advisory council was formed to act as a forum to improve communications between the managing units. This council meets semi-annually to review service areas and advise the management committee on policy changes and enforcement techniques. The unique system that Price Waterhouse set up will be described in detail in another chapter.

## THE TRAVEL MANAGER AND CORPORATE CULTURE

The savvy corporate travel manager will be able to tell you how travel fits into the entire corporate philosophy. The role of travel in the corporation is dictated by the corporate culture. For some companies, travel is a part of their overall commitment to service. Other companies keep their sales people out in front of the buying public through travel. In an effort to help companies understand the various roles that travel plays in corporate philosophy, the American Express Travel Consulting Group came up with the following schema to categorize the role that travel plays in various companies' strategies. These categories express the fact that all companies do not or should not manage travel in the same manner. The corporate culture is the key.

1. *Liberal Optimists.* These companies express a high level of concern for their employees and strive to be more flexible in terms of employee benefits. This segment considers the traveler's comfort and convenience to be more important

than the cost of travel and views business travel as a burden for their employees. Liberal Optimists are optimistic about their future growth prospects. Their plans to invest in their own growth reflect their confidence in their ability to outperform their industry over the next few years, as well as their confidence in the strength of the US economy.

2. *Administrative Activists.* These firms believe that administrative controls are the best management tools for profitable growth. Their very active approach to travel and entertainment (T&E) management stems from an awareness of the importance of business travel to corporate growth and of the need to effectively control costs. Their efforts occur in a climate of corporate optimism for the future. Administrative Activists use the widest range of policies and techniques for managing travel and entertainment of any of the five categories described by American Express. They do not believe they can significantly cut T&E costs (or R&D, manufacturing, marketing, or employee benefits, for that matter) without limiting their business—hence their emphasis on carefully controlling necessary spending.

3. *Complacent Winners.* These companies believe that they can cut costs in most major areas—employee benefits, marketing, R&D, manufacturing, and T&E—without limiting their business. It is their generally optimistic outlook and their intention to invest in their business that distinguish this group from the Sensitive Pessimists, the other segment that believes it can cut T&E costs without limiting its business. Their belief that cost containment is not the best way to increase their profitability—even though they believe they could cut costs without impeding growth—is evidence of their managerial self-confidence and complacency. In contrast to the Administrative Activists, the Complacent Winners show less concern for the comfort of their employees and tend to believe that strong bottom-line results come from superior management rather than from the efforts of a small group of employees.

4. *Sensitive Pessimists.* These firms believe that their industry and the US economy in general are headed for rough times and that there is little they can do about it. They have experienced no growth in recent years, and they

view cost containment, rather than revenue growth, as
their main avenue for increased profitability. Their plans
do not include heavy investments for growth in the near
future. Sensitive Pessimists are reasonably concerned
about their employees, but at the same time expect them
to share the corporate burden in the years ahead. It is
their appreciation for their employees—and their feeling
that business travel is a burden for their staff—that distinguishes them from the Oppressive Depressives.

5. *Oppressive Depressives.* These corporations are characterized
   by their low level of concern for their employees and their
   relatively gloomy business outlook. They do not believe
   that their obligation to their employees is as important as
   their obligation to shareholders, and they display little reluctance to impose controls on their personnel. Not surprisingly, employee turnover is a significant problem for
   this segment. Oppressive Depressives are unlikely to have
   experienced real growth in recent years, and they tend to
   believe that cost containment will be their best avenue to
   increased profitability. While the Sensitive Pessimists wish
   they could do more for their employees but are con-
   strained by weak business performance, the Oppressive
   Depressives express little allegiance to their personnel.

With respect to the diversity of corporate cultures and the universal need for corporate travel management, Margie L. Grace,
NBTA chairperson and travel manager for the Cincinnati-based
Chemed Corporation, states: "Each of these collective groups can
still benefit from a comprehensive travel policy, specifically developed and implemented to support a particular corporate strategy.
Many elements of a travel policy are common to corporations of
any size and scope."

According to the American Express Travel Consulting Group:
"Detailed and effective two-way communication is a key to building a travel management program that is consistent with company
values and objectives that reflect senior management's viewpoint.
Staff responsible for directly managing travel costs must make
every effort to learn precisely what top management is asking
them to accomplish, and then ensure that the travel management
program supports the views and objectives of the company. At the
same time, senior management should rely on the expertise

of their travel management staff to communicate to them the implications of their thinking in the real world of corporate travel."

Ongoing communication is also critical because corporate culture is in a constant state of flux. Slowing corporate or industry growth, or on the other hand, a desire to take a more aggressive competitive posture could change the company's business stance. If travel management staff are in close contact with top management, this will ensure that changes in corporate culture are quickly reflected in the firm's approach to travel management. This is also why it is strongly recommended that all firms, no matter what their current approach to business travel, have a written policy and review it at least annually. In the event that corporate objectives change, the mechanism will already be in place to clearly communicate any necessary changes in required travel behavior to all employees.

## THE JOB OF THE CORPORATE TRAVEL MANAGER

The job of the corporate travel manager is management. The corporate travel manager does not exist to make reservations or perform secretarial duties. The travel manager should be considered a middle- or upper-management position because of the vital role the manager plays in controlling a large corporate expense. Unfortunately, one of the jobs performed by the travel manager is the constant justification of the travel department. In addition to basic job justification, the corporate travel manager has five specific functions to perform:

1. Control corporate travel expenses through the design, implementation, and control of the travel policy.
2. Ensure that the relationship between the travel management company and the corporation complies with the agreement.
3. Maintain the relationship with the various airline, hotel, and car-rental vendors.
4. Manage the payment of all travel expenses.

5. Maintain accurate records through the proper use of management information systems, which ensure that corporate travel policy is being followed and that exceptions are discovered and reported.

## THE DUTIES OF THE CORPORATE TRAVEL MANAGER

The position of the business travel manager, as defined by the NBTA, is as follows: "The primary function of the business travel manager is to provide the most effective means of corporate travel, at the greatest economic advantage for the corporate consumer, taking into account every practical consideration for the safety, comfort, and convenience of the business traveler."

The American Express Travel Consulting Group offers the following as a sample job description:

### Summary

The corporate travel manager is a corporate staff position. The incumbent's key responsibility is to propose, implement, and manage strategies to control and reduce the company's annual travel expenditures.

### Principal Accountabilities

A. This position is responsible for management of the corporation's annual travel and entertainment budget. Activities include:

1. Identify actual annual T&E spending by category (air, lodging, car rental, meal and entertainment, miscellaneous).
2. Identify trends relating to rise or fall in T&E spending; determine causes; develop and implement corrective action plans as appropriate.
3. Liaison to all operating departments for determination of annual T&E budgets, budget variance tracking, and corrective department level action as appropriate.

B. This position is responsible for ensuring that appropriate corporate travel policies are developed, monitored, and enforced.

1. Review all corporate travel policies annually. Coordinate adoption of revisions with other responsible departments (purchasing, human resources, etc.). Present revisions for approval by senior management. Oversee annual distribution of approvers and travel accounts-payable staff. Ensure travel policy distribution is executed for all new hires expected to perform any of the above-mentioned functions.

2. Ensure that appropriate and current information is available to all parties charged with monitoring compliance to policy, including travel expense authorizers, department managers, travel accounts-payable staff, and the incumbent for this position.

3. Ensure that travel policy enforcement is executed by the appropriate parties (travel expense authorizers, travel accounts-payable staff, department managers).

C. This position is responsible for managing the relationship between the corporation and its contracted travel agency(s), including all employee customer-service issues arising therefrom.

1. On a periodic basis as approved by management, the Corporate Travel Manager will direct all activities relating to selection, contracting, and implementing corporate travel agency services.

2. On an ongoing basis, this position will monitor and document agency performance, and implement corrective action as needed.

3. Direct any on-site agency presence.

4. This position is the principal focus for employee customer-service inquiries and issue resolution.

5. Ensure appropriate distribution of travel agency related management information reports.

D. This position is responsible for managing the company's relationships with direct travel vendors (airlines, hotels, car-rental firms, etc).

1. Identify and conduct contract negotiations with appropriate vendors on an annual basis.

2. Ensure that all employees are directed to use preferred vendors; monitor and ensure enforcement of preferred-vendor usage policies.

3. Maintain ongoing contact with preferred vendors for customer-service issues resolution and vendor support for fulfillment of all corporate requirements.

E. This position is responsible for overseeing all corporate group and meeting planning activities.

1. Ensure professional purchasing practices are applied to all travel-related contract negotiations for company-sponsored groups, meetings, and incentives to minimize costs.

F. This position is responsible for administering the company's corporate charge-card program.

1. Manage the company's relationship with the corporate charge-card vendor.
2. Ensure that all employees expected to travel two or more times per year are issued a corporate charge card.
3. This position is the principal focus for all customer-service issues arising from the corporate charge-card program.
4. Liaison to human resources to ensure that all new employees expected to travel are issued a corporate charge card, and that charge cards are canceled for all terminating employees.
5. Ensure appropriate distribution of charge-card-related management information reports.

G. This position may include responsibility for staff management, for positions such as travel coordinator(s), analyst(s), and travel operations personnel. The position is responsible for recruitment, training, performance measurement, and coaching for all direct report positions.

H. This position may include a direct liaison role relative to the following travel-related activities:

1. Employee relocation
2. Scheduling and inventory management for corporate aircraft
3. Company owned/managed fleet management
4. Travel accounts payable
5. Travel management for divisions and subsidiaries that are based in foreign countries

Other areas of responsibility of the travel manager may include:

- Airline reservations.
- Ticketing.
- Hotel reservations.
- Confirmations.
- Car-rental reservations.
- Documentation.
- Rate negotiation.
- Corporate leased room arrangement.
- Rail and bus arrangements.
- Corporate aircraft scheduling.
- Expense account auditing.
- Dinner reservations.
- Tickets to entertainment events.
- Visas and passports.
- Management reports.
- Meeting and convention planning.
- Employee relocation.
- Training meetings.
- Per diems.

## Expanded Job Description

**Serve as liaison between the company and the travel management firm.**   One of the biggest responsibilities of the travel manager is maintaining the relationship between the company and the agency. The travel manager is the day-to-day point person in this relationship. It is not unusual for the travel manager to have a major role in the selection of the travel management company.

**Function as a communications center for employees.**   Most travel managers conduct routine surveys of the corporate travelers to find out how they evaluate the vendors (airlines, hotels, and car-rental companies). It is this communication link between the travel manager and the travelers that directs a great deal of the vendor selection and helps in measuring the success of the corporate travel policy.

**Review company travel policy annually and make recommendations to top management.**   There are a number of reasons why travel policy will need annual reviews. First of all, as the travel manager communicates with the corporate travelers, shortcomings in policy may become apparent. Another reason for annual reviews of travel policy is that the structure of the industry may change. An example of this occurred in the mid-1980s, when it became apparent that there was a long-term oversupply of hotel rooms, which brought about a major restructuring in the way hotels dealt with corporations. The same thing has also happened in the airline industry recently. The last reason for an annual review is that information obtained from MIS (Management Information Systems) reporting may indicate areas of weakness or opportunities.

**Issue a company newsletter on business travel and/or memos or bulletins with travel policy recommendations.**   Almost all of the travel managers at large corporations who were interviewed for this book issue a quarterly newsletter for their corporate travelers. The issues covered a wide range of topics, including how to pack a suitcase, an explanation of yield management, the fine points of policy, and things to do in various towns during the evening.

**Analyze the firm's management information needs.**   The massive computers of the travel industry will present the travel manager with a mountain of numbers. This mass of information is not necessarily related to anything. The modern corporate travel manager will need to keep broad questions in mind, such as What information will I need to be able to negotiate with the vendors? What information will I need to ensure policy compliance?

**Review MIS reports, consolidate data, and report the key findings to management.**   It is difficult to imagine a company having a successful travel policy without the overwhelming support of top management. Reports to senior officials detailing the savings and other details of the travel department are essential.

**Conduct informative seminars for travelers and secretaries.** It is not unusual for the travel management company to present seminars on timely topics in cooperation with the travel manager. These seminars usually discuss in more detail issues covered in the newsletter.

**Negotiate airline, hotel, and car-rental discounts.** Most of the savings that a corporation realizes from the use of a travel manager will result from vendor negotiations for discounted prices. The travel manager's input is vital because the manager is the source of travel information in the company. A number of major corporations use their purchasing department to do the actual negotiations or for the submission of requests for proposals, but the travel manager is usually on the staff that submits or reviews proposals.

**Develop company-vendor relations.** After the vendor deals are cut (including deals with the travel management company), the next important step is establishing a relationship with these vendors. This is important to ensure that if any problems arise they can be settled quickly. Travelers often complain that they will have a confirmation number for a hotel room only to find when they try to check in that the hotel has no record of the reservation.

**Assist senior management in developing travel budgets.** The travel manager has to look at a number of important issues when helping to develop the travel budget. Most important, the manager must understand the role that travel plays in the company. Is the money to be spent a part of operations? In some instances it may be an investment in the future. Another important element in the budgeting process is the forecast of travel prices. Is it reasonable to expect the same mileage the corporation flew last year at the same prices? Will rising prices put a pinch in this year's travel budget, or will the budget have to be increased?

**Maintain city files for travelers' benefit.**   The city files contain more than just the best places to eat. The city files are an invaluable resource for the corporate traveler entering a city for the first time. How does this traveler get from the airport to the city? Is there reliable public transportation, or will the traveler need to rent a car?

**Function as a liaison with the auditing department.**   The travel audit is important because it gives the travel manager a handle on how well the corporate travelers are following policy. The travel management company serves as a first line in this audit as they are usually required to inform the traveler if the request is not in line with company policy. Most travel management firms will report exceptions to their supervisors, as it is not the role of the travel management company to enforce policy. The travel exceptions are then reported to the travel manager, who forwards the violation to the appropriate supervisor.

**Identify cost-reduction opportunities and recommend action plans to management.**   Cost reduction seems to be the impetus in the growth of the position of corporate travel manager during the last ten years.

**Administer the company's incentive travel programs.**   There is a growing trend for the travel manager to administer the corporate incentive programs. This includes nontravel incentives.

**Plan company meetings or serve as liaison with the meeting planner.**   Sources at U.S. Travel Data estimate that as much as one-third of corporate travel is for meetings and conventions. This area of travel management responsibility is great enough to warrant an entire chapter in this book.

**Administer the company's corporate card program.**   A major problem and expense in administering corporate travel is the issuance of cash advances. To minimize cash advances and to simplify payment, the corporate credit card is often used for traveler assistance in case of lost luggage or medical emergencies. Recently corporate credit cards began offering insurance benefits for car rental and other important programs.

**Conduct orientation on travel policy for new employees.** An important task of the travel manager is to orient the new employees as to travel policy. These meetings are important to both the employee and the travel manager because they set the tone for compliance.

**Monitor legislative developments.** Monitor legislative developments that are likely to impact the firm's travel budget through taxes and surcharges that do not improve the quality of the transportation system. It is important for a business travel manager to be able to recognize legislation (national or regional) designed to prey on the business traveler as a source of revenue and to recommend the most appropriate stance for upper management to take on these issues.

## ADDITIONAL DUTIES OF THE TRAVEL MANAGER

Lyn Froclich, travel manager at Fred Meyer Stores, located in Portland, Oregon, states that her job description is similar to the one presented by American Express and adds that she spends about 50 percent of her time administering those duties. In addition, she spends about 40 percent of her time scheduling corporate aircraft and 10 percent with miscellaneous special projects, such as incentive and event scheduling.

## HOW TO HIRE A TRAVEL MANAGER

The NBTA recommends that corporations looking to fill the business travel manager function seek seasoned individuals with a thorough background in office management, negotiating skills, travel system expertise, a fair degree of computer literacy, the ability to interpret the value of travel purchasing statistics, the capability to manage the flow of these statistics, and expertise in evaluating travel agencies, the proposals of mega-agencies, and the claims of travel management firms. A skilled business travel management executive can pay tremendous dividends to a progressive corporation, while keeping sales teams and representatives in the mainstream of commerce and enhancing travel options.

The NBTA's guidelines can be expanded as follows:

• **The ability to understand the travel industry.** Be able to absorb what is necessary to know, in a short time. Just because someone can use a reservation system or has worked as a travel agent does not necessarily mean he or she understands the travel industry.

• **A sensitivity to the needs of the travelers.** Many travel managers have never traveled on business themselves and therefore don't always understand the difficulties that can arise while a company employee is on the road. Be sure your travel manager is aware of your travelers' needs as well as the firm's objectives.

• **Personal integrity.** As is the case in any position responsible for making major purchases, your travel manager will be exposed to many inducements by vendors trying to gain your company's business. You should be confident that the individual you select will act in the best interests of your company. Many firms have found it helpful to require their travel manager to sign a statement promising not to accept any free gifts or trips, etc., over an established dollar value without management approval.

• **The ability to recognize cost-saving opportunities.** A good travel manager must be creative enough to identify ways to control all costs related to travel—not just obvious opportunities like negotiating corporate hotel rates and making sure employees use them, but inventive approaches as well, such as arranging ground transportation to take travelers from the office to the airport in groups when this approach could reduce the company's local transportation bill.

• **An understanding of statistics.** Your travel manager is likely to receive a wide range of management information reports. He or she must know which statistics are important and how to use these reports to control costs and communicate critical issues to senior management.

• **Excellent communication skills.** Since the travel manager will be serving as a liaison among management, vendors, and the company's travelers, he or she must have excellent written and verbal communication skills.

## ONGOING TRAINING FOR THE CORPORATE TRAVEL MANAGER

The NBTA offers a series of comprehensive educational programs specifically designed for travel management personnel. The association's Certified Corporate Travel Executive (CCTE) program provides a formal classroom approach to topics like travel management strategies, negotiation, and communicating with upper management, to mention just a few. The NBTA also sponsors an annual convention and exhibition, featuring seminars conducted by the leading authorities in the business travel management industry.

## TRAVEL MANAGEMENT TIPS

- For most companies, the first step in controlling corporate travel and entertainment costs will be realizing the need to control all costs.
- Top management commitment to and support of the program is vital because travel-expense control and management often runs counter to personal benefits lavished on travelers by airlines, car-rental companies, and hotels. Without a firm resolve by company management to enforce policies and procedures, a corporate travel management agenda can achieve only relative effectiveness.
- The savvy corporate travel manager will be able to tell you how travel fits into the entire corporate philosophy. The role of travel in the corporation is dictated by the corporate culture.
- It is strongly recommended that all firms, no matter what their current approach to business travel, have a written policy and review it at least annually.
- The job of the corporate travel manager is management. The corporate travel manager does not exist to make reservations or perform secretarial duties. Travel manager should be considered a middle- or upper-management position because of the vital role the manager plays in controlling a large corporate expense.

- One of the biggest responsibilities of the travel manager is maintaining the relationship between the company and the travel management firm.
- Most travel managers conduct routine surveys of corporate travelers to find out how they evaluate the vendors.
- The NBTA recommends that corporations looking to fill the business travel manager function seek seasoned individuals with a thorough background in office management, negotiating skills, travel system expertise, a fair degree of computer literacy, the ability to interpret the value of purchasing statistics, the capability to manage the flow of these statistics, and expertise in evaluating travel agencies, the proposals of mega-agencies, and the claims of travel management firms.

# SECTION

# II

I n this section you will learn in chapter 3 how to conduct a study of your company's travel patterns and how you can use this information to make up policies that will help your company better manage its travel.

Chapters 4 and 5 will take you through the process of choosing a travel management partner. This process includes sending out a request for a proposal, and the ways in which proposals can be evaluated will be discussed.

# Chapter Three

# Using Corporate Policy to Control T & E Costs

I n making corporate travel policy, it is helpful to be philosoph-
ical. Philosophers ask pointed fundamental questions that others
who are tied up with the normal day-to-day routine ignore. It can
be argued that the best place to begin contemplating corporate
travel policy is with the fundamental questions such as, Why do
our employees travel?

When we ask the question, Why are we traveling? we are
asking, How do we handle the logistics of our people-to-people
business? According to Walter Freedman, president of IVI Travel,
"The evolution of travel policy is similar to that of distribution
management back in the 1960s. The distribution traffic manager
started out just moving the freight. Today distribution management involves the analysis of every step in getting the product to
the marketplace. What is the most effective way? During the
1960s, the distribution manager was the person on the deck moving boxes. Now he or she plays an important role in deciding the
most profitable way to get products to the final consumer."

Travel management deals with people logistics—What is the
most profitable way to get people together? Is it travel? Is it E-mail
or the telephone? These are some of the fundamental issues travel
managers should be concerning themselves with.

The same forces of evolution that changed the role of the distribution traffic manager are impacting the role of the travel manager in relation to policy. The role of the travel manager and the
travel council in initiating travel policy is more involved. It begins
with the central issue, Why do we travel? People logistics is what
corporate travel management and policy is all about.

In analyzing people logistics, one of the fundamental questions is, What is the purpose of the trip? It may come as a surprise to those who believe all corporate travel is done to meet with clients, but for many companies, the primary purpose of most trips is to meet with another company employee.

When the travel manager understands the purpose of the trip, then it is possible to set up parameters to guide decisions. One of the current problems in implementing a trip-purpose analysis is that management information systems do not properly account for this data. This reporting deficiency can be handled by conducting surveys or by making changes in expense reports.

In essence, the written travel policy serves as an extension of the firm's corporate travel policy, which in turn exists as part of the overall corporate strategy. The purpose of the travel policy is to keep the cost of traveling within predictable, projectable, and realistic parameters, while still remaining an effective conduit of communication. While the business travel philosophies of small and mid-sized corporations with 20 or 30 business travelers may permit the consideration of personal travel preferences, this quickly becomes a highly unmanageable situation with 50, 100, or 200 travelers.

It is important to note that the most effective business travel policies carefully allow for contingencies and corporate rank. However, their effectiveness is directly proportional to the degree to which they are enforced by upper management. IVI's Freedman says, "When senior executives assist in communicating the reasoning behind the rules, policy compliance will follow." One major manufacturer of electronic components believes that business travelers are entitled to some perks and benefits because the company's business calls them away from home and family. As every business traveler comes to know, living out of a suitcase and a hotel room loses its glamour rather quickly.

On the other hand, a substantial number of corporations emphatically state that travel constitutes a major portion of some job requirements, and the stringent control of travel costs is necessary if the company is to remain profitable. As a result, frequent flyer benefits are returned to the corporation and expense accounts are carefully reviewed. It is safe to say that the current economic climate in the United States has done much to prompt companies to study the need for travel and to find ways to control travel expenses. The slack travel policies of the past are no longer condoned.

## THE CORPORATE TRAVEL STUDY

The travel manager uses concepts like corporate culture and employee types to make an effective corporate travel policy. In addition, it is vital to collect facts to put into the corporate travel study.

The corporate travel study will be used not only for the analysis and making of policy, but in negotiations with the appropriate vendors and in the request-for-proposal process. The corporate travel study should cover, as a minimum, these areas:

A. Travel Costs
  1. Current travel patterns and costs
     a. Ratio of travelers to total employees
     b. Ratio of frequent travelers to total employees
     c. Ratio of local entertainers to total employees
     d. Travel destinations (city-pair analysis)
     e. Number of company locations
  2. Current travel policies
     a. Scope of control
     b. Frequency of review
  3. The components of T&E spending
  4. Recent and anticipated T&E cost increases
  5. Billing of travel expenses to clients
  6. The travel budget
B. Travel Policies
  1. The policy-making process
     a. Existence of control by headquarters locations
     b. Frequency of policy review
     c. Perceived employee compliance
     d. The components of travel policy
  2. Air-travel policies
     a. Senior executives
     b. Rank-and-file employees
     c. Definition of lowest available airfare
     d. Airline service issues
  3. Hotel policies

        4. Car-rental policies
           a. Nature of policies
           b. Car size limitations
        5. Per diems/spending guidelines
           a. Per diem amounts
           b. Per diems per region
           c. Updating per diems
           d. International per diems

    C. Travel Arrangements
        1. Use of outside travel agencies
           a. Number of agencies used
           b. Satisfaction with current agency
           c. Services provided by current agency
           d. Perceived value of travel agency services
           e. Rebating/revenue sharing
        2. Involvement of company employees in making travel arrangements

    D. Payment Methods
        1. Cash advances
           a. Temporary advances
           b. Permanent advances
        2. Limited-purpose cards
           a. Air-travel cards
           b. Car-rental cards
           c. Telephone credit cards
           d. Oil-company cards
        3. Company-sponsored multipurpose corporate cards
           a. Selection of corporate credit cards
           b. The role of corporate credit cards
        4. Other payment methods
           a. Employee funding
           b. Self-reimbursement methods
           c. Other billing methods

    E. Information and Expense Reporting
        1. Information management needs
        2. Expense reporting practices
           a. Use of spot checking
           b. The basis for auditing expense reports
           c. Receipt requirements

(This outline was adapted from The 1991 American Express Survey of Business Travel Management.)

The corporate travel study is an in-depth analysis of the ways in which the company currently handles its travel. After completing the study of how the corporation currently handles its travel, the travel manager can identify the company's travel needs and any changes that have to be implemented.

The corporate travel study should be used in making up the request for proposal (RFP). Making a RFP without first identifying corporate travel objectives is an exercise in futility.

According to E. J. Hewitt, manager of travel administration for a Midwest-based firm, "No one particular outline can serve as the basis for every firm's initial corporate travel analysis. The geographic location of a company, the number of travelers between highly competitive city pairs and remote locations, and the frequency of travel may serve to dramatically limit the return of any travel policy from the outset."

The NBTA recognizes that no two companies are exactly alike in their travel requirements or their travel philosophies. As a result, the association commits a considerable portion of its annual convention and exhibition to seminars that address conducting corporate travel studies for small, mid-sized, and large companies. The multilevel approach is considered important, since the analysis procedure will very often require an in-depth re-evaluation of the travel management firm or travel agency working with the company. Naturally, this places a greater emphasis on the value of corporate-placed personnel who understand this complex process.

## THE AVERAGE-FARE MYTH

One area in which a great number of people err in conducting a corporate study is the use of averages. If there is one area in statistics that is misused it is averages. Averages are supposed to be used to report the central tendency of a group of numbers. Some statisticians use words like "most likely event" in place of an average. The average was never meant to be the only descriptive number of a group. Actually at least two statistics are needed to describe any group. The average is one, and the other is the variance. The variance in many cases conveys more information than the average.

An example will clarify the issue. Let's examine two groups of numbers that have approximately the same average and show how this statistic will mislead us as to what is happening.

| GROUP 1 | GROUP 2 |
|---------|---------|
| 200 | 1 |
| 210 | 2 |
| 220 | 3 |
| 230 | 4 |
| 235 | 1,000 |

The first group of numbers has an average of 221 and the second group an average of 202. If we had seen only the averages, we would conclude that the two sets of numbers are actually quite similar. In fact they are not. The average of the second group bears no resemblance to any of the numbers and is biased, even though identical mathematical methods were used. The discrepancy involves the range or variance of the numbers.

Further examples of incorrect uses of averages include describing how the average employee travels. A little examination reveals that the average employee does not travel. If we begin to be more specific in our requests for information, then statistics can be invaluable (e.g., we may wish to describe the average trip to Boston by a salesperson or the average trip to Detroit by the president). This data has relevance and can be used in formulating corporate policy.

None of this is meant to say that averages should not be computed. Rather it is to suggest that the way they are commonly used in the travel industry is incorrect. Properly, an average is one number that is used as a proxy for a lot of other numbers. Averages are meaningful when the unit of measurement is very similar and the figures are broken down into groups where the variance is small relative to the size of the average (if the variance is greater than the average, then the average is meaningless).

Again an example will help show the proper use of averages. A number of leading magazines and consulting firms report statistics such as the average cost of an airline ticket in the United States. As was explained in the first chapter, there are over 300 different fare classifications, with the difference in price between the highest and the lowest being 75 percent. It is quite clear that the average airline fare is a useless statistic that describes a trip that never happens.

On the other hand, if we were to report the average fare between Washington, D.C., and Sarasota, Florida, for an unrestricted ticket or a V-class ticket, then this figure is meaningful. Instead of reporting the average hotel expense, break it down into various hotel types or brands. A good rule of thumb in analyzing data is that the more specialized the unit the more meaningful the data will be.

## CASE STUDY: AVERAGE FARE IS AN INAPPROPRIATE MEASURE OF AIR-TRAVEL COST PERFORMANCE

The following comments on using average fares are offered by James Carey, senior vice president of Kurth & Co., an airline consulting firm located in Washington, D.C.

As corporations expand into multiple facilities and become more involved in international operations, business travel has become a more significant part of total corporate expenditures. It has become increasingly important to closely manage travel costs by implementing policies that control or cause reductions in travel expenses from year to year. With the help of improved computer capability, the corporate travel manager now has the tools to effectively monitor and measure the travel patterns of the company and to modify policy to effect a travel cost savings or to achieve cost-containment.

Recently, the corporate travel industry has adopted average price per corporate trip as a standard measure of corporate travel cost. Average cost per trip is most widely used as a relative measurement of corporate travel expenditures between a company's divisions or to compare expenditures with those of other companies or industries. For example, during the year a company's purchasing department had average trip costs of $1,500 per person, while the manufacturing unit traveled for $1,300 per trip. In this simplified example it would seem obvious that developing a policy for the purchasing department to travel at $1,300 per trip would save the company $200 per trip in the coming year. However, without an understanding of the cost components of these trips, implementing this policy may not produce the desired result.

As part of a comprehensive method of analysis, a comparison of average costs can be appropriate as a measure of the relative size of expenditures. Since the average describes the price in the middle of a range of prices that are most frequently paid, any costs above this point can be characterized as excessive and any costs below the average as beneficial. The caveat to this logical assumption is that the costs that are being compared must be uniform. This means that the trips that are being examined must be in the same narrow range of prices. If this can be proven to be true, selecting lower price terms from a range of prices will result in lower total costs.

In order to establish an accurate measure of relative cost, it is necessary first to understand the reasons for price variations between products and then to find a method of measurement that accurately reflects the differences in the components of the cost. This can be done by understanding the relationship between the pricing policy of the supplier and the price paid by the consumer for the product or service. Understanding the pricing strategy for a product provides the basis for developing an appropriate measurement of purchasing effectiveness.

In general, the price of a product or service is directly related to the cost of development, production, promotion, and investment. In most businesses, these costs can be summarized in six basic categories:

1. The cost of research and development of a service or product.
2. The cost of promoting and selling the product to the ultimate consumer.
3. The cost of providing the service and maintaining assets at peak efficiency.
4. The cost of capital needed to support the production and sale of the service or product.
5. The amount of profit desired above costs for product improvement and creation of new products/services.
6. An acceptable amount of retained earnings to pay investors an acceptable return on their investment.

For different types of businesses, one or more of these cost categories will have a greater degree of influence on the price of each unit produced. For example, for a hotel operator, recovering the investment in the property and the building has a large impact on the basic price charged for a hotel room. The level of quality of facilities and service are the primary factors in setting a price above the basic room price.

The travel manager who understands these hotel pricing considerations knows that there should be a range of choices from lower- to higher-priced hotel rooms in each city. Also, the manager knows that prices will vary with the quality of service, the location in the city, and the cost of living of each city. With this basic knowledge, the travel manager can now establish a travel policy based on an acceptable quality of service, location, and price for future business trips. It will also be necessary to consider all three of these factors when measuring the future performance of the travel policy.

For example, an accurate cost analysis for hotel rooms used by the purchasing department versus the manufacturing division would begin by collecting data for all trips where a high-quality hotel was allowed for each group. A second set of data to compare would be available hotel-room prices for all competing high-quality hotels in the cities that were visited. Comparing the distribution of prices for purchasing department hotel use with the available room prices in the cities visited will give the manager a better picture of why the purchasing department hotel costs were higher. If it is found that the purchasing department has been consistently selecting hotel rooms from the highest-priced vendors, the policy for the coming year can recommend the selection of specific high-quality hotels or require that purchases be below the average price of the quality hotels in each city.

As can be seen from this example, each part of a business trip can be analyzed on the basis of its distinguishing characteristics of cost that affect price. From this information, an accurate measurement of acceptable performance can be devised. It is important to recognize that each portion of the trip must be measured by the appropriate combination of factors that accurately reflects the pricing strategies for that industry.

With this in mind, let's consider the differences in hotel pricing characteristics and airline seat costs. For an airline, the large capital cost of the aircraft, costly aircraft fuel, labor-intensive inflight and ground services, and the cost of operating multiple-city facilities are the primary drivers of basic seat price. Above this basic price, the cost of flying between cities at different distances is a highly variable cost for each airline. Fundamentally, the further the airline seat is flown, the higher the cost of providing the seat. This is caused by the added fuel burned per seat over the longer distance and the fact that a larger percentage of pilot and flight-attendant salaries are allocated to each seat on fewer trips per year.

As discussed before, the airline pricing process considers a substantial number of additional factors. This is made possible by the use of sophisticated computer-driven yield management and distribution capability. Beyond these elements of costs, the airline must also consider the pricing actions of competitors, as well as the levels of business and pleasure travel in each market.

The analysis in Figure 1, comparing two sets of airline trips, illustrates several problems with using average fare as a measure of airline costs. Both sets of trips result in the same average fare as a measure of airline costs, with Sample Two only 80 cents higher than Sample One. In Sample One, the trips were over vastly different distances and more importantly, all of the trips except for one were significantly below the total average fare. In Sample Two, all but one of the trips are below the average, with the one trip of $450 forcing the average to $291.80. Obviously the average fare provides very little information about the differences between the two trip samples. For the travel manager, it would be more important to understand why all the 700-mile trips in Sample Two had different prices than to know that they were all below the $291.80 average price.

The travel manager must be prepared to anticipate the impact of these types of events in order to quickly adjust travel policy and minimize the impact on the travel budget. This may seem to be a formidable task, but with careful examination of past pricing actions under similar circumstances, it is possible to anticipate the probable pricing actions of the carriers during future similar events.

Fortunately, a variety of information management technologies are available today that provide the resources to develop sophis-

**FIGURE 3.1**

| Air Fare Sample One | | | Air Fare Sample Two | | |
|---|---|---|---|---|---|
| | City Miles | Air Fare | | City Miles | Air Fare |
| Trip 1 | 100 | $    45 | Trip 1 | 700 | $   260 |
| Trip 2 | 300 | 60 | Trip 2 | 700 | 280 |
| Trip 3 | 500 | 100 | Trip 3 | 800 | 450 |
| Trip 4 | 700 | 250 | Trip 4 | 700 | 220 |
| Trip 5 | 900 | 1,000 | Trip 5 | 700 | 249 |
| Total costs | | $ 1,455 | | | $ 1,459 |
| Average fare | | $291.00 | | | $291.80 |

ticated systems for monitoring and measuring purchasing performance. However, it requires an initial commitment of time and financial resources to develop a system that provides realistic and accurate information to gain the benefits of the technology. As travel budgets grow at ever increasing rates, the potential savings from a comprehensive analysis system grow as well. But these savings cannot be realized until appropriate measures of performance are devised and implemented.

## THE TRAVEL BUDGET

One of the most puzzling aspects of travel management is the travel budget. Michael Woodward at American Express Travel Management Services offers the following outline to use in determining the travel budget:

    A. Getting Started
       1. What is the company's fiscal year?
       2. Who establishes budgets?
          a. Cost center manager
          b. Division and corporate finance departments
          c. Senior management
       3. What is senior management's strategic direction?
          a. Investment budget
          b. Cost reduction
          c. Flat or within 10 percent of previous year

    4. Will you use zero-based budgeting or incremental?

B. Travel Manager's Role in Budgeting
1. To provide travel-related information (industry trends and internal travel patterns), which will help budget managers establish appropriate allocations
2. To help company meet its travel budget goals (set and implement cost-reduction strategies)

C. Specific Information Travel Manager Should Provide
1. Changes in traveling population: How many employees travel currently and will this number increase next year? (For example, if a department has 29 people and plans to add three new employees, travel dollars will need to be allocated.)
2. Changes in travel patterns: What are the key cities and are there any expected changes? (For example, if international travel has been infrequent in the past, but the company recently acquired a new client in London or Tokyo, the travel budget must reflect this increase in average travel spending.)
3. Changes in travel frequency: how many trips have been taken in the past year and do you anticipate changes in this number?
4. Industry price forecasts: What are the anticipated increases (or decreases) in costs for air fares, lodging, car rental and meals?
5. Inflationary variables: While the company's finance area will include budget increases due to inflation, the travel industry may have (or expect) deviations from this standard.

D. Other Issues
1. Budget process will reflect strategic goals of senior management.
    a. There will be investment budgets in which the company is committed to increased levels of spending to achieve strategic goals.
    b. There will be budgets that reflect reduced spending levels from the previous year.
    c. There will be flat budgets, in which the increase reflects only inflation.
2. If management requests reduced travel spending from the previous year, the travel manager should under-

stand and document what it will take to meet those reduced budget goals. This will mean changes in travel policies and guidelines.

## WRITING A CORPORATE TRAVEL POLICY

In the December 1990 issue of *Corporate Travel* magazine, Kathy Passero gives the following ten tips for a first-time travel policy:

1. Determine management's goals and get their support. Get them to set an example for other travelers.
2. Analyze your corporate culture. Is cost control, comfort, or company visibility the number-one goal? Shape policy to reflect that.
3. Get feedback from travelers at headquarters and branch locations. Which vendors are travelers working with? How much are they spending and how often?
4. Gather travel data. Collect agency reports, traveler expense reports, credit-card reports, and any other information that could help show savings potential to management or aid in creating policy.
5. Use examples from travel consultants at firms similar to yours as a rough outline that you can tailor to your travelers' needs.
6. Prepare a proposal for senior management. Explain the benefits of a written travel policy. Point out the potential for current and future savings, backed up with solid facts and figures whenever possible.
7. Decide who will be responsible for monitoring compliance to the policy and what disciplinary actions will be taken for repeat offenders.
8. Create a standardized expense report that follows the policy.
9. Get management to meet with travelers to explain the need for a policy and to answer any questions. Create a brochure with a condensed policy to put in travelers' ticket jackets.
10. Hold follow-up meetings to explain policy, answer questions, and make sure executives' needs are met. Be pre-

pared to revise or extend the travel policy as your
corporation grows.

The staff at *Corporate Travel* magazine give the following outline
as a guide to what to include in a corporate travel policy:

A. Areas to Cover
   1. Method of making travel arrangements
      a. Individual travelers contact travel agency or travelers
         contact travel department, which in turn makes
         arrangements or contacts agency.
      b. Include telephone numbers of agency.
   2. Air travel
      a. Explain class of service allowed according to
         personnel levels.
      b. Are lowest fare routings and reservations required
         or just encouraged?
      c. List maximum number of executives allowed per
         plane.
      d. Determine policy on travelers' enrollments in
         frequent flyer programs; will they be allowed to
         keep the benefits for personal use?
      e. Explain when corporate charter aircraft may be
         used.
      f. List preferred carriers, if any.
      g. Other subjects to consider include: any flight
         insurance offered by company; accounting
         procedures on prepaid lost or unused air tickets;
         frequently flown city pairs listed when fare
         discounts are applicable.
   3. Lodging
      a. Establish per diems or spending guidelines
         according to city, type of hotel, or level of
         personnel.
      b. List suggested hotel types to be used—luxury,
         economy, etc.
      c. List preferred hotels or chains (if any).
      d. State policies on guaranteed reservations/cancella-
         tions; for instance, explain what a traveler with
         "guaranteed" reservations should do if he or she
         gets bumped out of a room.
      e. Other subjects to include: Are executive floors and
         other extra services permitted? Company policy on
         frequent guest memberships.

4. Ground transportation
   a. Rental cars
      1. Primary/preferred vendor and corporate negotiated rates.
      2. Establish what car size and vehicles are permitted; are luxury vehicles ever used?
      3. Cover policy on collision damage waiver and other insurance; is traveler permitted to take this out as a company expense?
      4. Explain refueling charges and company's procedure on them.
   b. Other transportation
      1. Is personal automobile use allowed and what is the amount of reimbursement?
      2. Explain use of company cars.
      3. Establish spending limits for cabs, limousines, van services.
      4. State policy on parking and valet service costs.
      5. Determine policies on rail transportation, as well as other forms of transport (bus, ship, etc.) and when use is appropriate.
5. Meals
   a. State per diems/spending guidelines allowed per meal, per day, and/or per city.
   b. List receipt requirements for meals; what dollar amount requires a receipt?
   c. Are alcoholic beverages includable as an expense?
   d. Explain the IRS definition of business meal—what is a business meal as opposed to a personal meal?
6. Entertainment
   a. Define level of personnel permitted to claim entertainment expenses.
   b. Include IRS definition of deductible entertainment expenses.
7. Payment methods
   a. Are cash advances permitted? How soon must traveler reimburse company?
   b. Corporate or personal charge cards; when they should or should not be used.
   c. Is direct billing to company ever permitted?
   d. State employee responsibility and liability for payment in use of cash advances and company charge cards.

8. Documentation
   a. Determine and explain specific documentation and expense breakdown required.
   b. State definition of acceptable receipts and for what dollar amount receipts are required.

B. Expense Reporting
   1. Sample forms
      a. Should be included with policy and should cover:
         1. Cash-advance form
         2. Pre-trip authorization
         3. Detailed expense report
         4. Other forms—special international travel authorization, damage waivers, etc.
   2. Report processing
      a. How soon after trip is filing required?
      b. Who must approve the completed reports?
      c. Where in the company should completed forms be sent?
      d. What is the average time after filing that travelers can expect reimbursement?
      e. Name of supervisor to contact in case of processing problems or questions.

C. Distribution of Policy
   1. Determine policy format—loose-leaf, booklet, memo.
   2. Include cover letter from senior management.
   3. Enclose/explain sample forms.
   4. Where to send/get approval of expense reports.

Peter Sontag, chairman of the board and chief executive officer of U.S. Travel, located in Rockville, Maryland, offers the following sample policy components. The recommendations for each category are listed as low control, medium control, and high control. Which one of the components is used depends largely on the corporate culture.

## Pre-trip Authorization Requirement

1. Low control. No written authorization required.
2. Medium control. Written authorization required by immediate supervisor for all trips. Authorization attached to the expense report.

3. High control. Written authorization by supervisor required for domestic trips, by second-level manager for international trips. Agency requires authorization number to complete reservation. Copy of authorization required to deliver ticket.

### Agency Usage

1. Low control. Travelers are encouraged to use one of the company's designated agencies.
2. Medium control. All travel reservations shall be made through the designated agency whenever possible.
3. High control. All travel reservations for airlines, hotels, and rental cars must be made through the designated agency. The company will not reimburse expenses for arrangements not made through the designated agency.

### Reservation Requests

1. Low control. State required departure or arrival time, airline, and flight number, if known.
2. Medium control. State desired departure time and arrival time, as well as airline preference.
3. High control. State desired departure time or required arrival time only. Do not request a specific airline or flight.

### Advance Planning

1. Low control. Travelers are encouraged to make reservations as far in advance as possible to take advantage of discount fares.
2. Medium control. Reservations should be made at least 7 days prior to departure, if possible.
3. High control. Travelers are encouraged to make reservations at least 14 days prior to departure.

### Reservation Changes

1. Low control. No mention.
2. Medium control. Changes should be made through the agency or an 800-number after-hours service.

3. High control. All reservation changes must be made through the agency or the 800-number after-hours service. Changes should be made at least 24 hours prior to departure for delivery of new tickets.

### Airline Class of Service

1. Low control. Domestic trips—coach. International trips—business class. First class permitted for director level and above.
2. Medium control. Domestic trips—coach. First class authorized in specific circumstances (e.g., traveling with a client.) International trips—business class.
3. High control. Domestic trips—coach. International (less than five hours)—coach. International (more than five hours)—business class. Authorization from a company vice president required for first-class travel.

### Low-fare Utilization

1. Low control. Traveler should always try to utilize the lowest available fare.
2. Medium control. Agency will offer traveler the lowest available fare within two hours of the desired departure or arrival time. All air travel should be at the lowest available air fare short of endangering the reason for the trip.
3. High control. Must accept lowest fare on any airline arriving within two hours of desired arrival time for domestic flights or six hours for international flights. Second authorization required for utilization of a higher fare prior to ticketing.

### Use of Connections

1. Low control. No mention.
2. Medium control. Connecting, rather than nonstop flights, should be used if there is a substantial fare saving.
3. High control. Connecting flights must be used if (1) they add no more than 90 minutes to the total trip time, and (2) they result in a fare saving of $100 or more.

### Airline Choice

1. Low control. No mention.
2. Medium control. Traveler may designate one airline he or she chooses not to fly.
3. High control. May not specify airline or flight.

### Frequent Traveler Benefits

1. Low control. Traveler allowed to accrue benefits.
2. Medium control. Award travel belongs to the company, and should be turned in to the company for business use.
3. High control. All travelers enrolled centrally by the company. Statements and awards delivered to the central company address.

### Hotel Reservations

1. Low control. The designated travel agency can handle hotel bookings.
2. Medium control. Reservations should be made through the designated travel agency. May specify a property.
3. High control. All hotel reservations must be booked through the designated agency, both prior to and during a trip, whether or not an airline flight is involved. May request a location, not a specific hotel.

### Hotels—Negotiated Rates

1. Low control. No comment.
2. Medium control. Hotels with company- or agency-negotiated rates should be used whenever convenient.
3. High control. Hotels with company- or agency-negotiated rates must be used within X miles of the work location if use does not require additional ground transportation charges.

### Hotels—Corporate Rates

1. Low control. Whenever possible, rooms should be reserved in hotels with a corporate rate.

2. Medium control. Always identify yourself as a Company X traveler and request a corporate rate when making a reservation or checking in.
3. High control. The designated travel agency will secure the lowest negotiated rate when making a reservation. Upgrades at check-in, at a rate higher than the rate confirmed, are not permitted.

## Class of Hotel

1. Low control. Moderately priced hotels should be used for company travel.
2. Medium control. First-class hotels, such as Sheraton, should be used. Concierge and executive floors should not be reserved unless no other accommodations are available. Deluxe or luxury hotels are not approved for company travel.
3. High control. Mid-priced hotels such as Holiday Inn, Ramada, or Choice are approved for the company traveler. Concierge and executive floors will not be reimbursed.

## Rental Cars—Company

1. Low control. Should use designated company, but may take advantage of local specials.
2. Medium control. Must use designated primary and secondary company.
3. High control. Must use designated primary and secondary company. Others are not reimbursed.

## Rental Cars—Class

1. Low control. No class specified.
2. Medium control. Compact or intermediate cars should be used.
3. High control. Economy or compact cars should be used unless there are three or more traveling together, then intermediate or full-sized cars are approved. Luxury cars are not approved.

### Meetings

1. Low control. No specific direction on meetings.
2. Medium control. Department heads should contact the designated agency to arrange a discount meeting airfare.
3. High control. The designated agency must be notified of all company groups involving ten or more travelers to the same destination. The agency will negotiate a meeting fare, which must be used by attendees.

### Travel Time

1. Low control. Employees should travel during normal business hours.
2. Medium control. Employees may travel during normal business hours.
3. High control. Employees should travel outside of normal business hours whenever possible.

### Meal Costs

1. Low control. Reimbursable within reasonable limits.
2. Medium control. Reimbursable within reasonable limits.
3. High control. Per-meal reimbursement required.

### Receipts

1. Low control. Required over $25.
2. Medium control. Required over $15.
3. High control. Required for all expenses.

### Payment for Air Fares

1. Low control. Personal charge card or accounts receivable.
2. Medium control. Ghost account (central air billing).
3. High control. Company-issued individual charge card.

### Payment for Hotel Rooms

1. Low control. Personal charge card or travel advance.

2. Medium control. Personal charge card.
3. High control. Company issued charge card.

### Travel Advances

1. Low control. Permanent travel advances for frequent travelers.
2. Medium control. Travel advances issued on a per-trip basis.
3. High control. No travel advances.

### Expense Reports

1. Low control. Must be completed and signed by immediate supervisor.
2. Medium control. Must be completed within 7 days of trip and signed by immediate supervisor.
3. High control. Must be completed within 7 days of trip. All expenses exceeding pre-trip estimate must be explained.

### Unused Tickets

1. Low control. Should be returned to agency upon completion of trip.
2. Medium control. Return to travel coordinator for return to agency.
3. High control. All coupons—even if of no apparent value—must be returned to agency. Agency receipt for returned coupon must be attached to expense report.

## COMPONENTS OF A CORPORATE TRAVEL POLICY

According to the American Express Consulting Services Group, "Forty-four percent of private companies (and a higher percentage of light spenders) still do not have formal, written policies; only about one-third review their policies at least annually; and one-third are unsure of the degree of employee compliance with policy. This is unfortunate because policy-related measures account for four of the most frequently taken steps to reduce or control T&E costs. These four steps are:

1. Require travelers to take the lowest logical airfare.
2. Tighten receipt requirements.
3. More strictly enforce existing T&E policies.
4. Create a travel policy.

(Adapted from the 1991 American Express Survey of Business Travel Management.)

Most formal policy manuals cover the major expense issues, such as airline travel, hotel accommodations, car rentals, and per diems. Generally, it is accepted that company headquarters should establish travel policy, as this offers the company the greatest opportunity to control travel expenses.

## TRAVEL ARRANGING

According to Runzheimer International, a Rochester, Wisconsin-based travel consulting firm, travel arranging refers to the function of reservation and ticketing activities. It includes how employees book their trips as well as how and where travel staff perform booking tasks, how tickets are delivered, and who performs these functions.

Essentially, companies have different choices in arranging travel. Those choices, which were listed earlier in this book, involve the various corporation/travel management company partnership configurations.

In the Runzheimer 1990–1991 Survey & Analysis of Business Travel Policies & Costs, it was reported that only 38 percent of the survey respondents require all travelers to use the organization's travel department or designated agency. If the company has a travel department or designated agency, it tends to require rather than encourage travelers to use the preferred reservations office. Two major reasons for centralizing reservations are to provide better service to travelers and to control direct travel dollars. The first goal may be met even if travelers are not required to use the centralized unit, but the second one typically is not.

The Runzheimer survey also pointed out that in travel arranging, the commission-sharing rage of the last few years has led firms to focus primarily on earning more dollars when changing their methods of booking travel. Now, however, companies are taking a more balanced view, broadening their focus to include three priorities:

1. Controlling the travel function.
2. Improving service.
3. Managing travel costs.

Improving service to travelers has become a more important priority in deciding how reservations and ticketing should be handled. In the 1984 Runzheimer survey, only 40 percent of the organizations placed major emphasis on travelers' services, while in 1990 about three in five cited this as a reason for changing systems. Runzheimer also discovered that the percentage of companies that intended to change how travelers booked trips in 1990 had declined substantially from the 1986 and 1988 surveys. During the 1986 and 1988 survey years, companies were restructuring their travel-arranging systems to share in commissions and to consolidate their travel volume to increase discounts. The fact that so few companies were planning to change systems in 1990 compared with the previous surveys provides further evidence that the frenzy for change, resulting from companies' abilities to share in commissions, has subsided.

Of the few firms that intend to change their travel-arranging systems at headquarters in 1990, more than half (58 percent), were planning to change to a system in which reservations and ticketing are handled on-site, counteracting the trend toward off-site relationships. The respondents that stated they were anticipating a change in travel-arranging methods at branch offices said that all travelers would soon book trips through headquarters.

According to the Runzheimer survey, of the remaining firms that expected to change travel-arranging methods in 1990, 26 percent planned to switch to on-site arranging, the largest percentage plan. Among these respondents, 15 percent planned to install satellite ticket printers, creating satellite plants.

## TRAVEL AGENCY USE

Data analyzed in the Runzheimer survey reveal that client-agency relationships are far from stabilized. Companies are continuing to consolidate their travel through fewer travel agencies and are switching agencies to improve services. Price, or commission-sharing, seems to be a less important factor driving company decisions to change agencies, because companies assume that the chosen agency will rebate some level of commission.

"Full service" has become the new catchword among travel management companies, and some of the service components have caught the attention of corporations. Particularly interested in these services are companies looking for ways to control rising travel costs. Management reports from travel agencies help companies identify their travel cost—the first step to controlling costs. Clients are also expecting their agencies to play an enhanced role in enforcing travel policy-monitoring and reporting on traveler noncompliance to policies. Also, as deregulation has opened airfares to negotiations, more companies are relying on their agencies to help them negotiate with airlines for better fares or services.

Despite reports to the contrary, rebating and commission sharing are clearly here to stay. Although any company that can shoulder some of the work usually delegated to an agency can get a better deal than those that prefer to let the agency do it all, travel volume is also a tool to use when negotiating with travel agencies.

## VENDOR RELATIONS

Corporations spend the largest portion of their travel dollars with three types of vendors: airlines, hotels, and car-rental firms. Thus it comes as no surprise that companies focus most of their energies on negotiating with these three vendor types for cost-effective rates.

The Runzheimer survey lists some important highlights in this area:

1. Fewer respondents report negotiations with hotel companies. National travel management companies have used the combined clout of their clients to negotiate greater dis-

counts, contributing to the decline in the number of companies that have negotiated their own rate discounts. For
those firms that negotiate hotel rate discounts, the average
discount off the corporate rate is 14 percent.

2. Since 1986, the percentage of respondents that negotiate
   with car-rental firms has declined further. As is the case in
   hotel-rate negotiations, travel management companies have
   established "preferred vendor" relationships with car-
   rental firms that may provide more attractive discounts
   than those negotiated by companies on their own.

Discount and price should not be the only considerations in
negotiating with vendors. After a value is placed on a client's volume, the client can further negotiate additional services. Companies can consider negotiating for a combination of a lower rate
plus free or reduced service costs. This combination can have a
stronger impact on bottom-line travel expenditures than negotiations that produce a reduced rate only. For example, when a company is negotiating airfares, additional bargaining may result in
the waiver of cancellation penalties, which could result in substantial savings. In hotel negotiations, an extra push might yield
free continental breakfasts for all corporate travelers, resulting in
additional savings in meal reimbursements. In car-rental negotiations, free collision damage waivers (CDW) or upgrades could
also help keep travel costs in check.

## EXPENSE PAYMENT REIMBURSEMENT
## AND REPORTING

For a business trip, employees are reimbursed for travel expenses
that generally fall into six categories: airfares, lodging, meals,
telephone, entertainment, and incidentals. Even without a formal,
written travel policy, virtually all companies have procedures for
travelers to follow in reporting these expenses to receive reimbursement. Expense reporting and reimbursement are typically
the first areas of travel for which companies document procedures. Often, corporate accounting oversees travel expense administration, reconciliation, and reimbursement. In recent years,
however, expense reporting has taken on a new importance as an

increasing number of companies are relying on this traditional accounting procedure to identify company travel costs, with the ultimate purpose of managing them more effectively.

The Runzheimer study outlines three main trends in reimbursements:

1. Most respondents to the Runzheimer survey have established guidelines for reimbursing employees for most of their travel costs incurred during a business trip. Although a growing segment of corporations is becoming stricter when establishing reimbursement limits, most respondents still allow reimbursements for any cost that is considered reasonable.

2. Fewer than one in five respondents have altered their meal expense reimbursement policies in response to the 1986 tax changes, which limit the deductibility of meal expenses to 80 percent. By not addressing this change, companies have, in some cases, made employees responsible for declaring part of the meal-expense reimbursement (20 percent) as taxable income. In other cases, companies have missed an opportunity to limit meal expenses by implementing restrictions as a result of the tax law change.

3. Company-issued charge cards remain the primary method used by respondents to reimburse and reconcile travel expenses. T&E charge cards (e.g., Diners Club, American Express, 1st Bank, Visa, and Enroute) are the most commonly issued cards. Pre-trip travel advances are also a common method used to reimburse travelers for incidental travel expenses.

Runzheimer comments that an efficient system of travel expense reimbursement is the key to the effective management of corporate travel costs. According to the consultants at Runzheimer International, an ideal reimbursement system will:

1. Allow employees to arrange travel without delays.
2. Take advantage of economies in the marketplace.
3. Minimize any inconvenience to the traveler.
4. Afford corporate controllers and financial personnel the ability to identify and monitor travel expenditures for purposes of controlling and managing company travel dollars.

5. Minimize any cash outlay on the part of the company because cash advances can tie up investment or operating
   capital.
6. Produce consistent, reliable billing from vendors.

Runzheimer comments further that an ideal system is cashless
travel with accurate billing and without interest payments. Employee abuse of corporate credit cards has not materialized to the
extent that many business travelers feared. Meanwhile, market
acceptance of business travel cards has spread, enabling business
travelers to charge expenses at virtually every phase of their trip—
from air travel to ground transportation to airport parking. To the
credit of the charge-card companies, efforts to provide useful management reports have aided many travel managers in improving
their determination of where travel dollars are spent and who is
spending them. Vendors have also made significant strides in understanding the corporate market. Centralized billing, automated reservations, and direct negotiations of corporate rates have produced
significant savings for those companies eager to pursue them.

Yet business travel cost payment, reimbursement, and reporting
are far from reaching what travel managers would term a utopia.
Vendors' corporate rates are often confusing, ambiguous, and in-
consistent. Vendor and charge-card billing systems are too inflexible to help many companies because of a lack of standardization
in data-gathering among North American corporations. Moreover,
many of the present generation of vendor management information reports are more complicated than necessary, somewhat self-
serving, sometimes meaningless, and therefore, as the drop in the
number of respondents who use the reports suggests, unusable
by clients. Contributing to this lack of enthusiasm for vendor reports is the fact that many companies do not have the skilled
employees or the time to put all the information contained in
these reports to effective use.

## POLICY COMPLIANCE

Corporations report a wide variance in the degree to which they
police exceptions to policy. Joe Laughlin, director of sales at United
Airlines, comments, "Our policy on reimbursement is very strict.

If the flyer does not stay at one of our approved hotels, they do not get reimbursed, no exceptions."

In the December 1990 issue of *Corporate Travel* magazine, the American Express Consulting Group reports that:

> *Including these allowable instances of forfeited savings, 13% of all business travel bookings analyzed this month contained segments which did not meet companies' lowest fare objectives. Therefore, non-complying trips cost 31% more than available alternatives would cost. Out of the total air purchasing trips for the month, non-complying trips meant a forfeit of 7% of readily available discounts. A closer look reveals four areas—carrier preference, late booking, and class and routing exceptions—that corporate travel departments can crack down on to squeeze more savings out of business trips.*

One of the most common exceptions to policy is frequent flyer preferences. The American Express group reports that travelers who use their own favorite carrier cost their companies 23 percent more than the lowest available alternatives. In the same article, American Express comments that the most controllable exception to policy is class of service. Class of service exceptions occur when a traveler requests an open ticket or a full-fare coach ticket, possibly to allow upgrading to first using frequent flyer mileage awards.

The corporate travel manager will be given a report called the exceptions report by the travel management company. This report will detail the employees who have not followed policy. Generally, it is not the travel manager's job to discipline the errant employee. However, it is the duty of the travel manager to report exceptions to the employee's supervisor. The supervisor is in charge of disciplining exceptions. The range of actions vary from warnings, to nonreimbursement, to termination.

## CASE STUDY: UNITED TECHNOLOGIES

One way of preventing exceptions to corporate policy is through strong communication to travelers. According to Carol Salcito at United Technologies, "Communication is one of the key elements in a successful travel program." Carol's plan to manage UTC's travel program was to get the word out to the largest audience possible (UTC has 190,000 employees located in over 105 countries). In order to accomplish this task, UTC produced a video. This video was to accomplish two objectives:

1. Basic education to new employees.
2. Marketing awareness.

According to Salcito, "I wanted to provide employees with a brief overview of the features of our travel program and why it would be beneficial to participate. While the video would serve as a basic education vehicle, it would clearly be a marketing effort. I wanted to increase awareness of the travel program benefits and features to current employees as well as new employees."

After obtaining approval from senior management, the next step was to go forward with the help of an outside producer of videos. The producer interviewed Salcito, and an outline for the video was developed.

The travel council provided the producer with a script plus recently written articles on travel and copies of the car-rental agreement, preferred hotel program, and charge-card program.

Once the producer provided UTC with a hard copy of his outline, Salcito provided him with a script on each of the suggested topics of discussion. A UTC employee edited the script, and it was turned back to the producer for creative work, after which the script was returned to Salcito. Each of the members of the travel council added their input. The final version involved roles for all of the travel council members, developing a sense of ownership and pride in the video.

The role each member would play was to discuss one particular aspect of the travel program. The topics were:

1. Designated travel agencies.
2. Travel policy.
3. Car-rental contract.
4. Travel charge card.
5. Preferred hotels.

It was decided to keep the video short (no more than 15 minutes) and humorous parts were added. The producer suggested a simple story line conveying the experience of one individual who is preparing for, arranging, and engaging in a hypothetical trip, with before and after situations.

Before the video could be produced, it was necessary to obtain approval of the travel vendors because most of the video was filmed on location. They all agreed as long as their names never appeared during the mishaps of the traveler.

A professional actor was chosen to portray the traveler; another professional actor was to present the details.

After the video was completed, other questions had to be answered, such as who should receive the video. The director of human resources for the corporation worldwide was brought into the decision-making process at this time. It was decided that a brochure would be produced along with the video.

Salcito comments, "I had 10,000 copies of the brochure printed; prepared a memo to all recipients of the video asking how many they wanted; explained that the pocket in the rear of the brochure was for their addition of their division's travel policy; and asked them to contact me directly if they had any questions or concerns. At this moment we have distributed over 3,000 brochures and shown the video to the same number of employees. We have received excellent comments through our quality-control cards and I believe the downswing of complaints is a direct result of this video. The video showed our employees that senior management was willing to invest money to communicate, educate, and inform the business traveler of a corporate program designed to make their travel easier."

## CASE STUDY: COLGATE PALMOLIVE

Colgate Palmolive is a 200-year-old company with global headquarters located in New York. Colgate Palmolive hired Sheila Bender to be director of the Travel & Meeting Management Group eight years ago. Colgate Palmolive gave Bender broad mission statements, such as "make our money work smarter." Bender set about to accomplish this task through a careful analysis of the Colgate Palmolive corporate culture. According to Bender, "Our company has a rich heritage that our employees are very proud of. Colgate Palmolive is also a market-driven company. The employees understand concepts such as market share and how important this is to a company's bottom line. My task was to discover the corporate culture and control it to the extent they want it controlled. My sales job was to find what would fit Colgate Palmolive and sell it to them."

The travelers out of the New York office would be on the road for as long as three weeks at a time, usually to foreign destinations with as many as ten to fifteen segments on each ticket. Bender wanted to accomplish a number of objectives in formulating policy. One of these was to build strategic relationships with vendors because Colgate Palmolive is not in the travel business. This meant that no time lengths were set on most contracts, including the travel management company they chose. In order to build long-term strategic relationships with the vendors, Bender states that she would never promise more than could be delivered.

Bender was given a great deal of control over policy, but the various departments made their own travel budgets. Even though she had considerable authority, she decided to allow key employees and divisions to buy into the programs before they were announced. This way it was easy to get compliance. Bender states that their policy compliance rate is 98 percent.

Based upon Bender's analysis, which covered an eight-month period, it was decided that a number of changes should be made in the existing corporate travel policy. Previously, the company had collected frequent flyer miles from the employees. Bender recommended that the frequent flyer points be given back to the employees and that instead they use a recommended airline.

It was explained to the employees that the airline choice was based on a negotiated deal in which Colgate Palmolive promised to move market share to certain carriers. This method was in line with the company's being market-driven, so the employees would easily understand the reason for the airline deal. Employees were not required to use the airline and could use another carrier if they were willing to pay the difference between the negotiated rate and the full fare. Employees were also given the chance to use other carriers if they felt the ones chosen were not suitable for any reason.

## CASE STUDY: PROFESSIONAL BASKETBALL

According to Charles Roumas, marketing vice president at Travel One, Inc., located in Mt. Laurel, New Jersey, and account manager for a professional basketball team, there are important cultural factors in managing a sports team that make a difference in its performance. The whole idea of corporate culture and of having policy reflect it is best typified in professional sports.

Roumas states that there are three main factors that make sports travel management different from most corporate travel:

1. Basic arrangements.
2. Players' needs.
3. Logistics.

## BASIC ARRANGEMENTS

"Basic arrangements" refers to the use of scheduled airlines versus charter air flights. A great deal of the time, scheduled airplanes are not a good choice to use in professional sports because games may run long and the team will miss the plane. Unlike most business people, they cannot leave in the middle of a game to make their flight. There are also other considerations, such as that most players require first-class seats if for no other reason than that they have very long legs. Another consideration is that in many of the players' contracts they are guaranteed certain types of space and accommodations when they travel. If there are not enough first-class seats available, then certain seniority clauses in the players' contracts take over.

## PLAYERS' NEEDS

It is no understatement when professional basketball players are described as big boys. The centers for many of the teams are 7 feet tall and can fit only in seat 1B in an aircraft because their feet stretch to the door of the cockpit. In the charter bus that takes the players from the hotel to the sports arena for practice and games, the center often sits at a window and stretches across four seats on the bus.

Because professional athletes are in the same class as entertainment stars, they are accorded certain privileges, such as special menus and open bars. Hotel selection is critical because extra-long king-size beds are usually required. In the case of many of the centers, two king-size beds are put together and the player sleeps diagonally.

The players also go through a ritual known as carbo loading before a game. They load up on high-carbohydrate foods to provide ample energy for the game.

## LOGISTICS

Getting to and from the planes and hotels in private buses is an important aspect in sports travel. The players of many winning teams attribute some of their recent success to the fact that now they have a bus pick them up right at the airplane, bypassing the airport terminal and the crowds of fans waiting to stop them. Hotel rooms are generally preregistered and keyed so that the players can also bypass the lobby and go straight to their rooms.

## TRAVEL MANAGEMENT TIPS

- People logistics is what corporate travel management is all about.
- In analyzing people logistics, one of the fundamental questions is, What is the purpose of the trip?
- When the travel manager understands the purpose of the trip, then it is possible to set up parameters to guide the decisions.
- The purpose of the travel policy is to keep the cost of traveling within predictable, projectable, and realistic parameters, while still remaining an effective conduit of communication.
- It is important to note that the most effective business travel policies carefully allow for contingencies and corporate rank. However, their effectiveness is directly proportional to the degree that they are enforced by upper management.
- The travel manager uses concepts like corporate culture and employee types to make an effective corporate travel policy. In addition, it is vital to collect facts to put into the corporate travel study.

- The corporate travel study will be used not only for the analysis and making of policy, but in negotiations with the appropriate vendors and in the request-for-proposal process.
- The corporate travel study should be used in making up the request for proposal (RFP). Making a RFP without first identifying corporate travel objectives is an exercise in futility.
- In order to establish an accurate measure of relative cost, it is necessary first to understand the reasons for price variations between products and then to find a method of measurement that accurately reflects the differences in the components of the cost. This can be done by understanding the relationship between the pricing policy of the supplier and the price paid by the consumer for the product or service.

*Chapter Four*

# Choosing a Travel Management Partner

## THE TRAVEL MANAGEMENT CORPORATE PARTNERSHIP

Five years ago, the megas bid on practically every piece of business that came across their desk. At that time, it was not unusual for companies to put their travel business up for bid every year. Both of these conventions are changing. It is becoming commonplace for the large companies not to bid their travel business every year because it is unprofitable.

## THE INCUMBENT

Many corporations have successfully consolidated their travel with a single agency. These companies should ask themselves if they are satisfied with the level of service the incumbent is providing. It takes a great deal less time to correct a problem with an incumbent than to put out a request for proposal. It is an unfortunate trend that too much time is spent on choosing a travel management company.

Travel managers who have a satisfactory relationship with a travel management company should concentrate on all of the other issues that they face and consider themselves fortunate.

Corporations are becoming more interested in maintaining long-term relationships with vendors. At some point, the cost of going out to bid and the time involved every year in analyzing bids becomes counterproductive. An example of this trend is Texas Instruments, who recently hired a consulting group to examine alternatives to the bidding process.

## PARTNERING

The concept of partnerships was addressed in the September issue of *Corporate Travel* magazine in an article by Loren Ginsburg. The article reported that General Electric Power Systems had just renewed its three-year contract with Rosenbluth after a few informal meetings with competitors. Northrop Corporation forged a five-year American Express deal, and Kodak added two years to its Rosenbluth pact without requesting a bid.

According to Loren Ginsburg, "partnering" is the latest purchasing trend. Mega-corporations are consolidating business with one partner for multiyear deals.

The benefits are clear to Ginsburg: "Partnering eliminates the administrative hassle and expense of competitive bids; locks in long-term rates; keeps internal processes consistent; and eases traveler compliance. And in a time when budgets and manpower are being streamlined, it's simply easier to stick with preferred vendors."

Matt Nozzolio, spokesperson for United Technologies, agrees with Ginsburg: "In purchasing travel or other products, we're looking to align ourselves with quality suppliers for an extended period of time, rather than continuing to open up contracts."

The concept of partnering does not preclude shopping. E. J. Hewitt, travel supervisor at Libbey-Owens Ford in Toledo, Ohio, states, "We tend to stay with the same vendors when contracts expire, but we will go to other vendors informally and ask them what they have to offer. Phil Tedeschi at Reliance Electric offers similar advice: "Generally, when the contract is up, we'll try to renegotiate with the original supplier before we take it to the street. That is, unless we have service problems, then we would go out to bid."

One way to implement partnering is to write roll-over provisions into contracts. According to Gerard Smith, corporate travel administrator at Northrop Corporation, "Options to extend the deal allow for longer-term relationships without going through a bid process." Another method used by corporations to implement partnering is guarantees. Loren Ginsburg states: "To encourage clients to roll over contracts, agents are supporting efforts to audit their services and work to improve glitches."

In creating a true partnership between the corporation and the travel management company, the choice of which travel company to use is one of the most important decisions facing the corporate travel manager. The form of the relationship between the corporation and the travel management firm will decide to a large extent the relationship between the two. The legal relationship and the payment form are of vital importance. The payment form is critical because under the commission agreement, the travel management company is an agent of the travel vendors, not the corporation.

There are a variety of options available to the corporation with which to forge a partnership with the travel management company. The majority of these options require an understanding of the Airline Reporting Corporation (ARC) and the accreditation process and its relationship to airline ticket stock.

The airline ticket is a unique document in that it has a monetary live status. This means that a ticket once issued or stolen can be used by anyone, and the issuing travel agency has a legal obligation to pay for it. The airline ticket is a standard document issued by the ARC. The main activity of the ARC is managing the Area Settlement Plan. The Area Settlement Plan is the world's oldest centralized ticket processing and reporting system. It helps airlines and travel agents by providing a simple and unified system through which airlines can market their services to the consumer. The ARC provides three primary services to the travel industry:

1. Travel agency accreditation.
2. Printing and distribution of standard ticket stock.
3. Centralized reporting, processing, and settlement of tickets issued.

The ARC traffic documents, or tickets, are the key to establishing the relationship between carriers, travel agents, and the public. The standardized ticket provides a simple and efficient means for agents to sell travel on all participating carriers. Each time an agent issues a ticket, the name of the carrier is imprinted on a blank form. The ARCs processing centers can then identify the carrier or travel agent to receive funds or commissions for that ticket. Each week all participating carriers receive one check from the ARC for all travel sold on that carrier.

## TRAVEL AGENCY ACCREDITATION

Before a travel agency is opened, it must go through an accreditation process administered by the ARC. Only after completing this process can an agency begin to issue tickets. The location for which the application is intended must have at least one person who is employed full time by, and on the payroll of, the agent at the place of business. This person must be either the owner, a partner, the manager, or an officer, and must fulfill each of the following qualifications:

1. Exercises daily supervision of the responsibility for the operations of the agency and has authority to make decisions.
2. Must pass a written examination covering material in the Industry Agents' Handbook.
3. Has had at least two years' full-time experience in selling general travel services or supervising the operation of a travel agency.
4. Has had at least one year's experience in airline ticketing within the last three years.

The place of business must be used primarily for the retail sale of passenger transportation and must be clearly identified to the public as a travel agency. In addition to the personnel and location requirements, there are also financial requirements that must be met before a travel agency can be established. The financial requirement is in the form of a bond, which is held against the failure of an agency to make timely payments for airline ticket sales to the ARC.

## PRINTING AND DISTRIBUTION OF STANDARDIZED TICKET STOCK

The standard ticket is a contract between the carrier indicated on the itinerary of the ticket and the passenger. There are seven important items on each ticket:

1. Authorizes passage between the points and via the routing indicated.

2. Serves as evidence of payment of the fare shown on the ticket.

3. Serves as evidence that an interline agreement exists between the carrier named in the routing and the ticketing agent.

4. Indicates the class of service, the flight number, and the date of travel.

5. Contains all information necessary to ensure expeditious and proper handling of the on-line and interline customer and his or her baggage via the routing shown.

6. Contains a record of all conditions that must be known at the time of reissuance or refund.

7. Contains all information necessary for billing purposes between the issuing and carrying airlines' revenue accounting departments.

## CENTRALIZED REPORTING, PROCESSING, AND SETTLEMENT OF ISSUED TICKETS

The process by which the airlines get their money for the tickets sold by travel agencies is very interesting. In essence, the ARC acts as a settlement house that collects all the money paid to travel agencies for airline tickets and then pays this money to the airlines. Each week every travel agency sends in a report to the ARC detailing all of its cash and credit-card transactions. Under the ARC agreement, the ARC has the right to draft the travel agent's trust account at the agent's bank for the amount owed the airlines, less any commissions the agent is to receive. The ARC sends the agent a commission check for credit-card transactions. The ARC then consolidates all of the money received from the travel agencies and sends each of the 136 participating airlines one check for the week's business. All of the money transfers are done electronically.

## AUTOMATED TICKETING

For the overwhelming plurality of travel agencies, the printing of an airline travel document along with the boarding pass and travel itinerary is now a very simple process. The ticket printers are provided with the CRS, along with the reservation equipment. Because of this, it is only necessary for the travel agent to do a few simple keystrokes on the CRS to go from a passenger name record (PNR) to a printed ticket. This is a major improvement in productivity. Many agents can still remember the days only one decade ago when all tickets had to be printed by hand, a long and tedious task. At the same time, getting the ticket to the final user remains a problem that is receiving the attention of automation specialists.

One such attempt to speed up the process of delivering airline tickets to corporate clients involves the use of satellite ticket printers (STPs). A satellite ticket printer is simply a ticket printer that is located in a corporate office and that is electronically linked to the travel agency's main location.

STPs are a late but welcome development. The ARC, bowing to the unstated but ever-present pressures of the Department of Justice, approved the concept of commissionable ticket printers for travel agents and their clients on December 3, 1985. Although the volume necessary to make placement of these devices economically viable is significant, they are multiplying in numbers, with an attendant reduction in the dollar value of tickets that must be generated to make them practical. They provide an excellent alternative to former ticket-delivery techniques, and they improve service capabilities with no reduction in a company's ability to gather complete data for management reporting. The use of STPs is growing rapidly. These ARC-appointed locations account for a substantial number of the new agency locations accredited in the past three years.

The host travel agency retains full control over the STP and sends signals to the STP to activate it. In order to set up an STP, a travel agency must go through an ARC approval process, much like the agency undergoes when first opening. This approval process also includes bonding. This is necessary to maintain strict accountability.

An STP location must be such that the ticket printer is located in a "secure" area where the general public does not have access to the ticket stock. The STP is maintained at the corporate site by an individual who has been trained in its operation and who assumes responsibility over the ticket stock. STPs represent a tremendous savings in time and labor to travel agencies in that it is no longer necessary to have delivery cars running all over the city to deliver tickets to large corporate clients. At the same time, it is still necessary for travel agencies handling smaller corporate accounts and leisure travelers to have delivery networks.

In order to facilitate the delivery of airline tickets to clients not served by STPs, the ARC recently gave the go-ahead to the development of a detailed plan to form a new accreditation category. This work arose from the emergence in the marketplace of companies that indicated a wish to provide electronic ticket delivery services (ETDN) to ARC-accredited travel agents, utilizing networks built upon STP technology.

The ARCs accreditation system has, up to now, provided only for the approval of retail travel agent outlets and STP locations uniquely dedicated to individual ARC agents. For this reason, the creation of a new category would be necessary to allow the ARC to place its ticket stock in accredited third-party network locations.

One such plan proposed for ETDNs (electronic ticket delivery networks) was to use services like Western Union, who would assume accountability for airline ticket stock. A customer would make a reservation through a travel agent and then pick up the ticket at a Western Union office close by. Another plan was developed by Susan Gunther in Phoenix, Arizona, utilizing automated travel teller machines (ATMs), which can produce tickets and itineraries.

The banking industry was revolutionized by automated teller machines, which reduced waits in long lines for simple transactions; such machines will soon be available to the travel industry.

The travel-teller machines will be manufactured by EDR Systems of Beachwood, Ohio, a maker of computer-based hardware and software systems. EDR is using a computer terminal manufactured by Diebold, Inc., a maker of bank automated teller machines.

Gunther said the idea for the teller machine came to her while she was delivering airplane tickets to a client. "I knew there had to be an easier way to do this. If you can withdraw money from a bank at the automatic teller machine, why can't you access tickets from your travel agency in the same manner." The automated ticket machines represent a major departure from the STPs in that they are fully automated and do not require an agent present to print the ticket stock.

## ATB TICKET STOCK

As the ticket-printing process becomes more automated, it is also necessary to change the basic travel documents. One such recent advancement is the introduction of automated ticketing and boarding pass (ATB) ticket stock. The ATB is made of a heavier paper so that it can go through the printers easier without jamming and also have the boarding pass included on the end of the ticket.

In response to the industry's growing need to reduce ticket theft and fraud, the ARC is developing the ATB-2. The new ticket will utilize magnetic-strip technology to facilitate the detection of stolen tickets at airport departure gates. The magnetic strip will also contain the traveler's PNR and other useful information.

## OPTIONS FOR CORPORATION/TRAVEL MANAGEMENT PARTNERSHIPS

Prior to the deregulation of the airline industry, travel agencies serviced both leisure and business clients from full-service locations. Relationships that were undreamed of just a few years ago are now possible. Travel agencies can service their clients in a host of different ways. There is no one best means of providing services. Many large corporations are served by a single agency with multiple operating configurations based on the needs of each location requiring service.

According to Harold Seligman, president of Management Alternatives, Inc., located in Stamford, Connecticut, there are many hybrids, but the basic lineup is as follows:

1. An on-site accredited or nonaccredited facility staffed by company personnel.
2. An on-site accredited or nonaccredited operation staffed by agency personnel.
3. A dedicated off-site location.
4. A full-service off-site location assisting multiple clients.
5. A business travel center with client dedicated staff.
6. A staffed or unstaffed satellite ticket printer.

Each of these options can be configured with differing financial and operating arrangements. To select the best working relationship for your company, you must define and prioritize your objectives, which can include the following:

1. Service to travelers.
2. Improved purchasing capability.
3. Rebate from the agency.
4. Consolidation with a single-source supplier to better control travelers.
5. MIS and data collection.

A variation on the above themes, suggested by some travel management companies, is to allow them to come in and be the corporation's entire travel department. However, according to John Hintz, president of the NBTA, "This is not an acceptable solution to corporate travel management, because it is like having the fox guarding the henhouse."

## OWNING YOUR OWN AGENCY

The federal government established the Civil Aeronautics Board (CAB) in 1937–38 to oversee the development of a budding aviation industry. In 1945, following World War II, the CAB permitted the Air Traffic Conference (ATC) to act as the voice of the airline industry, free of the constraints of antitrust laws and other anticompetitive practices. The CAB/ATC was the dynamic duo that oversaw the dramatic growth of air travel from 1945 to 1978. Beginning in 1978 and concluding in 1985, the CAB and the ATC were replaced by the Department of Transportation and the Airline Reporting Corporation (ARC). In a protected environment, free of normal competitive influences (markets and pricing), a few airlines controlled the bulk of US aviation.

The Deregulation Act of 1978 changed these procedures. Airlines were now free to enter and exit domestic markets and to charge whatever price they wished for transportation without government oversight. After January 1, 1985, agencies were free to use their domestic commissions in any manner they wished—to offset client costs, to give discounts to customers, or for any other scheme they could hatch.

Sharing international commissions is technically still a violation of the agency/airline agreement, but the Department of Transportation has stated that they see no harm to the traveling public if agencies wish to reduce prices by sharing commissions.

Whether owning an agency is a financially sound idea requires careful study. It is a marginal proposition at best, and without sufficient volume, it will be a money-losing venture. For a short time, corporations set up their own travel agencies. This practice was cut short when the megas began the practice of revenue-sharing.

Instead of starting up their own travel agency, some companies have considered buying an agency. Some of the issues that arise in determining a course of action are:

1. ARC appointments through change of ownership rather than a new application.
2. Ongoing business.
3. Assets, including proprietary software.
4. Former owners or staff can act as qualifiers.
5. Liabilities.
6. Buying stock versus buying the assets.

There is no simple answer to the question of owning your own travel agency. Harold Seligman comments that "Several corporations have been visibly successful, others have been successful but have never been identified. Most, however, have determined that travel is not the business in which they are engaged and therefore they will be better served by a third-party travel agency. The spread of commission sharing has done a great deal to eliminate any economic benefits that used to accrue to corporations that owned their own agency."

## TRAVEL CONSOLIDATION

One of the main reasons for bringing travel services into the corporation is the centralization of travel management. According to Peter Sontag, CEO of US Travel, "By centralizing its travel management program, a corporation can save money, gain purchasing control, and receive consistent and improved service." Sontag further states that "Centralization can save a corporation money in several ways, including rebates from agencies and better prices from suppliers. It will also bring a corporation several types of service improvements, including upgraded communication and leverage with agencies and suppliers because of the volume involved."

Centralization is one of the keys to a corporation's being able to take control of its travel costs. Successful negotiation with travel suppliers depends to a large extent upon the company's total travel volume—the more business the company can give the supplier, generally the better the deal. Phil Tedeschi, travel manager at Reliance Electric, states: "The perception that a corporate program cannot be as successful as one instituted locally is often the biggest obstacle in the way of successful travel management."

Many national or multinational companies have examined the opportunities to "network," or consolidate, their travel purchases and have implemented very successful programs to accomplish cost containment and traveler control through single-supplier arrangements. Using a single agency to secure all of the corporation's travel through one source has been the most dramatic change in corporate travel purchasing resulting from deregulation. This permits the company to maximize buying power and to receive reports from a single entity to enhance control of travelers and vendors. Many companies, having experienced substantial success with domestic consolidation, are now beginning to undertake global unification of travel activity. This is the next major trend in travel management and is rapidly gaining momentum.

## THE CONSOLIDATION OF PRICE WATERHOUSE'S TRAVEL

The Price Waterhouse Travel Systems Department was formed in May 1987. The firm's management committee (similar to a board of directors) authorized the department in late 1986, following an extensive two-year review of its buying practices. The design project addressed all issues of travel and entertainment, including the introduction of a corporate travel card, changes in the processing of expense reports, and the introduction of a central travel reservation facility serving all Price Waterhouse (PW) offices.

Prior to the introduction of this program, each Price Waterhouse office throughout the country procured its own travel. Over 300 agencies were used nationwide. Since many offices were small, they were unable to obtain volume-buying programs or have access to accurate management reporting. Even offices large enough to receive reports were unable to share in volume buying since there was no vehicle for sharing this information within PW. Collectively, PW was unable to track its total travel expenditures, but estimates indicated that total airline, hotel, and rental-car volume was approximately $30 million per year. Since the beginning of implementation and management reporting, this figure has been refined to over $45 million. Total travel and entertainment is now estimated at over $65 million.

Price Waterhouse faced the challenge of consolidating travel within a totally decentralized corporate environment. PW, one of the "big six" accounting firms, is a partnership of over 900 persons. Each managing partner is free to make his or her own decisions on virtually all matters, including travel. Since little in a partnership is absolutely mandatory, centralizing travel management was particularly challenging.

It was considered essential that the travel management program offer a full range of travel services and volume-rate programs while being responsive to local control. As such, enforcement of travel policy was retained at these varied offices with the travel systems department acting as consultant. In this role, the department advises the agency and individual travelers of cost alternatives and subsequently reports variations to managing partners as either savings attained or lost opportunities for profit. Price Waterhouse has dubbed this arrangement the "travel management alliance" with specific responsibilities as follows.

The travel systems department:

1. Sets policy.
2. Monitors reservations.
3. Administers charge-card program.
4. Negotiates volume-rate programs.
5. Negotiates local-rate programs.

The practice office:

1. Enforces policy.
2. Requests reservations.
3. Enforces charge-card usage.
4. Requests and uses volume rates.
5. Requests local rate assistance.

The travel management company:

1. Advises on policy.
2. Confirms reservations.
3. Accepts charge card for travel services.
4. Administers volume-rate programs.
5. Administers local-rate programs.

The travel systems department resides at the travel reservation center in order to be physically close and responsive to the needs of all parties, both PW's and the travel management company's. Department supervisors monitor their own CRS terminals, the management information system terminal, and the Price Waterhouse mainframe computer in order to coordinate all activities of the users and the contractor. It is easy to see that communications is the key to making the "travel alliance" system work.

The travel reservation center is located at the firm's national administrative center in Tampa, Florida. The on-site branch of Lifeco Travel Services is dedicated solely to the needs and use of Price Waterhouse. Services are divided into three main areas: staff travel, partner services, and a meeting and group travel desk. Specialized areas take care of personal and vacation travel, passports and visas, and quality control. A special services group handles hotels, car rentals, and special requests such as handicapped assistance, special meals, and international travel.

Three "800" phone numbers feed directly into the main service areas, with all calls monitored by a communications supervisor. Phone calls can be transferred between the various groups, and agents can be switched from one area to another electronically to compensate for overloads. Reservations can also be made by electronic mail or fax.

Tickets are delivered by a variety of means, including overnight pouch for small offices and direct delivery from other Lifeco offices.

Or they can be printed at 43 PW locations by STPs. STPs are the preferred method since they are operated by PW personnel and are located at practice offices, offering hands-on travel management.

According to John Hintz, Director, travel systems at Price Waterhouse, "The most important benefit of the consolidated travel program is the collective buying programs." The primary collective buying programs are:

1. Educational programs for continuing education (required of tax and audit personnel).
2. Administrative and business-development meetings (held on a regional basis).
3. National recruiting program.
4. Semi-annual partner conclaves.

These meetings are the types common in most major industries—training, marketing, recruiting, and managerial. Taken collectively, these programs represent significant ongoing costs to a company, and they provide major opportunities for volume-rate programs.

## SELECTION CRITERIA

Many factors will enter into the process of selecting a travel management company: size, cultural compatibility, financial and purchasing arrangements, stability, references, and a host of other issues. According to Harold Seligman, the senior travel industry consultant and president of Management Alternatives, Inc., there are at least 11 factors a travel manager should take into consideration when choosing the travel management company.

1. Size of the company.
2. Proportion.
3. Service.
4. Local presence.
5. Override (bonus) commissions.
6. Purchasing power.
7. Distribution.
8. Management Information Systems and automation.

9. Globalization.
10. Financial stability.
11. Selection process.

1. Size. Seligman says that size is one of the many important criteria that differentiate agencies. Size is possibly the most discernible difference, and it helps categorize possible contenders for your business very quickly and in a very definitive manner. For descriptive purposes, we will identify travel management companies in three different categories: mega, large regional, and small.

The mega-agencies are those dealing on a national basis, with approximately $200 million plus in annual air sales. The large regionals are below the $200 million range and, depending on the region where they are located, will handle air sales down to the volume of $20 million a year. The small agencies are those doing less than $25 million. They represent more than 99 percent of the total agency locations in the country. In the 1991 *Business Travel News* annual survey of commercial agencies, those with sales exceeding $20 million numbered only 79 agencies.

Aside from all else, cultural fit and service capabilities are the most important elements to consider in attempting to achieve a long-lasting relationship. Picking your travel partner requires at least as much care and consideration as selecting the right accounting, legal, or advertising agency to serve your corporation. Each of these services needs capable professional experts to supplement the in-house capacity that exists in your company.

The size of the travel management company is only one of the many important factors to consider in making the right choice. Size for size alone is not necessarily a valid consideration. It is a subject that has received considerable exposure, both pro and con, in the trade publications.

Travel management companies have reached mega-proportions undreamed of just a few years ago. The consolidation that has taken place in the travel business was anticipated by a few far-sighted businessmen. They are the founders of several of the mega-agencies: Don Sohn of Heritage Travel, now a part of Thomas Cook; Barney Kogen of Lifeco Travel, who acquired a small agency for $30,000 after deregulation; Peter Sontag, who acquired large regionals and folded them into a mega; and Hal Rosenbluth, who took a family business into a mega. The large regionals are generally presided over by people of the same category as those who run the megas.

As in other service businesses, a "big six" (or some similar number) was bound to evolve as the giants of the industry. Accountants, advertising agencies, and law firms have witnessed the emergence of a small number of very large firms that typically service the Fortune 500 list of companies. Like other service businesses, the travel agency community has coalesced into a number of very large agencies primarily serving the giant users of travel. However, for their survival they require a substantial share of the traffic originating from smaller client companies.

Some 30-plus years ago, *Travel Agent* magazine published the first list of agencies by size. There were less than 100 agencies listed with volumes of over $1 million annually in the US and Canada, and most of their business came from transatlantic steamship tickets. In 1991, an agency doing $20 million in air sales did not make the top eighty. To join the most august group, the top ten, you now have to exceed a quarter billion dollars in annual air sales.

2. Proportion. The agency must be in correct proportion to the size of the corporate travel budget. According to Harold Seligman, there is no magic formula one can employ. However, he suggests there are some yardsticks that can be applied: "Common sense suggests a company with a $25 million air travel budget is not going to select an agency with $5 million in annual sales volume. The risk to both is enormous. The company would be ill-served while the agency grew its capabilities to the size necessary to provide the services."

Many corporations will not award a contract to a vendor whose sales are not at least triple the size of the award. They are concerned that any company relying on a single customer for more than 50 percent of its business would be in jeopardy if the customer were for any reason to pull the account. Some corporations like to be the largest client of an agency, but not so large that the agency's survival is at stake if they lose the business.

An agency that is small relative to the size of the client awarding the contract might be able to phase in the new business over an extended period. But the time required for an agency to achieve multiples of its present size could undermine the realization of the benefits of consolidating with a single agency.

Such an arrangement would place the agency's future in jeopardy. They would be required to invest heavily in staff, space, equipment, infrastructure, etc., to up-size. If the account is pulled for whatever reason, they would have expended the costs of start-up and continuing overhead but would have no business to service.

A multimillion-dollar account could choose between a mega and a large regional with the confidence that each of them can provide the resources essential for a complete service package.

A small-budget company has the option of selecting from all three categories. Each one has the resources to serve their needs. The mega and large regional agencies are all pursuing smaller, local accounts and will aggressively seek relationships with potential clients in the $100-thousand category and up.

The large regionals and mega-agencies serve many small accounts and do it well. When they compete for a small account, they do so, for the most part, on a local basis, winning or losing the business on the strength of their local management and not on their regional capabilities. The playing field is more or less level in these instances.

3. Service. One of the benefits of the megas and large regionals is their purchasing power with the airlines, hotels, and car-rental companies. This will be especially true for the company trying to manage its travel budget for the first time. Many neophyte travel managers have learned their initial lessons in the industry from skilled travel management firms. Though purchasing, rebates, and other issues discussed later in this chapter will all play a role in the selection process, none is more important than service.

The quality of the service necessary to satisfy travelers, travel arrangers, and travel management should always be in the forefront when choosing the travel management company. As an offset to the superior automation, purchasing clout, etc., of the larger agencies, the small agency can offer the highly personalized attention of the owners or of very senior management without regard to account size.

The small agencies ability to service and retain clients has a dramatic influence on the viability of their business. They are much more directly involved in the service package they provide a client than are the senior officers of a mega or large regional agency. The senior personnel with the largest agencies are on call for their largest accounts. This is as it should be. In the periodic review meetings that follow implementation, the larger the client, the more senior the officer participating in such sessions.

This is not to suggest for a moment that the large agencies cannot deliver personal service to the client. They do it very well for many small companies, but usually on a local level. Local management is the answer. When the large agencies have the right manager in place, they can be as effective as any of the smaller agencies.

4. Local presence. Other important aspects of the service equation are hand-holding and problem-solving. Local presence, regardless of the agency, is a concern. When the agency is a full-service location of a regional or local agency, or the national agency's account executive is present, local management can be much more effective in dealing with pre- and post-travel problems. If satisfaction or resolution of problems must come from some remote headquarters location, the smaller client will not be as well served as the large corporate customer.

Identification is usually the issue. The smaller client is well-known and highly valued at the local level, but may be a nonentity at the distant headquarters. Only the pressure of local management can assist with the resolution of such problems.

Small agencies dealing on a local level can be more responsive, since the lines of communication are much shorter. But regardless of the agency's size, the degree of authority at the local level is of the utmost importance.

The best method for determining the agency's dedication to fulfillment of this service commitment is through careful checking of references. Don't just question references regarding telephone response time and ticket delivery, but ask penetrating questions about travel trauma and how the agency resolves problems. An example of travel trauma would involve a traveler who has a confirmation number and a reservation trying to check into a hotel, but the hotel has no record of the reservation and no rooms available.

5. Override (bonus) commissions. Since the early days of deregulation, a company awarding a contract to a travel agency may

share in the agency's override commissions. Airlines pay a bonus (override) to agencies, based on the volume of business they generate for them. This override is usually calculated on the basis of incremental volume. For example, if an airline has a 30-percent share in a particular market, and the travel management company sends 33 percent of its travelers on that airline, then that agency is paid an override for generating additional volume. Overrides range from 1 to 5 percent of volume. A typical bonus schedule is as follows:

1.  100% to 110% of local market share . . . 1% override.
2.  111% to 115% of local market share . . . 2% override.
3.  116% to 120% of local market share . . . 3% override.

In many instances override arrangements are based on the specific market. Sometimes, smaller agencies may be able to extract the same or better concessions from the carriers than the larger management companies. In those instances, the district or regional manager of the airline had a budget for securing a greater share of the business originating in his or her territory. A national agency with no significant presence in the community would not have participated in such an override arrangement.

Initially, the airlines began paying overrides to their higher-volume travel agencies with the expectation that the agency would pass these on to the corporate customer. As will be shown later in this book, the overrides are less expensive to the airline than negotiating corporate deals. For a long time, the travel agency community served as a buffer between the airlines and the corporations. The corporation would approach the agency asking for discounts and the agency would respond by sharing override commissions. Before the advent of sophisticated corporate travel managers, this worked well for the airlines. However, now most travel managers will negotiate directly with the airline for special airfares and with the travel management firm for a percentage of the override commissions.

With this change in the structure of negotiations, airlines are looking very closely at the practice of paying overrides when most large corporations have negotiated fares. One point is sure. In the future the airlines will be very careful with the overrides paid to travel management companies.

A variety of methods have been set forth to compensate the travel management company. All of these pricing schemes have one element in common: The travel vendor pays the travel management company. In almost all cases, the travel vendor pays the travel management company a commission for booking the business on their behalf. The exception to this rule is that some software used in management reporting is sold by the travel management company to the client.

For all practical purposes, commissions paid by the vendors to the travel management company make up the bulk of their compensation. Every pricing scheme revolves around the amount of commissions the travel management company will earn, their costs in servicing the account, and how many transactions there will be. The more common pricing schemes are:

1. Cost-plus.
2. Management fee.
3. Hourly fee.
4. Fee for service.

Pricing schemes 2 through 4 fall under the general heading of fee-based pricing. Fee-based pricing was introduced to the travel industry by IVI Travel headquartered in Northbrook, Illinois. Peter Sontag, president and CEO of US Travel, is also a big promoter of fee-based concepts.

According to Mark Pestronk, a Washington, D.C.-based attorney specializing in travel-related law, "Fee-based pricing means an arrangement in which the travel agency rebates 100 percent of its commission to the client and then deducts fees for services rendered on a per-transaction basis.

"The benefit of fee-based pricing for the travel agency is that it is assured it will be profitably compensated for its services, regardless of the number of voided transactions, deliveries, changes, noncommissionable sales, hours of counseling, and general running around. The benefit for the commercial account is that the client pays only for what it receives; it can save money by avoiding extra transactions." In short, Mark Pestronk believes the benefit to both parties is fairness.

Of course, fee-based pricing can only work if the travel agency knows its costs. Conversely, ignorance of costs makes fee-based pricing a shot in the dark. Just a one-percent rebate can cripple if the agency does not know its cost structure.

Rebates of commissions on hotels and car rentals are, and always have been, legal. Rebates on domestic air transportation have been legal since January 1, 1985, when all of the major carriers stated that they would remove antirebating provisions from their contracts with travel agencies. However, for international air sales, the regime in effect since 1938 still applies: Rebating on international air sales is a violation of Section 902(d) of the Federal Aviation Act. Accordingly, fee-based and rebating contracts cannot promise to return international air commissions to the client.

Walter Freedman, president of IVI Travel, argues that the biggest benefit to the client is that it levels the playing field when it comes to issues like "are you trying to get me the best deal?" In a commission-based environment, if the agency writes a ticket for $1,000, they get a commission of $90.

$1,000 ticket
   100 tax (10% tax)
   900 gross ticket price × 0.10 commission
    90 commission

If the same agency writes a $500 ticket, they earn

$500 ticket
   50 tax
  450 gross ticket price × 0.10 commission
   45 commission

Under the straight-commission pricing scheme, there is no incentive for the agency to work on the side of the corporation. In essence, why would the travel company work to get the client a lower fare when it reduces its income? There is a very real conflict here. If the travel company charges a flat fee, supposedly they no longer care what the price of the ticket is. If you add base incentives to the fee, then there is an absolute motivation for the travel company to reduce travel costs.

The travel management company no longer worries about losing commissions because they are getting the client better deals. Money is made by charging fees for transactions. The fee-based pricing concept helps to better define the relationship between the travel management company and the corporation. With a fee, the travel company no longer is the agent of the airline or hotel, but becomes an extension of the client.

During the early 1980s, as the competition for commercial accounts intensified, travel companies began a practice known as rebating. A better term than "rebate" is "revenue sharing" because the corporation does not pay the travel management company directly. Revenue sharing has been used to entice a corporation to switch travel management companies. The increased demand from corporations for revenue sharing is also a signal from corporations that they wish to reduce their service charges on booking travel. The amount of the rebate can be a straight percentage based on volume, or some other formula such as the average ticket price.

According to Mark Pestronk, there are thirteen varieties of revenue sharing:

1. Straight percentage of sales.
2. Straight percentage of commissions.
3. Percentage varying with volume.
4. Percentage varying with ticket size.
5. Percentage varying with agents assigned.
6. Percentage varying with performance grade.
7. Percentage varying with savings.
8. 100% credit with fee per ticket.
9. 100% credit with fee per menu items.
10. 100% credit with cost-plus-%-of-gross management fee.
11. 100% of credit with cost-plus-dollar management fee.
12. Percent of BTD's costs.
13. Percent of profit-center profits.

To engage in revenue sharing, a travel management company must know its costs. On the corporation's side, it is important to be realistic. As more and more smaller agencies wish to do corporate travel, some have offered revenue-sharing programs that have ensured that they would be bankrupt within a short time. Corporations eager to reduce travel expenses have accepted these deals only to find that their travel expenses have gone up because the agency booked them for more-expensive airfares or the agency was unable financially to make its commitments. The truth is that some revenue-sharing agreements can raise overall travel costs and must be approached with caution.

It is fairly easy to spot a revenue-sharing agreement that is no good. Simply look for one that offers two or more points more than any of the competitors. Revenue sharing has also brought some unfortunate trends, such as the use of outside travel consultants. It is not uncommon for a travel manager to enlist the help of a travel consultant in evaluating requests for proposals. Sometimes the consultant's sales pitch is that he or she will beat the travel company out of an additional point in revenue-sharing, which will more than make up for their fee.

## REVENUE SHARING AND THE WINNER'S CURSE

During the late 1970s, a term was coined in the offshore oil leasing business—the "winner's curse." The winner's curse refers to the fact that those who won the bidding rights in a sealed-bid auction were also those who were most likely to overvalue the potential earnings of that lease.

In the travel industry, the winner's curse arises because there are so few standards. The reason there are so few standards is that the industry is young. As of yet nobody has taken the time to question the claims made by various parties. Excessive promises of revenue sharing can certainly be one case of the winner's curse. Another example of the winner's curse in the travel industry is claims made about software. Because of these claims, many corporations have bought software or services only to receive something other than what they were sold. One of the signs of the maturing travel industry will be the setting of standards and bench-marking of software.

One way for a corporation to protect itself against the winner's curse is to place very restrictive covenants in all contracts regarding performance and service. It is fine to talk about partnering; however, prudence is best.

6. Purchasing power. Purchasing power has become one of the main focal points of competition among travel management companies. Harold Seligman maintains that the ability of the

agency to assist the client reduce its overall travel and entertainment costs through preferential pricing is a core element in the selection of a travel management company. The larger agencies have the advantage that comes with size. Many mid-sized and smaller agencies are learning to overcome their size disadvantage by becoming skilled negotiators on behalf of their clients. This has reduced what would otherwise be a significant handicap for the smaller agencies in their ability to compete. In the July 1991 issue of *Corporate Travel* magazine, an article addressing carrier discounts suggests that many $3- to $5-million agencies are achieving remarkable results.

Another factor that reduces the advantages of the two larger categories of agencies is the desire of the carriers for their discount arrangements to be client-specific. To avoid proliferation of the discounts, the client is usually a party to the negotiated agreement. The carriers understand that the agency has little influence over vendor selection and that the mandate to use a specific airline, hotel, or car-rental company must be client-generated.

Certainly, in entering negotiations with a carrier it would be much better to have one of their top-ten producers than their 200th-ranking agency on your team, but it is the client's ability to direct its travelers to a preferred vendor that will be the most telling factor in the negotiating session. As mentioned elsewhere, the autonomy vested in local and regional management by the primary suppliers frequently works to the benefit of regional/local agencies.

Size does provide the megas and the very large regionals with ready access to the most senior management at primary suppliers. This entrée can prove advantageous in negotiations. In an article on airline deals in *Corporate Travel* magazine, Delta Air Lines clearly stated that all negotiated arrangements must be cleared with headquarters. Under those circumstances, it is better to make the deal at headquarters than in the field. The more important the agency is to the carrier, the greater the likelihood of an audience with the decision-makers.

The statistical data on the advantages of the larger agencies over the small ones on the hotel side is somewhat cloudy. In bidding, all three categories of travel companies will compete aggressively, using every available resource. Each will demonstrate its superior capabilities. Aside from confusing the client with their statistical detail, the agencies will often contradict each other's data, leaving the client wondering if there is any truth to their figures.

The problem with all of the consolidated programs is that if they don't include the hotels you use, the size of the agency may be of little or no consequence. If other clients use the hotels your travelers do, then the agency should have secured a preferred rate. If their other clients are not patronizing those hotels, chances are you can get a better deal than can an agency.

7. Distribution. Once again, the needs of the client will determine how important a factor ticket distribution will be in the selection of the agency. A few years ago, there were only three agencies with a national branch-office system. The agencies wishing to compete with them on a national basis had to be innovative if they were to retain their clients. They formed consortiums and other strategic alliances, but technology has all but leveled the playing field in most instances.

Almost eight years ago, a Connecticut-based company was faced with a common problem. Much of their travel originated from the Fairfield County region, using the four New York metropolitan airports, but locations around the country accounted for one in three tickets. Because they were trying to consolidate data to better control both travelers and vendors, they sought a distribution technique that would enable them to use the headquarters-based agency to serve their outlying locations.

The agency they used was Robustelli Travel of Stamford, Connecticut, which had another client, Emery Airfreight, one of the earlier overnight express-mail services. To service the client's wishes, Robustelli established a ticketing location at the Emery facility in Dayton, Ohio. This enabled Robustelli to accept reservations on a WATS line until almost midnight and still deliver tickets the next morning. This was the forerunner of the system that other agencies have duplicated with Federal Express or other overnight services.

Satellite ticket printers (STPs) and other sophisticated arrangements and relationships are helping the smaller and mid-sized agencies compete with the megas with regard to distribution. Nothing will offset the edge the larger agencies have with a local presence in many markets, but the advantage they once had in the pure physical act of placing travel documents in the traveler's hands has been significantly neutralized.

8. Management Information Systems and Automation. Management information and automation capabilities are other ways to distinguish between agencies of differing sizes. The corollary between size and automation sophistication is usually demonstrated, but not always. Most of the regionals have access to the necessary financial resources to either develop their own version or purchase third-party software, and they can afford hardware that makes them very competitive with the national agencies.

Systems such as AQUA, created by Associated Travel of Los Angeles, and several systems with similar capabilities were developed by regional agencies and subsequently sold to agencies of any size willing to pay the price, including the mega agencies. Recently introduced compilation programming enables companies to gather data from several serving agencies to produce management reports internally. This may further erode the automation advantages of the mega-agencies. At the same time, the megas are able to fully staff data-processing departments that have the ability to customize any software to fit a client's particular needs.

The mega-agencies and some large regional agencies do have resources to invest in development that exceed by substantial margins the abilities of the lesser agencies. Many extremely innovative offerings have been developed by larger agencies. Vision (Rosenbluth), SAFE (IVI), Quest (Maritz), Maestro (US Travel), and PDQ from Lifeco are the innovative offerings of a few of the megas.

No one has ever kept score, so it is difficult to measure where the creative juices flow most, but I suspect the larger agencies have contributed disproportionately to the imaginative new offerings that have emerged in recent years.

9. Globalization. For most agencies, overseas representation involves a loosely structured arrangement with an agency selected to service the needs of American travelers when in the country of the correspondent. The emerging relationships now involve originating traffic in those countries in which multinational clients have operations. Attempting to realize the same results that have been achieved domestically, many companies are now seeking agency relationships that will enable them to accomplish the same programs internationally.

Seligman asserts that globalization appears to be a trump card held by the largest agencies. Although the regional and large local agencies have correspondent relationships with international agencies, they do not duplicate the capabilities of the largest agencies. Wagon-Lits and American Express have representation that is unparalleled internationally. Lifeco, US Travel, Rosenbluth, IVI, and Maritz are, through acquisition or a structuring of partnerships, assuring themselves of a greater voice in the servicing of the overseas branches of their North American client companies than has been typical in a travel agency's arrangements with its international counterparts.

The consolidation of global travel purchases is just beginning. Whether the megas will retain the advantage or whether it will be overcome through the development of creative overseas relationships by their smaller competitors has yet to be determined. A global computer reservations system, combined with a spread of satellite ticket printers could quickly dissipate the edge the multinational agencies appear to have. However, a truly global CRS is decades away. The recession and the Gulf war seem to have slowed somewhat the interest in global consolidation, but it is happening and will continue to expand.

10. Financial stability. Financial stability is another concern in the selection process. Though some of the mega-agencies are public companies and their financial status is readily accessible, many are privately held. Many regional and large local agencies are sub chapter "S" corporations with few tangible assets. Careful evaluation of competing agencies' financial strength is important. Seligman warns that size is no guarantee of stability. Ensuring that your agency has the ability to withstand the ups and downs of the economy and has the resources to provide all of the services you require is a new challenge in the selection process.

11. Selection process. The process of selecting a travel agency partner can vary depending on size. For the large-budget organization, the development of a formalized request for proposal or quotation is the preferred method. The degree of sophistication will differ, based on the company's bidding practices.

For the mid-range-budget company, the selection process can fluctuate widely—a formal RFP (request for proposal), or an RFI (request for information) before the RFP, or just site inspections of a small number of select agencies, which will be followed by price negotiations for the contract.

For the company with a small budget, the options are even more varied. Depending on company culture, a formal bidding may be undertaken, or management may select the agency, choosing to give the business to a friend or relative. Once again, there are no set rules that must be followed to achieve the best results.

There are advantages and disadvantages to each category of agency. Every agency grouping has certain strengths that are offset by shortcomings. As stated at the outset, there are no established rules that enable a client of a certain size to focus only on agencies of a specific size. It requires a customized effort to achieve the program that will realize your travel program objectives.

In addition to the points mentioned by Harold Seligman, Bary Berglund, the travel manager and senior vice president at The Center For Creative Leadership in Greensboro, North Carolina, offers the following points:

1. Communication. This is a critical component of the corporation/travel management company relationship, and it begins with the first meeting. Despite the tendency to depersonalize the business world, it is important to find a company where the reservationists will treat your corporate employees with due respect.

2. Contract Deliverables. Resist temptation. If a promise sounds too good to be true, reject it.

3. Performance of On-Site Personnel. Some corporations will require on-site personnel. The employees who staff these offices should have the ability to make independent in-house decisions that are compatible with the client's corporate culture.

4. Automation Support. More and more, large corporate clients are specifying which CRS is to be used. They have internal systems that perform accounting and data-processing functions that interface with a particular CRS.

5. Program Review Sessions. On a set schedule, preferably quarterly, the travel manager and the travel management company should assess the past, present, and future of their relationship.

Unfortunately, there is no one-size-fits-all solution. You must try on the different sizes to ensure a perfect fit. So how do you choose the appropriate-sized agency to serve your organization? Networking with your peers is a very effective means. Learn about the agencies serving others with similar travel requirements.

Question other travel managers and then invite those agencies with good reputations for serving companies with travel that closely parallels yours to compete for your business.

## TRAVEL MANAGEMENT TIPS

- Companies who have already consolidated their travel with a single agency should ask themselves if they are satisfied with the level of service the incumbent is providing. It takes a great deal less time to correct a problem with an incumbent than to put out a request for proposal.
- Corporations are becoming more interested in maintaining long-term relationships with vendors. At some point, the cost of going out to bid and the time involved every year in analyzing bids becomes counterproductive.
- Partnering is the latest purchasing trend. Mega-corporations are consolidating business with one partner for multiyear deals.
- Partnering eliminates the administrative hassle and expense of competitive bids; locks in long-term rates; keeps internal processes consistent; and eases traveler compliance.
- The Airline Reporting Corporation acts as a settlement house that collects all the money paid to travel agencies for airline tickets and then pays this money to the airlines. Each week every travel agency sends in a report to the ARC detailing all of its cash and credit-card transactions.
- One attempt to speed up the process of delivering airline tickets to corporate clients involves the use of satellite ticket printers (STPs). A satellite ticket printer is simply a ticket printer that is located in a corporate office and that is electronically linked to the travel agency's main location.
- One of the main reasons for bringing travel services into the corporation is the centralization of travel management.
- When a corporation centralizes its travel management process, it can save money, gain purchasing control, and receive consistent and improved service.
- Centralization can save a corporation money in several ways, including rebates from agencies and better prices from suppliers.

*Chapter Five*

# Sending Out a Request for Proposal, Evaluation, and Implementation

I n the preceding chapter, the pros and cons of choosing agencies of differing sizes were discussed. Once the decision has been reached on the type of agency you wish to consider as your service partner, the next step in the process is to find, among the appropriately sized agencies, the one that best matches your corporate needs. This will be the agency that has all the requisite tools, the cultural compatibility, and the geographic structure that corresponds to the agency profile you have developed. The decision of which travel management company to use will be one of the most emotional your corporation ever makes. The reason for this is that it will affect more of your employees than any other vendor decision.

Once a determination has been made that a total or partial consolidation of travel purchasing is practical, the best way to select the right agency is by competitive bidding. For most companies, the most effective approach is the development of a request for proposal that elicits the most comprehensive combination of service and price. Small-budget companies can develop shortcut approaches to selection, including site visits, interviews, reference checks, etc., but for an organization with a substantial budget, the RFP is the best technique.

Harold Seligman suggests that an effective RFP should include at least the following:

1. General Information
   a. Credentials of bidding agencies, geographic location of branch offices and staffing at each site, financial stabil-

ity, and any other issues that may affect a long-term relationship. If originating international travel is a part of your requirement, then ask the appropriate questions concerning the agencies' overseas affiliation and capabilities.

b. Inquire about the agencies' personnel and training techniques. Also find out about compensation programs and incentives to staff.

c. References are possibly the most pertinent part of this section. Require the bidders to provide current references from clients whose travel purchases approximate your own. If you buy a million dollars in air tickets annually, references of the size of AT&T or IBM will be of little use. Also ask the agencies to furnish the names of at least two former clients, including an explanation of the reasons for loss of patronage. Before contacting the references, develop a questionnaire with a numeric evaluation to permit you to arrive at the most objective comparison possible.

2. Automation

a. Require the agencies to provide full details of their automation, both airline reservations and back-office management systems. More and more companies are relying on the agencies to provide statistical analysis of booking patterns, volume, favored suppliers, etc., to enable them to negotiate preferred primary vendor arrangements more effectively. The agencies' data can be sorted in numerous ways to enhance the purchasing efforts of the travel manager.

b. Question the agencies concerning their future plans. Will they be able to provide on-line access to your data? Can they customize the reports you require?

3. Supplier Relations

Inquire about the agencies' ability to provide negotiated prices with airlines and hotels. Ask them to be specific about the carriers and routes your travelers fly most frequently and the hotels that are most popular with your employees. Most preferential pricing arrangements require the agency to maintain confidentiality, but they can in their proposal describe their ability to reduce the gross price of travel without betraying the confidence of the suppliers.

4. Communications

   Ask the bidders to provide as much information as possible about their communications capability—telephone systems; 24-hour emergency service for travelers, both in the US and abroad; use of fax or E-mail to accept reservations; and the possibility of direct access through computer link-up.

5. Document Delivery

   Question the agencies about their in-town and remote delivery programs. Also quiz them about the use of STPs at those locations where they may be appropriate.

6. Special Arrangements

   Ask about special services that agencies provide, such as:

   • Meet and greet.
   • Complimentary airline club membership.
   • Customer service representatives.
   • Traveler newsletters.
   • Preferred pricing for vacation or other personal travel.
   • Passport and visa services.
   • VIP programs.
   • Other special services that differentiate the agency from competitors.

7. Meeting and Group Travel

   If group travel of any type (meetings, incentives, conferences, etc.) is a part of your travel package, question the agencies about their ability to deliver such services. Ask for separate references from group travel customers.

8. Revenue Sharing

   a. The travel agency industry has become very sophisticated in its rebate offerings. It requires considerable knowledge to interpret precisely what is being proposed. Figures are manipulated to appear far more generous than can be realistically achieved. Be sure your agency proposals can be quantified. If you have a preferred revenue-sharing method, ask the bidders to provide quotations that specifically meet your goals. Depending on your size and travel patterns, override commissions should also be addressed.

    b. Hotel and car-rental commissions, though not as im-
portant in most bids as air commissions, nonetheless
should be included in the request for revenue sharing.

9. Site Visit/Negotiations
After evaluating the proposals and reducing the number of
contestants to manageable proportions, conduct interviews
and site visits with the best of the bidders. This will be
followed by negotiations with the agency that appears best
suited to serve your needs. When agreement is reached
with the selected agency, the next stage of the process is
negotiating the final contract. Be certain to include a
skilled purchasing executive on your team.

## THE ROLE OF CONSULTANTS IN SELECTING A TRAVEL MANAGEMENT FIRM

As more and more corporations are using the RFP process to select
a travel management company, an entire industry of consultants
has arisen to advise corporations on this process. As yet, there are
no standards of ethical behavior or guidelines for what a reasonable proposal should include. Because the consultant can play
such a vital role in the selection process, a number of "double-
dipping" deals have received notice. In the May 1990 issue of *Corporate Travel* magazine, Loren Ginsberg writes, "Many agencies
are wooing consultants with everything from gourmet dinners to
a percentage of the profits if they are selected. And firms who put
their trust—and their money—in consulting services must be sure
the expert they choose is not 'on the take' with an agency or vendor."

Loren Ginsberg offers these five rules on how to hire a clean
consultant:

1. Ask for a list of the past 10 corporate bids, with the agencies selected. If the same agency appears consistently, be
suspicious.
2. Call corporate references. Ask about their experience
working with the consultant.
3. Ask about the consultant's experience. How long has he or
she been in the business?
4. Is the consultant between jobs? Anyone can hang out a
shingle while looking for employment. While these people

may be competent, they may not be available to see a project through or provide ongoing service.

5. Add a clause to the contract stating that the consultant is to take nothing of value from the agency or vendor in a bid process.

One point is very clear: A written code of ethics that is to be adopted by all consultants is necessary. This code will be adopted by all reputable consultants. The violation of this code by those who subscribe to it must carry a penalty.

It is hoped that none of this is interpreted as disparaging comments against consultants. A consultant can provide an invaluable resource to the corporation under the following conditions:

1. The consultant must understand the nuances and travel behavior of the corporation he or she represents.

2. The RFP must reflect the particular needs of the corporation. If possible, the consultant should work with the corporate travel manager during the research for the corporate travel study. If the consultant knows firsthand the current level of travel management in the corporation and where the corporation wants to be in the future, then an effective RFP can be prepared and a reasonable selection process can be accomplished.

3. The consultant should be retained to help in the implementation of the account and to be a partner in the evaluation process once the travel management company is selected.

4. The consultant is independent of the corporation and therefore should not be in on the decision-making process. The consultant can advise, but the corporation's travel council should make the decision as to whom they wish to work with.

## CASE STUDY: THE TRAVEL CONSOLIDATION OF THE CENTER FOR CREATIVE LEADERSHIP

The Center For Creative Leadership is a nonprofit educational organization located in Greensboro, North Carolina. The following case study is adapted from their experience in sending out an RFP. The RFP used in this example is based on the one that was used, but none of the actual participants in the bidding process are named.

## REQUEST FOR PROPOSAL

### Section 1—General Agency Information

1. Name, address, telephone number.
2. Annual airline ticketing volume.
3. Total number of employees (full- and part-time, by category).
4. Officers (names and titles); local sales representatives.
5. Length of time in business/leisure/group sales markets (as applicable).
6. Number of full-service locations (in what major cities?).
7. List of international locations (if applicable).
8. Type of billing and accounting systems available.
9. Do you offer group travel services?
10. Do you offer meeting and convention planning services?
11. How many commercial accounts over $500,000 do you service annually? over $1 million?
12. Provide your business mix in the following format (list each category as a percentage of total volume).
    a. Business travel
    b. Commercial travel
    c. Vacation travel
    d. Group travel
13. Please attach a list of your five largest commercial accounts and indicate whether you serve all or part of their commercial business.
14. Please list at least three commercial accounts that have discontinued business with your agency in the last one to three years.
15. If our company were one of your accounts, what percentage of your total business would our volume represent?

### Section 2—Automation Capabilities

1. Which airline reservation system(s) do you use?
2. What other equipment do you use in your agency that we could benefit from?

3. What is your philosophy regarding the employment of satellite ticket printers for key clients? At what point in a customer's sales volume would you consider installation of an STP? At what cost to the client, if any?
4. Comment on any additional automation features.

### Section 3—Management Reporting Systems

1. Do you provide management reports? Are they individually designed or do you use a prepared package?
2. Do your management reports
   a. summarize by department?
   b. summarize air-travel, hotel, and car-rental spending by vendor, passenger, city pair, and destination?
   c. provide data on lowest fare opportunities, acceptance or reason for decline (savings and exception reports)?
3. Are your management reports
   a. issued on a monthly or quarterly basis?
   b. able to reflect fiscal year-to-date figures?
4. Do you have the capability to reconcile actual rates charged against rates reserved?
5. Do you provide complete itineraries and agency contact telephone numbers with each ticket?
6. Are you developing any new information features?
7. Please attach a copy of a recent management report.

### Section 4—Client Deliveries

1. Do you employ a delivery service?
2. How many full-time delivery personnel do you employ?
3. Number of company-owned delivery vehicles?
4. How do you handle delivery prior to and after normal working hours (8 A.M.–5 P.M.)?

### Section 5—Special Services

1. Do you provide 24-hour service? An 800 number? (If yes, please describe.)
2. How do you handle itinerary changes while the passenger is en route?

3. How do you handle emergency airline ticket needs?
4. Do you give immediate credit for unused tickets?
5. Do you have the capability to issue prepaid tickets to any location?
6. Describe your international service capabilities (e.g., passport/visa preparation, travelers checks, foreign currency, etc.).
7. Do you reconcile client travel expense statements against your own billings?
8. Please describe any experience you have with obtaining and managing bulk-fare ticket purchases.

### Section 6—Employee Training

1. What ongoing and specialized training do you provide for your staff?
2. Have all your agents been through airline training school? Do they have previous travel or airline experience?
3. Please provide a listing of your agents with the following information provided for each: name, agent credentials, years in the travel business, number of years with your firm (this applies only to the local area).

### Section 7—Client Quality-Control Fulfillment

1. What internal controls are in place to prevent unauthorized travel from being charged to clients?
2. What internal controls or checks do you have to assure accuracy in rate application and mathematical calculations on airline tickets?
3. What controls do you have for assuring calculation of most-current airfare before issuance of ticket?
4. Do you have the capability to conduct an automatic audit of existing reservations to screen for lowest possible fares and rebooking at lower rates, as appropriate?

### Section 8—Innovative Management System/Revenue Sharing

1. Provide your general philosophy on revenue sharing, rebating, management fee arrangements, etc.

2. You are invited to submit any proposal for travel service that would uniquely meet the client's needs, but that might not be described in any other section of this proposal.

## EVALUATION OF THE RFPs

After the RFPs were returned by the various agencies, Berglund made up a spreadsheet. Figure 5.1 is based on the one he used. On this spreadsheet, he identified 22 criteria that were to be evaluated. These criteria were specific to The Center for Creative Leadership and their location. For example, Berglund felt that it was important to consider how long the respondent had been

**FIGURE 5.1**
*Detailed Evaluation: Criteria and Rules*

| | |
|---|---:|
| 1. Time in business travel management | 100 |
| 2. Avg.tx/day/agt | 85 |
| 3. Percent business travel | 65 |
| 4. Largest commercial accounts | 84 |
| 5. Discontinued accounts | 76 |
| 6. Percent account our company is | 100 |
| 7. Individual reporting systems | 100 |
| 8. Rebate | 10 |
| 9. Other hard-dollar offers | 44 |
| 10. 24-hour service | 100 |
| 11. Itinerary change en route | 100 |
| 12. Agents' experience | 88 |
| 13. Automatic audit | 100 |
| 14. Agents with international experience | 49 |
| 15. Number of accounts greater than $500k | 38 |
| 16. Number of accounts greater than $1M | 38 |
| 17. Control of unauthorized travel | 75 |
| 18. Accurate ticket calculation | 60 |
| 19. Annual volume | 75 |
| 20. Soft dollar items | 50 |
| 21. Late ticket delivery | 75 |
| 22. Delivery services | 50 |
| TOTAL SCORE FOR MASTER TRAVEL | 1562 |

**FIGURE 5.2**
*Summary Evaluation: Criteria and Rules*

1. Master Travel ........................................................................ 1562
2. Seacoast Travel .................................................................... 1379
3. Professional Travel .............................................................. 1247
4. Easy Way Travel .................................................................. 1069
5. Guest Travel ........................................................................ 686

managing business travel because many of the respondents were local agencies that had previously managed only leisure travel.

Based on the responses, Berglund rated each agency on a scale of 0 to 100. Figure 5.1 shows the results for an imaginary agency named Master Travel. Another spreadsheet (Figure 5.2) was compiled to rank-order the points of the various respondents. From Figure 5.2 it is easy to see the winner of the bidding process.

## CASE STUDY: RICHARD D. IRWIN, INC.

Richard D. Irwin, Inc., is a seventy-year-old publishing house located in Homewood, Illinois (they are the publisher of this book). They are like thousands of other companies in the United States in that they have a fairly substantial travel expense ($1 million) and they had made little attempt in the past to manage this expense. Irwin had been using a local travel agency for the last fifteen years. Each time Irwin purchased an airline ticket, the agency sent them a bill. During the recession of 1990, they formed a committee to investigate ways of reducing travel costs. One of the members of the committee remarked that he had heard that some travel agencies offer rebates. Thus the search for an agency began.

The search for a new agency was begun under the condition that first of all, the long-term relationship with the local agency should be saved. But after discussions were held, the consultant recommended that the relationship be terminated because the local agency had little to offer in terms of management reporting and had little power with any of the vendors.

A four-member travel council under the direction of Margaret DeWald was formed after consulting with the vice president of finance to make sure top management would be supportive of the consolidation. Various local representatives from regional and mega-agencies were invited to preliminary meetings. After these visits, a short list was made, based largely on how well the travel council members liked the local representatives. Follow-up visits were scheduled to receive presentations from the short-listed agencies. The agencies were given the task of recommending an agency configuration to Irwin that would help the company reduce travel expenditures.

Like most medium-sized companies, Irwin had little information to give to the agencies other than the aggregate travel expenditure and the best guess of the top-five city pairs. The participants in the presentations were given one hour to explain their programs, and their proposals were limited to not more than ten pages. The council members were agreed on the fact that none of them wanted to read 100-page proposals. For the travel council members the presentations were their first opportunity to become familiar with the terminology of the industry. Their questions revolved around differences between the various CRSs and how the travel management company would best serve their interests.

After the presentations, the travel council met for a preliminary vote. Each council member was given two votes: first place and second place. The first-place vote was worth ten points and the second-place vote five points. The voting was interesting in that the choices were based more on personality types than on proposal specifics. The reason for this was that the council members decided that any of the respondents would be able to offer more services than they had ever thought possible. The council members also felt it important that they choose based on personality because they wanted somebody they would not mind spending a great deal of time with as they learned travel management.

Site visits were scheduled, and a final vote was taken. By this time, all the members were in agreement as to which company to choose.

## AGENCY/CORPORATION LEGAL ISSUES

In the August 6, 1990, issue of *Travel Weekly,* John Caldwell, a Washington, D.C. based attorney specializing in travel legal issues states:

*Contracts for legal services between corporations and agencies are receiving attention overdue in today's litigious society. Only recently, a large corporation sued its former agency for rebates after expiration of the "formal" written contract but during an agreed extension period. Although the old adage that a written contract is no better than the trust between the parties is still true, both sides are always better off with a detailed contract which anticipates foreseeable contingencies. Misplaced trust can be expensive.*

Caldwell continues by suggesting that the parties to the agreement develop a letter of intent based on the RFP as a basis for start-up. According to Caldwell, "The letter of intent is a method for agreeing first on general concepts and ideas before attempting to flesh out all details in the first writing. Another advantage is to discover generic issues not considered or discussed in negotiating sessions. Better to uncover major 'hang-ups' before starting work on a detailed contract which could flounder on basics."

Mark Pestronk, a Washington, D.C. based attorney specializing in travel contracts suggests that the following points should be negotiated in every contract:

1. Where will services be performed?
2. When will services begin?
3. What travel arrangements will be performed?
4. What travel management will be performed?
5. Payment terms.
6. Term and termination.

John Caldwell offers the following outline draft of a travel management agreement:

1. Appointment and services.
2. Consideration.
3. Billings and payment terms.
4. Refunds and voids.
5. Airline/supplier charges.
6. Term of contract.
7. Termination with cause.
8. Scope of services—exhibit "A".
9. Confidentiality of travel data and business/financial information.

10. Relationship of the parties.
11. Software produced for exclusive use.
12. Dispute resolution/attorney's fees.
13. Indemnification.
14. Liability.
15. Notices.
16. Insurance.
17. Choice of law/choice of forum.
18. Nondiscrimination.
19. Entire agreement.
20. Severability.
21. Notice of insolvency, merger.
22. Assignability.
23. Headings for convenience.
24. Signatures.

### Exhibit A—Scope of Services

1. Provide and consult on all travel services.
2. Assist in monitoring travel expenses.
3. Assist on request with policies and procedures.
4. Plan and arrange group and meeting travel.
5. Create and maintain traveler profiles.
6. Guarantee use of lowest-available fares.
7. Provide 24-hour, toll-free telephone service.
8. Timely issue and deliver all travel documents.
9. Provide automated accounting support.
10. Provide lost-baggage assistance.
11. Assist with visas and passports.
12. Establish and staff on-site retail branches.
13. Meet all telephone standards.
14. Provide and maintain STPs where appropriate.
15. Provide qualified, experienced personnel.
16. Not reassign personnel to new accounts.
17. Create and review MIS reports on request.

18. Credit-card reconciliation.
19. Frequent flyer tracking.
20. Electronic/magnetic transmission of data.
21. Discount hotel program/negotiated rates.
22. Support company discount negotiations.
23. Assist with consolidation of company travel.
24. Cooperate with fare and service audits.
25. Ensure a smooth transition to any successor.
26. Traveler information bulletins.
27. Timely payment of revenue sharing.

Often, "boilerplate contracts" are used between parties to the contract. In the September 10, 1990, issue of *Travel Weekly* John Caldwell gives the following examples of critical issues that are often overlooked in boilerplate contracts:

1. What happens in the event of loss or theft of ticket stock at a satellite printer location where the Airline Reporting Corporation (ARC) imposes a 100-percent obligation on the agency? Automated ticket and boarding-pass stock is considered negotiable by the ARC. Options for negotiated ticket-stock liability include the agency's assuming 100 percent of the risk, shared responsibility, or a specifically tailored indemnity clause.

2. How long should the service arrangement last, and what provisions will be drafted for termination with or without cause? A contract for one year, which can be canceled by either side on 30 days' notice, is a month-to-month deal in today's industry. There is a trend emerging in the business travel marketplace toward longer-term contracts of three or five or more years, but cancellation without cause remains a delicate issue.

3. How will low-fare guarantees and savings guarantees be constructed, applied, and, importantly, enforced?

4. Service standards, including telephone response maximums, hold times, call-backs, abandoned-call rates, experience minimums, right to approve and/or request assignment of on-site personnel, approval of off-site premises and operating scenarios, "critical-path" implementation schedule, and all other working details should

be developed in the body of the contract or in an attached schedule.

5. Provisions should be added for service and financial audits. There should be no doubt about who pays, when
the audits can be scheduled, or the audit's scope. You
should have access to all source documents. Access to
individual office financial documents, budgets, and pro-
formas is critical to fee-based guarantees.

6. How will overrides and hotel and car commissions be
verified? Will relying on third-party confirmation be
effective? These issues need to be faced directly, and
contract provisions must be drafted to minimize later
misunderstanding.

7. Risk of disclosure of company travel data to third parties
should be faced. A clear duty not to disclose data should
be imposed and the company should assert its ownership
rights.

8. How long will direct deals negotiated with airlines be
handled? What is the agency's role in direct deals, and
will it be paid a fee for noncommissionable discounts?
Should this be factored as a management fee or a reduction in hard-dollar rebating?

9. What happens when the agency fails to pay rebates on
time or remains in default for two or more consecutive
quarters? What responsibility exists on the part of the
agency to dun hotels for commissions and how will this
be enforced? Terms need to be spelled out defining how
long rebates continue and for what categories of sales.

10. When the contract terminates, responsibility for continuing service prior to a cut-over to the new provider should
be explained. A date should be set for ticketing out passenger name records for future travel. The corporation
should protect itself against gaps in service.

Pestronk agrees with Caldwell that there should be written contracts between the travel management company and the corporation and in the November 26, 1990, issue of *Travel Weekly* outlines
the following issues that travel agencies will want included:

1. *Exclusivity.* Above all, the corporation should promise
that all of its business travel will be handled by the

agency. Alternatively, when the account is to be shared among agencies, the contract should specify the geographic or other basis for the division of its business. The failure of the corporation to honor its commitment to give one agency all of the corporation's business is probably the largest source of litigation in corporate travel today.

2. *Outstanding contracts.* The second biggest source of litigation derives from claims by an incumbent agency that the corporation and the new agency conspired to break the incumbent's contract. Therefore, the corporation should warrant to the new agency that there are no such existing contracts, or that entry into the new contract will not constitute a breach of the present contract.

3. *Payment.* Just as the corporation wants specificity regarding rebate payments, the agency needs specificity regarding when and how the corporation will pay for airline tickets.

4. *Debit memos.* If payment is by credit card, the agency should get a promise by the corporation to pay for all debit memos from card chargebacks due to a lack of signature or imprint on the ticket charge form.

5. *Term.* When an agency must invest time and money to set up new offices, train personnel, or add equipment, the corporation should commit to a long-term contract, with no 30-day, no-cause termination.

6. *Termination by the corporation.* If the corporation terminates early, it should at least have to pay for the agency's ongoing automation expenses. At best, the corporation should also be liable for all lost commissions.

7. *Termination by the agency.* Regardless of the length of the contract, the agency should be able to terminate if the levels of airline commissions change materially, or if the corporation fails to purchase a stated, minimum quantity of airline tickets.

8. *Satellite ticket printers liability.* Caldwell notes that contracts should cover who assumes the risk of loss from theft of stock at STPs. However, he might have added that the Airline Reporting Corporation always holds the agency absolutely liable for all such theft, even when committed by an employee of the corporation. Therefore, when the

corporation is operating the STP, the corporation should agree to indemnify the agency against the latter's liability to the ARC.

9. *Service standards.* Caldwell's approach is to recite all of the service standards in the contract. If the standards were set forth in a proposal, it is preferable merely to incorporate the proposal by reference. Otherwise, the corporation may try to raise each standard as part of the negotiations.

10. *Transition.* The corporation with on-site computer reservation systems should agree not to remove personal name record data and profiles at the end of the contract.

## THE IMPLEMENTATION OF A CONSOLIDATED ACCOUNT

According to Walter Freedman, president of IVI Travel, "Employee support is a key factor in a successful travel program. For companies that are just beginning the consolidation process, some divisions and locations will be more ready for consolidation than others. It is important for the implementation team to be sensitive to the questions and concerns of travelers at each location." The following implementation plan is for full-service reservations at a reservation center with a satellite ticket printer located at the account's headquarters.

| Task | Resources | Start by Week | Complete by Week |
|---|---|---|---|
| company meets the implementation team | account mgmt. | one | one |
| review implementation plan | account mgmt. | one | one |
| review proposal of services to be provided | account mgmt. | one | one |
| apply for STP ARC appointments | operations | one | one |
| determine telecom needs | corporate services | two | two |
| determine automation needs | operations | two | two |
| determine management reporting needs | account mgmt. | two | two |
| determine staffing needs | operations | two | two |

| Task | Resources | Start by Week | Complete by Week |
|------|-----------|---------------|------------------|
| determine training needs | operations | two | two |
| develop and review travel policy | account mgmt. | two | two |
| review air, hotel, car-rental contracts | account mgmt. | three | three |
| finalize distribution configuration | operations | three | three |
| distribute profile cards | account mgmt. | three | three |
| develop seminars for travelers/planners | account mgmt. | three | four |
| review implementation process | account mgmt. | three | three |
| establish account review schedule | account mgmt. | four | four |
| develop specific training | human resources | four | four |
| develop customized reservation scripts | operations | four | four |
| assign ARC rep. and accounting team | accounting | four | four |
| secure VIP list | account mgmt. | four | four |
| check status for ARC approval | operations | four | four |
| implement mgmt. report requirements | MIS | four | four |
| finalize credit-card reconciliation | accounting | four | four |
| conduct seminars for travelers/planners | account mgmt. | four | six |
| train company client service staff | operations | four | eight |
| review implementation progress | account mgmt. | four | four |
| review prepaid policy | account mgmt. | five | five |
| establish 24-hour emergency procedures | account mgmt. | five | five |
| establish quality procedures | operations | five | five |
| input negotiated rates | operations | five | five |
| establish visa/passport procedures | operations | five | five |
| collect profiles | account mgmt. | five | six |
| coordinate MIS reporting needs | MIS | six | six |

| Task | Resources | Start by Week | Complete by Week |
|------|-----------|---------------|------------------|
| build corporate profile | operations | six | six |
| build automation table | operations | six | six |
| receive ARC STP appointments | operations | six | six |
| install telecom | operations | six | seven |
| install automation | operations | six | seven |
| input profiles | operations | six | seven |
| notify vendors of start-up | operations | seven | seven |
| finalize ARC/refund processing | operations | seven | seven |
| test process controls | operations | seven | seven |
| install automation and STP | operations | seven | seven |
| train STP attendant | operations | seven | seven |
| distribute hotel directories | account mgmt. | seven | eight |
| start-up | operations | eight | eight |

## HAVE RFPs GOTTEN OUT OF HAND?

Once corporations realized that corporate travel could be managed better through consolidation, a rush to using larger and larger RFPs began. At a certain point the costs of larger RFPs will begin to outweigh the benefits. According to an article in the October, 1990, issue of *Corporate Travel* magazine by Kathy Passero, "Controversy over new trends in the Request for Proposal (RFP) process is making the corporate travel industry a battleground of clashing opinions. Critics argue that corporations' efforts to create detailed RFPs are resulting in irrelevant redundant questions and forcing agencies to respond with foggy answers. Consultants, too, are adding fuel to the fire by using boilerplate RFPs asking as many as 160 essay questions, sources claim."

Arlene Macchia, manager of travel and meetings at Allied-Signal in Morristown, New Jersey, states that, "They've gotten too long and involved and expensive." There is some sentiment that travel consultants are justifying their fees through over-lengthy proposals.

On the mega side of the argument is the fact that responding to a large RFP may cost between $20,000 and $30,000. For a mega this translates into a cost figure of approximately $100,000 for obtaining a new account. On the corporate side of the argument, the travel manager's first worry is not what the megas are paying for an RFP, but what their costs are. It is easy to realize that the corporation must be spending equally large sums in the evaluation process.

Laurie Berger in the August, 1991 issue of *Corporate Travel* magazine writes:

> *Pressed to meet ever-shrinking budgets, corporate travel managers do not have the luxury of doing business with friends, sticking with long-time vendors or building new relationships, particularly when new, unfamiliar competitors come calling with sizzling new offers.*
>
> *So, many firms are hopping from one vendor to the next, desperately seeking the best deals. But this promiscuity has earned criticism from jilted partners and suitors across the industry. And rightfully so.*
>
> *Long term, this behavior will hurt both buyers and suppliers. Quantity will decline, vendors will go out of business and ultimately corporations will pay for poorer service.*

## TRAVEL MANAGEMENT TIPS

- Once the decision has been reached on the type of agency you wish to consider as your service partner, the next step in the process is to find, among the appropriately sized agencies, the one that best matches your corporate needs.
- The decision of which travel management company to use will be one of the most emotional your corporation ever makes. The reason for this is that it will affect more of your employees than any other vendor decision.
- The best way to select the right agency is by competitive bidding.
- As more and more corporations are using the RFP process to select a travel management company, an entire industry of consultants has arisen to advise corporations on this process.
- The failure of the corporation to honor its commitment to give one agency all of the corporation's business is probably the largest source of litigation in corporate travel today.

*Chapter Six*

# Service and Quality Issues

T he travel manager does not deal in a physical product, yet what the travel manager does will in some way affect how efficiently a large number of corporate employees are able to perform their duties. The travel manager is in a service position. Service, quality, and performance are the essential ingredients for evaluating how well the travel manager performs tasks.

## THE SERVICE IMPERATIVE

In Karl Albrecht and Ron Zemke's best-selling book *Service America*, the authors argue that service is "very much a primary product. It is, indeed, this argument that service is not a single-dimensioned thing that is at the core of our contention that service is as much a commodity as an automobile and as much in need of management and systematic study."

Harvard Business School professor Theodore Levitt agrees that the service and nonservice distinction becomes less and less meaningful as our understanding of service increases. He writes, "There are no such things as service industries. There are only industries whose service components are greater or less than those of other industries. Everybody is in service. At Citibank, half of the organization's approximately 50,000 employees work in back rooms, never seen or heard by the public. They spend their time writing letters of credit, opening lockboxes, processing transactions, and scrutinizing everything done by the public-contact people. Is Citicorp any less a manufacturer than IBM? And is IBM, half of whose 340,000 employees deal directly with the public, any less a service provider? Service is everybody's business."

Management expert and social scientist Peter Drucker is even more emphatic that the term "services," as used to describe the largest portion of our contemporary economy, is a singularly unhelpful description. In a recent column in *The Wall Street Journal*, he surveys the world economy, the slump in commodity prices, and the slow recovery of manufacturing compared to the rapid growth of the service sector and states:

> We may—and soon—have to rethink the way we look at economics and economies, and fairly radically. "Information" is now classed as "services," a 19th-century term for miscellaneous. Actually it is no more services than electrical power (which is also classed under services). It is the primary material of an information-based economy. And in such an economy the schools are as much primary producers as the farmer—and their productivity perhaps more crucial. The same in the engineering lab, the newspaper, and offices in general. (January 9, 1985)

## THE THREE DIMENSIONS OF SERVICE

Albrecht and Zemke outline various dimensions or levels of service. The first is what they refer to as "Help Me": help me with my taxes, help me get from point A to point B, help me find a house, help me pick out a new pair of shoes. Albrecht and Zemke think the "Help Me" level of service masks the full impact of service in today's marketplace.

## "FIX IT" SERVICE

The second dimension, according to Albrecht and Zemke, is service in the "Fix It" sense. It sometimes seems that we are a nation of broken toys. The car is in the shop, the phone is out of order. Service in this sense is underaccounted for in the economy and in the marketplace, but it is seldom undervalued in the eye of the consumer. The quality of a company's "Fix It" service is already a significant factor in its marketplace success. The capacity of a travel management firm, or the travel manager, or the hotel chain, or the car-rental company, or the airline to deliver "Fix It" service as a matter of routine sets each apart in its industry and in the marketplace as a whole.

The attitude that "This would be a wonderful business if it weren't for all the damned customers," is a costly error in judgment.

An unusually incisive set of studies of consumer complaint behavior was carried out during the Carter administration for the White House Office of Consumer Affairs by a Washington, D.C., company, Technical Assistance Research Programs, Inc. (TARP). These studies spoke volumes about the positive economics of first-class service. According to their findings, manufacturing organizations that don't just handle dissatisfied customers but go out of their way to encourage complaints and remedy them, reap significant rewards.

Among TARP's key findings are the following:

1. The average business never hears from 96 percent of its unhappy customers. For every complaint received, the average company in fact has 26 customers with problems, 6 of which are serious problems.

2. Complainers are more likely than noncomplainers to do business again with the company that upset them, even if the problem isn't satisfactorily resolved.

3. Of the customers who register a complaint, between 54 and 70 percent will do business again with the organization if their complaint is resolved. That figure goes up to a staggering 95 percent if the customer feels that the complaint was resolved quickly.

4. The average customer who has had a problem with an organization tells 9 or 10 people about it. Thirteen percent of people who have a problem with an organization recount the incident to more than 20 people.

5. Customers who have complained to an organization and had their complaints satisfactorily resolved tell an average of five people about the treatment they received.

As TARP president John Goodman put it in an address to the Nippon Cultural Broadcasting Company in Tokyo:

*The fundamental conclusion is that a customer is worth more than merely the value of the purchase a complaint concerns. A customer's worth includes the long-term value of both the revenue and profit from all his purchases. This becomes particularly important if the customer could potentially purchase a range of different products from the same company.*

Travel managers who have trouble getting subsidiaries to consolidate or to implement new company policy need to be aware of
"Fix It" service. Fix it service will be one of the key elements in
keeping people happy.

## VALUE-ADDED SERVICE

The third dimension discussed by Albrecht and Zemke is value-
added service. They refer to this as the most intangible aspect of
the service imperative. Value-added service has the feel of simple
civility when delivered in a face-to-face context, but it is more than
that. When it shows itself in such an ingenious and successful
product as the American Express platinum card, it looks like
perceptive marketing.

Albrecht and Zemke state that value-added service is more
easily understood in experience than in definition: you know it
when you see it. In response to an off-hand comment you made,
a corporate calling officer from one of the hotels or airlines sends
you information on a leisure trip you are planning. Perhaps the
account manager from the travel management company you use
stays late into the night helping you prepare a presentation to your
corporate travel council. This is value-added service.

## VALUE-ADDED SERVICE
## IN THE TRAVEL INDUSTRY

One example of value-added service is given by Walter Freedman
of IVI Travel.During the recent Middle East crisis, a special 24-
hour service center was set up to handle calls related to the crisis.
Agents were aided with a database of information about airline
check-in procedures and the use of electronic devices. In addition
to the hot line, IVI, with the help of their overseas partner Hogg
Robinson, set up a contingency plan to assist USA reporters in
Saudi Arabia to receive clothing and equipment from BBC charter
flights to Riyadh. IVI's partner, National Australia Travel, used
their banking relationships in Riyadh to provide emergency cash
for the *USA Today* team.

Another example of value-added service is the inserts that Peter Sontag of US Travel in Rockville, Maryland, places in each ticket jacket. Peter offers a challenge to anyone to look in the glove compartment of the car and find the toll-free number to the chairman of the car's manufacturer. "Next to your house, a car is the single most important purchase that people make, but there's rarely even a hint that auto makers want to hear from their customers." Bad service and inaccessible management are frustrating to Sontag. To prove his service commitment to US Travel's clients, he has a toll-free, private hot line that rings to his desk. To encourage clients to call, Sontag's phone number and a personal message are included with some 100,000 tickets each month. If a customer calls, Peter will either handle the problem on the spot or, if it needs additional work, send it out to field staff.

In 1988, Rosenbluth Travel (located in Philadelphia, Pa.) issued one of the industry's first guarantees of service. Rosenbluth's Performance Promise guarantees that the components of a travel reservation—lowest fare, seat assignments and boarding passes, schedule changes communicated, car-rental and hotel confirmation—will be delivered to the traveler's satisfaction or Rosenbluth returns their commission to the traveler's corporation. Hal Rosenbluth notes, "Our confidence in our people led us to issue our promise and we feel strongly that we should not accept payment for services not rendered to the client's satisfaction."

Another striking example of the type of value-added service that is necessary for the travel manager to put the travel management department on the corporate map is the service provided by Carol Salcito of United Technologies, who is known to offer continuing assistance to her fellow travel managers in helping them set up their departments.

## THE IMPORTANCE OF VALUE-ADDED SERVICE IN PLACING THE TRAVEL MANAGEMENT DEPARTMENT ON THE CORPORATE MAP

With value-added services carrying more weight in corporate life, it is here that the corporate travel manager has the greatest opportunity to solidify his or her position. Of the three types of service outlined by Albrecht and Zemke, "Help Me" is currently the most prevalent in the travel management business. This is not a demeaning statement. First of all, many corporate travel managers are just trying to get a department set up and operating. In a very real sense, those of us who make our living in this industry are all learning at the same time.

The "Help Me" type of service is important and will continue to be as more and more corporations begin to seek the benefits of travel management. Because both the travel management companies and large corporations are beginning to tire of the annual bidding process, the "Fix It" type of service will become more important. The astute travel manager will place more emphasis on finding out problems and fixing them. This will assure a better relationship with travelers and also with the travel management company.

As was pointed out in the TARP study, few people with complaints actually voice them. Because of this, the lack of complaints does not mean that grievances do not exist. Therefore, part of the travel manager's job will involve researching areas in which problems may exist. A number of well-managed travel departments conduct focus groups and regularly survey their travelers to keep on top. The active travel manager will give value-added service to the corporation by fixing problems that a non-service-oriented travel manager will miss.

The common thread of service-oriented travel managers is customer-focused service. None of these examples represents a new definition of what service means. It is rather the value and power they have in the marketplace that is new.

John Nasbitt's "high-tech/high-touch" concept has a lot to do with the development of the need for customer-focused service. As new technology is introduced into our society, there is a counterbalancing human response. For example, Nasbitt points out, "The high technology of heart transplants and brain scanners led to a new interest in the family doctor and neighborhood clinics." In that same vein, the advent of automated tellers in banking gave rise to a counterdemand by many customers for access to a personal banker. The more we are faced with high tech, the more we want high touch. The fewer contacts we have with the people of an organization, the more important the quality of each contact becomes. All contacts with an organization are a critical part of core perceptions and judgments about that organization. The impressions made by the people contacts, however, are often the firmest and most lasting.

Russell Ackoff sees another dimension to the demand for value-added service: a shifting focus from concern for one's standard of living toward a concern for the quality of life. If some aspects of this phenomenon represent a shift away from materialism and the "I can have it all" credo, as some claim, other factors that fall under the quality-of-life category certainly signal that with a secure standard of material life, the accessories become more important. A young person's need for a car gives way to a desire for the right kind of automobile. Access to discretionary funds sufficient to support frequent air travel gives way to a desire for a first-class setting and the best possible amenities. The total experience of obtaining a product or service becomes integrated with the real and palpable quality of the product or service itself.

## DESPERATELY SEEKING QUALITY

In a very interesting article by Loren Ginsberg in *Corporate Travel* magazine, entitled "Desperately Seeking Quality," Loren reports that those who bid on Motorola's $100M account in 1989 were told something they had never heard before—If they wanted the business, they'd have to apply for the Malcolm Baldrige National Quality Award. According to the *Corporate Travel* magazine article, "Motorola's stance reflects a growing commitment to real quality. Corporations are not only building quantifiable service standards into vendor contracts, they're putting specifics into their request for proposals (RFPs). Those who don't measure up simply won't win the business."

Other corporations such as Union Carbide and KPMG Peat Marwick put quality standards in their agency RFPs. Loren adds, "In addition to spelling out quality requirements in their service agreements, these firms required key agency contacts to sit on corporate quality teams with representatives from various corporate divisions."

Andy McCormick, spokesperson for IBM, was quoted in Ginsberg's article as saying IBM will dedicate a portion of its agency

RFPs to quality standards, and that the 1991 bid process would revolve around corporate-quality ideas. IBM's agencies are asked to conduct lowest-fare checks when the reservation is booked, when ticketing is completed, and 24 hours before departure. In addition, IBM relies on a third-party vendor to check for lowest-fare bookings. Agencies are offered incentives for high compliance, and they are penalized for exceptions.

Agencies must also provide monthly phone-call reports by location, as well as overall phone performance for agency sites nationwide. Traveler surveys are issued and analyzed.

According to the *Corporate Travel* magazine article, other corporations—such as Dr. Pepper/Seven-Up Companies, Price Waterhouse, United Technologies, Storage Technology Corp., and Wm. Wrigley, Jr., Company—actually specify quality standards in the RFP process.

## SERVICE AS A MANAGED ENDEAVOR

Historically, the terms "service" and "management" haven't rested easily side by side. Service delivery was something most self-respecting business school graduates shunned—with the exception perhaps of rising young bank officers. The concept of management seemed to encourage an orderly image antithetical to service in the "Help Me" sense.

Ronald Kent Shelp, vice president of American International Group, a multinational insurance company based in New York City, and chairman of the Federal Advisory Committee on Service Industries, attributes those perceptions to a confusion of personal services—such as those provided by housekeepers, barbers, and plumbers—with the concept of service as the provision of intangible products in general. Consequently, service has been misperceived as always involving a one-to-one relationship between provider and receiver, as labor-intensive, and as having productivity characteristics not readily increased by capital and technology.

According to Shelp:

*While personal-service jobs were declining, industrialization was calling forth a whole range of new services. Some of these were the result of new-found affluence, as more and more people could afford more and better health care, education, amusement, and recreation. Other services were needed to increase the productivity of production-wholesale trade, information processing, financial services, communications. These services and others like them became highly productive when modern technology supplied them with computers, satellite and other rapid communications, and systems analysis.*

*Thus service jobs moved away from the low end of the economic spectrum toward the other extreme. Much of the service-oriented job growth in advanced nations has taken place in professional, managerial, administrative, and problem-solving categories. Increasingly, education became the name of the game in service jobs.*

## THE EVOLVING NATURE OF SERVICE IN THE TRAVEL INDUSTRY

Steve Taylor, COO of Lifeco Travel Services, points out that the travel management industry has passed through a number of different stages, in each of which the concept of service has changed.

Before deregulation, the functions of the industry were really nothing more than order-taking and delivery of documentation. There was very little "value-added" to the travel process and no overt need for management. Fares were strictly regulated by the government: first-class, coach, night coach. The government approved a bold new concept called "super saver," which was highly restricted. It was designed to stimulate the leisure traveler and was unusable by the business traveler. During regulation, service and quality revolved around taking reservations and delivering tickets.

The second stage was from 1980 to 1985. During this period, the evolution of travel management actually began. Corporations began to focus on consolidation of their travel business under the direction of a travel management firm in order to take advantage of volume buying and policy control. The different CRS systems began to penetrate the market.

It was during this time that the travel management concept began to penetrate corporate America. With the increased sophistication of corporate travel managers, there was also a demand for more and better data. During this time period, travel managers began to develop more stringent travel policies.

For better control, more corporations began to recognize that it's better to consolidate as much travel as possible under one travel management vendor.

In 1986 there was a major development in CRS policy that allowed "foreign devices" to be attached to their systems. A foreign device is simply software provided by a third party vendor that is able to access a CRS. Now the megas were able to differentiate the product they sold to corporations by developing their own software to help manage travel. This is a significant development because the airlines had no real incentive to manage or reduce corporations' costs.

The megas began to develop software that has to a large extent shaped the direction of travel management. This software allowed corporations to further consolidate their travel by enabling them to track it more efficiently than ever before. This foreign software allowed the mega-agencies to further expand geographically as they attracted larger corporations that were consolidating their travel with one travel management company. The other significant development brought about by third-party software was the continued evolution of the nature of service in travel management. One point became painfully clear: The modern travel manager had become tied in to automation, and without a thorough knowledge of the automation systems available, the manager's capability to manage travel would be seriously compromised.

Beginning in early 1988, the concept of travel management began to evolve into what is called "total T&E cost containment." This was pushed by increases in the fares available to the business traveler. The fare increases were brought about by the continued growth in the economy and by more and more airlines taking control of their yield.

As corporations continued their push to consolidate travel, they became worried about the global aspects of travel. One of the more interesting developments in third-party software was the beginnings of pre-travel trip management.

Currently a number of mega-agencies and third-party software vendors are in various stages of developing and implementing pre-trip software, which can be a powerful tool in the hands of corporate travel managers willing to use it actively. Previously, travel had been managed almost after the fact, with companies auditing the trip after it had taken place. Pre-trip management puts information at the disposal of the travel manager before the travel takes place. Once a trip is taken, it is difficult for the travel manager to go to the airlines and other vendors and tell them that this turned out to be an unnecessary trip so please do not bill us for it. The time for the manager to control expenses is before they are incurred.

Pre-travel management delivers reports to the travel manager's desk the first thing every morning with the details of every active PNR. This pre-travel data is updated nightly on the travel manager's PC, and the software's user-friendly format can generate reports over a wide range.

As reported in *Travel Weekly* magazine in June 1991, this information can be used in a number of areas.

1. *Policy compliance.* A pre-travel manager will know when a traveler has done anything outside travel policy guidelines as they relate to that specific traveler.
2. *Trip necessity.* Pre-travel software has the ability to deliver a report to a department head detailing, for example, the fact that three people from the same department will be in Seattle next Monday.
3. *Corporate aircraft.* If a corporate aircraft is going someplace where two or three other employees are booked to fly on commercial airlines, these passengers can be placed on the corporate aircraft.
4. *Safety issues.* Many corporations will permit only so many employees on one flight. Pre-travel software can monitor this situation. The same software can also locate any employee anytime or anywhere in the event of some type of disaster.
5. *VIP travel.* All VIP travel can be checked to make sure the VIPs have been handled properly.

## QUALITY INITIATIVES FOR THE TRAVEL MANAGER

According to Rolfe Shellenberger, senior consultant at Runzheimer International, the following are the quality initiatives for a travel manager, organized on the basis of the four functions of management—planning, organizing, directing, and controlling.

## *Planning*

Travel management is part of all management at your company because travel is integral to all business operations. A key role of travel management is to provide planners with accurate data on travel service availability and costs so that realistic budgets can be developed for both marketing and operations. The planning process involves:

1. Developing a database on destination costs for the use of departmental planners.
2. Developing and offering a library of information on destination services to be used by marketers and operations executives in planning remote coverage for anticipated projects.
3. Designing a pro-forma travel budgeting system for departmental planners, using data developed from travel agencies and charge-card companies.
4. Establishing a plan for travel management, based on control of destination costs. Establishing goals for reducing or optimizing costs at frequently visited destinations, including airline, hotel, and car-rental expenses.

## *Organization*

1. Review the organizational relationship of travel management in each company location; recommend changes that will improve communications between department heads and travel specialists as well as between travelers and travel service suppliers, whether they are inside or outside your company.
2. Review each travel operation in terms of its efficiency. When volume suggests financial and service advantages, evaluate alternative travel arrangement scenarios, e.g., in-house versus full-service, "Rent-a-Plate" versus full-service or in-house. Consider traveler convenience first, but also consider costs and offsets from commission-sharing, accuracy of information available to travelers, volume and peaking problems that might reduce overall quality of service, and the impact on policy implementation and adherence.

3. Question where travel management really belongs in the organization. It may vary as to division but could be part of Purchasing, Personnel, Finance, Marketing, Administration and General Services, or even the Executive Department.

4. Expand the scope of travel management so that it incorporates other functions, which can enhance its effectiveness as an operating and buying unit within the corporation. For example, meeting planning will often be more effective as part of the travel department; also, relocation and fleet management involve disciplines routinely involved in travel management.

5. Be sure that travel arrangers are equipped with the tools they need to order travel services more efficiently and in a manner that will make travelers feel secure and aptly served. Conduct training regularly, particularly when new hires are suddenly responsible for arranging travel for their supervisors. Be sure that a pipeline from Personnel is established so that this training can be effectuated as soon as possible.

### *Directing*

Corporate travel managers must direct their own staffs, travel arrangers, and travel agency personnel who service your company. A less obvious obligation, one crucial to quality assurance, is to design and execute strong communications programs to inform departmental executives and travelers of late-breaking developments in the specialized field of travel. The travel manager must

1. Establish performance standards for staff members that will assure quality. Some critical elements are:
   a. Prompt response to telephone inquiries. Set a standard for answering the phone within so many rings.
   b. Callbacks. In any business, a key determinant of quality is a commitment from people to follow up on phone calls from within and outside the company. A standard of 24 hours should be the minimum. If the manager cannot do it, then he or she should delegate it to someone.

     c. Promise fulfillment. If you have said you will provide information, set a time for it and follow through. Be sure commitments are realistic and then assure prompt delivery.

2. Establish performance standards for agencies, then measure results in a consistent, objective fashion. These standards will include such items as answering time, holding time, ticket delivery, and follow-up on complaints.

3. Develop a systematic way of keeping travelers informed of things they ought to know—newly negotiated hotel, airline, and car-rental rates; travel conditions in frequently visited cities; changes in travel service patterns; procedures travelers are to use in assuring value of accommodations and efficiency to their travel.

4. Develop and maintain a continuing training program on travel services, destination information, procedures to optimize travel values (e.g., planning in advance to take advantage of lower fares) for travelers, travel arrangers, and department heads.

5. If not already accomplished, prepare a handbook for travelers that will show them how to book more easily and more efficiently.

6. Initiate reports on travel activity to inform senior executives of cost trends and travel management performance.

7. Hold regular meetings with travelers, not only to inform them of changes, but also to acquire knowledge of their needs and preferences.

## Controlling

1. Review the content and organization of management reports from travel agencies, charge-card companies, car-rental firms, and other travel service vendors. Make such reports consistent among divisions and capable of consolidation.

2. Develop procedures to inform department heads when travelers request policy variances so that policy can be amended or enforcement action can be taken.

3. Look for ways to consolidate travel information with the expense-account process. Start with the assumption that you can eliminate duplications in keying travel data.

4. Review authorization and approval procedures on expense reports to see if all are needed and useful.

5. Be sure your agencies are using quality-control procedures, whether they are automated or not.

6. Develop error/complaint reports for travel transactions, not necessarily to reprimand anyone, but to identify areas for additional training or procedures revision.

## THE MALCOLM BALDRIGE AWARD

The US Government offers companies an opportunity to vie for the Baldrige Award, which is granted in three categories— manufacturing company, service company, and "small company" (either manufacturing or service). The following items are listed in published guidelines for organizations who wish to compete for the award. If you want a complete copy of the guidelines, you may order it free from:

Malcolm Baldrige National Quality Award
National Institute of Standards and Technology
Administration Building—Room A537
Gaithersburg, MD 20899
Phone: 301–975–2036

The Baldrige Award contains the following sections that pertain to service companies:

### Business Process, Operational and Support Service Quality Improvement

1. Develop quality standards and measure them. They will include the following:
   - Response time to inquiries; also answering time.
   - Callbacks.
   - Accuracy of reservations records.
   - Library maintenance and update (destination costs, etc.).
   - Coverage of office.
   - Ticket delivery.
   - Turnover of volume (number of reservations before ticketing a trip).

- Calls per reservation/ticket.
- Complaints related to volume.
- Complaints related to preferred suppliers.
- Accuracy of records.

(Note that many of the above are handled by agencies; travel management must see to it that standards exist and are properly measured.)

2. Institute training programs designed to minimize adverse reports. These may include the following:
   - Training travel arrangers on procedures to minimize frequency of calls and length of transaction time per reservation.
   - Training travelers to use reference material that will save time and minimize errors on travel requests.
   - Training accounting/auditing people on documents returned as receipts with expense reports.
3. Set up preferred-supplier program and communicate it to travelers.
4. Involve travel suppliers—airlines, hotels and car-rental companies—in your internal communications programs to offset administrative costs and keep the program interesting.
5. Establish a "zero defects" program. Offer rewards to all participants for accomplishments in exceeding quality goals. Suppliers may be happy to provide rewards in return for the promotional value.

### Supplier Quality Improvement

1. Conduct regular meetings with travel agencies to get them to "buy in" on the quality program, including all standards covered above.
2. Monitor supplier performance by surveying travelers with questionnaires and phone calls.
3. Develop a quality-award program to reward suppliers when they meet and exceed requirements. Have an "airline of the month," "hotel of the month," and "car-rental company of the month" award based on traveler reports.
4. Periodically inspect preferred suppliers (hotels, airlines, car-rental and limousine services, etc.) to be sure of the products you're advocating. Enroll suppliers in your

quality-control program by having them join you in measuring their performance related to your travelers.

5. Circulate to suppliers information on your program's initiatives and on the results of your own quality-improvement activities; it will motivate them to do the same.

6. Require prospective suppliers to inform you of their quality-assurance procedures as part of their bid for your patronage. Be particularly attentive to motivational issues, i.e., how employees are compensated for quality performance, and what their employee turnover is.

## EMPLOYEE QUALITY ISSUES

Despite the increased use of automation in the travel industry, the key person who will interact with your corporate travelers is the reservationist who talks with the traveler on the telephone. This overworked and underpaid employee is the person who will have the most interaction with your travellers. It should be of immense concern to all of us that the front-line personnel in the travel industry, who have the greatest impact on the comfort of our travel experience, also receive the lowest wages. The corporate travel manager should take a major interest in how the travel management company treats its employees because its travelers can probably expect the same treatment.

IVI Travel, based in Northbrook, Illinois, has developed an employee recognition program called *The Mark of Excellence*. Service standards are established jointly with customers, and employees receive recognition and rewards for achieving the highest level of service excellence. According to Jim Venskus, IVI's Director of Education and Development, "Recognition of a job well done is very important to our employees."

Arrington Travel, located in Chicago, Illinois, ensures employee quality control through the use of the following checklist, which reservationists must use when completing a passenger name record (PNR).

1. *Form of payment*. Compare the record with the corporate profile for the correct form of payment and the credit-card expiration date.

2. *Lowest fare*. Check against company policy to ensure application of the lowest fare or the lowest-cost routing.

3. *Waitlist/Fare conversion*. Confirm that all waitlisted fares have been converted.

4. *Tickets remark*. Check the account number, savings codes, and remarks section regarding codes.

5. *History field*. Contains complete agent documentation regarding policy exceptions, e.g., denied airports and lower fares.

6. *Cars field*. Check the corporate and personal profile to ensure that proper car size and vendor was requested.

7. *Hotel field*. Check the corporate and personal profile to ensure that proper hotel, room category, and rate was requested.

8. *Seats field*. Check the personal profile to ensure that the correct seat was requested or waitlisted.

9. *Mileage numbers*. Verifies that all frequent flyer numbers are on the profile and have been appended to the record.

10. *Flight service*. Displays information relative to specific flights, such as connecting flights, and contains documentation reflecting this information.

11. *Confirmations*. Check for confirmations from airlines (seats, meals, special requests, etc.), hotels, and car-rental companies.

12. *Special instructions*. Check for VIP notice or instructions to airlines.

13. *Schedule changes*. Verifies if schedule changes have been made and that all information is corrected for date continuity.

14. *Delivery field*. Check for correct delivery information and number of characters and to verify that the ticketing date is correct for that date of travel and within policy.

15. Check corporate and personal profiles for special delivery or accounting instructions.

## EVALUATING VENDORS AND SOFTWARE

Because of the complexity of the travel assignment, quality issues are rapidly becoming automation issues.

In the May 1991 issue of *Corporate Travel* magazine, Jeff Hoffman developed an outline to be used in evaluating automation equipment and the vendor before purchasing.

### Basic RFP Outline

1. Purpose: statement of RFP's goal.
2. Statement of confidentiality: agreement between your company and vendors to protect both parties from disclosures.
3. Background information: overview of your company and organization.
4. Automation requirements: overview of your automation requirements, detailing problems to be solved with automation.
5. Timetable: list of milestone dates for such events as bidders' conference, proposal-due dates, vendor presentation dates, contract award date, start date, etc.
6. Evaluation criteria: explanation of evaluation criteria, including definition of required versus optional features and relative weighing of each.
7. Overview of automation requirements: description of average and peak transaction volumes, reporting requirements, response time requirements.
8. Contractual issues: description of any contractual requirements (i.e., CRS approvals needed for software, etc.)
9. Vendor proposal description: outline of desired proposal responses, including required system features and performance parameters, cost, assistance in required conversions, ongoing support, performance guarantees, proposed contract and reference lists.

### General Evaluation of Vendor

1. Corporate overview
   a. What is vendor's financial position and long-term stability?
   b. What is vendor's total automation development budget?
   c. What is the average technical experience level and travel industry experience level of vendor's employees? Ask to see actual résumés of people who will be assigned to the project.

    d. Has the vendor separated the research and develop-
ment team from the standard MIS/operations functions? What is the budget ratio for the two organizations? How do the employees differ?

2. Systems approach
    a. What is the vendor's system-design methodology? How
much influence will you or other corporations have
over the design of new automation that is compatible
with the vendor's product methodology?
    b. What is the vendor's product development methodol-
ogy? Make them convince you that their approach to
projects is organized and will meet your deadlines.
    c. Will you have signature approval authority on product
technical specifications to ensure that they meet your
needs?

3. Implementation and support
    a. During product implementation, what will be the spe-
cific breakdown of responsibilities between you and the
vendor? How will those responsibilities carry over into
initial testing and product support? What similar implementation experience does the vendor have?
    b. What are the vendor's product-testing techniques? Will
acceptance test parameters be defined before you accept automation products?
    c. How will the vendor assist you in conversion from
your existing products, if any? What previous conversion experience does the vendor have?
    d. What level of product support will the vendor provide
for all automation products? Include commitments for
on-site installations, training, help desks, and documentation. Is the product support staff dedicated to
support only?
    e. How and when will product updates and enhance-
ments be delivered?

4. Costs and benefits
    a. What are all the applicable product acquisition and im-
plementation costs? Include purchase/license costs,
product modification costs, required hardware and software costs, supplemental documentation costs, conversion costs from existing automation products, testing
costs, and training costs. Separate annual from one-

time costs, and consider the cost of employee time for involvement of your employees.
  b. What are all the applicable operating costs for each automation product? Include data-collection costs, system-processing costs, and programming support costs.
  c. What ongoing contractual or maintenance costs will be required? Include such costs as CRS access fees and data lines, and make sure that required CRS contracts and approvals are in place.
  d. What other costs will be required, such as telecommunications costs?
  e. What are the benefits of using the vendor's automation products?
5. Planning considerations
  a. In the event of a disaster of any kind, what disaster recovery or contingency plan does the vendor have?
  b. In general, what is the vendor's overall long-term strategic system's plan?
  c. What is the vendor's past track record with similar systems in similar environments on similar technical platforms?
  d. Are the vendor's products parameter-driven (versus hard-coded) to allow for continued refinement and customization by you?
  e. Can the vendor provide you a complete list of references with names?

## FRONT-OFFICE PRODUCT EVALUATION

1. Reservations process
  a. Which CRSs does the vendor work with, and who can you contact at each CRS to discuss this vendor and its products?
  b. Does this vendor provide any automated travel-requesting tools, such as a link to an office automation/electronic mail system? Which systems in particular?
  c. Does the vendor provide any corporate booking tools to facilitate corporate travel planning?
  d. Does the vendor have an automated policy compliance or travel authorization system?

e. What type of agent productivity tools/techniques has the vendor developed? Does the vendor have any automated quality-control tools?

f. Does the vendor have an automated telephone-call tracking and reporting system for use with automatic call distributors (ACDs) to ensure proper service levels?

2. PNR monitoring and control

a. Does the vendor have a PNR monitoring system? Does it do fare checking, seat assignments, or alternate routing analysis? If so, what algorithms and parameters are used to make selections, and what type of management/ statistical reports are available from the system? Does the system use direct access or total access to other CRSs?

b. Are the PNR monitoring and quality-control systems for air only, or also for car-rentals and hotels?

c. Can PNR monitoring and agent productivity tools automatically input negotiated fares? Can international fares and itineraries be handled? Are all systems parameter-driven to allow traveler-customized operation?

d. Has the vendor developed a standardized PNR format? How is PNR integrity protected when PNRs are handled by automated systems? Is there an interface by automated systems? Is there an interface to the back office to guarantee that PNRs remain valid throughout the record's life cycle?

e. Does the vendor have a pre-travel reporting system for you to examine current PNRs? Does the system provide canned or faxed reports, or ship you the actual data for your use?

3. Scheduling systems

a. If you own or operate any corporate aircraft, does the vendor have any automated tools to help you plan and schedule the use of these aircraft?

b. If you plan your own meetings, does the vendor have any automated meeting-planning tools? Can these tools link itineraries in PNRs with ground-based reservations?

4. Implementation and distribution

a. What are the operational implications and requirements of your using the vendor's systems? Are significant profile changes or similar set-up activities required?

    b. Is the vendor required to assist you in dealing with conversion trauma? Does the vendor have automated conversion tools for such operations as movement of traveler profiles from one CRS to another?

    c. Do the vendor's products use CRS-stored profiles or locally stored profiles? If local, how is "800 number" phone support provided to customers by agents away from the local profile system?

    d. Is the vendor connected to a ticket distribution network? What about itinerary distribution? Can itineraries be transmitted via your company's existing electronic mail/office automation system?

## BACK-OFFICE SYSTEMS

*Interfaces*

1. Is the vendor using custom-built or industry-standard back-office software, or some of each?
2. What CRS interfaces does the vendor's back office have?
3. What PNR versions is the vendor using with each CRS?

*Record Integrity and Reconciliation*

1. How does the vendor reconcile PNRs through the back office?
2. Can back-office records be reconciled with previously generated pre-travel reports?
3. How well does the back office system handle special fields used by your company in PNRs? Does the back-office system filter out or lose certain data elements that you need to pass through (e.g., employee/department numbers, comparison fares)?
4. Does the vendor have an automated quality-control process to ensure the integrity of back-office records?
5. Does the vendor have an automated accounting interface to such functions as general ledger and accounts receivable? What about interfaces to T&E expense management systems?

*Back-Office Reporting*

1. Will you receive back-office printed paper reports or actual data?
2. What is the timeliness and availability of back-office data to you? Are data delivery and turnaround times guaranteed?
3. How is the accuracy and completeness of back-office data guaranteed?
4. What security measures are in place to protect the integrity of, and access to, your back-office data?
5. Is the available back-office data what you really need? Does the data come in a usable format, or is a programmer required to retrieve and review it?
6. Is the data available on-line?
7. For on-line systems, can you generate custom reports at your site without the vendor's assistance?
8. Are built-in graphics available to you, or must they be hand-produced?

*Advanced Reporting Functions*

1. Are there any built-in reporting mechanisms to assist you in identifying exceptions and policy violations?
2. Can the reporting system identify travel trends automatically?
3. Is automated reporting available to assist in travel budgeting and forecasting? Future cost avoidance? Override and commission tracking?
4. What type of historical statistics are available from the back-office reporting system?
5. Is there an automated or structured feedback loop from the back-office reports to the reservations and travel planning process itself?

*Conversions and Consolidations*

1. What experience does the vendor have in conversions from your existing back-office automation systems to the vendor's automation systems?

2. What would be your role and responsibilities in the conversion versus that of the vendor? What are the total conversion costs?

3. Does the vendor have national consolidation experience? What about global consolidation? What is the vendor's methodology for domestic consolidations and plans for global consolidations?

## TRAVEL MANAGEMENT TIPS

- Service, quality and performance are the essential ingredients for evaluating how well the travel manager performs.

- With value-added services carrying more weight in corporate life, it is here that the corporate travel manager has the greatest opportunity to solidify his or her position.

- The mega travel agencies have developed software that has to a large extent shaped the direction of travel management. This software allows corporations to further consolidate their travel by enabling them to track it more efficiently than ever before.

- Currently, a number of mega-agencies and third-party software vendors are in various stages of developing and implementing pre-trip software, which can be a powerful tool in the hands of corporate travel managers.

- Pre-trip management puts information at the disposal of the travel manager before the travel takes place.

# III

This section of the book deals with vendor relations. I choose to begin this section with a very short chapter on meals and entertainment. Unknown to many, this is the easiest place to begin cutting costs. For smaller companies that do not have the volume for negotiated deals, this information will be worth the price of this book.

Chapter 8 deals with the many unknowns of the airline business. At this time, none of us know what will happen during the coming year, or two years or even six months in the future. Of all the material in this book, this chapter is the most volatile. What the airlines are doing today is no indication of what they will be doing in the future. Therefore, I have described both the new fares and negotiated deals, even though some of the major airlines have backed away from these. As far as we know, they may come back next fall (or perhaps never).

Chapter 9 tells about the new field of globalization. This is a mystery area for many travel managers. Hopefully, this information will prove valuable to those who deal with international travelers.

Chapter 10 gives the travel manager rules concerning the use of charter air travel, and chapter 11 goes into the black hole of travel management: frequent flyer programs.

*Chapter Seven*

# Managing Meal and Entertainment Expenses

T his is the smallest chapter in this book, but it has tips that can be some of the fastest routes to reducing and controlling expenses, especially for smaller companies. One of the most ignored aspects of travel management is the control of costs for meals and entertainment. The American Express Consulting Group identifies meals (16 percent) and entertainment (11 percent) as the second-largest components of principal travel costs. Despite this, travel managers often disregard these expenses in policy considerations. Even though most corporate entertainment is done with a meal, we will use "meal" to refer to a traveler eating alone.

According to Jeff Lang, director of American Express Consulting Services, "Meal and entertainment expenses are the most loosely controlled, but the most controllable of all travel expenses. A simple act such as lowering receipt requirements can save a corporation a great deal of money."

## IRS REQUIREMENTS

For meals and entertainment to be deductible, the following conditions must apply:

1. Receipts must be saved for expenses of $25 or more.
2. The expense must be ordinary and necessary to conducting business.
3. The expense must be directly related to or associated with business activities.
4. Purely goodwill expenses are no longer deductible.

An example of a purely goodwill expense is taking a client to play golf and not discussing business. Malcolm Forbes's birthday parties were considered goodwill expenses. Even though those who were invited were business associates, business was not discussed.

## CONTROLLING MEAL AND ENTERTAINMENT EXPENSES

Three methods will be examined for controlling meal and entertainment expenses:

1. Per diems.
2. Spending guidelines.
3. Tightening substantiation, reporting, and approvals.

The travel manager should keep certain issues in mind when formulating policy for meals and entertainment. These concerns include:

1. Payment methods.
2. Auditing procedures.
3. Travel patterns.
4. Types of expenses being incurred.
5. Level of the employee.
6. Company culture.

## PER DIEMS

According to the American Express Consulting Group, a corporate per diem has the following characteristics:

1. Established daily allowance.
2. Requires no receipts.
3. Total reimbursed for each day (or portion thereof).
4. Does not include business meals and entertainment expenses.
5. May not be broken out by breakfast, lunch, or dinner.
6. May vary by city.

The main advantages of per diems is that they put a limit on total potential expenses and limits administrative costs associated with auditing receipts.

The main disadvantages of per diems is that they are too low, imposing a hardship on the traveler and forcing the traveler to make up the difference in other areas, or they are too high. In this case, the corporation's expenses are higher than necessary.

There are certain tax implications to per diems. The 1990 amendment to the Family Support Act states that meal per diems in excess of federal government levels will be taxed as income unless actual expense is fully documented.

## SPENDING GUIDELINES

The second method of controlling meal and entertainment expenses is by imposing spending guidelines. Jeff Lang comments that spending guidelines have the following characteristics:

1. May set maximum reimbursable limits.
2. May be used to determine reasonableness range.
3. Receipts required.
4. May vary by city.
5. May or may not be published by policy.
6. Can be daily or per meal.

There are a number of advantages to using spending guidelines rather than per diems. These advantages include:

1. Can establish a maximum cap on spending.
2. Eliminates excessive reimbursement.
3. Can help to establish reasonableness.
4. Can be used to track differing patterns or areas of abuse within a single company.
5. Eliminates inconsistencies company-wide.
6. Requires substantiation.

While spending guidelines have these advantages, there are also disadvantages. The disadvantages are that they require additional administration, they can be arbitrary, and they may encourage travelers to spend or report maximum amounts.

## TIGHTENING SUBSTANTIATION, REPORTING, AND APPROVALS

Receipt levels, types of receipts, reporting expenses, and second-level approvals are the four main considerations in tightening substantiation, reporting, and approvals, according to Jeff Lang. Lang comments further that the main advantages of tightening documentation are:

1. Reduces exposure to guesswork.
2. Reduces upward rounding.
3. Helps traveler reconstruct actual expenses.
4. Diminishes likelihood of adverse IRS audit.
5. Reimburses only for actual expenses.
6. Allows flexibility, with proper explanations and approvals.
7. Helps to reduce cash advances.
8. Increases scrutiny for entertainment expenses.

Lang adds that the two disadvantages to this method are that it increases administration through review of receipts and that employees perceive it as a hardship.

In addition to the methods discussed above for controlling meal and entertainment expenses, The American Express Consulting Group studies indicate that using a corporate credit card is an excellent method for reducing average meal expenses. In a study conducted with four companies, the following was discovered:

### Average Meal Costs (per trip)

|  | Travelers With Credit Cards | Travelers Without Credit Cards |
| --- | --- | --- |
| Company A | $ 59.00 | $ 74.00 |
| Company B | 180.00 | 273.00 |
| Company C | 140.00 | 203.00 |
| Company D | 57.00 | 66.00 |

## TRAVEL MANAGEMENT TIPS

- For medium and smaller size companies, a well defined expense program is the quickest way to reduce costs.
- The quickest way to reduce meal and entertainment costs is through a well defined policy using a corporate credit card.
- Cash advances should not be used for entertainment expenses.

*Chapter Eight*

# Managing Domestic Airline Programs

J ust when you think you know what the airlines are doing, they change their minds and try something else. Material explaining the recent changes in the fare structure is included in this chapter; however, the reader is cautioned that the airlines change promotional schemes every spring. The material in this chapter may well be outdated by the time it is published. Some airlines are currently offering corporate deals as outlined; some are not. What they will be doing next year is anybody's guess.

In order to deal effectively with the airlines, it is important to understand concepts like yield management and certain nuances of airline economics. Attention must also be paid to the main method of airline ticket distribution: the CRS. One of the problems corporations have had in dealing with the airlines is the misunderstanding that airlines welcome deals. The typical purchasing manager is accustomed to working with companies that welcome volume discounts because their unit costs decrease with increased volume.

This is not the case in the airline industry. This misunderstanding of the basic nature of airline economics has far-reaching consequences. The misunderstanding of the very nature of the industry flows down to the purchasing managers of many corporations, who seldom understand why sales managers of airlines do not welcome volume deals. In manufacturing, as volume increases unit costs generally decrease. This is not so in the airline industry.

According to Laurie Berger, editor of *Corporate Travel* magazine, the airlines currently negotiate volume discounts because they are "forced to deal." A deal with an airline will be the most hard-fought deal your purchasing team ever wins, and it requires considerable knowledge on the part of the negotiator. Critical to this is an understanding of the way airlines price their product. The pricing process is referred to as yield management. The second area of importance to the travel manager is the CRS because it is through the CRS that the airlines distribute their products.

## INTRODUCTION

Yield management, or revenue management (the terms are used interchangeably), is one of the hottest topics in travel circles today. For an airline, yield is the revenue that it receives per passenger mile (RPM).

Yield management is concerned with maximizing this revenue. Yield-management systems help airlines obtain the greatest revenue possible by assigning different prices to the seats in an airplane according to what price different types of travelers (business, leisure, etc.) are willing to pay. These prices are then loaded into the CRS.

Revenue increases are generally achieved in three different areas: overbooking, improving the fare mix, and segment control. Overbooking sets sales levels with more precision, allowing airlines and others to reduce the revenue shortfall that occurs when confirmed passengers fail to use reservations and when reselling the space is impractical. "Fare mix" refers to the practice of charging customers according to their willingness to pay. Segment control deals with the revenue impact of a particular booking, and applies only to the airline industry.

The benefit of revenue-enhancement systems is that they can significantly improve profits because they only marginally increase expenses. There are other factors influencing yield, such as the type of aircraft used and marketing methods, but yield management so far deals only with the schedules, the inventory of seats, and the prices assigned to them.

Historically, yield management has been used primarily in the airline industry, but the potential users range from the rental-car industry to concert promoters.

## CAPABILITIES OF YIELD MANAGEMENT

Originally promoted to the industry as a cure-all, yield management is now undergoing a period of re-examination to decide its actual position in our business. If you were to believe all the hype that has been generated over yield management since its inception, you would have the mistaken assumption that the airline industry is awash in profits. Nothing could be further from the truth. Currently the airline industry is very weak financially. Although an effective tool, yield management is not a guarantee of profit, since there are areas affecting profits that it does not deal with, and costs are completely outside its realm. Furthermore, yield management cannot ensure that people will call a particular airline or hotel for a reservation. What yield management can do is help a company better manage what it can control.

Even though the concept of yield management has been instrumental in lowering air fares to a large portion of the buying public, there is a great deal of resentment by various consumer groups, mainly because the process of pricing an airline ticket has become one of the most complicated procedures in the world. Because of yield management, three people sitting in the same row of an airplane may have paid radically different prices. A fare from D.C. to Atlanta might be higher than one from D.C. to Sarasota, Florida (which is a longer flight). This causes pricing confusion because the price of an airline ticket is no longer dependent upon distance. It is no longer possible to track fares with any degree of certainty.

## THE ECONOMICS OF YIELD MANAGEMENT

The economic justification for yield management rests on a concept known as elasticity of demand. Economists have long recognized that different people are willing to pay different prices for the same product. Imagine that you are a company based in New York that manufactures computers. Your biggest customer, located in Orlando, is having problems and needs to be serviced immediately or they will lose a big job. It is reasonable to assume that your company will lose a major customer if you don't get a service person down to Orlando right away. Contrast this with a young married couple with a brand-new child they wish to show off to grandparents. They want to travel, but have less money to spend.

The business traveler in the above example has no choice but to travel. This is known as inelastic demand. Inelastic demand simply means that within certain bounds, the consumer will pay any price. There is little reason to discount the price of any product to this type of customer because they are willing to pay relatively high prices. If the product were discounted, the airline would experience an "opportunity cost" because the end user would have paid more for the same product. If a businessman is willing to pay $200 to travel from Detroit to Boston, there is no reason to charge only $150. If the airline charged that person $150, they would forfeit a $50 opportunity cost. The opportunity cost represents how much more the airline could have charged for the same ticket without losing the sale.

The pricing strategy for inelastic customers is to charge them as much as possible. Of course, there is an invisible line which when crossed will cause the airline to lose sales, but the point is that with inelastic demand there is little need to discount prices. Business travelers travel out of necessity and are generally a good example of inelastic demand.

Leisure travel is a good example of elastic demand. The term "elastic demand" refers to the fact that the customer is very sensitive to price changes. In other words, if there is a small downward change in the price of travel, there will be more people traveling, and the quantity increase will make up for the lower price. This means that if the airline is facing an elastic demand curve, it will actually bring in more revenue by lowering its price. Conversely, raising the price to market segments that are price elastic will cause a decrease in total revenue. When the price of airline tickets rises above a certain point, vacationers look to other means of travel such as the automobile, and they generally travel closer to home.

With inelastic demand, an airline makes more money by charging a higher price, while with elastic demand it makes more money by charging a lower price. An airplane is filled with passengers, some of whom are priced elastic and the others inelastic. This presents us with a very interesting problem. Given that there are a fixed number of seats in an airplane, how many do we allocate to high prices and how many to low prices? More importantly, how do we distinguish between those who are willing to pay high prices and those who won't? The airlines have devised some simple methods to differentiate between these two groups of consumers.

The typical business traveler makes travel reservations less than two weeks in advance, but the leisure traveler schedules a vacation months in advance and plans accordingly. The time a booking is made prior to travel is one of the main tools used to estimate demand elasticity in the travel industry.

There are varying degrees of time and price sensitivity, and the allocation of the different classes can be graphed. It is easy to see that virtually no passengers are time/price indifferent. If an airline used only one fare to address this wide range of consumer desires, it would probably choose a fare in the middle. This fare, however, would not be low enough to attract discount seekers on the flights for which there is very low demand or high enough to shift demand from the peak flights.

It is easy to see that yield management involves charging different prices for essentially the same product. It is what economists call price discrimination. It would be very difficult to price most consumer products like this. Imagine going into a grocery store and seeing a different price on every loaf of Wonder Bread. One of the reasons airlines and hotels are able to price discriminate is that prices are not marked on the product as they are on most retail goods. Some form of price concealment is vital for implementing yield-management systems.

## AIRLINE YIELD MANAGEMENT

To help further illustrate the concept of airline yield, two examples will be given to help show how it is calculated. The most common method of calculating airline yield is based on the revenue passenger mile (RPM). This refers to one revenue passenger being transported one mile. The sum of RPMs is the customary measure for total airline passenger traffic.

RPMs = aircraft miles flown × passengers carried

Sometimes costs are measured in available seat miles (ASM), which is one seat flown one mile. For an airline's total system, available seat miles are the sum of the seat miles flown by all aircraft. It is a measure of an airline's total capacity.

ASMs = aircraft miles flown × seats available for sale

A third commonly used statistic is the load factor (LF), which is the percent of available seat miles that revenue passenger miles represent in revenue passenger service.

LF = RPMs ÷ ASMs

Yield is calculated by dividing the revenue into either RPMs or ASMs.

The concepts of ASM and RPM are vital to the airline industry and are used in analyzing airline operations. Almost all of the wide variances in the profitability of the airline industry can be accounted for in the following four items:

1. Traffic—usually measured by RPMs.
2. Capacity—usually measured by ASMs.
3. Unit revenue—called yield, and usually measured as cents per RPM.
4. Unit costs—normally measured as cents per ASM.

A significant change in either traffic, capacity, yield, or costs that is not offset by a change in one of the other elements will cause a sharp swing in profits. An airline monitors these figures carefully because its products are extremely perishable, that is, they are consumed or wasted at the moment of production and cannot be stockpiled or inventoried.

Since yield management does not guarantee that an airline will make money, the best that most systems can do is to minimize losses during periods of economic downturns. Yield management is concerned only with revenues and cannot control or materially affect costs, such as fuel, which greatly affect airline profitability. This is why even the most sophisticated yield-management systems cannot guarantee profits. In the airline industry there are a number of factors that affect yield.

## FACTORS AFFECTING YIELD

According to airline industry analyst Dr. George James, the two greatest considerations are the fare level and the seat mix. Other activities that affect yield are scheduling, overbooking, and traffic flow. In terms of being able to implement a yield-management system, the most important ingredient is accurate forecasting of passenger demand by fare class.

## PRICING STRATEGIES

The pricing system used in implementing yield-management is called segmental pricing. Essentially, there are two forms of pricing in air transport: uniform pricing and market, or segmental, pricing. Uniform pricing involves setting a single price for all passengers on a route or flight. This is the approach generally adopted by charter operators, where in the final analysis the charter airline is under no obligation to operate planned flights if there is not sufficient demand at a uniform price to make them an economic proposition. To a lesser extent this is how the airline industry operated before deregulation. There were coach fares, first-class fares, and super-savers. Segmental pricing occurs when the air ticket is priced according to how elastic, or sensitive to the fare, the customer is. With segmental pricing, business travelers pay higher prices and leisure travelers are offered discount tickets.

Prior to deregulation, competition among carriers was limited by the Civil Aeronautics Board (CAB) in two of the three major areas of airline marketing—route authority and pricing—leaving only the number of flights to be made available by any one carrier over any one route up to the individual carrier's judgment. Competition was limited to frills and the number of departures.

Pricing policies were generally viewed and analyzed from an industry standpoint because the CAB would not permit any carrier to offer a lower fare that was uneconomic for the industry as a whole. Thus, even though a particular fare might benefit a particular carrier at the expense of another carrier, the CAB would not permit the offering of the proposed fare without an extremely strong justification showing clearly that the fare would benefit the general public. The carriers who stood to lose revenue as a result of the lower fare would argue in rebuttal that their loss of revenue would have to be offset by a general fare increase in all fares, thereby harming the general public by requiring them to pay a higher fare, and in effect, subsidizing those few passengers who would benefit from the lower fare proposed by their competitor.

With the advent of deregulation, carriers suddenly found themselves facing new forms of competition. Airlines responded by creating the hub-and-spoke system. In the hub-and-spoke system, airlines bring many flights from "spoke" cities into a central "hub" airport, interchange the passengers, and send the flights back out to their final destination in one of the "spoke" cities. Airlines using hub-and-spoke operations maintain a large presence at each airport and often dominate traffic at the hub. An example of the hub-and-spoke system would be a flight from Washington, D.C., to Sarasota, Florida. If you flew Delta, you would go first to Atlanta. In Atlanta, all of the Delta passengers going to Sarasota from the "spoke" cities disembark and get on a Delta flight going to Sarasota.

In addition to the hub-and-spoke system, new, low-cost, non-union carriers have sprung up in major markets, offering transportation at unrestricted fares priced from 30 percent to 70 percent below existing fares. Smaller regional carriers whose route structure had been limited by the CAB to short-haul, feeder-type operations hubbed around a single airport. After deregulation, these smaller feeder airlines began to expand into other major cities and compete with the large trunk carriers whose route structures had been designed by the CAB to carry passengers over the longer distances between the major hub cities.

In addition to expanding their services to large cities beyond their old route structure, the regional airlines realized that they could also compete effectively for a portion of the long-haul market. Long-haul customers had historically traveled on the trunk carriers because of their nonstop flights. Regional airlines competed by offering lower fares on their multistop or connecting flights.

Since the individual airlines were no longer limited in their pricing policies by industry orientation, true price competition expanded dramatically. But the rewards associated with filling seats (that might otherwise be empty) with low-fare passengers that an airline would not otherwise have carried must be balanced against the risks of displacing higher-fare passengers that would otherwise have been carried.

The problem is further complicated by the existence of a multitude of fares, with varying degrees of restrictions limiting the availability of all but the highest-priced seats. These restrictions include the day of the week on which the travel occurs, the length of stay, and the willingness to accept a layover in lieu of a direct nonstop flight. In addition, the number of flights operated by the various airlines over different routings, and the varying degrees of demand for seats at different times and during different seasons also have an impact.

In the late 1970s the CAB allowed up to 35 percent of any flight to consist of discount seats. These discount seats (super-saver fares) soon spread throughout the system, and the CAB placed no specific limits on the number of seats that could be sold. The US airlines were, for the first time, responsible for their own yields. By 1982, 75 percent of the nation's traffic was flying on discounted fares.

Within certain bounds, airlines are obligated to operate the flights they plan, at least in the short run. With that obligation, and given that additional passengers add only very small amounts to the cost of operations, it is wise to use segmental pricing to create additional demand that would not otherwise exist and to realize more revenue.

In other words, if not all seats are filled at a single uniform price, then revenues can be increased if additional passengers can be attracted by offering the empty seats at a lower price. As long as the discounted price is higher than the additional cost of carrying the extra passengers, the airline comes out ahead.

This adds a new wrinkle. According to Robert Cross, president of Aeronomics, Incorporated, "If the empty seats are filled by additional passengers, profits are improved. But if some of the formerly higher-fare-paying passengers now pay the lower fare, then overall revenues will decrease. Total revenue will decrease or increase depending on the extent to which former higher-fare-paying customers slide over to the new lower fares and the extent to which the new low fares generate new traffic. The pricing objective is to maximize new traffic growth while at the same time minimizing the amount of slideover."

The simplest way of limiting the slideover of traffic from high fares to low fares is through the use of low fares and restrictions such as advanced-payment requirements, length-of-stay requirements, travel on selective days or flights, age qualifications, and so forth.

As was stated earlier, yield management does not guarantee that an airline will make money. Hopefully, yield management will minimize losses during a downturn. Yield management is concerned only with revenues. There is yet little that can be done to control costs such as fuel that greatly affect airline profitability. This is why even the most sophisticated yield-management system cannot guarantee profits.

Many analysts believe that the number of seats offered at different prices (the seat mix) is the greatest determinant in arriving at the airline's yield. An airline's seat mix is the percentage of seats sold in the various discount classes or for full fare.

If an airline allows its flights to fill up early, then it experiences what is known as high-yield spill. Critical to the concept of spillage is understanding the demand patterns that occur for a given flight. In a very real sense, the ability to forecast travel demand accurately is one of the key ingredients in successful yield management. If the seat mix is not accurately controlled, a flight could fill with discount passengers, resulting in the spillage of later-booking high-yield traffic.

This spill can be prevented by forecasting the high-yield demand and reserving enough seats for later higher-fare business traffic. However, if too many seats are saved and the late-booking traffic fails to materialize, the flight will depart with a low load factor.

We can generally characterize those who buy their tickets more than two weeks before departure as leisure travelers. It is easy to see that the number of bookings increases, with most of the bookings occurring just two weeks prior to departure.

Seat mix improvements generally come from reducing the spill of higher-yield traffic that occurs when flights book full prior to departure, and the generation of incremental revenue from offering additional discounts on flights that would depart with empty seats.

The specific type of computer program used to handle some revenue-management systems is called an expert system (ES). Expert systems are used to perform a variety of extremely complicated tasks that in the past could be performed by only a limited number of highly trained human experts. Perhaps the most intriguing and powerful characteristic of ESs, and that which distinguishes them from more-traditional computer applications, is their ability to deal with challenging real-world problems through the application of processes that reflect human judgment and intuition. These expert systems are tied into the company's CRS, which extracts the necessary information. These ESs have the ability to categorize an airline's many diverse flights to fit optimized booking paths.

Zones defining acceptable flight performance are then constructed around the optimized path. These are referred to as threshold criteria. If the flight exceeds the threshold criteria, the computer analyzes the seat mix and recommends an inventory change that is designed to put the flight back into the optimized range. For example, if a flight is selling faster than the indicated optimal rate, the recommendation would probably be to reduce discount seats and add full-fare seats. On the other hand, if a flight is selling slower than expected, the addition of discount seats might be indicated.

It is easy to see that to be successful, the yield-management system must accurately control those elements that affect the revenue picture. This includes overbooking levels. Overbooking is a strategic component of any yield-management system. Airlines overbook certain flights because they expect a certain number of people not to show up for the flight. If they did not overbook on these flights, they would incur an opportunity cost because a certain number of seats would be vacant when the aircraft departed even though it was 100-percent booked.

Many airlines still manage their overbooking levels only by looking at measurements such as the number of passengers denied boarding per 10,000 passengers boarded. Seat spoilage, i.e., the number of seats that departed empty on an aircraft booked full prior to departure, is frequently measured simply by looking at the percentage of seats that flew empty.

Studies have shown that flights that are booked completely full and actually depart with a 100-percent load factor incur a significant risk or probability of having denied boarding.

These probabilities can be quantified as costs. Oversale costs include not only the out-of-pocket expense of handling the rejected passenger, but also intangible costs such as the loss of goodwill and flight departure delay.

Conversely, if overbooking levels are set in order to reduce the possibility of departing with less than 100 percent, then the load factor is increased. Spoilage occurs when a flight is fully booked on the days prior to departure, yet operates with many of its seats vacant. The cost of spoilage can be quantified by multiplying the number of empty seats by the average fare in the market. The probable cost of spoilage goes down significantly as the load factor on flights that were booked full approaches 100 percent. At a 100-percent load factor, spoilage costs equal zero.

The objective for the airline is to minimize the sum of these two costs. This can be done by understanding the oversales and spoilage-cost curves on each individual departure. The point at which the sum of the costs is minimized is at the intersection of the two curves. The airline's goal is to ensure that its flights balance the risk of oversales and spoilage by constantly striving for the minimal sum of oversales and spoilage costs.

Computer models that look at the risk of denied boarding and spoilage costs to minimize the sum of the costs can have a significant impact on revenues. A 1-percent improvement in a major airline's spoilage rate can add $10 million to its bottom line annually.

Another element that must be managed by the yield-management systems is traffic flow. Consider Delta Airlines, which has a hub in Atlanta, Georgia. The amount of revenue made from carrying a passenger from Washington National to Atlanta Hartsfield will vary tremendously, depending on whether that passenger is a local Washington to Atlanta passenger, or connects on Delta to Sarasota, Florida, or connects to another overseas airline. This happens because yield management is a demand-based pricing system, not a cost- or mileage-based one. Traffic-flow problems exist because of the hub-and-spoke nature of the airline business. The solution to traffic-flow problems is calculated by some of the most sophisticated mathematical techniques in existence.

## INCOME ELASTICITIES

Even though airlines have spent most of their time investigating airline price elasticities, this is probably not the most important economic determinant of travel. In beginning economics, we were taught that income elasticities were generally stronger than price elasticities. This means that how much income a person or a corporation has will influence how much they react to a price change. When income decreases, there is simply less money to spend. In the decreasing-income scenario, prices have to be decreased more than under an increasing-income scenario to have the same effect.

## OTHER AIRLINE ECONOMIC ISSUES

In the April 1991 issue of *Air Transport World*, Joan Feldman outlines other important economic issues that a corporate travel manager should be aware of when negotiating with an airline. If the travel manager does not understand these issues, the district sales manager will be happy to explain them and tell the manager that they cannot discount because their airline does not make money. According to Feldman, "By comparison with other industries, airline employees were notoriously well paid before deregulation. They often topped the government's list of wages by industrial sector."

Besides labor costs, airlines are also struggling with the problem of rebuilding an aged fleet. Feldman comments that, "The fleet renewal is so expensive that even the strongest carriers are leasing more. That means a reduction in cash flow from depreciation, fewer interest deductions, and an increase in rental expense. The capital shortage will result in higher ownership costs even when airlines qualify for credit. One projection suggests that aircraft costs could increase from 10 percent–12 percent of the total now, to 20 percent."

While all of these costs are increasing, none has done so to the degree that marketing has. The Air Transport Association says its members paid $1.9 billion in commissions in 1981. By 1989, that figure had climbed to $4.76 billion. Whereas commissions were 5.4 percent of operating expenses in 1981, they were up to 10.6 percent by October 1990. These figures do not include items such as CRS incentives, under-the-table deals, rebates, and other incentives designed to steal traffic from competitors.

One point is clear: The airlines are in serious trouble. According to Bob Cross, "The airline industry is currently dying a slow death and things are going to have to change." The common denominator for managing airline travel for the 1990s will be change, as the domestic airlines maneuver to survive. There is no guarantee that the methods described in the rest of this chapter will be in vogue for long. Charles Roumas, executive vice president at Travel One, Inc., states, "One of the most important elements in dealing with an airline is the time of day. If you do not like the airline's current position, wait one hour and they will change it. When the sales manager gets a monthly report showing low traffic, they will lower prices; the next month, when they get their financial report showing all the traffic is unprofitable, they will try to withdraw their low prices."

## AIRLINE RESERVATION SYSTEMS

Airline computerized reservation systems are the primary form of travel agency computerization in the world. Approximately 85 percent of all airline tickets in the United States are sold through CRSs. This number increases for business travelers. These systems manage the millions of reservation requests and cancellations and fare and reservation pricing requests that are initiated by travel agencies using these systems—not to mention the thousands of database changes that occur daily. The CRSs function as extremely powerful and valuable distribution and marketing tools for their airline owners. The competitive environment of today's travel agencies is largely defined and controlled by airline CRSs.

The following topics are important for the corporate travel manager to understand:

1. Airline reservation and distribution systems.
2. CRS processing and communication concepts.
3. Relationships between the CRS and other industry components.
4. CRS and airline competitive strategies, as these pertain to reservation technology.

Airline distribution has been greatly shaped by deregulation and the rise of travel agency computerization. Critical to understanding how travel distribution is managed is an appreciation of the influence computerization exerts over travel agency reservation and purchasing practices.

The role of automation in this area must not be underrated, as automation provides the vehicle for airlines to effectively create their own dealer networks among the travel agency community.

These dealerships play an important role in broader carrier distribution strategies. Computers are routinely cited as representing significant competitive barriers to domestic US and international carriers operating within the US, as well as in other areas, when in reality market leverage is gained through much more subtle and effective means, as will be detailed in the chapters on regulation.

The marketing relationships described here are supported by automation within the travel agency community, based on the conditions existing in the US market. Although not directly applicable to many areas of the world, these US experiences are indicative of what other markets may expect as regulation is relaxed and competition increases. As US carriers expand beyond their national boundaries, both as to routes and agency distribution, other countries may expect US-style distribution practices to be introduced and competition to become more aggressive.

The fundamentals of airline reservation handling have not changed substantially for decades. From the first basic, no-frills scheduled air service between Amsterdam and London, inaugurated May 17, 1920, by KLM Royal Dutch Airlines using a leased airplane, passengers have required reservations and reservation record management of some type.

## OBJECTIVES OF A RESERVATION PROCESS

The systemization of commercial air travel in the 1920s and 1930s introduced the same basic trip components that are used today. These are: (1) scheduled services that may involve a number of intermediate stops, where a passenger may desire to travel only a portion of the aircraft's complete route, (2) fares that apply to each portion of the passenger routing, (3) documentation, in the form of tickets, certifying that payment has been made and that a traveler has a right to transportation on a specific flight schedule between a specific origin and destination, and (4) the necessity of managing reservations and cancellations, so that passengers may rely upon the airline's ability to accommodate them on their desired flights.

Commercial aviation and retail travel services revolve around the public's desire for certainty of accommodation on airline flights, and therefore, the necessity of reserving and pre-issuing airline tickets. Some air services, such as no-reservation air shuttles, eliminate the need for pre-planning and the need for complex ticketing, as a single or very simple fare structure is used. In general, the role of airline tickets and ticket issuance has not changed in 70 years.

In 1968 American Airlines modified and implemented a Programmed Airline Reservation System (PARS) on its System 360. Other airlines had launched similar, but unsuccessful, reservation system development projects. These eventually adopted the basic PARS system, and modified it to meet their own needs.

PARS concepts, designs, and features still form the primitive foundation of most airline reservation processing and management systems today. An international variant of the PARS system, IPARS, followed the initial PARS project.

PARS was designed to run on IBM's latest 1960s-vintage commercial processor, System 360, and used a variety of existing and proprietary tools and software systems. Since its introduction, IBM has assumed a leadership role in developing, enhancing, and upgrading airline systems, supportive programs, protocols, and the hardware on which they run.

System 360/370 architecture assured PARS's usable life in the 1990s. As IBM upgraded its commercial mainframe processor line, newer, faster, more powerful machines replaced older systems in existing PARS installations. This was made practical because upward compatibility was an important feature of the System 360 concept. Even though many essentials of the PARS environment remained fundamentally unchanged over the years, hardware advances allowed PARS to continue meeting the needs of ever expanding CRS networks.

## WHAT IS PARS?

Rather than a monolithic program set or product, PARS is the essential foundation and conceptual basis for airline systems. Because these concepts were replicated in later modifications and revisions of the original PARS, there is great similarity among all PARS systems, particularly the major US CRSs. This applies to operational practices, operator formats, system capabilities and limitations, and ongoing enhancements. There has been significant cross-sharing of PARS functionality because of IBM's role as developer and maintainer of software tools that comprise much of the PARS environment.

Although this text speaks of PARS and IPARS systems, it does so in a generic sense, as there is frequently little or no real difference in the software of one PARS-based system as opposed to another. Where there are fundamental or architectural distinctions, these are clearly identified. In reality, all major American CRSs have operated as independent systems since the late 1960s.

## INVENTORY VERSUS PASSENGER SYSTEMS

The initial airline automation efforts, including PARS, were inventory systems and not passenger systems. Based on the management priorities defined in the late 1950s, gaining centralized inventory control was the most important priority. These early transaction systems processed reservation requests against declining inventory allotments, but lacked even the relatively simple passenger record, service request, and file access capabilities of later PARS-type systems. The extensive schedule information for off-line (nonhost) airlines was also lacking.

More-extensive databases were partially visualized, but were incorporated only into later PARS software releases after the initial inventory systems had been operative for some time. These were also implemented in varying degrees of sophistication, depending upon the airline and the system in question. There is more commonality between the schedule, reservation, and booking modules of various PARS-type systems than there is in other databases and functions.

## COMMUNICATION LIMITATIONS

Early airline systems lacked the sophisticated communication capabilities that are taken for granted today. Large public data networks, sophisticated data-transfer protocols, and standardized interfaces were unknown. System planners operated in an environment where even long-distance telephone calls were relatively rare and expensive.

This necessitated low-cost, reliable, easily implementable and maintainable communication methods to support information exchange between airline host systems. Because of their role as product distribution tools, not just inventory systems, airline computers in particular rely on data communications to exchange information rapidly and effectively. This is because interline ("interline" refers to tickets issued by one airline on behalf of another) reservations and ticketing have been fundamental to world travel for many years. An airline's biggest customers are other airlines' internal reservation centers and computers, who make reservations for passengers and serve as a source of passengers who may transfer or connect from these airlines.

Communication between airline systems is necessary because the operator of one system needs the ability to update the inventory and create reservations in another system that operates independently of the one the operator is using. The system functions as a computerized work environment and productivity tool for the operator. If inventory sales and updates in off-line systems can be accomplished electronically, the reservation process is much faster. The alternative is for the CRS operator to use the telephone, which always increases the time required to make a passenger's reservation.

The passenger also wants reliable schedule, availability, and reservation information as quickly as possible. Particularly in the US, travelers are accustomed to instant results and are dissatisfied if lengthy delays are introduced. Electronic messaging, together with airline database practices, make virtually instant reservation confirmations practical.

Early airline communications used teletypewriter-based messages that could operate reliably at low transmission speeds, using existing, inexpensive communication circuits. These communications operated in a network-based mode, thus eliminating the need for dedicated circuits between each reservation system.

These basic communication formats and practices are another legacy from the early days of airline computerization and still serve much of the industry today. While the original interline communication methods are practical, they are neither flexible nor particularly efficient and have been replaced by modern communication technology.

## CURRENT AIRLINE AUTOMATION

Some idea of the complexity that current airline reservation systems have achieved can be gleaned from the following description of TWA's PARS system:

"TWA's system has about 50,000 communication terminals in the field worldwide. The size of the database is about 850 gigabytes (a gigabyte [GB] is one trillion bytes). It is fully duplicated for performance and availability reasons. About 8 percent of the 850 gb is occupied by passenger records.

A typical daily workload is about 20 million transactions. The peak performance rate is about 800 transactions per second (TPS). The average rate is 552 TPS, with a response time of 1.5 seconds.

The reliability of these systems is also an important parameter. A partial database recovery (recovery from transaction or system program failure) takes about two minutes. A cold start (starting the system from scratch) takes about eight hours."

## TRANSACTION-PROCESSING FUNDAMENTALS

Today all airline systems operate as online transaction processing systems. A transaction system allows operators to initiate queries and requests for specific applications, view the results of these applications in real time, act upon the results of this process, initiate follow-on transactions that are determined by the results, and update files or records based on information resident with the user rather than within the system. These events are driven by a series of independent interactions between the user and the system, known as transactions.

Transaction-based systems differ from other conventional computer applications in a number of ways:

1. Transactions are discrete and independent. While the information contained within one transaction may affect other transactions, one transaction is usually not dependent upon another, nor connected with another.

2. Transaction-based systems are batch-oriented. This means they manipulate data elements as a group. There may be extensive data dependencies in such systems, and omissions of some elements would require the entire application to be rerun.

3. The transaction system works by using information stored in a database, and the results of online data entry are usually recorded in a database.

4. Transaction systems also function without regard to where their users are located. Users working on the same system may be separated by thousands of miles.

5. Data integrity—Each part of the CRS database, particularly passenger reservation records, must be current at all times and must reflect the best possible condition of the data; no delayed updates are acceptable.

6. Concurrent sessions—Because transaction systems usually must support many users, they emphasize performance and throughput. Since many system users may require access to the same databases simultaneously, transaction systems must support user sessions running concurrently, while maintaining performance and the integrity of individual data elements.

7. Queries and requests for applications respond to real-time. Thus, the timeliness of data supporting an online system becomes critical, as old data cannot be used to make reliable decisions. Data must also be synchronized within the system, so that databases are consistent for all users and transactions initiated or updated by one user are available to other users and do not conflict with updates made by other users.

8. Limited functionality—Airline CRSs attach functions to the database query and update portions of the online system. These functions act upon data retrieved online from the CRS, or input online at the user's site, and produce specific responses, such as calculated prices for traveler itineraries, or tickets. Online transaction systems offer few functions to their users, as compared to the range of functions that could be designed for the system, and these have limited, specific purposes.

9. Data accessibility—Most required CRS data are available continuously while the system is operating and can be accessed at random. This contrasts with batch-oriented systems, in which data necessary for one application may not be available unless that application is running, and where offline storage and sequential data are required.

10. Event-driven—Transaction systems must undergo regular maintenance, as must all complex systems. CRSs also have scheduled database updates for schedule changes, among other purposes. The CRS will also schedule certain applications affecting many transactions to be executed at specific times. This helps shift system load to off-hours.

11. Point-of-entry editing—Online transaction systems reject incorrectly formatted instructions or data blocks as these data are entered and return an error message to the users in real-time, so that a correction can be made and the entry reattempted. This must be done because interaction with the user is essential to the online transaction system's successful operation.

12. Transaction size—Most batch or single-application computer systems take several minutes to execute all but the simplest applications. Many larger programs can take hours or days to complete. The real-time, event-driven nature of the transaction system requires responses within seconds. This means that systems must be designed and programmed for optimal speed, and transactions must be kept small to achieve the best responsiveness. CRS reservations, for example, are compilations of many individual transactions, each executed individually but that together complete the traveler's desired reservation.

## UNDERSTANDING TPF

TPF is a proprietary development and processing environment specifically designed to facilitate entry and processing of a large number of simultaneous transactions from multiple network terminals, when extensive database queries must be managed accessing large quantities of data and where overall responsiveness is a critical factor. A transaction is defined as a single entry, or a series of entries that are assembled in an electronic work area and completed at one time and that, in turn, initiate other actions within the system.

It is more important to define TPF's role as a transaction management system, rather than a database system. TPF controls terminal-based queries and responses, and disk access, while other programs are developed or purchased and integrated to handle true database functions.

## ROLE OF PARS TODAY

All this contributes to the characteristics that still shape PARS-based systems:

1. Careful, intricate design, in which many programs and applications work in concert to produce desired results.
2. A relatively inflexible structure that must incorporate modernized versions of very old programs with new applications to meet today's business needs.
3. A TPF basis that is intrinsically expensive and difficult to maintain, and very challenging to update and that does not always have the latest technology tools available to it.
4. Nonstandard communication protocols and interfaces that are unique to the airline industry, are character- rather than data-oriented, and are not efficient when used to support modern applications.

The limitations of PARS-type systems have been very frustrating to CRS suppliers and users. Agents appreciate the basic commonality between PARS-type environments, which makes it fairly easy to learn a new system once one has been mastered, but do not appreciate the cryptic formats PARS uses. Suppliers like the high reliability that has been achieved through constant refinement and diligent maintenance of their PARS environments, but agents are dismayed at the difficulty and expense of introducing modern functionality.

Many agents believe that PARS systems are nothing more than antiquated 1960s technology and must ultimately be replaced by current technology. Several years ago this was a common theme, particularly among misinformed government regulators who criticized airline software development and management practices as not being in the public interest.

All airline CRSs use the most modern communications, storage, processor, and related technology available. PARS-based systems preserve the remnants of their beginnings, but each CRS has developed along different lines and operates and is maintained independently. Today's CRSs often struggle with significant expense and effort to free themselves of their inbred limitations, but each works with programs that are comparatively modern and bear the mark of their unique developmental histories.

## WHAT IS A CRS?

Although the term "CRS" has been used a great deal in this book, no attempt has been made to define what it is. Several large airlines have created CRS entities that make reservation and related-function systems available to travel agents. These are sophisticated online transaction processing systems and databases that are specially designed to meet the needs of travel agents. A CRS provides:

1. Airline and AMTRAK (rail) schedules.
2. Availability for transportation carriers that have agreed to pay booking fees (the CRS primary revenue source) for reservations through the CRS.
3. Fares for services (air and rail) maintained in the CRS.
4. Storage of user and custom-specific databases.
5. Communication facilities necessary to support interline reservations and special messages that users initiate on

behalf of travelers whose reservations are made through the CRS.

6. Storage of traveler reservation files (PNRs).
7. Applications, such as ticketing and itinerary issuance, that produce printed documentation based on reservations files and other CRS data.

These services are adapted for travel agency needs. While the airline's own reservation and ticket office operations require similar functions, they are not the same. For instance, there are strict, federally mandated rules that specify how the CRS may display flight availability, in order to give all airlines participating in the CRS equal access to potential customers based upon the merits of their flights. An airline is under no such limitations for its own reservation system and will display availability and schedules for its own flights to the exclusion of competing services.

Thus the airline's own reservation system is a different application, even if it shares computer resources with a travel agency CRS. The early attempts at travel agency automation preceded the development of the CRS, and agencies were simply given terminals for the airline's system.

So far, we have presented the basics of the airline industry. Both pricing and distribution issues were discussed at length in order to give travel managers a greater understanding of the forces they have to contend with. With this knowledge it is now time to discuss ways in which the corporate travel manager can deal with the airlines.

## CORPORATE TRAVEL ASSUMPTIONS AND ATTITUDES

To begin this section it is important to remember the airlines viewpoint that corporate travel demand is inelastic and, thus, it should command the highest price. On the other hand, corporate travel managers feel that all airline discounts should be accessible to all market segments.

Most corporate policies dictate use of the "lowest convenient airfare." However, corporate travelers' carrier preferences (often because of frequent flyer programs) are used as an excuse to waive selection of lowest-priced services. Discussions with corporate travel managers around the country have revealed stories of legendary proportions of travelers who come up with schemes to waste corporate assets to circumvent lowest fares in favor of frequent flyer programs. Bruce Roggenheim of AQUA Systems in Santa Anna, California, comments that he has seen as many as 90 percent of lowest-fare options rejected by flyers in favor of frequent flyer miles.

According to Rolfe Shellenberger, senior consultant at Runzheimer International and one of the most experienced corporate airline negotiators, the two most common ways that travelers reject lowest fares to serve their own interests are:

1. Selecting a time of departure that assures use of their favorite airline, and
2. Finding reasons to avoid a nonfavorite airline, such as "their restrooms are dirty."

## NEGOTIATING CORPORATE AIRLINE DEALS

With recent changes in air fares by American Airlines, many airlines have dropped their negotiated rates. At the same time, there are still airlines that will negotiate. One point is clear. From the beginning almost all airlines denied ever having a negotiated deal with any company. To find out what an airline's policy is, you will have to contact them because what is told to the press seldom has corresponded with reality.

According to Rolfe Shellenberger, "The strongest appeal in negotiating corporate airline deals is for market share improvement." Shellenberger continues, "Airlines feel that they must have a presence in some markets even if their operations are only marginally profitable. In these cases, the weaker carrier will make generous concessions to improve traffic and load factors."

Shellenberger gives guidelines for what to expect in these negotiations: "A 20 percent discount must produce a traffic increment of at least 25 percent for an airline to break even on the transaction, and a 40 percent discount must produce a traffic increment of 66⅔ percent. Furthermore, a significant discount is unlikely from a carrier that is already handling 50 percent or more of a corporation's traffic on a given route."

In the above examples, Shellenberger develops a principle some have come to refer to as Share Shift. "Share Shift" refers to a corporation's ability to move incremental traffic from one airline to another. Incremental volume is the single most important concept used by airlines in managing their revenue systems. It is obvious that the airlines that have the weakest presence in a market are the ones most willing to deal. Revenue improvement of any type is a compelling offer to an airline.

Shellenberger continues, "If a corporation can guarantee increased total expenditures on an airline, after price concessions are taken into account, the airline will be motivated to deal, regardless of its public posture against corporate discounts. Usually, at any price level, corporate traffic is more profitable than leisure travel to most destinations; assurance of even deeply discounted traffic (say, at 40 percent below standard coach) is more favorable than selling seats in advance at 60–70 percent off coach."

## TRAVEL MANAGEMENT INFORMATION NEEDED FOR NEGOTIATION WITH AIRLINES

Shellenberger states that the following information is needed for a travel manager to begin negotiations with an airline:

A. Total airline expenditures.

B. Expenditures by airline.

C. Expenditures by city-pair by airline.

D. Cost per mile by city-pair and overall.

## DEVELOPING A PROPOSAL

The starting point for beginning an airline proposal is with the local sales representative. It is best for the corporation to make the contact. As in any sales-oriented situation, the airline wants to deal with the ultimate decision-maker. The corporate travel manager, with the advice of the travel management firm, should make the first contact on behalf of the corporation. For the travel manager who is just beginning a career, the travel management company is an invaluable resource. For those companies who consider the travel company a partner, it is important to work closely with it. Ultimately, all negotiated deals have to be booked through the use of the travel management company's CRS, and this necessitates their working with the corporate travel manager.

One of the biggest problems in negotiating with airlines is convincing them that you will be able to actually shift market share to them. The corporation has to be able to show firm determination in the form of a commitment that it will deliver. The role of the travel management company is to gather data and to serve as consultant to the corporation.

Even though the local sales representative is the starting point, it should be remembered that he or she typically knows little about airline costs and problems except on a superficial basis. According to Rolfe Shellenberger, "Most sales representatives are not exposed to yield data and most have limited exposure to staff functions dealing with profitability."

The travel manager should also meet the sales manager. Depending on the geographical scope of the corporation, a national sales representative may be assigned to your account. The corporate officer empowered to do national airline negotiations will vary from airline to airline. This is one area where the smaller corporations can expect invaluable help and assistance from the travel management company. The more experienced, savvy corporate travel managers negotiate their own deals. The local sales managers for almost all of the airlines have the power to make decisions on free tickets, but not on price adjustments. However, having the local sales manager as an ally will be a necessary part of getting the concessions.

According to Rolfe Shellenberger, airline negotiations are quite different from other vendor negotiations in that the corporation takes a proposal to the airlines. Shellenberger states, "Do not expect airlines to initiate price concessions except on international routes, where the typical concession is about 10 percent." This means that the travel manager has to do a considerable amount of homework before approaching the airlines.

This homework involves knowing the specific routes used by corporate travelers and also knowing how the corporation will guarantee the traffic. According to Shellenberger, the most important rule in airline negotiations is having policy in place to insure the incremental traffic. If the policy is not in place before the airlines are approached, your position will be weakened. At best, the airline will dictate the type of policy your corporation will need to have in place for them to meet your proposal.

Shellenberger also advises that while city-pair deals are more common, some airlines will entertain broader concessions based on overall market share. It is important for the travel manager to specify in the airline proposal what traffic and revenue the airline will receive if it accedes to your proposal. Local sales representatives from various airlines advise corporations to be very flexible. The more flexible the corporation can be in terms of delivering incremental travelers to the airline on the flights it desires, the more likely the airline will agree.

The corporation should be ready to accept "soft dollars" (free tickets) instead of price adjustments. Soft-dollar deals are specifically advised if the corporation is sending fewer than 25 travelers per month on a specific city-pair.

Rolfe Shellenberger says that the travel manager's job will be easier if you can control travelers' travel timing. "Airlines will be much more generous if you offer to use off-peak flights (e.g., after 7 P.M., mid-morning, early afternoon, Tuesdays, and Saturdays.)"

## TYPES OF CORPORATE FARES

There are at least eight commonly used corporate fares:

1. City-pair.
2. Specific meeting fares.
3. Continuous meeting fares.
4. Incentive fares.
5. Relocation fares.
6. Training fares.
7. Conversion fares.
8. Prepaid fares.

Because of the recent fare restructuring some airlines are currently not offering these fares. At the same time, others do.

## CITY-PAIR FARES

A city-pair airline contract is an agreement between the airline and the corporation to offer special fares between a specific origination and destination. For example, a company may negotiate a deal between St. Louis and Nashville. This deal is usually stated in terms of a discount for "Y" class, which is an unrestricted coach ticket (Y-class is a benchmark price, which is used to calculate most of the other fares on an airplane); or "Y-9," which is an airline's method of offering unrestricted coach pricing without moving the Y-class benchmark; or V-class, which is the lowest fare–highest restricted ticket.

An example of a corporate deal might be:

1.  20 percent off Y-class tickets.
2.  5 percent off V-class tickets.

As a rule of thumb, airlines offering corporate fares want at least 20 travelers per month on a specific city-pair to offer a discount. But if an airline is introducing new service to a city, they might work a deal with as few as 10 travelers. Unless the corporation is very large and offers the airline large amounts of traffic on a route, the discounts will be in the range of 20 to 25 percent. Contracts can last for as short as six months with a 90-day review to one year with a 90-day review. The contracts are company-specific. Travel management companies that offer to piggyback one company's traffic on another deal run the risk of having a company's corporate fare revoked.

The most important thing for the new corporate travel manager to remember about the city-pair deal is never to sign a contract with an airline when you cannot perform what you have promised. The airlines have very long memories.

The city-pair fare is also dependent upon the corporation's keeping a certain percentage of its travelers on the airline's flights. An airline might specify that in order to get 25 percent off Y-class fares, the corporation has to use the airline for at least 50 percent of its total travel.

## SPECIFIC MEETING FARES

The most common type of corporate airline fare is the meeting fare. Meeting fares are usually very generous and discounts can run as high as 45 to 50 percent off Y-class fares. To qualify for a meeting fare, the corporation informs the local sales manager of the meeting and its location. Generally, a company needs to have at least 10 employees traveling to a meeting to qualify for a meeting fare. Meeting fares are not booked through the CRS, but are booked through special "meeting fare desks." The meeting fare is usually good for a time period of plus or minus 72 hours from the meeting and then expires. The meeting fare is good from any destination to the meeting.

Meeting fares have special restrictions attached to them. For example, many contracts have a minimum-volume requirement and a percent-of-deviation clause. A percent-of-deviation clause specifies that if the company has fewer than a certain percent of the travelers that it promised, the fare changes. For example, a corporation might promise an airline that it will deliver 100 travelers. The airline may specify in the contract that to qualify for the meeting fare, the corporation has to deliver at least 50 employees, and if there is a deviation of more than 20 percent from what is stated in the contract, the fare will be raised. In this case, if there were fewer than 80 passengers, the fare could be raised, and if the corporation had fewer than 50 travelers, the contract would be void.

It is good policy for the travel manager to use at least two airlines for larger meetings, as the number of seats in an airline for meetings fares is restricted.

## CONTINUOUS MEETING FARES

The continuous meeting fare is a contract used when a company holds a number of meetings throughout the year and does not want to negotiate a contract for each one of them. The continuous meeting fare is also used as a pseudo-corporate fare. Many airlines state it as their policy not to offer corporate fares. However, because some offer them, they must all follow for competitive reasons. In order not to break policy, they use the continuous meeting fare as their corporate fare. The contract states that the meeting time is for Wednesday of any week and the fare is good for plus or minus 72 hours from the time of the meeting. This is the same as saying that the fare is good any day of the week.

## INCENTIVE FARES

An incentive fare is usually a high-discount fare offered to a corporation that is using travel as an incentive. For example, an insurance company may offer the top ten salespeople a free trip to the Caribbean for a week. These fares are good for a specific time period, but the originating city is not specified because it is unknown at the time of the contract. The restrictions are that it is good to a specific destination and is usually to be used within a plus or minus 72-hour window.

## RELOCATION FARES

The relocation fare is a seldom-used fare because it is generally not under the control of the local sales representative, so the information is not always conveyed to the travel manager. To obtain a relocation fare, the travel manager is advised to contact the corporate headquarters directly. The person in charge of relocation fares has a different corporate calling in each airline. The relocation fare has fewer time restrictions than the meeting fare. These fares are usually good for 90 to 120 days, and it takes at least 10 people moving within this time period to qualify.

## TRAINING FARES

The inbound training fare is another seldom-used fare that can be an important cost-saving tool to the travel manager. This fare is good when segment usage is not high enough for a corporate fare. The travel manager must present some type of documentation to the airline that training meetings are to be held.

## FARE CONVERSIONS

Fare conversions are unique in that they are not offered to corporations, but rather to travel management companies. A travel management company with fare-conversion rights can book tickets that normally would qualify as Y-class (tickets with no restrictions and high costs) as tickets with lower costs and no restrictions.

## PREPAID TICKETS

United and American airlines recently offered, and then cancelled, prepaid or mileage purchase programs. These programs are better for companies that do not have the volume traffic to qualify for the other corporate deals. These programs suffer from the fact that the company must prepay and tie up cash. As an example, both the United Pass Plus program and the American AAIR Pass have contracts ranging from six-month trial packages to lifetime deals. The six-month trial program costs $4,300 and is good for 12,500 miles (34 cents per mile). These fares are used for a single traveler or a small group (less than five). These fares can be a good deal if the traveler flies on routes where the cost per mile is very high (New York to Boston). The danger of these fares is that the travel manager never knows when a fare war may break out. Charles Roumas, vice president of marketing and planning at Travel One, Inc., located in Mt. Laurel, New Jersey, offers the following example:

A client has three travelers. Their top city pairs annually are: 40 one-way segments from Philadelphia to Los Angeles at an average price of $550; 30 one-way segments from Philadelphia to Denver at an average price of $420; and 12 one-way segments from Philadelphia to Chicago at an average price of $280. The total dollars spent in these markets are $37,960 one-way; $75,920 round-trip. In these instances the client's average cost per mile is:

To Denver (26.8 cents per mile)
To Chicago (34.4 cents per mile)
To Los Angeles (22.9 cents per mile)

The average cost for these routes is 25.2 cents per mile. In this example, it is not realistic for the client to purchase this pass because it is not cost-effective.

## MANAGING A CORPORATE FLEET

Some of the larger corporations maintain a corporate fleet of aircraft. These fleets are much more than just a perk to those who use them. According to Frederick J. Bernard of Jet Aviation, located in Teterboro, New Jersey,

> "The corporate fleet and the use of air charter is an important business tool which helps support the company's vision and mission. It serves the following functions:
>
> 1. Allows senior management nonstop service to factories that are located in rural areas away from major airports.
> 2. Creates opportunities for flexible scheduling to serve passenger requirements.
> 3. Enhances managerial productivity by creating a travel environment suitable for accomplishing work privately or conducting meetings and discussions.
> 4. Eliminates other nonproductive passenger activity such as traveling to and from airports to meet commercial airline schedules, waiting in airports for connecting flights, and retrieving luggage or filing claims for lost baggage.
> 5. Provides increased level of security by eliminating exposure to potential dangers at airline terminals.
> 6. Allows managers to arrive free of tiring, frustrating or emotionally draining effects which frequently attend commercial travel."

## RECENT CHANGES IN FARE STRUCTURES

On Thursday, April 9, 1992, American Airlines' chairman, Robert Crandall, announced that the airline would revamp the industry's fare structure, dropping top fares used by business travelers by as much as 40 percent. Whether this is a long-term restructuring or a very clever way to increase fares was not clear at that time. "This is not a sale," Crandall promised in unveiling the restructuring during an elaborately produced New York press conference via satellite to reporters, travel agents, and American Airlines employees around the country. "This is a permanent revision of the fare structure."

According to the April 10th, 1992, issue of the *Aviation Daily*, "Reaction from competitors to American's pricing overhaul, which will eliminate more than 85 percent of the 500,000 fares that the airline currently offers in 13,000 domestic markets, was mixed. Delta and USAir said they would remain competitive on fares, but they stopped short of saying whether they will revamp their pricing systems to bring them in line with American's new four-tier fare structure. United and Northwest yesterday announced its own four-tier simplified system. Simplifying air fares for the business traveler makes great sense to us, United said."

Continental said it planned to match both the fare levels and the fare structure in competitive markets. The carrier said it was continuing an economic analysis to see if the levels and structure make sense for Continental in the long term and said that it could conceivably introduce its own system changes at a later date. America West said, "We are pleased that one of the big three airlines has made a move to simplify the overly complicated fare structure in our industry and America West plans to respond to these initiatives." Southwest, the US industry's low-cost, low-fare leader, said the only way it could match American's action would be to raise its own fares.

The revamped fare structure established four basic fare categories—first class, a new coach category called "AAnytime" fares, and two advance purchase, discount categories called "PlanAAhead" fares. New first-class fares would be 20 to 50 percent lower than existing first-class fares, depending on the length of the flight. New unrestricted coach, or AAnytime fares, would be at least 38 percent lower than existing full-coach fares and would be available on all flights, in all domestic cities, at all times. These fares do not carry blackout dates, advance purchase-requirements, seat limitations or Saturday-night stays.

Both PlanAAhead fares are nonrefundable, but they are reusable, according to Crandall. For a fee of $25, holders of the restricted fares can change their travel plans. A fee also applies to the other fares when it comes to refunds or reissuing tickets. In other cases, travelers, regardless of fare level, who have their tickets refunded or reissued will be required to pay the $25, $5 of which will go to the travel agent, if any, involved in the transaction. American is also eliminating all corporate, meetings, and

conventions discounts as those contracts expire. Crandall said that
the only special fares that will be retained are those the airline
needs to remain competitive, such as discount coupons for senior
citizens.

Crandall said the underlying economic assumption of the new
fare structure is that "as we offer a product of greater value, we
will sell more." Crandall said that although yields under the new
structure will remain flat, the new pricing system will stimulate
traffic, which, in turn, will drive revenues upward.

## NBTA'S REACTION TO THE
## FARE RESTRUCTURING

On April 14, 1992, the National Business Travel Association
(NBTA) reacted to the new fares with the following statement:

> The new simplified fare structure introduced by American Airlines
> last week is being received with mixed emotions by business travel
> managers and their companies, according to a statement issued by the
> NBTA, as travel managers alternately discover that their budgets either
> make modest drops or surge upward as high as 8 percent.

"There are actually two issues here," said Norman Sherlock,
NBTA executive director. "While the first seems to be the question
of how much extra firms are going to be charged or save on the
price of travel, the second issue is how badly does the simplified
fare structure defeat the spirit and purpose of deregulation."

The NBTA states that while the simplified fare structure seems
to offer equal benefits on the surface, it effectively turns the clock
back to the days of a regulated fare structure.

The degree of acceptance of American's new fare structure by
travel managers largely depends on a company's air volume and
on whether or not it has a substantial number of negotiated fares.
Companies locked into utilizing a single carrier or hub are finding
unanticipated relief in the simplified fares. Yet, other firms who
had up to 45 percent discounts as a result of volume considerations are facing instant travel cost increases as high as 8 percent.

The NBTA maintains that a carrier's sudden decision to ignore
a segment of its client base that has traditionally paid the highest

conceivable fares for years becomes anticompetitive when that standard is forced upon the industry.

"It can always be argued that a supplier has the right to charge what the market will bear in any given instance," said John Hintz, president of the NBTA. "But business will go where it's welcome and there are hundreds of business travel managers who no longer feel welcome, or respected in this fare program."

A compromise that would virtually guarantee the acceptance of this simplified fare program need only entail some extra consideration for high-volume travel service purchasers and a more realistic approach to meeting fares, according to a consensus of travel managers.

In a statement offered to business travel managers, several airline representatives claimed that the reduced and simplified fares were developed in response to corporate client claims that the disparity between business and leisure fares was too broad.

"You cannot serve the interests of one corporate segment and claim you have solved the problems confronting all," said John Hintz. "Business travel managers adversely affected by this situation are looking for alternatives. A sizable portion of our membership believes these fares could just as easily disappear in a month or so, right after eliminating the competition of several other struggling airlines. It is in the best interests of our entire membership to provide the best environment for all business travelers and their companies."

## CASE STUDY: EASTMAN KODAK

The following comments are taken from Gerald Ephraim, corporate manager of travel and fleet services at Eastman Kodak, located in Rochester, New York. According to Ephraim, "Before you can go to the airlines, you need to have your act in place. Our first step was to consolidate over 70 locations with one agency (Rosenbluth) and study our travel patterns. We felt consolidation was important in order to have negotiating strength."

The second step was to network with other similar companies and try to determine what fares are reasonable in various markets. Ephraim refers to this as "benchmarking." Ephraim states, "This is not a perfect way to do business, but it is the best way available since there is so much uncertainty about airline fares." Ephraim considered the benchmarking and consolidation process essential for three reasons:

1. Ensures consistency of service.
2. Enables collection of volume data.
3. Enables the company to move market share.

Ephraim's next move was to bid out the largest city-pair routes to the various carriers. For the most part, the bidding process was carried out over the phone and during personal meetings. Ephraim insists that the most critical factor in dealing with the airlines or any vendor is that every deal is win-win. Unless everybody comes away with something they need, the deal will not last very long. "Without credibility, you cannot live long in this business." Ephraim continues, "In the beginning we started out with four city pairs. Before we went to the airlines we knew which ones would be interested in dealing and which ones would not. We sat down and presented them with our information and worked out our deals."

One of the airlines that negotiated with Ephraim had less than a 10 percent market share when the deal was concluded. Over the next two months, that airline's market share for the city-pair increased to 40 percent. When the other airlines saw how Kodak was able to move market share, others approached Ephraim and offered better deals than he was currently obtaining. In a true spirit of partnering, Ephraim declined these offers, believing they would not last long, and continued with the same vendors. Ephraim now manages 80 to 90 negotiated city-pair fares.

In addition to the city-pair deals, Ephraim uses other negotiated fares. He states, "Kodak does a great deal of training in Rochester. We provide the airline with the title of the class and the listing of the participants. The training-fare discount is just higher than the group fare, with the group fare being the best. The training fares come up quickly with less lead time for planning."

Ephraim also makes use of incentive fares. He states, "We use incentive fares three different times a year, such as for the Coaches

All America. The incentive fares are nice in that the prices are about the same as for groups, but there are less restrictions."

According to Ephraim, it is the most difficult to work with the airlines in the international arena: "The difficulty arises because the airlines operate as many different companies. If you want fares both ways originating both in Tokyo and America, for example, there is no one person who can decide for both ends of the business. The deal is different even though the company is the same. There is no international focus regardless of where you originate the meeting. International airlines run their own show."

## TRAVEL MANAGEMENT TIP

- The travel manager should maintain a close relationship with each airline and with the travel agency.

# Chapter Nine

# The Globalization
# of Travel

## GLOBALIZATION

According to Stephen Taylor, "The race to build global travel management networks is on. The participants are varied, each bringing different resources, strengths, and implementation strategies to the playing field. The race is likely to continue throughout most of the 1990s. In the end, only a virtual handful of 'winners' will emerge."

Like most things in the free-enterprise system, the drive to build service networks capable of handling travel management clients worldwide is a response to the perceived needs of the marketplace. One can hardly pick up a business magazine today without reading a couple of articles about the globalization of commerce in general, as multinational companies struggle to position themselves to compete in the global marketplace. These multinational companies are expanding their networks in their respective fields, and the assumption is that they will be looking for travel management firms capable of servicing their travel needs worldwide.

The analogies to what happened with consolidation in the United States in the 1980s are significant. That process was driven by the service advantages and efficiencies that could be achieved through consolidating travel under one travel management company nationwide. After several years of jockeying for position, a half dozen or so companies emerged in the US with the requisite networks and marketplace critical mass to meet all the travel needs of nationally based clients.

## BENEFITS TO MULTINATIONAL CORPORATIONS

The consolidation process is driven by the marketplace in the attempt to achieve two primary objectives. The first benefit is the desire to provide uniformly high service levels for travelers worldwide. When traveling to international destinations, travelers are already surrounded by a wide array of unfamiliar cultures and uncertainties. Having a local travel office with a reservations agent who knows how to handle that particular customer and understands the corporation's travel policy requirements is vitally important. Obviously, the business traveler in an international location has plenty of other business issues to deal with and should not have to worry about travel arrangements and last-minute changes. Increasingly, the international traveler's expectation is that he or she will be recognized and dealt with in a uniform manner, and meeting this expectation is one of the primary objectives of the globalization process.

To accomplish this uniformity, a great deal of emphasis must be placed on the "front office," or the reservations process itself. Given the way the industry operates, this means there must be a high degree of PNR connectivity among CRS systems from one country to the next. While it will be years before we get to a point where all the various CRS systems are truly seamless, similar results can be achieved to one degree or another through interoffice procedures that minimize the amount of manual interface between systems. Of course, this can also be accomplished by utilizing a single CRS system worldwide. Either way, there are significant training issues involved in making the chosen approach work.

The second key benefit to multinational corporations revolves around worldwide data collection. Data collection is at the heart of the travel management process, both in terms of the implementation and enforcement of travel policies worldwide and the gathering of comprehensive data for travel-supplier negotiations. Here again, the analogies to the consolidation process in the US in the 1980s are obvious. Most people would agree that the US consolidation process would not have been possible without the ability to collect reservation and ticketing information from the various CRS systems into single back offices for the production of travel management reports for nationwide clients.

Today's multinational consolidation is further complicated by the uncertainty surrounding global CRS systems and the alliances that continue to emerge. While recent events have solidified the process enough to give at least some idea of where it is all headed, the shakeout is still going on. This uncertainty hinders the rapid formation of the service systems needed by global travel management firms to meet the worldwide travel needs of multinational corporations.

## THE GLOBAL PLAYERS

The participants in the global travel management consolidation race are a rather diverse lot, each bringing different strengths and capabilities to the playing field. The list of players begins with the US mega-agencies. Having emerged from the consolidation process within the US during the 1980s, these players are anxious to bring their respective strengths into the international arena. Moreover, they are approaching the global consolidation process from different angles.

As in many other areas of commerce, the other main players are entering the race based on the relative strengths they have in their home markets in Europe and the Far East. These players bring with them the inherent advantages of enormous size and large market shares in their home countries. In addition, they frequently possess governmental tie-ins, which they have long since learned to use to their advantage in the broader marketplaces of the world.

Other marketplace strengths that each of these players brings are: long histories and the advantages that come with broad name recognition; overlaps into other travel service areas, such as credit cards and travelers' checks; and cross-ownerships with airlines, banks, and even governments. Still others, primarily the US players, bring their histories of technological innovation and the entrepreneurial agility upon which they must rely.

## GLOBAL STRATEGIES

Even though we are only in the early stages of the race, a number of different strategies have already emerged. The first is an extrapolation of the consortium approach employed by many regional agencies in the US in the early 1980s as US consolidation unfolded. This approach is more marketing-oriented than anything else. It relies on establishing a brand name and on at least some degree of ability to recognize travelers whose agencies participate in the consortium/association through established service procedures.

The consortium/association approach has the advantage of being the least expensive and the quickest way of getting together what can be called a "global network." For multinational companies that are concerned only with having some sort of loosely affiliated entity in a distant location to which a traveler may turn in a given scenario, this approach will work. The issues of uniformly high service levels and global data collection obviously are difficult to address with this approach.

At the other end of the spectrum, some agencies are approaching consolidation from a wholly owned network point of view. Building these networks requires the outright purchase of regional agencies in local markets or the opening of new offices in key business centers.

Agencies that use the wholly owned approach have a unique set of challenges with which to deal. Most of these challenges center on the issue of integrating international locations into a cohesive worldwide network. There are the obvious technological issues in terms of front-office CRS capabilities and back-office data collection. But far more important are the human issues that result from the cultural diversities that exist from one country to the next. Blending people from different countries with different attitudes toward adaptability into an integrated international network takes a lot more effort and time than one might expect.

The advantages of the wholly owned approach are that travelers will receive a uniformly high level of service, and travel data will be collected in a much more comprehensive, cohesive manner. The disadvantages are that building wholly owned networks takes a lot more time, and they are more expensive to build.

A third approach that has begun to emerge recently is the joint-venture. Entities with substantial local market presence take equity in a joint-venture company that focuses on finding ways to integrate the service and data-collection systems of each of the respective shareholders into a network to provide worldwide travel service for multinational companies. These joint-venture companies have the advantage of significant market strength in their respective home countries. In addition, they will be working hard to establish sufficient uniformity among their components in service systems and data-collection capabilities. They will meet the needs of global consolidation by building interconnected CRS and customer-service systems.

In essence, the joint-venture approach falls somewhere between the loosely affiliated consortium/association approach and the wholly owned network approach. As previously mentioned, the advantages are the relative strengths of the joint-venture participants in their home markets. The disadvantage is that no one knows yet for sure how willing the respective participants will be to adapt their own local ways of doing business to the requirements of the global network. In other words, it remains to be seen how much they will be willing to change what they do locally, perhaps even to their local disadvantage, so that a cohesive international network can be created.

## WHERE WE ARE NOW

The strategies of the race participants have become fairly clear. The abilities of the respective approaches to provide truly global travel management services is less clear. With respect to the consortium/association approach, they probably are not far away from reaching the end of their capabilities. The real question is whether these consortia/associations will continue to adapt sufficiently to get beyond the mere marketing-relationship level. The ability of these consortia/associations to compete with the US mega-agencies in the 1980s is not even debated anymore.

The joint-venture approach has many advantages that relate to the relative strengths of the home-market players. However, they have a long way to go in establishing the kind of uniformity in their service systems and their data-collection capabilities that will meet the needs of multinational corporations. Again, the key question here will be just how willing these players will be to change what they do on a local basis to meet the greater needs of the international network. The jury is still out.

The wholly owned approach has the advantage of being highly integrated, but it affords a lesser degree of market penetration than do the other two approaches. The wholly owned approach focuses on a high degree of service and technological integration from the very start, and it is in place in a number of countries today, especially in North America and Europe. However, this process will take time to develop as it expands one country at a time.

## TIMING ISSUES

The key issue here is whether or not agencies are ready to handle the global consolidation of multinational corporations' travel management under any of these approaches. Depending upon the degree of penetration the consolidating multinational corporation desires, the answer is probably "not really." If a corporation is looking to consolidate all of its worldwide travel, for example, at 100 locations around the world, with true data-collection and uniform service standards, the answer is that no one is ready yet. But the number of companies that are likely to attempt this kind of massive consolidation on a worldwide basis all at once can probably be counted on one hand. Rather, the more likely approach is that companies will consolidate broad areas one by one over time. These areas can be divided into North America, Europe, and the Far East.

As the liberalization of travel in Europe in 1992 becomes more of a reality, enabling a pan-European consolidation to gather steam, the first step will probably be the consolidation of travel management in North America and Europe. This will be driven to a significant degree by the fact that the largest CRS vendors are forming their alliances and establishing significant market penetration on a North American/European basis. This means that companies may have to travel among 100 locations around the globe, but the first step in "globalization" will be to consolidate, for example, 40 locations in North America with 40 locations in Europe. It will probably take another three or four years for this process to become commonplace.

In this arena, the wholly owned networks are well on the way to having established this type of North American/European capability. The data-collection issues should be resolved within the next year. The front-office issues related to uniform service systems are also well underway, again driven by CRS interconnectedness, which is now becoming a reality as a result of CRS alliances now coming into place.

The approach of the joint-venture companies will also undoubtedly focus on getting these kinds of issues resolved on a North American/European basis first. The more difficult issue for them will be integration of diverse operating procedures into a uniform service system.

## CASE STUDY: THE GLOBALIZATION OF A MAJOR GLASS MANUFACTURER

The following material was submitted by E. J. Hewitt, travel manager for a midwestern glass manufacturer. Recently, E. J. Hewitt and the travel manager of the company that acquired her employer (a British corporation) got together in the United States to discuss how travel is handled in the parent company and how it is handled where Hewitt works. This meeting was especially important considering what is happening with the liberalization of travel in 1992. The meeting included local vendors and the travel management company that handled Hewitt's travel.

Even though it turned out that both companies were using the same travel management company, E. J. Hewitt found out that there was little consolidation of management information reports between the two countries. There was limited ability to bring all of the information under one reporting system.

One of the first things that E. J. and her counterpart did in their meeting was to compare their respective travel policies. Fortunately there was a great deal of similarity. There was not a wide span in culture. One of the benefits that came out of this meeting was that some of the contracts that E. J. had negotiated could be extended to the parent company's travelers in the United States, and some of the contracts the parent had secured in Europe were made available to the travelers Hewitt managed in Europe. E. J. Hewitt comments, "It seems that the car-rental companies had a better handle on putting the contracts than the airlines did. The airlines were not prepared to do this at this point in time."

Another area that was discussed was hotels, as the parent had been very successful in negotiating preferred arrangements. It was found that the hotels would not readily exchange programs, but E. J. and her counterpart each set up their own communications to help the other work with their respective vendors.

The issue that kept coming up in all of the discussions was that you must have good data. You must be able to identify the travel dollar. E. J. comments, "There is no point even sitting down and trying to put together an international program if you cannot identify your travel dollar."

## CASE STUDY

Consolidating travel globally is akin to expanding any other business function abroad. The same business principles and practices must be applied. Keys to success are:

1. Willingness to modify the travel program country by country to address local needs and expectations.
2. Establishing realistic goals, expectations, and timetables.
3. Remaining flexible to the constantly evolving technological enhancements and changes.

Mary Kay Dauria is first vice president of the National Business Travel Association and currently directs the global consolidation for a Fortune 500 company. According to Dauria, there are five areas that differentiate international travel programs from domestic ones. These are:

1. Culture.
2. Regulatory issues.
3. Front- and back-office automation.
4. Negotiations.
5. Billing procedures.

Dauria begins her discussion of international travel management with this advice: "I thought I knew a lot about international
until I started my present job. Every country represents a new
challenge. When you go into a new country, you use what you
have learned from your domestic program as a basis to ask
questions as to what possibilities are available. I am leery of anybody who claims to be an expert as there are too many things we
do not know yet. What I look for is an agency and vendors who
are willing to go through the learning curve together and be
realistic about the challenges that are to be faced."

## CORPORATE CULTURE

Dauria emphasizes that you cannot assume that a program will
work anywhere else in the world just because you have had success in the United States. Even when policies are the same for
your off-shore companies, they could be implemented more le-
niently or strictly. Dauria offers an example to make this clear: "In
the United States we are accustomed to having people answer the
phone after only two or three rings. In contract negotiations with
domestic travel agencies we specify how many rings. However, it
is nothing for a phone to keep ringing many times off-shore. The
expectation of service is entirely different. Another difference in
service is that the customer pays for the call. Within each country
there is some 800 service, but overall there is little. Even the airlines do not offer the same US standards of telephone service."

There are a lot of other issues that must be dealt with culturally.
In Europe, train travel may be more common than air, or in some
countries it is important that the business traveler arrive in first
class. Dauria states that in some cases, business travelers travel
economy until the last segment of the trip and upgrade for the last
leg of the journey.

## REGULATORY ISSUES

Most of the regulatory issues Dauria discusses involve automation. According to Dauria, cross-border ticketing is prohibited.
Because of this, there are no European reservation centers. Even

STPs are of limited use because they have only been approved on a selective basis. At present it is not possible to establish a major reservation center because of the cross-border ticketing prohibition. Other regulatory issues that will be investigated by country include BSPs, commission structure, and international price controls.

## AUTOMATION AND BILLING SYSTEMS

"System links are still a difficulty off-shore," states Dauria. She continues, "Linking up systems and opening gates is a problem since where back-office systems exist they are not currently networked. This is a major problem in off-shore systems because it restricts the amount of consolidated information available to the travel manager. Even with all of the advances that have taken place in the last ten years in travel automation, data is still faxed from location to location and manually input into a PC. Even the credit-card companies cannot provide detailed data off-shore. Credit-card operators are not under the control of one worldwide company. There is great variance among the foreign subsidiaries to supply data. Credit-card companies can often tell total expenditures in a country, but cannot provide country break-out by vendor. As with most things in this industry, this is customer-driven, and until the customers express a need, the vendors will not provide it."

A common mistake is the assumption that the US-based CRS systems provide identical capabilities off-shore. Although capabilities are constantly being enhanced, particular operating rules should be verified with each country. Additionally, with the high usage of train service in some parts of the world, provisions must be made for servicing this travel need. US CRS systems do not currently have this capability off-shore. Other services common to CRS systems in the US that are not readily available off-shore include seat assignments, boarding passes, and automated quality control and fare checks.

## VENDOR NEGOTIATIONS

In the current global business environment, major focus is placed on cross-cultural training for employees doing business abroad. The travel arena is no different. Research on doing business in the targeted country is essential for success both within your own company and with vendors abroad. Nuances for the proper conduct of business and negotiations vary from country to country. Approaching business deals with the appropriate style is essential to successful programs off-shore.

"The idea of single-source vendor negotiation is not available in the global arena. Most all of the vendors operate on a profit-center basis, so they can only speak for business that affects their own market. This means the local country sales rep cannot see the revenue go up in their area when a deal is completed for traffic originating in another country. Because of this, there is little incentive for better deals in one country based upon performance in another. This gets complicated fast. In the Transpacific area you deal with one contact going into the Orient and another representative from the same vendor going out. Even though it is the same company, there is little communication among vendor reps, so there are a lot of missed opportunities. Single-source representation for worldwide programs is a concept that is only in the beginning stages."

The area of complicated vendor negotiations extends to the travel agencies. Commission structures vary from country to country. Dauria advises travel managers to be wary of across-the-board commission-sharing agreements.

Dauria comments, "Negotiated programs are very time intensive and are conducted on a country-by-country basis. Because there are limitations in the networking of information systems, everything has to be built country by country. It is a nightmare without one integrated database. If I make a program change, I have to cover many bases and that leaves room for slipups. The focus on global relationships has to be long-term because on a global system there is no short-term.

## CASE STUDY: MARITZ TRAVEL

Scott Guerrero, vice president of corporate travel at Maritz Travel Company, located in St. Louis, offers the following advice for those intending to manage international travel:

Significant interest in purchasing travel on a global basis is being expressed in various parts of the world. This interest is being driven by certain vendors, or by various corporations, or by the success that consolidation of US domestic travel purchasing has achieved.

When there is a temptation to rush into a global purchasing program, it is strongly recommended that various elements be closely examined to determine the feasibility of such an approach within each corporation's structure. We begin this analysis by discussing the objectives of a global purchasing approach. Four key elements of any such global program will then be examined to determine whether all four are at work to provide an environment, and a higher degree of probability, for a successful program.

The objectives of a global program should be the same as those of any other major purchasing endeavor—lower costs and improved service levels. In looking at the cost elements, we will refer to "cost" as the components of travel's "raw materials"—airplane seats, hotel rooms, and rental cars.

## LOWER COSTS

Lower costs can take a variety of forms in the travel purchasing area.

1. An absolute reduction in the cost of a hotel room night (at the same hotel) or a seat on a flight (same airline, departure, and cabin) or an identical rental car.
2. Alternate rooms, seats, or cars at a comparable hotel, flight, or rental-car company at a lower cost.
3. Reduced cost due to the use of lower-quality raw materials. For example, a one-stop flight, a hotel with fewer amenities, etc.

## BETTER VALUE

In addition to an absolute reduction in costs, another way of looking at the travel purchasing element is to provide an upgraded room, airline seat, or rental car at the same cost as a basic service.

## IMPROVED SERVICE LEVELS

This includes the services provided by the travel management company (distributor) and features group and VIP services, 24-hour emergency numbers, assistance at airports, preferred hotel programs, tape hand-off of data, local performance reviews, executive summaries, management information, and a designated person with the experience and resources to make it all work.

In looking at ways of achieving these objectives, it is suggested that a corporation examine four quadrants that bear on the likelihood of success of an effective global travel program. The quadrants are:

1. The corporation's policies and culture.
2. The economic impact—dollars to be affected.
3. The raw-material vendor's policies and scope.
4. The effectiveness and capabilities of the travel distributor.

In the following sections we will discuss each of these quadrants.

## CORPORATE CULTURE AND POLICY

As a first step in examining the likelihood of success for a global travel purchasing effort, a corporation must examine its current practices in buying services on a global basis. What has been the success of buying other services on a worldwide basis? Is a worldwide purchasing organization in place to effectively identify the opportunities and manage the process? Does the corporation provide a high degree of local autonomy to division or regional management, which would have the right to ignore a purchasing directive from headquarters? Are there locations in the world that have supportive management and that would provide meaningful "success stories" in launching such an endeavor? Is nationalism a factor? The answers to these and other questions are essential prerequisites before embarking on the difficult, time-consuming tasks of studying and implementing the global travel management process.

Another issue to examine is the travel policy within a corporation, including frequent flyer programs. Is vendor choice something that is directed by the corporation or left to the employee's own decision making? Are employees allowed to make airline and hotel choices based on their own frequent flyer program versus the best interests of the corporation? What kinds of savings are considered meaningful enough to shift people away from frequent flyer loyalties? Is the corporation prepared to reward employees for saving the corporation money when giving up frequent flyer benefits?

## ECONOMIC IMPACT

If an effort is to be made to cope with global purchasing of travel, it is important to identify the dollars (or marks or yen) which would be impacted by a program to lower the cost and/or improve the service. When this is done, a correlation to the first quadrant (corporate culture) needs to be made. Do the corporate culture and the travel policy that will support a global purchasing effort match with those areas where the greatest expenditures are being made? It is also suggested that a corporation not try to harness more than 80 percent of its travel expenditures in the first three or four years of a program. The return on the time and effort required to capture the last 20 percent might not be worth it. Again, the early "success stories" of some larger units with the greatest economic impact are important.

In order to determine where the greatest expenditures are being made, a basic sampling of expense accounts, airline charges, and other management information from credit-card vendors or local travel management companies should be able to provide some general data. It is suggested that the locations spending 60 to 80 percent of the total amount be identified and prioritized and then analyzed within the context of the four quadrants.

## VENDOR POLICIES, SCOPE AND PROGRAMS

Once the corporate culture has been assessed and the largest opportunities for savings have been identified, it is essential that meetings be held with the major providers of "raw materials." At this early stage in the development of global travel purchasing, very few vendors, airlines, hotel companies, or rental-car firms are truly organized or prepared to be dealt with on a global basis. It may be necessary to bridge several departments within an airline or a hotel chain in order to get decisions made on a worldwide level.

## Hotels

In particular, many hotel chains are operated by one company but, in fact, are owned by many individuals. Decision-making is often done on a regional or even individual-hotel basis, although some North American representatives have negotiating authority. The willingness to "trade off" support in one city or in one part of the world for support in another will be a challenge for many hotel companies to manage. It may be necessary to address the hotels regionally as well as globally. It might also be in a corporation's interest to involve two or three chains in the process without trying to meet global needs through one preferred chain.

The opportunity to trade off savings in the US market, for example, in exchange for availability and rate guarantees at more heavily used locations (London, Hong Kong), is one approach. A secondary aspect to consider is the leveraging of meetings and other group bookings. Many chains place a high value on this source of revenue and by combining the room nights and food and beverage expenditures from such meetings, a corporation might improve its negotiating posture. Seasonality—support in off-peak periods—is also relevant.

## Airlines

While not as complex in structure and ownership, airlines also present a challenge in taking a global approach to purchasing. Commissions vary between countries and airlines. Decision-making is not always centralized. Among the relevant issues are the following:

1. A corporation must be willing and able to shift volume from one carrier to another, to use alternate gateways (London to Los Angeles via Dallas), etc., if truly effective

negotiations are to occur, and meaningful savings are to be realized.

2. Understanding the international airline market, key carrier objectives, marketing tools, and gateways is crucial to managing varied and often short-term "windows of opportunity."

3. The influence of the CRS systems may be an important factor. Certain carriers with a large stake in the CRS system (and its resultant revenues) will be interested in the possible linkage of CRS usage to airline usage. In the US, laws preclude an open linkage in such negotiations, but use of the CRS can be a factor even if not directly a part of the contract.

4. The payment system to be used for the airline purchases is another potentially significant factor. The possibility exists for direct, advance purchases, using cash. Another alternative is the use of an airline's air-travel card, which provides additional float to the airline of record. This needs to be weighed against the financial benefits of using other charge cards.

5. The ability to identify and include any international participation in the corporation's meetings and meeting planning.

6. Certain IATA (International Air Transport Association) and bilateral regulations will limit a carrier's ability to sell below the "published price."

7. Potential shift of air-cargo volume.

8. The targeted carriers must have the scope of service to cover a high percentage of city-pairs.

9. In addition to absolute price concessions, amenities such as club memberships, upgrade calls, etc., should be sought.

All of these factors need to be studied and raised in discussions with the airlines.

In meetings with the US-owned airlines, the most obvious area of trade-off is between support for US domestic routes versus international routes. Carriers such as Delta, American, and United, that are just expanding into Europe but have very high domestic load factors, provide a target for such negotiations—again, if a corporation is prepared to consider alternate gateways (Dulles, in the case of United).

With the international carriers, the trade-off will involve high-density routes (such as the routes between the UK and Africa) versus support on more highly competitive routes, such as the North Atlantic in the peak and off-peak periods.

## TRAVEL DISTRIBUTOR CAPABILITIES

The fourth quadrant that has to be evaluated in analyzing a global travel management process is the degree of sophistication and support to be provided both locally and globally by the travel management organizations, who must help identify the opportunities and implement them, and then provide ongoing service.

One way to start is to identify a list of criteria that a corporation considers to be ideal for the management of their travel. The list should include such features as 24-hour services, dedicated account management, effective data management, regular performance reviews, VIP services, group and meeting capabilities, airport assistance, a specialized hotel program, collection of data, and systems capabilities—telecommunications and data, etc. Once a list of these criteria can be made, you can determine the degree of consistency (for example, data handoff) that is available around the world and what unique opportunities exist locally.

A second step will be to determine the role that the travel management organization can play in the global purchasing program. Once service has been raised to the highest level available in each country, the travel management company as well as the vendor organizations must assist in the data gathering and analysis. The travel management company must also be capable of providing localized cost-savings programs through effective local airline negotiations, hotel and rental-car rates, etc.

## CASE STUDY: THOMAS COOK TRAVEL

The following advice is offered by Thornton Clark, senior vice president of Thomas Cook Travel, located in Cambridge, Massachusetts.

For most US corporations, being able to do business effectively worldwide will become increasingly important in the decade ahead. The country's need to export more products and achieve a balance of payments with other countries drives individual US corporations to focus on our ability to sell products effectively outside of the United States. Much more than in this country, rules of behavior will have a noticeable impact on a business traveler's success in obtaining corporate objectives abroad.

Traditionally, most American business people have had problems dealing in foreign countries because of a wide variety of long-established differences, high among them being Americans' widespread lack of sophistication in foreign languages. Americans are frequently less capable in multiple languages and much less aware of cultural differences, especially those emanating from the world's major religions. An American business traveler may not even be aware of having committed a major faux pas; but a serious error may not just cause personal embarrassment, it could cost the traveler's company a multimillion-dollar deal.

There are many lengthy books that delve in great detail into all of the different rules that a business traveler needs to know before attempting to do business in a new country. These rules differ from country to country, and in many cases a rule in one country is a gaffe in a different part of the world. In addition, the rules are changing. Not too long ago you had to be careful about using the right terminology in describing parts of Germany. Although Russia was only one part of the Soviet Union, most Americans were guilty of referring to the USSR as Russia, and this could have been offensive to people in other parts of the USSR. The objective is to alert travelers to the importance and need for a thorough study of each country's idiosyncrasies before traveling on business. Although this chapter touches on some of the rules, it is extremely important to note that these also change from time to time. The purchase and study of a recent book or guide to each country is necessary.

For starters, let's take a look at the use of names. Everywhere outside the United States, especially in Europe, business traditions tend to be more formal than those to which Americans are accustomed. A mistake with somebody's name can get everything off on the wrong foot and cause a serious business problem. Americans, used to calling people by their first names at their first meeting, should be very careful not to lapse into such informality outside the United States. You should not even ask someone if you can call them by their first name. This puts them in an awkward position if their preference would be to say no. Don't make the switch unless they bring it up and suggest it.

Even when you know to call someone by their last name, in some places, such as China and numerous Spanish-speaking nations, you may have difficulty determining which is the last name. In some countries the last name is in the middle of the three and in some it is the first of the three. You should determine where the last name falls in the country you are about to visit or, if you are unable to do that, ask your business contacts by what name they would like to be called.

Hand in hand with the subject of names is the use of titles. In most countries outside the United States, the use of titles is much more important and expected than it is within the United States. You probably know all of the stories about the importance of business cards in Japan, the volume of cards used, and the formality of presentation expected instead of just sliding a business card down the table. It may not be as well-known as the case of Japan, but everywhere in the world business cards should be used during the introduction process as a way of making your name and title clear and, for this reason, many more cards should be taken than you would normally carry.

In many countries, everyone with whom you are likely to meet at a business meeting is likely to speak several languages. Americans rarely speak two languages well, unless you count English as noticeably different from American. English is taught in the schools of most countries and in many countries it is required at an early age. You are likely to be amazed, and certainly pleasantly surprised, by how many people with whom you are likely to deal in business are fluent in English. Unless you are truly confident that you are fluent in the language of the country in which you are attempting to do business, you should stick with English. Almost everyone will understand you, and most will be willing to respond in English.

You probably have heard the advice that Americans are thought to be lazy about foreign languages and that it will be most appreciated if you try to memorize and speak a few words in the language of your host country. This, however, can be amusing and in some cases catastrophic. Many years ago I had the occasion to give a formal presentation to the German commission in Berlin responsible for the control of all banking activity in the country. Needless to say, this was quite a formal group. In my opening comments I attempted to interject a few words in German including the German abbreviation *GmbH*, which is their equivalent of *Inc.* for "incorporated" in America. GmbH is the abbreviation for the phrase *Gesellschaft mit beschraenkter Haftung*, which means "company with limited liability." I made it through the first three words reasonably well, but accidentally said *Hoffnung* at the end. This resulted in gales of laughter from this very staid group. I was representing a cause that they considered to have little prospect of success and I had inadvertently called my company a company, not with limited liability, but with "limited hope."

Almost as important as language are movements of the body— placements of the hands and feet and gestures. In many parts of the world the left-hand side of the body carries with it the evil connotation expressed in the word *sinister,* which is derived from the Latin for "left." Apparently this goes back to ancient days when most people carried their sword in their right hand and the extension of the right hand showed that you were unarmed. A person who extended his left hand was suspected of concealing a weapon in his right. In any event, actions such as eating food with one's left hand are considered highly improper and should be avoided carefully in Arab countries in the Middle East and in parts of Asia and Africa. It's very difficult for Americans who are accustomed to leaning back and crossing their legs to remember rules such as not crossing your legs in such a way as to show the dirty soles of your feet.

Relaxing gestures can also get you in trouble. You have to remember to be aware of such actions as a big friendly wave of the hand in Greece. A female marketing officer of a company for which I once worked was attempting to signal to a Portuguese gentleman controlling the sound system in the remote projection booth of an auditorium in which I was scheduled to give a speech. She was using hand signals to wave up or down to adjusting the volume levels. When everything was fine, she touched her thumb to her forefinger to signal the standard "OK." Unfortunately, in Brazil, this was the equivalent of pointing a different finger up in the air, and the man involved was quite displeased, in addition to being puzzled about what he had done to deserve such a reaction.

On the subject of business meal etiquette, rules that you learned as a child may be totally inappropriate in some foreign countries. I was always taught to finish the food on my plate, and was criticized for wasting good food and not thinking of all the hungry people in the world. This admonition did me no good on my first day in Korea. At a luncheon hosted in a private club by senior executives of Korean Airlines, I was presented with course after course of delicious specialties. After several courses and what appeared to be a full meal, my hosts reverted to speaking in Korean and called the waiter. After 15 minutes, another course arrived and was served around the table. It was quite good, so I finished this portion, too. My two hosts spoke in Korean again and, after some discussion, called the waiter again. Luckily, this last course was more than even I could finish and some food remained on my plate. Only the next day did I learn that completion of everything on one's plate clearly signals that you have not had enough to eat and require more food.

In other parts of the world, business meetings begin with informal conversation accompanied by relatively formal service of coffee, and that usually means much stronger coffee than that to which Americans are accustomed. In Japan, tea is frequently served with great formality before any business discussion is undertaken.

Even for people who don't normally drink, alcoholic toasts almost always need to be answered, and should never be declined. This can be a real test of the mind and body in countries where the downing of significant quantities of alcoholic beverages is considered proper business decorum. For Americans who have been accustomed to an increasingly smoke-free environment, the frequency and volume of smoke, especially in restaurants, can come as a real shock outside of the United States. There are some countries in which a ritual smoking ceremony is as appropriate to the start of the meeting as coffee is during the day or a toast may be in the evening. Here again, even though it may cause physical difficulty, it is important that participation in such a ceremony not be declined.

Although errors in tipping do not directly lead to business problems, it is an area so frequently questioned that it warrants comment here. Who should you tip, when should you tip, and how much should you tip? An additional question, especially upon arrival, is how much all those funny-looking coins are worth. Even in the United States, where the bigger coins are usually worth more, this is not always the case. Abroad, it is possible to tip too little, but the more common problem is tipping far too much for fear of tipping too little. Until you are certain of the currency, simply avoid the problem by tipping in US dollars. Dollars are highly acceptable to almost everyone in the world, and in many cases are much more valued than the local currency. You eliminate the risk of not knowing how much you gave and, of course, make expense-account computation much easier.

In some countries, tipping is expected if not demanded. In a few cases, such as Japan, it is considered improper, and a tip should not be offered. Many books comment that tipping is illegal in China; but, probably because of unknowing tourists' violating the rule, it may be approaching acceptability. Be careful.

Especially in restaurants, travelers must be careful not to grossly overtip by failing to notice that a service charge has been added on to the bill. In many foreign countries, the words indicating "service included" are easily recognizable, even to someone who does not speak the local language. This is certainly an area that you should check on before going to a country, including learning the words that would apply. Even in a restaurant where service is included, asking the waiter if the tip is included all too often will result in the answer that it is not, even when it is. Many people suggest that 5 percent in cash should be left in addition to the 15 percent that is typically added to one's bill. The rules here differ from country to country, and even within countries, so checking in advance will be helpful.

Only a few countries have been mentioned, and only a few of the things you need to know about each country were touched upon. To accomplish your business objective, you should obtain the information and familiarize yourself with each country's traditions before you begin your trip. Even the most-seasoned traveler cannot remember all of the rules and sort out which ones apply in which countries.

US travelers don't even have to think about avoiding scheduling business trips on holidays such as Thanksgiving, Christmas, or the Fourth of July; but most don't even know what the holidays are in other countries, much less when they occur. This information must be obtained even before you ask for appointments and plan your trip.

Our entire country needs to be more effective in selling our goods and services abroad. Knowing and following the rules of the game in foreign business is essential if success is to be achieved.

## TRAVEL MANAGEMENT TIPS

- The consolidation process is driven by the marketplace in the attempt to achieve two primary objectives. The first is the desire to provide uniformly high service levels for travelers worldwide.
- The second key benefit to multinational corporations revolves around the worldwide data collection. Data collection is at the heart of the travel management process, both in terms of the implementation and enforcement of travel policies worldwide and the gathering of comprehensive data for travel-supplier negotiations.
- There are a number of different strategies for global consolidation. The first is an extrapolation of the consortium approach employed by many regional agencies in the US.
- Some travel agencies are approaching consolidation from a wholly owned network point of view.
- A third approach that has begun to emerge recently is the joint venture.
- One of the key timing issues is whether or not agencies are ready to handle the global consolidation of multinational corporations' travel management.
- As the liberalization of travel in Europe approaches, enabling a pan-European consolidation to gather steam, the first step will probably be the consolidation of travel management in North America and Europe.
- One of the most important facts to remember is that you cannot assume that a program will work anywhere else in the world just because you have had success in the United States.

- The idea of single-source vendor negotiation is not available in the global arena.
- When there is a temptation to rush into a global purchasing program, it is strongly recommended that various elements be closely examined to determine the feasibility of such an approach within each corporation's structure.
- As a first step in examining the likelihood of success for a global purchasing effort, a corporation must examine its current practices in buying services on a global basis.
- Another issue to examine is the travel policy within a corporation, including frequent flyer programs.
- Once the corporate culture has been assessed and the largest opportunities for savings have been identified, it is essential that meetings be held with the major providers.

*Chapter Ten*

# Charter Air Flights

## THE *AIR CHARTER GUIDE*

The most important source of information on air charters for travel managers is the *Air Charter Guide*. It contains all of the flight and price information available. This invaluable information can be purchased on a subscription basis by writing to:

The Air Charter Guide
P.O. Box 2387
Cambridge, MA 02238
(617) 354–7655

## PLANNING A CHARTER TRIP

According to the *Air Charter Guide*, there are many reasons for using air charter, such as the opportunity to use the airport you wish and to save time while maximizing convenience and flexibility. The editors explain, "Scheduled airlines utilize a mere 500 airports compared to over 5,000. With literally thousands more arrival and departure points available, air charter travelers can significantly reduce time spent getting to and from airports."

It is important to realize that many of the airports listed in the *Air Charter Guide* are private, although nearly all are available for public use. Therefore, it is important to call ahead to confirm plans.

The *Air Charter Guide* states that in many cases, the air charter operator selected will be able to assist in choosing an airport, since determining the suitability of the airport becomes his responsibility once the flight plan has been filed.

According to the editors of the *Air Charter Guide*, "Many of the aspects of the airport will affect your eventual choice. When are you going? If the trip is being planned well in advance, you may want to pick a destination airport with an instrument landing system (ILS), which is shown in the listings in boldface type. Usually limited to higher volume airports, this navigation device will insure your ability to land in weather or very low cloud cover. If the trip is important, choosing an ILS-equipped airport may be easier than changing plans at the last minute due to weather. A second advantage is that most ILS-equipped airports are big enough so that other services are better—passenger lounge, car rentals, snack bar, and other amenities are generally available."

The editors of the *Air Charter Guide* advise that since half of the total trip time is often spent on the ground getting to and from the airport, it makes sense to pick an airport within a 15- or 20-minute drive. If there is an alternative, try not to choose one of the big internationals because you will have to pay higher landing fees, and you will probably be held longer on the ground by the air-traffic control. The editors of the *Air Charter Guide* recommend a nice suburban airport with ILS, car rentals, restaurant, and plenty of free parking.

Many criteria apply to the selection of the right charter operator. A one-way trip makes an operator at your destination just as good a choice as an operator at or near your home airport, since the aircraft still has to go round-trip no matter where it originates. The term "positioning" refers to ferrying aircraft for departure from other than the home base for the aircraft and crew.

The editors at the *Air Charter Guide* give the following advice, "Whether to position, or ferry an aircraft at the airport of your choice from an adjacent area, will usually depend on economics, although the logistics of waiting for a plane to arrive for an early morning departure can be a consideration in poor weather. The cost of positioning for a trip may be affected by any number of factors, including the type of equipment used, the absolute distance to the adjacent airport, the amount of air traffic in the area, the weather at the time of positioning, and the competitiveness of the operator."

Many of the charter operators listed in the *Air Charter Guide* advertise free positioning in the remarks column of the guide's main listing. In effect, such a move broadens their client market. It is important for the travel manager to understand that positioning involves added expenses. Jet equipment, for example, burns a disproportionate amount of fuel at low altitude and while taxiing. Therefore, what might make good sense as a positioning distance for a helicopter or propeller-driven light airplane is going to be much too short for a jet. There will be instances when, despite the inconvenience, the cost of moving that jet will not be worth it compared to an additional 20-minute drive by car to a different airport.

For the travel manager who uses the *Air Charter Guide*, picking an operator can be made easy. Simply pick a few different operators from the Operator Locator section, so that you will have several choices to compare within the main listings. Next turn to the Detailed Listings in the *Guide*, where a wealth of data will allow informed judgment. Look at the operator's experience, his years in business, and the age of the aircraft.

Regarding the age of the aircraft, the *Air Charter Guide* states, "It is important to understand that equipment age is a relative factor, not at all like the longevity of an automobile. Aircraft last 20 to 30 years. Instead of being replaced, they are refitted with entirely new engines and instruments. Like boats, aircraft age as gracefully as they are maintained. However, you are entitled to expect that a 1985 aircraft will be in better condition than a 1948 model."

For the travel manager who is using the *Air Charter Guide*, a quick check of the Aircraft Listings will tell you whether the aircraft is pressurized, what general category it fits, its speed, and what it looks like. Variations on specific type probably affect the number of seats and the speed more than the basic configuration. Speeds shown in the *Air Charter Guide* are maximum cruise speeds. For planning purposes these numbers should always be downgraded.

The editors of the *Air Charter Guide* advise that the basis for computing the planning speed is the cruise speed, which also influences trip price. Though the actual travel speed will also be a function of trip length, a general rule of thumb for calculating average speed on a trip of 300 miles would be to subtract 5 percent from the speed of a helicopter or airplane flying 100 mph or less, 10 percent from the posted speed for an aircraft in the 200 to 250 mph range, and as much as 20 percent for aircraft whose cruise speed is listed in excess of 400 mph. This new speed comes much closer to the gate or block speed. Your operator will be much better able to give you a precise cost quotation when you have agreed on the aircraft to be used and the route to be taken, and have defined all of the variables that make generalizations on this topic so difficult.

Credentials are important. Do not hesitate to review the operator's operating certificate or insurance policy. If your company has unique insurance policies, discuss them.

Food can often be provided on board. Those operators who normally provide catering services generally have indicated this service in the *Air Charter Guide*. If your travelers have special dietary needs, inform the operator of them. Some of the better-equipped and larger jets can accommodate on-board cooking. Aircraft smaller than ten-seat capacity are not equipped to handle this. Some charter operators, such as MGM Grand out of Los Angeles, offer extravagant dining with stand-up bar facilities.

Advance coordination of food service is necessary for anything much more complicated than drinks and pretzels or coffee and doughnuts. The editors of the *Air Charter Guide* point out, "You own the aircraft while you have it, so you are entitled to request something special."

With some aircraft, toilet facilities can be a problem. You should understand that the "lav" in the detailed listings in the *Air Charter Guide* simply means that some sort of toilet facility is on board. The smaller aircraft are limited to a chemical flush toilet with a privacy panel or curtain, whereas the larger jets may have a toilet compartment with sink—as is customarily found on board airliners. The presence or absence of a toilet compartment or "lav" has planning significance because it limits the range of any given leg on the itinerary. In general, aircraft should be selected so as to limit a trip leg to no more than 2½ hours, if possible. By today's standards, that is a long time in any vehicle and is tiring. If it takes longer than that in a propeller-driven plane, it might be better to hire a jet for the trip.

## HELICOPTER CHARTER

The helicopter charter business is expanding rapidly, particularly in built-up areas such as the Northeast Corridor. Special consideration must be given to the planning of a helicopter trip. In return, it can provide you with special flexibility.

The editors of the *Air Charter Guide* state, "Helicopters operate under different weather flying criteria than other aircraft. While it is possible to fly "visually" in a helicopter on a trip that would require use of instrument flight rules in an airplane, you should not depend on this margin from the travel planning standpoint. If your helicopter leg is lengthy, you should pick an operator who has instrument-flight-rule-equipped helicopters and can schedule you in one if needed."

Just as there are single and twin-engine airplanes, there are also single and twin-engine helicopters, though the absence of a second rotor makes them less obvious. Both single and twin engine aircraft have their economies and safeties, limitations and advantages. The editors of the *Air Charter Guide* recommend that the travel manager discuss the relative merits of single versus twin engine helicopters with operators. Assess the travel implications, economies, and availability of both and decide with an open mind. Single-engine and multi-engine helicopters are different. They each have their own place.

One of the problems with helicopters is finding heliports. Hospitals, police departments, and media often have their own, and just as often won't share. Ask your charter operator to research landing requests. An off-airport helicopter landing has to be planned and often must be cleared through local municipalities. In metropolitan areas, it may be more difficult to land at other than approved heliports. This restriction is much less in rural areas. In any event, you must ask first. In metropolitan areas, helicopter charter will generally be between approved heliports or between heliports and airports.

## PRICING CHARTER FLIGHTS

The expense of air charter must be evaluated against the trip at hand. How many are going, and how does the cost compare to other forms of travel? What is the savings in time, lodging, ground transportation, and gained business opportunity? Air charter, properly used, brings all the advantages that air travel is supposed to offer: rapid transportation with real convenience and service. When you really have to be somewhere in a hurry, it is worth every penny.

According to the *Air Charter Guide*, "Aircraft are usually chartered by the hour, with rates varying according to many factors. Hourly rates are figured against the time the aircraft is actually in the air. A strong tailwind, therefore, will actually lower the cost. Air traffic delays, holding patterns, and en route deviations will increase it."

Many operators try to make their pricing more appealing by charging on a distance basis against the actual trip length. Some will qualify this length, however, by charging for trip length as extended by expected deviations. The editors of the *Air Charter Guide* comment that, "Since there is no way for a passenger, who is not actually performing the flight, to check this distance, it becomes a specious form of pricing because the unit (i.e., mileage) cannot be measured."

Most unit-pricing charges (hourly or distance-based) relate to an operator's actual hourly expenses—aircraft lease, fuel, maintenance, crew wages, plus the profit margin. Prices guaranteed in advance are like any other lump-sum agreement: a bet on the part of the vendor that he can do the job within the sum quoted and still make some money. To the extent the market will bear, a prudent operator will charge extra to give some margin.

## SURCHARGES

While many charter operators include all surcharges in their base price, some bill other aspects of the trip as extra charges. The *Air Charter Guide* lists these as:

1. Handling fees (landing and takeoff).
2. Municipal landing fees.
3. Ramp (parking fees).
4. Waiting time.
5. Overnight charges.
6. De-icing.
7. Preheating of cabin and/or engines.
8. Hangar storage.
9. Federal and state taxes.

Hourly and overnight waiting charges vary widely by aircraft type, country, and personnel. European hourly waiting charges generally range from 3 to 7 percent of hourly flight charges. Typical US rates: $50–$100/hr. standby; and $75–$300 overnight.

Landing and ramp fees are regarded as pass-along expenses to the customer. The fees vary widely. Though usually quite reasonable (it costs more to park a car in Manhattan than to land and park a Lear Jet at the average airport), the expense to land at the major metropolitan airports can be very high. Inquire before you make the trip.

The *Air Charter Guide* comments, "The presence or absence of surcharges should be regarded only as a variation in pricing policy which reflects the operator's choice of how to do business. Each operator has different equipment and markets. Prices are structured accordingly."

## PRICING USING THE *AIR CHARTER GUIDE*

Basic charter prices are shown in the *Air Charter Guide* in several ways. A specific hourly price is listed opposite an operator's aircraft, as a single figure, with no qualifications about pricing method in the remarks section. Two prices for the same aircraft type indicate that the price was unavailable to the *Guide* or that the *Guide* was requested not to print the information. The high and low regional prices for that type of aircraft are shown on the line instead. This still provides a good indication of what to expect, and a basis for comparison when discussing the trip quote with the operator. Where prices based on distance are converted to the *Air Charter Guide*'s hourly format, a note in the Operator Comments section indicates that this has been done.

## CASE STUDY: THE MESCON GROUP

The following comments are offered by Peter V. Agur, Jr., general manager, aviation management systems of the Mescon Group, located in Atlanta, Georgia.

There are some very important "key people" in every organization. They are the people who open or protect the windows of opportunity for their business. Often they are top executives. Sometimes they're engineers or technicians who can get a production line or a customer's problem solved. No matter who they are, their time-place mobility can be essential to the success of the company. As more and more companies wade into the turbulent waters of down-sizing, right-sizing, and a flood of other major challenges, the impact and importance of key people multiplies. Leveraging that impact is critical. Many organizations are making heavy capital and cultural investments in video-conference centers and other electronic communications systems to improve access to key people. But the key people still have an imperative need to be where the action is. They often get there by air.

The choices are the airlines or business aircraft. The term "business aircraft" refers to both corporate aircraft and charter aircraft. So, when is it best to use business aircraft to get them there? As one top executive put it, "Use business aircraft for what the airlines don't do well." In other words, when the benefits of using business aircraft exceed their costs. And that depends on the type of "strategic" and operational costs and benefits involved in a specific trip. Strategic or special travel involves significant opportunities and/or risks that require urgent response or attention. They can be characterized as "911" trips. Strategic trips normally generate very little concern for the cost of air services because the time-place mobility of the passengers is so important. Examples include the initial phases of acquisitions, divestitures, and real or potential disasters.

Operational or routine travel can directly enhance the performance of the company. Typically, there is significant concern for the time and cost savings provided by air travel.

The most widely perceived application of business aircraft is in getting senior executives to and from important meetings. However, these versatile aircraft are used for a wide variety of other purposes, too. A southeast-based company is up to its ears in another merger. To accelerate the transition, a team of senior operational managers is going to each major facility throughout the region to define the company's new expectations and direction as well as to answer the questions of concerned employees and managers. Unfortunately, the airlines don't go to all the places they need to. In fact, it seems that air travel anywhere in the southeast includes a stop in Atlanta, no matter what. They figured it would take them more than two weeks to complete the circuit on the airlines. The schedule was condensed to four days using a business aircraft. One of the most important advantages they cited in their decision to use the business aircraft was their ability to have some control over the schedule.

Among other examples of successful business aircraft uses are Hewlett-Packard and Steelcase. H-P has an open and egalitarian approach to using air travel resources. Anyone who demonstrates a net direct and time-cost benefit from the use of business aircraft may request it. This policy includes line personnel as well as managers. Steelcase, the office furniture manufacturer, has an enviable reputation for excellence in marketing and customer service. Business aircraft bring customers to Steelcase's plants and headquarters. The company is committed to the belief that performance is people-based and business aircraft help get people together.

So how does a travel manager help a customer select the most effective air travel mode? It depends upon the specific needs of the passenger, the trip's itinerary, and the air travel value each mode can create. That value is measured as a blend of costs and benefits. The components of air travel value are:

1. Confidentiality—Minimizing the personal or organizational risk of financial harm or embarrassment.
2. Cost effectiveness—Providing the specified service or product for a reasonable direct price.
3. Safety/security—Minimizing the risk of injury, fright, or physical damage or harm.
4. Service—Meeting the traveler's needs for reliability, predictability, responsiveness, flexibility, etc.
5. Time effectiveness—The measure of traveler productivity and time saving during the entire door-to-door travel experience.

Special or strategic trips cause passengers to have extremely high concerns for time effectiveness. Those passengers also have very high interest in safety/security, confidentiality, and service. Considering the importance of their mission, they have relatively low concern for cost effectiveness. Most executives say that business aircraft can create high travel value for special or strategic-trip passengers.

Routine or operational-trip passengers tend to have very high needs for time effectiveness, safety/security, cost effectiveness, and service. The nature of their travel doesn't usually include a significant requirement for confidentiality. Depending on the itinerary and the number of passengers, either the airlines or business aircraft could be very effective for routine trips.

If a trip has special or strategic value, the lead passenger (usually the senior person involved) will often request the air travel mode of preference. However, routine trips are not necessarily as cut-and-dried. In fact, many managers prefer to have some sort of analytical tool that helps them make the best decision between airlines and business aircraft. The concept of an air travel premium can do the job. Essentially, the air travel premium is the full cost differential between moving the passenger, or passengers, on the airlines or in a business aircraft. The full cost is measured from door to door in terms of direct and time costs.

Direct costs of door-to-door travel usually include:

1. Ground transportation.
2. Room and board.
3. Ticket or aircraft costs.

Time costs can include:

1. Direct flight availability.
2. Ground transportation to the airport.
3. Parking, check-in, and security checks.
4. En-route productivity.
5. En-route stops/connecting flights.
6. Trip time differential due to any speed difference between the airlines and a business aircraft.
7. Typical unscheduled arrival delays.
8. Debarking and baggage claim.
9. Ground transportation from the airport.

The costs and data necessary to calculate the air travel premium can be gained from the passengers, airline schedules, and business aircraft performance charts (or for the more practical of mind, from the flight department's scheduling personnel).

Time-cost can be a rather sensitive issue if it's not treated conservatively. Most senior managers are uncomfortable with time-cost multipliers. The idea of a multiplier is to provide some understanding of the opportunity cost associated with time. They normally range from two-and-one-half to ten times the traveler's hourly compensation rate. Most financially oriented mangers are much more comfortable with measuring the real cost of a person's time. For example, an executive whose W-2 income is $74,000 per year may have a full compensation cost to the company of $100,000 when benefits are considered. This equates to $50 per hour for a 2,000-hour business year (50 times the 40 hours in the work week).

Let's take a look at an example of how to apply the concept of air travel premium. A company in Shreveport, Louisiana, had a group of three senior managers who needed to go to Dallas, Texas, and back on Monday. On Wednesday they had to do an out-and-back to Baton Rouge, Louisiana. They asked their travel manager to give them guidance as to the most effective mode of travel: take the airlines or charter an airplane. Using direct-cost and time-cost measurement, the manager determined the following:

1.  The cost of three round-trip tickets to Dallas was $2.79 per mile, and the time differential cost of these three people to travel on the airlines instead of a charter aircraft was $0.96 per mile, for a total direct and time cost of $3.75 per mile to fly on the airlines to Dallas and back.

2.  The cost of three round-trip tickets to Baton Rouge was $3.03 per mile, and the time differential cost of these three people to travel on the airlines instead of a charter aircraft was $1.38 per mile, for a total direct and time cost of $4.41 per mile to fly on the airlines to Baton Rouge and back.

The available charter airplane cost $4.50 per mile. Monday's trip to Dallas had an air travel premium of 20 percent ($4.50/$3.75). Wednesday's trip to Baton Rouge had an air travel premium of 2 percent ($4.50/$4.41). The lead passenger was able to decide if the benefits of time effectiveness, safety/security, service, and confidentiality more than offset the cost differential.

Some interesting patterns can be noted in air travel premiums:

1. The more passengers the better for business aircraft.
2. Airline travel between non-hub cities has relatively high time and ticket costs.
3. Longer trips have smaller time-premium-per-mile costs on the airlines because the large fixed-time costs are spread over greater distances.

The bottom line is that the airlines clearly do a very cost-effective job between hub cities and on legs of 500 miles or more. Company and charter aircraft can't be matched for meeting the needs of passengers on special or strategic trips, and they can be very cost-competitive for groups of three or more on many routes, especially those within 500 miles or so between non-hub cities.

One of the most frequent uses of charter aircraft is to support the flight departments of companies with their own fleets. They charter aircraft to supplement their capacity. Otherwise, the corporate flight department is in the awkward position of turning key people away or investing in enough equipment and people to meet peak-demand requirements. This can leave substantial excess capacity during nonpeak times. Either case can be very expensive in its own way. The use of charter aircraft creates convenient and relatively inexpensive elasticity of business aircraft supply.

Once the decision has been made to use charter aircraft, managing the quality of performance is the first priority. A lot of charter operators get their business from phone inquiries. That's sort of like picking a heart surgeon from the yellow pages. They're both highly trained and certified, but some are better than others. And the stakes are pretty high.

There really is variability of quality among charter suppliers, but most are professional. Talk with business aircraft operators you respect and ask them which charter operators they use or recommend. Get references from the ones you're interested in and check them out. Select the two or three charter suppliers who impress you the most and visit them. If you really want to be certain of the highest-quality possible, hire an aviation consultant to do an inspection of the top candidates. Even so, you should still visit their facilities and the facilities your key passengers are going to use. You should expect cleanliness and order. It's amazing how the very best operators of business aircraft have a passion for the neat and tidy.

Once you've picked the operator with whom you're comfortable, you can either let him run the show his way or help him meet the travel expectations of your passengers. Explain to the operator the service expectations your company has for their crews. Be specific about such things as the greeting process, baggage requirements, catering needs, passenger profiles, and ground transportation requirements.

Cost management is the next priority. One of the most basic cost-saving actions you can take is to be sure to match the trip needs to the equipment you charter. Renting a faster or bigger aircraft than you need can be very expensive. If the trip is less than 500 miles, a turboprop or a light jet can be nearly as quick and a lot less expensive than a high-speed jet. Another source of savings is volume discounts. If you anticipate buying more than 50 hours of charter service in a 12-month period, you may be able to purchase a "block" of time from your preferred operator at a reduced rate. You may also be able to make reservations for a trip with a long lead time. Some charter operators, like the airlines, give discounts for customers who plan in advance. Charter services often have a 5 percent fee in reserve for paying brokers who bring clients to them. There's no harm in asking for that margin to be returned to you if you're acting in your own behalf.

The most important point about cost management of charter operations is that it's a very competitive marketplace. Charter pricing tends to be very similar in most regions. You should be able to get the aircraft you want from the best-quality operator available for within 10 or 15 percent of the cheaper sources. That's a small price to pay for getting top performance, especially when you're paying for the assurance of service and safety.

Intelligent air travel strategies and policies can help ensure the service and safety your passengers expect. Having a single clearing point within your company for hiring charter services can make a lot of sense. That single source can select the operators who most closely match your organization's requirements for technical, service, and financial performance. You can also improve your bargaining position. Sometimes a naive traveler will assume that reasonable quality is assured by FAA certification and purchase charter services on price alone. That's not necessarily a valid assumption. An involved company travel manager can play a vital role in assuring safety and performance.

An important point that is occasionally tragically reinforced is, Who should be allowed to travel together? Unrestricted grouping of key people leaves the organization at risk for catastrophic loss in the case of an accident. It's important for your policy makers to be deliberate about the risks the company is willing to accept and the safeguards it wishes to employ. As an example, many large companies won't let their top two people, or more than three senior executives, travel together. Some companies even restrict people with vertical relationships within functional areas from traveling together. On the other hand, the chairman of one Fortune 100 company said he wasn't willing to put up with the inconveniences incurred when his senior management team had to travel in small groups to the same destination. When he was asked about the potential risk to the company if the worst should happen, he replied that no one was irreplaceable and, besides, there would be a sudden surge of vertical mobility for the survivors. His humor may not be appreciated by everyone, but his position represents one end of the spectrum. Whatever works best for your company is fine. Just be deliberate and be consistent. Apply whatever restrictions your company chooses to all modes of travel—airlines and business aircraft as well as cars and trains.

Another important policy to consider is the number of engines your company requires on aircraft carrying employees. This was particularly important when engines and subsystems were not as reliable as they are today. However, it's still a major issue and needs to be given the attention it deserves. Westvaco Corporation, a renowned paper, packaging, and chemicals manufacturing company headquartered in New York, has a very firm commitment to their multi-engine aircraft policy: When conducting Westvaco business, Westvaco employees are required to travel in multi-engine aircraft. This policy is particularly impressive when you consider today's challenging economic business conditions.

The obvious follow-on question is, What about one pilot versus two? Most turboprops and a few jets are certified to be flown single-pilot. The rest require at least two pilots. Is the second one worth the extra money? Only if you need him or her. Flying in today's crowded skies requires sharp eyes and many cockpit duties. There are other reasons, though. A few years ago Dr. Mike Mescon, the well-known keynote speaker, had a talk to give in a south Georgia city. On the morning Dr. Mescon boarded the chartered twin-engine airplane he'd used on previous occasions, the weather was more befitting of Seattle than Atlanta. When Mike greeted the pilot, he got little response. He didn't think much about it until they were climbing into the gloom. He leaned forward and asked the pilot, the one and only pilot, if he was feeling okay. The answer was chilling: "Have you ever wanted to kill yourself?" Mike says he put his materials down, eased into the co-pilot's seat, and gave the finest motivational speech of his life. Two pilots are not a bad investment.

Speaking of pilots, a large computer company in the northeast is managing the quality of its charter trips in a very direct way. One of their own pilots flies as a crew member on charter flights. Although this requires some planning, effort, and extra cooperation from the charter operator (the pilot must be certified to fly charter, insurance coverage has to be set up, etc.), the passengers are delighted to see a familiar face on an unfamiliar aircraft. The result is more certainty of the levels of service provided by an outside vendor and customers' (passengers') perceptions of service and safety are greatly improved. That air travel services group thinks it's worth the effort.

If you don't or can't put your own pilot in the cockpit of charter aircraft, you can and should specify the qualifications of the pilot(s). Charter flying is a traditional way for young or new pilots to build flight time. You may want to designate the minimum experience levels you are willing to permit on your trips. Any reputable operator will respect and honor this kind of request.

Another important crew member on larger aircraft is the flight attendant. Some passengers object to having a flight attendant on board for appearance's sake. Others don't wish to be coddled or interrupted. These are valid concerns. All executives' concerns are valid. But, the most important purpose of a flight attendant is not service. It's safety. These highly trained people can assist in either an aircraft emergency or a passenger's medical emergency. In either case the pilots are busy flying the aircraft.

A practice in some parts of the charter industry is worth noting. Some operators may not tell you when they can't fulfill your trip needs. Instead they'll call around to other charter companies until they find one who can. The operator you contacted first will most certainly receive a finder's fee for the business. They may not even tell you that your trip is being handled by someone else. Without your consent, how can you manage the services you receive?

A relatively recent and rapidly growing innovation in the charter industry is something generically referred to as "umbrella" charter operations. This occurs when one operator is the central holder of a charter certificate. That certificate holder gets other operators, often corporate flight departments with excess capacity, to perform charter trips under their umbrella. The concept is designed to maintain traditional safety standards and has the benefit of reducing the government paperwork necessary for small, high-quality departments to fly charter. It has the drawback of removing the customer one more step from the supplier.

The surest way to be certain of charter safety and service is to take care of the basics. Use a select pool of suppliers with whom you deliberately develop a rapport. Make certain they understand your organization's specific needs and expectations for service. Have each supplier initially inspected and "certified" by a technical expert. Have that same technical expert perform re-inspections periodically. Once a year works well. Make it clear to your consultant that the objective of the inspections is not to catch the charter operator doing things wrong. It's to find opportunities for them to improve and succeed, for themselves and for you.

## TRAVEL MANAGEMENT TIPS

- The most important source of information on air charters for travel managers is the *Air Charter Guide*.
- If there is an alternative, try not to land at one of the big international airports because you will have to pay higher landing fees, and you will probably be held longer on the ground by the controllers.
- A one-way trip makes an operator at your destination just as good a choice as an operator at or near your home air-

port, since the aircraft still has to go round-trip no matter where it originates.

- It is important for the travel manager to understand that positioning involves added expenses.
- Equipment age is a relative factor, not at all like the longevity of an automobile. Aircraft last 20 to 30 years.
- The basis for computing the planning speed is the cruise speed, which also influences trip price.
- Credentials are important. Do not hesitate to review the operator's operating certificate or insurance policy. If your company has unique insurance needs, discuss them.
- Helicopters operate under different weather flying criteria than other aircraft.
- Aircraft are usually chartered by the hour, with rates varying according to many factors.
- The most widely perceived application of business aircraft is getting senior executives to and from important meetings. However, these aircraft are used for a wide variety of other purposes.
- The more passengers the better for business aircraft.
- Airline travel between non-hub cities has relatively high time and ticket costs.
- Longer trips have smaller time-premium-per-mile costs on the airlines because the large fixed-time costs are spread over a greater distance.
- One of the most basic cost-saving actions you can take is to be sure to match the trip needs to the equipment you charter.

## Chapter Eleven

# Managing Frequent Flyer Programs

O ne of the worst nightmares for the travel manager can be frequent flyer programs. The problems arise when corporate travelers circumvent cost-savings programs and refuse low fares in order to accumulate mileage. Both the traveler and the travel manager can be better off if they understand the system.

Airline frequent flyer programs are designed to generate customer loyalty. The dollar value of free tickets and other awards doled out by such programs is a staggering sum by any measure. But despite the costs incurred by participating airlines, frequent flyer programs serve as a cost-effective marketing tool for airlines struggling to retain or increase market share.

For the business traveler who passes airfare costs along to his or her employer, the quest for frequent flyer awards often takes precedence over shopping for the most economical airfares. While the airlines and their business travelers reap the benefits of frequent flyer programs, corporate travel managers are often faced with several unpleasant consequences: excessively high airfares, circuitous travel itineraries, and totally unnecessary trips.

Many companies—some motivated by foresight, others by economic depression—have taken steps to capture frequent flyer awards earned by their corporate travelers. Other companies encourage their travelers to keep frequent flyer awards for their personal use, recognizing the "perk" factor involved.

## PROGRAM OVERVIEW

The airlines instituted frequent flyer bonus programs over a decade ago in the wake of airline industry deregulation. While these programs vary slightly from airline to airline (and from one time of the year to another), all are similar in design. Travelers enrolled in these programs earn miles based on the distances they fly on a particular carrier. After a passenger accumulates enough mileage on the given airline (usually 20,000 to 40,000 miles), the mileage may be redeemed for free or discounted travel or for upgrades to first or business class.

The primary purpose of all frequent flyer programs is to build customer loyalty by rewarding individual travelers who concentrate their travel with one airline.

Since the inception of these programs, business travelers have been prime targets for enrollment, not only because they are such a lucrative portion of the airline's passenger loads, but also because business travelers usually have the prerogative of choosing carriers.

Typically, business travelers personally enroll themselves in a carrier's frequent flyer program. Consequently, regardless of whether tickets are purchased for business (and thus paid for by the traveler's employer) or personal purposes (and thus paid for by the traveler), the business traveler quickly accumulates mileage and personally benefits from the earned awards.

The benefit to an airline from enrolling business travelers is that the travelers have a strong incentive to stick with the airline, regardless of the cost to the company. But this mutually beneficial arrangement between airline and traveler is the nemesis of many corporate travel managers.

The corporate travel manager who is interested in staying current with changes in frequent flyer programs should subscribe to the monthly publication:

InsideFlyer
4715-C Town Center Drive
Colorado Springs, CO 80916
(719) 597-8880

For the corporate travel manager who requires an outside service for frequent flyer program management service, a company exists solely for this purpose. The company is aptly named:

Frequent Flyer Services
4715-C Town Center Drive
Colorado Springs, CO 80916
(719) 597–8899

An excellent overview of frequent flyer mileage programs can be obtained from:

Runzheimer International Ltd.
Runzheimer Park
Rochester, Wisconsin 53167
(800) 558–1702

## FIRST-CLASS UPGRADES

According to Randy Petersen, president of Frequent Flyer Services, located in Colorado Springs, Colorado, "Among frequent flyer program benefits, none is more revered than first-class upgrades. Not only are they considered premium benefits, but they are the most popular awards for many of the programs. The ability to move from the back of the plane to the comfort and work space of the cabin at the front should continue to be a primary reason in selecting and using a particular airline." Petersen states that there are three ways to take advantage of this benefit: award upgrades, elite-level upgrades, and purchased upgrades. Each has its own set of rules and its own "price."

### *Award Upgrades*

Although purchased upgrades are usually available only for the domestic market, award upgrades are available for international flights as well. In addition, upgrades from some programs are available for even the most economical ticket. Some upgrades involve only one class of upgrade—coach to business, business to first class, or coach to first class if there is no business class. These award upgrades are available under some programs for only 10,000 miles, which is within reach of most members. Petersen states that the most popular use of these upgrades is for international destinations or for transcontinental flights. Members can save many miles by realizing that business class on international flights is very comparable to first class on domestic flights and that business class on domestic flights will often provide the comfort they seek. Petersen advises that true first-class upgrades should be used only if business class or one-class upgrades are not available.

### Elite-Level Upgrades

Most airlines have or are moving in the direction of offering free stand-by and confirmed upgrades for their most frequent flyers. To reach the mileage level necessary for elite-level benefits, look for promotional periods that offer fast-track entry into these levels, or carefully plan flights during the latter half of the year to qualify. Petersen maintains that those who are members of elite-level programs appreciate first-class upgrades as the single most important benefit of their membership. Most programs have several levels of membership, and the benefits are enhanced the more one flies a particular airline. First-class upgrades for members of the "elite" vary from carrier to carrier and include free or low mileage redemption options and low cost. Members hoping to take advantage of space-available upgrades should check in early (upgrades usually are available within two hours of flight time), before fellow flyers flash their plastic.

### Purchased Upgrades

Currently, only eight airline programs allow purchased first-class upgrades. This type of upgrade is available to all members of the program regardless of the number of miles flown. The ability to purchase a first-class upgrade is dependent on the availability of the seat; airlines will not displace a paying passenger. Purchased upgrades usually include only the contiguous 48 states, although Hawaii is included in some.

## AIRPORT CLUBS

Most airport clubs have guest privileges, conference rooms, newsletters, flight-status monitoring, nonsmoking areas, and check-cashing privileges. Many offer spousal memberships at a nominal cost and also nonrefundable, nontransferable multiple-year or lifetime memberships. All airport clubs offer complimentary tea, coffee, soft drinks, snack food, work space, telephones, newspapers, magazines, and television.

## FOOD UPGRADES

According to Petersen, "Frequent travelers often feel all too familiar with airline food. Even frequent flyer program members are sometimes not aware that all major North American carriers offer special meals to all coach, business, and first-class passengers, although none have advertised the service widely."

Request specific information on meal service when making flight reservations. In-flight time will determine which menu options are available on a particular airline. Make selections from the available menus and request a special menu order. Usually, airlines must receive special requests approximately one day in advance.

Special meals are not the only option available; even the mealtime can usually be adjusted. Petersen states, "Though most people are aware that the way one feels at arrival time can be affected by what one consumes during flight, experts now believe that the timing of meals plays an equally important role in maintaining a traveler's well-being."

According to Charles Ehret, Ph.D., author of *Overcoming Jet Lag*, travelers need to eat at times coinciding with the normal mealtimes at their final destination. This enables the traveler to arrive in a healthy and alert state and to avoid the problems associated with jet lag. Ehret continually follows his own meal schedule during flights and says there are thousands of other frequent flyers who help reset their biological clock by ordering meals at special times. He explains that it is only necessary to inform flight attendants on board of a preferred mealtime and more often than not this schedule can be met.

Petersen claims that "frequent-flyers who keep these 'well-kept secrets' in mind can increase their enjoyment of airline dining, their levels of productivity and alertness, and their feelings of synchronicity with the local schedule upon arrival."

## AWARD REDEMPTION

Awards are meaningless unless the traveler knows how to redeem them. Numerous awards expire without being used simply because the recipient did not know what to do to reap the benefits. Petersen believes that "many travelers would be happy to transfer awards if he or she knew under what conditions the transfers could be made. Most frequent travelers also find themselves in the position of needing an award 'ASAP.'"

Frequent flyer and frequent guest programs have grown tremendously in the last few years; that growth, combined with the 1988 triple-mileage promotion that inflated most account balances, has made it difficult to use free awards. Protecting profitability (not wanting to displace paying travelers), airlines and hotels have begun to enforce more-stringent limits on the use of free awards. Although blackout dates are routine, the use of capacity controls is another matter. More often than not, fewer seats are available on international routes because of the smaller number of flights and because an airline typically enjoys a greater profit margin on these flights. Petersen offers the following points about redeeming awards:

1. Free-award seats and rooms are handled the same way "yield management" is handled for fare-paying passengers: availability changes daily. If the preferred travel dates are not open, ask to be waitlisted on a free award; call back periodically to check availability.
2. Try flights other than nonstop. Routing through hubs takes longer, but more seats may be open than on more popular flights.
3. Schedule free-award travel for midweek; Friday, Saturday, and Sunday are peak periods of congestion for advance-purchase and discount fares.

4. Plan ahead to use free awards; two months in advance is not too early to make preliminary reservations.
5. Look closely at the international destinations of the airlines and their partners; more seats are often available to less popular destinations. Because tourists generally plan to travel around, this strategy can be very effective.
6. Consider paying for part of the cost. If free-award seats to Tokyo are filled, take a free trip to Tahiti and then pay the small connecting charge to Tokyo.
7. Airline awards usually include discounts off the rack rate at hotels. A better strategy may be to redeem a hotel award (usually for free rooms) and purchase the airline ticket. Advance-purchase airline tickets are generally less expensive than a week's hotel charges.
8. Search out insurance to cover free travel awards, which are not replaceable if lost or stolen. Travelers to international destinations should review their existing insurance coverage for claims outside the United States. Information on this can be obtained from Travel Assistance International.

## APPROACHES TO MANAGING
## FREQUENT FLYER PROGRAMS

The consulting group at Runzheimer International recently completed a survey on how corporations manage frequent flyer programs. According to Runzheimer, the corporate travel manager faces three options:

1. Ignore frequent flyer programs. Some companies hesitate to tamper with frequent flyer miles, so they allow their weary road warriors to reap the benefits of logging long hours on the road, without regard to the impact on the company's travel budget. Although this option prevents the company from capitalizing on a potentially valuable source of travel cost savings, it is a safe decision from the standpoint of employer/employee relations. It avoids confrontation with traveling employees and thereby sidesteps a potential morale problem.

Surprisingly, some companies would rather fire employees who abuse travel policy than confront the frequent flyer issue head-on by staking claim to awards. But such firings are sure to create morale problems of their own, even if disguised as downsizing.

2. Implement a voluntary program. Some corporations permit travelers to turn in frequent flyer mileage to the company, which buys awards from the traveler with some kind of incentive, such as cash or free upgrades. One variation is for a company to claim ownership of mileage points but offer its frequent travelers free flight certificates upon request. This approach allows the company to realize value from frequent flyer mileage points while minimizing employee friction. This approach would be useful in a situation involving very frequent travelers who accumulate an extraordinary number of mileage points, but seldom redeem their awards because they are weary of travel. This solution does have a downside: frequent flyer programs prohibit the sale or barter of awards, and a company suggesting such action is confronted with an ethics issue.

3. Capture most or all frequent flyer mileage awards. This approach designates all mileage points accrued on company-paid business trips as company property. Accrued mileage points are then exchanged for free travel on future company trips. The Runzheimer consulting group recommends three options to companies who decide to capture frequent flyer points.

The first option is to implement an in-house management program whereby the travel department administers collection of frequent flyer mileage points and their application toward company travel purchases. The second option recommended by Runzheimer is to contract with the travel agency to assist in developing and installing a frequent flyer management program. The third option is to retain an outside service organization (other than a travel agency) to administer a frequent flyer program.

## HOW COMPANIES CAPTURE
## FREQUENT FLYER MILEAGE POINTS

The following chart lists several of the more innovative ways that companies have found for dealing with frequent flyer awards. Whether companies administer the program themselves or seek

# SEVEN WAYS TO CAPTURE FREQUENT FLYER AWARDS

Here are some of the more innovative ways that companies have found for dealing with frequent flyer awards:

| IDEA | IMPLEMENTATION | ADVANTAGES | DISADVANTAGES |
|---|---|---|---|
| 50/50 | Traveler's first free ticket is used for future business travel; the next free ticket can be used for traveler's personal vacation travel. | a) Traveler receives substantial benefit.<br>b) Traveler has "clear conscience".<br>c) Company recognizes fringe benefit. | a) Company gives up 50% of savings.<br>b) Non-travelers are left out.<br>c) Travel benefit is taxable to employee. |
| Fly/Stay | Traveler's free airline tickets are used for future business travel; free hotel awards are used for traveler's personal vacation travel. | a) Company achieves 100% of savings.<br>b) Traveler receives substantial savings.<br>c) Traveler has "clear conscience".<br>d) Company recognizes fringe benefit. | a) Non-travelers are left out.<br>b) Travel benefit is taxable to employee. |
| Donation | Corporate policy requires employees to turn in all free tickets for donation to non-profit causes. | a) Creates positive employee morale.<br>b) Satisfies policy requirements.<br>c) Company recognizes fringe benefit of community support. | a) No direct financial benefit to company.<br>b) Employees may see it as unnecessary. |
| Credit Account | Corporate policy requires employees to turn in all free tickets; traveler receives 20% of face value as credit towards vacation travel; secretary receives 5% credit. | a) Company achieves 75% of savings.<br>b) Travelers receive some benefit and will work with the program.<br>c) Travel benefit not taxable to employee. | a) Company gives up 25% of savings.<br>b) Non-travelers are left out. |
| Ticket Bank | Corporate policy requires employees to turn in all free tickets, creating a corporate 'ticket bank'; all employees may buy tickets at a reduced rate. | a) Company achieves up to 50% of savings.<br>b) All employees may participate.<br>c) All employees 'police' one another.<br>d) Travel benefit not taxable to employee. | a) Company gives up 50% of savings. |
| Earn/Sell | Company offers to purchase free tickets from traveling employees at a reduced rate. | a) Company achieves up to 50% of savings.<br>b) Travelers receive monetary benefit and will work with the program. | a) Company gives up 50% of savings.<br>b) Non-travelers are left out.<br>c) Travel benefit is taxable to employee.<br>d) Company suggests the employee violate program rules against selling awards. |
| Ticket Lottery | Corporate policy requires employees to turn in all free tickets for monthly drawings; winners can be travelers or non-travelers. | a) All employees 'police' one another.<br>b) Creates positive employee morale.<br>c) Travelers receive some benefit and will work with the program. | a) No direct financial benefit to company; except by avoiding unnecessary trips.<br>b) Distribution of tickets wouldn't please everyone. |

FFS-318

an outside management service the steps to capture frequent flyer mileage awards are similar.

Randy Petersen recommends that the following five-phase program be used in implementing a frequent flyer program:

**Phase one.**   Petersen recommends that a carefully written memo, from top management, announce the new travel policy or changes in your present policy. A meeting should be held to introduce and explain the details of the new frequent flyer program management service and how it will work to save airfare expenses for the client. All corporate travelers should attend the session. The corporation's investment in initiating this program will ensure its success.

**Phase two.**   The following forms need to be filled out:

A. Corporate questionnaire (an update on the corporation's current travel situation; see Figure 11.1a and b).

B. Business traveler enrollment roster (a list of all business travelers to be tracked; see Figure 11.2).

C. Business traveler program enrollment and profile form (see Figure 11.3a for new enrollments or 11.3b for transfers and new enrollments).

**Phase three.**   Once the above items are received, the service can initiate the start-up procedure. This involves enrolling each individual in each travel program requested (see Figure 11.3a). The timetable for this procedure will vary, depending upon the airline and hotel programs desired, since several programs allow you to enroll individuals over the telephone, while other programs require a written application. Once all business travelers have been enrolled in all requested programs, the vendor of the frequent flyer program can supply your travel agency with their new program membership ID numbers, and it will be the responsibility of the travel agency to provide only these membership numbers when taking reservations.

If some business travelers are currently enrolled in the programs and will be allowed to keep their accumulated miles prior to this point, it will be necessary to re-enroll them under a separate corporate number, or the vendor can track these travelers'

## CORPORATE QUESTIONNAIRE

To properly begin the enrollment and administration of your new Frequent Traveler Program Management, we need your answers to the following questions, regarding your current Frequent Traveler Program situation:

1. Are your business travelers currently involved in the programs for personal use?
    ☐ All          ☐ Some        ☐ None

2. Are we to transfer their current program mileage/points into the new system?
    ☐ Yes         ☐ No

3. Are they to keep their current mileage/points and start from scratch in the new system?
    ☐ Yes         ☐ No

4. Due to the importance of 'elite-level' benefits, will we be managing combined accounts for selected travelers?
    ☐ Yes         ☐ No

5. Which travel programs will your company claim awards from?
    ☐ Airlines     ☐ Hotels       ☐ Car Rentals

6. Will your company be claiming all awards in the new system?
    ☐ Yes         ☐ No

7. Will your company be sharing the awards in the new system?
    ☐ Yes         ☐ No

    If "Yes", please give a brief explanation: _____
    _____

8. Please list the airline and hotel programs you have selected for us to manage:    _____
    _____
    _____
    _____

9. Please list the date you would prefer our services actually to begin on:   _____
    _____

10. Will claiming frequent traveler program awards become part of the company travel policy?
    ☐ Yes         ☐ No

    If "Yes", how can we assist you in rewriting your travel policy?   _____
    _____

11. Will your company require our monthly reports to be departmentalized?
    ☐ Yes         ☐ No

                                                                                    FFS-350

## FIGURE 11.1a

12. If you answered 'YES', to question 11, will you allow awards to be transferred between departments?
    ☐ Yes        ☐ No

13. Will your company require a cost savings analysis:
    ☐ Monthly    ☐ Quarterly    ☐ Annually

    Will these reports need to be departmentalized?
    ☐ Yes        ☐ No

14. Explain your travel agency's participation in the capture and use of frequent traveler program awards: _____
    _____
    _____
    _____

15. Which of the following will be our direct contact?
    ☐ Travel Agency    ☐ Corporate Travel Manager       ☐ Department Travel Managers

16. Will you be requesting the optional monthly "InsideFlyer" newsletter ($20. per subscription)?
    ☐ Yes        ☐ No

    If "Yes", how many subscriptions would you like?    _____
    Where would you like them sent?    _____
    _____
    _____
    _____

17. Will you be requesting the optional monthly Individual Consolidated Statement for each traveler ($7 per traveler per year)?
    ☐ Yes        ☐ No

18. Will you be requesting the optional Frequent Traveler Program Reconciliation Report ($10 per traveler per year)?
    ☐ Yes        ☐ No

19. Once the start-up fee has been received (25% of the first year total), which payment system will your company require?
    ☐ 9 equal monthly installments (we will send you a monthly invoice)

    ☐ 3 equal quarterly installments (we will send you a quarterly invoice)

    ☐ Balance within 90 days of start-up (earns a 2 $\frac{1}{2}$% discount)

FFS-350-1

**FIGURE 11.1b**

## BUSINESS TRAVELER ENROLLMENT ROSTER

Included in the services rendered by **FREQUENT FLYER SERVICES** are the enrollment or transfer of existing travel programs, for each individual business traveler, into the Frequent Traveler Programs you have determined most beneficial for your company through our discussions.

Please list below, each individual business traveler who will participate and complete the Frequent Traveler Program Enrollment Form, or attach a company personnel roster for the travelers we will be tracking.

| Business Traveler | Business Traveler |
|---|---|
| .......................................................................... | .......................................................................... |
| .......................................................................... | .......................................................................... |
| .......................................................................... | .......................................................................... |
| .......................................................................... | .......................................................................... |
| .......................................................................... | .......................................................................... |
| .......................................................................... | .......................................................................... |
| .......................................................................... | .......................................................................... |
| .......................................................................... | .......................................................................... |
| .......................................................................... | .......................................................................... |
| .......................................................................... | .......................................................................... |
| .......................................................................... | .......................................................................... |
| .......................................................................... | .......................................................................... |
| .......................................................................... | .......................................................................... |
| .......................................................................... | .......................................................................... |
| .......................................................................... | .......................................................................... |
| .......................................................................... | .......................................................................... |
| .......................................................................... | .......................................................................... |
| .......................................................................... | .......................................................................... |

Company Name _____ Date: _____

Corporate Travel Manager: _____

Authorized By: _____ Title: _____

p l e a s e     t y p e     o r     p r i n t

FFS-320

## FIGURE 11.2

# BUSINESS TRAVELER PROGRAM ENROLLMENT FORM

Your Name ...........................................................................................................................................

Company Name ....................................................................................................................................

Company Address ................................................................................................................................

City, State, Zip Code ...........................................................................................................................

**AND**

Home Address ......................................................................................................................................

City, State, Zip Code ...........................................................................................................................

## Corporate Program Enrollments

| | | |
|---|---|---|
| ☐ Air Canada ($20)[1] | ☐ Finnair | ☐ Northwest Airlines |
| ☐ Alaska Airlines | ☐ Hawaiian Air | ☐ Philippine Airlines |
| ☐ All Nippon (ANA) | ☐ Hilton Hotels | ☐ Ramada Hotels |
| ☐ Aloha Airlines | ☐ Holiday Inn ($10)[1] | ☐ Sheraton hotels ($25)[1] |
| ☐ America West | ☐ Hyatt Hotels | ☐ Southwest Airlines |
| ☐ American Airlines | ☐ Japan Air Lines (JAL) | ☐ Stouffer Hotels |
| ☐ British Airways | ☐ Korean Air (KAL) | ☐ TWA |
| ☐ Canadian Airlines | ☐ Marriott Hotels | ☐ United Airlines |
| ☐ China Airways | ☐ MGM Grand Air | ☐ USAir |
| ☐ Continental Airlines | ☐ Midwest Airlines | ☐ Westin |
| ☐ Delta Air Lines | ☐ National Emerald Club ($75)[1] | ☐ Other ........................... |

[1]This is the standard enrollment fee of this program, which will be charged separately to your company.

## Authorization

Because we are acting on both your behalf and the company which pays for your travel, there may be some instances when Frequent Flyer Services will be required to have your authorization to represent you when enrolling in programs, changing an address or the redemption of travel awards earned from employer paid travel.

**I HEREBY GRANT TO FREQUENT FLYER SERVICES, ACTING ON THE AUTHORITY OF MY EMPLOYER, AUTHORIZATION TO ACT AS AN AGENT TO ORDER CORPORATE ENROLLMENTS, ADDRESS CHANGES ON COMPANY ACCOUNTS, AND CORPORATE AWARD REDEMPTION TRANSFERS FOR ME IN WHATEVER FREQUENT TRAVELER PROGRAMS DEEMED SUITABLE BY MY EMPLOYER.**

Signature .....................................................................................Date .................................................

**FOR PROGRAM PASSWORD USE ONLY:**

Date of Birth ..................................................................Place of Birth ..............................................

Mother's Maiden Name ...........................................Social Security Number ................................................

FFS - 330-2

# FIGURE 11.3a

# BUSINESS TRAVELER PROGRAM ENROLLMENT FORM

Your Name ..........................................................................................................................
Company Name ...................................................................................................................
Company Address ...............................................................................................................
City, State, Zip Code ...........................................................................................................

**AND**

Home Address .....................................................................................................................
City, State, Zip Code ...........................................................................................................

## Current Program Memberships

| Travel Program | Membership # | Travel Program | Membership # |
|---|---|---|---|
| ............................. | ............................. | ............................. | ............................. |
| ............................. | ............................. | ............................. | ............................. |
| ............................. | ............................. | ............................. | ............................. |

## New Program Enrollments

| | | |
|---|---|---|
| ☐ Air Canada ($20)[1] | ☐ Finnair | ☐ Northwest Airlines |
| ☐ Alaska Airlines | ☐ Hawaiian Air | ☐ Philippine Airlines |
| ☐ All Nippon (ANA) | ☐ Hilton Hotels | ☐ Ramada Hotels |
| ☐ Aloha Airlines | ☐ Holiday Inn ($10)[1] | ☐ Sheraton hotels ($25)[1] |
| ☐ America West | ☐ Hyatt Hotels | ☐ Southwest Airlines |
| ☐ American Airlines | ☐ Japan Air Lines (JAL) | ☐ Stouffer Hotels |
| ☐ British Airways | ☐ Korean Air (KAL) | ☐ TWA |
| ☐ Canadian Airlines | ☐ Marriott Hotels | ☐ United Airlines |
| ☐ China Airways | ☐ MGM Grand Air | ☐ USAir |
| ☐ Continental Airlines | ☐ Midwest Airlines | ☐ Westin |
| ☐ Delta Air Lines | ☐ National Emerald Club ($75)[1] | ☐ Other .......................... |

[1]This is the standard enrollment fee of this program, which will be charged separately to your company.

## Authorization

Because we are acting on both your behalf and the company which pays for your travel, there may be some instances when Frequent Flyer Services will be required to have your authorization to represent you when enrolling in programs, changing an address or the redemption of travel awards earned from employer paid travel.

**I HEREBY GRANT TO FREQUENT FLYER SERVICES, ACTING ON THE AUTHORITY OF MY EMPLOYER, AUTHORIZATION TO ACT AS AN AGENT TO ORDER CORPORATE ENROLLMENTS, ADDRESS CHANGES ON COMPANY ACCOUNTS, AND CORPORATE AWARD REDEMPTION TRANSFERS FOR ME IN WHAT-EVER FREQUENT TRAVELER PROGRAMS DEEMED SUITABLE BY MY EMPLOYER.**

Signature ...............................................................................Date ................................................

**FOR PROGRAM PASSWORD USE ONLY:**
Date of Birth .............................................................................Place of Birth .................................................
Mother's Maiden Name ..........................................Social Security Number .................................................

FFS - 330

# FIGURE 11.3b

programs using their current ID number and actually manage both their personal mileage and the corporate mileage as separate accounts under the same ID number (see Figure 11.3b). This system offers management service to these corporate travelers and maintains their elite-level status within their most-frequented programs. If business travelers are currently enrolled in the programs, and their mileage will remain the property of the corporation, it will be necessary to do an address change on all current travel programs.

Individual computer files are created under the corporate umbrella for posting individual on-going travel program information.

**Phase four.** Phase four is the actual frequent traveler program management phase of the service. The frequent flyer traveler information from each program statement summary received is logged into the computer files of the corresponding individual. Any awards requested by the corporation are also logged, and all award certificates are mailed to the corporate client (see Figure 11.4).

**Phase five.** The last phase consists of management reports that are generated for the travel manager (Figures 11.5a to e).

Mr. Petersen also claims that once certificates are earned through travelers' mileage accounts, companies can use the awards in one of three ways:

1. *Traveler's discretion.* The company takes the award certificate and presents it to a traveler to use on a future business trip. In this case, the use of the award is at the traveler's discretion, but the travel department's database would spot the non-use of the travel certificate. The traveler might then be encouraged to use the certificate on his or her next trip to avoid billing the company for that flight.

Other companies encourage travelers to be creative in maximizing mileage awards. For example, a traveler might forego the use of the certificate on the next trip if he or she was anticipating a costlier trip in the future, which would make better use of the award. In this instance, the travel department would note that the traveler had not used the flight certificate at the next available opportunity, but would also recognize the possibility that the traveler might be opting to maximize the use of the award at a later date.

## REQUEST TO PROCESS EARNED AWARDS

Company Name _____ Date _____

Name of Business Traveler _____

Name of Travel Program Membership # _____

Award Code/Level _____

Deduction _____

Name of Companion Traveler (if applicable) _____

Choice of Partner Awards (if applicable) _____

Additional Comments

*(ALLOW UP TO 4 WEEKS FOR PROCESSING AND DELIVERY OF YOUR CERTIFICATES)*

---

Company Name _____ Date _____

Name of Business Traveler _____

Name of Travel Program Membership # _____

Award Code/Level _____

Deduction _____

Name of Companion Traveler (if applicable) _____

Choice of Partner Awards (if applicable) _____

Additional Comments

*(ALLOW UP TO 4 WEEKS FOR PROCESSING AND DELIVERY OF YOUR CERTIFICATES)*

FFS - 348

## FIGURE 11.4

4715-C Town Center Drive
Colorado Springs, CO
80916-4709

**INDIVIDUAL ACTIVITY STATEMENT**

Service Center
4715-C Town Center Drive
Colorado Springs, CO
80916

| Status | |
| --- | --- |
| statement date | |
| May 31, 1992 | |
| corporate code | |
| ABC-257 | |
| department code | |
| Marketing | |
| service plan | |
| 2 | |
| start date | |
| Dec 28, 1990 | |

Barry, Thomas
ABC Sky Corporation
101 East 52nd Street
Oakland , CA   91560

**Account Status**

| FFS Program Recap | Activity | Old Miles | New Miles |
| --- | --- | --- | --- |
| American #LME1910 | 2,686 | 93,860 | 45,516 |
| Continental #KN183890 | 1,000 | 0 | 36,593 |
| Delta #2088791817 | 4,000 | 0 | 15,000 |
| Midwest #181173536 | 0 | 0 | 5,000 |
| Northwest #346782665 | 3,010 | 0 | 12,395 |
| TWA #81912425 | 0 | 456,720 | 6,465 |
| United #01250162049 | 0 | 0 | 15,182 |
| USAir #833955672 | 0 | 0 | 4,611 |

Please Note:

**Activity Detail**

| Date | Code | Period Activity | Credit | Bonus | Total |
| --- | --- | --- | --- | --- | --- |
| 5 Mar, 91 | DL | DL #0327 Y DFW - COS | 1,000 | | 1,000 |
| 6 Mar, 91 | DL | DL #1511 Y COS - OAK | 1,000 | | 1,000 |
| 28 Mar, 91 | DL | DL #0306 L DFW - MCO | 1,000 | | 1,000 |
| 28 Mar, 91 | DL | DL #0262 L COS - DFW | 1,000 | | 1,000 |
| 27 Feb, 91 | AA | AA #1019 Y SAT - DFW | 593 | | 593 |
| 27 Feb, 91 | AA | AA #0619 Y DFW - COS | 246 | 254 | 500 |
| 2 Mar, 91 | AA | AA #0622 Y COS - DFW | 593 | | 593 |
| 2 Mar, 91 | AA | SH 3 DAYS DFW, TX | | 500 | 500 |
| 2 Mar, 91 | AA | HTZ 3 DAYS DFW, TX | | 500 | 500 |
| 11 Mar, 91 | OP | OP #1232 Y OAK - SFO | 500 | | 500 |
| 12 Mar, 91 | OP | OP #1664 Y SFO - OAK | 500 | | 500 |
| 18 Mar, 91 | NW | NW #0938 F MEM - MIA | 860 | 430 | 1,290 |
| 18 Mar, 91 | NW | 25% MILEAGE BONUS | | 215 | 215 |
| 19 Mar, 91 | NW | NW #0945 F MIA - MEM | 860 | 430 | 1,290 |
| 19 Mar, 91 | NW | 25% MILEAGE BONUS | | 215 | 215 |

FFS-360 (revised June, 1991)

**FIGURE 11.5a**

**Frequent Traveler Program Management Service:** *101 — Attained Program Awards*

**Prepared by:** *Frequent Flyer Services*                    **Report Date:** *July 1, 1992*

**Exclusively For:** *Ms. Deborah Reeves*                    **of:** *ABC Sky Corporation*

## Program Award Totals:

| Award Program | (A)<br>Class<br>Upgrades | (B)<br>Companion<br>Tickets | (C)<br>Coach<br>Tickets | (D)<br>Bus/1st<br>Tickets | (E)<br>Weekend<br>Nights | (F)<br>Airline/Car<br>Coupons | (G)<br>Multiple<br>Nights | (H)<br>Airline<br>Tickets |
|---|---|---|---|---|---|---|---|---|
| Air Canada | 0 | 0 | 0 | 0 | *N/A* | *N/A* | *N/A* | *N/A* |
| America West | 0 | *N/A* | 0 | 0 | *N/A* | *N/A* | *N/A* | *N/A* |
| American | 22 | *N/A* | 8 | 3 | *N/A* | *N/A* | *N/A* | *N/A* |
| Continental | 28 | 16 | 8 | 0 | *N/A* | *N/A* | *N/A* | *N/A* |
| Delta | 12 | *N/A* | 1 | 1 | *N/A* | *N/A* | *N/A* | *N/A* |
| Holiday Inn | *N/A* | *N/A* | *N/A* | *N/A* | 1 | 1 | 0 | 0 |
| Hyatt | *N/A* | *N/A* | *N/A* | *N/A* | 2 | 2 | 0 | 0 |
| Marriott | *N/A* | *N/A* | *N/A* | *N/A* | 4 | 4 | 1 | 0 |
| Northwest | *N/A* | *N/A* | 4 | *N/A* | *N/A* | *N/A* | *N/A* | *N/A* |
| Sheraton | *N/A* | *N/A* | *N/A* | *N/A* | 1 | 1 | 1 | 0 |
| TWA | 3 | *N/A* | 1 | 0 | *N/A* | *N/A* | *N/A* | *N/A* |
| United | 10 | *N/A* | 4 | 1 | *N/A* | *N/A* | *N/A* | *N/A* |
| USAir | 30 | *N/A* | 11 | 0 | *N/A* | *N/A* | *N/A* | *N/A* |
| **TOTALS:** | **117** | **20** | **40** | **6** | **8** | **8** | **2** | **0** |

**FIGURE 11.5b**

**Frequent Traveler Program Management Service:**   *110 — Consolidated Program Analysis*

**Prepared by:**  *Frequent Flyer Services*                    **Report Date:**  *July 1, 1992*

**Exclusively For:**  *Ms. Deborah Reeves*                    **of:**  *ABC Sky Corporation*

**Travel Program:**   *American AAdvantage*

| Name/Dept | YTD Credits | Legs/Stays | AIRLINE AWARDS | | | | HOTEL AWARDS | | | |
|---|---|---|---|---|---|---|---|---|---|---|
| | | | A | B | C | D | E | F | G | H |
| Altemus, S | 47,016 | 37 | 4 | N/A | 2 | 1 | N/A | N/A | N/A | N/A |
| Bertha, L | 8,700 | 10 | 0 | N/A | 0 | 0 | N/A | N/A | N/A | N/A |
| Butler, K | 41,160 | 33 | 4 | N/A | 2 | 1 | N/A | N/A | N/A | N/A |
| Daly, R | 10,914 | 4 | 1 | N/A | 0 | 0 | N/A | N/A | N/A | N/A |
| Dugan, T | 5,700 | 3 | 0 | N/A | 0 | 0 | N/A | N/A | N/A | N/A |
| Hall, H | 39,594 | 18 | 3 | N/A | 1 | 0 | N/A | N/A | N/A | N/A |
| McCullough, M | 8,922 | 7 | 0 | N/A | 0 | 0 | N/A | N/A | N/A | N/A |
| Moffett, M | 19,458 | 5 | 1 | N/A | 0 | 0 | N/A | N/A | N/A | N/A |
| Nye, D | 14,922 | 6 | 1 | N/A | 0 | 0 | N/A | N/A | N/A | N/A |
| O'Grady, P | 11,838 | 13 | 1 | N/A | 0 | 0 | N/A | N/A | N/A | N/A |
| Rooney, J | 4,398 | 5 | 0 | N/A | 0 | 0 | N/A | N/A | N/A | N/A |
| Sutter, D | 63,276 | 56 | 6 | N/A | 3 | 1 | N/A | N/A | N/A | N/A |
| Waldmann, T | 11,400 | 15 | 1 | N/A | 0 | 0 | N/A | N/A | N/A | N/A |
| **Totals - American:** | **287,298** | **212** | **22** | **N/A** | **8** | **3** | **N/A** | **N/A** | **N/A** | **N/A** |

**FIGURE 11.5c**

**Frequent Traveler Program Management Service:**   *210 – Traveler Program Analysis*

**Prepared by:**  *Frequent Flyer Services*                    **Report Date:**  *July 1, 1992*

**Exclusively For:**  *Ms. Deborah Reeves*                    **of:**  *ABC Sky Corporation*

| TRAVELER/Dept Program | YTD Credits | Legs/Stays | \| AIRLINE AWARDS A | B | C | D | \| HOTEL AWARDS E | F | G | H |
|---|---|---|---|---|---|---|---|---|---|---|
| **Altemus, S** | | | | | | | | | | |
| American | 47,016 | 37 | 4 | N/A | 2 | 1 | N/A | N/A | N/A | N/A |
| Continental | 18,744 | 25 | 1 | 1 | 0 | 0 | N/A | N/A | N/A | N/A |
| Delta | 15,492 | 13 | 1 | N/A | 0 | 0 | N/A | N/A | N/A | N/A |
| Hyatt | 2,670 | 5 | N/A | N/A | N/A | N/A | 0 | 0 | 0 | 0 |
| Marriott | 7,410 | 5 | N/A | N/A | N/A | N/A | 0 | 0 | 0 | 0 |
| Northwest | 5,622 | 6 | N/A | N/A | 0 | N/A | N/A | N/A | N/A | N/A |
| Sheraton | 1,440 | 3 | N/A | N/A | N/A | N/A | 0 | 0 | 0 | 0 |
| TWA | 5,394 | 6 | 0 | N/A | 0 | 0 | N/A | N/A | N/A | N/A |
| USAir | 6,750 | 7 | 0 | N/A | 0 | 0 | N/A | N/A | N/A | N/A |
| **Bertha, L** | | | | | | | | | | |
| American | 8,700 | 10 | 0 | N/A | 0 | 0 | N/A | N/A | N/A | N/A |
| Continental | 15,000 | 30 | 1 | 1 | 0 | 0 | N/A | N/A | N/A | N/A |
| Delta | 15,000 | 6 | 1 | N/A | 0 | 0 | N/A | N/A | N/A | N/A |
| Marriott | 18,144 | 12 | N/A | N/A | N/A | N/A | 0 | 0 | 0 | 0 |
| Northwest | 4,500 | 5 | N/A | N/A | 0 | N/A | N/A | N/A | N/A | N/A |
| USAir | 36,840 | 42 | 3 | N/A | 1 | 0 | N/A | N/A | N/A | N/A |
| **Butler, K** | | | | | | | | | | |
| American | 41,160 | 33 | 4 | N/A | 2 | 1 | N/A | N/A | N/A | N/A |
| Continental | 35,832 | 18 | 3 | 2 | 1 | 0 | N/A | N/A | N/A | N/A |
| Marriott | 38,226 | 25 | N/A | N/A | N/A | N/A | 1 | 1 | 0 | 0 |
| **Daly, R** | | | | | | | | | | |
| American | 10,914 | 4 | 1 | N/A | 0 | 0 | N/A | N/A | N/A | N/A |
| Marriott | 7,350 | 5 | N/A | N/A | N/A | N/A | 0 | 0 | 0 | 0 |
| USAir | 17,298 | 11 | 1 | N/A | 0 | 0 | N/A | N/A | N/A | N/A |
| **Dugan, T** | | | | | | | | | | |
| American | 5,700 | 3 | 0 | N/A | 0 | 0 | N/A | N/A | N/A | N/A |
| Continental | 6,000 | 12 | 0 | 0 | 0 | 0 | N/A | N/A | N/A | N/A |
| Delta | 57,000 | 47 | 5 | N/A | 1 | 1 | N/A | N/A | N/A | N/A |
| Hyatt | 10,590 | 19 | N/A | N/A | N/A | N/A | 1 | 1 | 0 | 0 |
| Marriott | 33,618 | 22 | N/A | N/A | N/A | N/A | 1 | 1 | 0 | 0 |
| Northwest | 36,534 | 36 | N/A | N/A | 1 | N/A | N/A | N/A | N/A | N/A |
| USAir | 40,500 | 52 | 4 | N/A | 2 | 0 | N/A | N/A | N/A | N/A |

**FIGURE 11.5d**

**Frequent Traveler Program Management Service:** *310 – Traveler Exception Report*

**Prepared by:** *Frequent Flyer Services*                **Report Date:** *July 1, 1992*

**Exclusively For:** *Ms. Deborah Reeves*                **of:** *ABC Sky Corporation*

## Missing Credits:

| Name/Date | Citypair | Program | Airline | Hotel | Car | Total |
|-----------|----------|---------|---------|-------|-----|-------|
| **Acker, J** | | | | | | |
| 5/10/90 | ATL/IAD | DL | 1,000 | MAR -1,000 | AVS -1,000 | 3,000 |
| 5/12/90 | IAD/ATL | DL | 1,000 | 0 | 0 | 1,000 |
| 5/22/90 | CLE/PIT | CO | 500 | MAR -1,000 | NTL -500 | 2,000 |
| 5/22/90 | PIT/ATL | CO | 528 | 500 | 500 | 1,528 |
| 5/26/90 | ATL/CLE | AA | 928 | 0 | 0 | 928 |
| **Beyers, R** | | | | | | |
| 5/09/90 | ATL/YUL | DL | 1,002 | HYT -1,000 | NTL -1,000 | 3,002 |
| 5/12/90 | YUL/BDL | DL | 1,000 | 0 | 0 | 1,000 |
| 5/12/90 | BDL/ATL | DL | 1,000 | 0 | 0 | 1,000 |
| **Caldwell, N** | | | | | | |
| 5/06/90 | BNA/YYZ | DL | 1,000 | 0 | NTL -1,000 | 2,000 |
| 5/06/90 | YYZ/BNA | DL | 1,000 | 0 | 0 | 1,000 |
| **Dugan, S** | | | | | | |
| 5/19/90 | ACY/PHL | US | 750 | 0 | HTZ -500 | 1,250 |
| **Fairfield, T** | | | | | | |
| 5/2/90 | ATL/CVG | DL | 1,000 | MAR -1,000 | NTL -1,000 | 3,000 |
| 5/2/90 | CVG/GRR | DL | 1,000 | 0 | 0 | 1,000 |
| 5/2/90 | Grand Rapids | MAR | DL 2,313 | 9,250 | 0 | 11,563 |
| 5/12/90 | GRR/DTW | NW | 750 | RAD -500 | BGT -500 | 1,750 |
| 5/19/90 | DTW/ATL | NW | 750 | 0 | 0 | 750 |
| **Grady, G** | | | | | | |
| 5/16/90 | ATL/DCA | DL | 1,000 | 0 | 0 | 1,000 |
| 5/16/90 | DCA/ATL | DL | 1,000 | 0 | 0 | 1,000 |
| **Kelp, B** | | | | | | |
| 5/09/90 | ATL/YUL | DL | 1,000 | HYT -1,000 | 0 | 2,000 |
| 5/12/90 | YUL/BDL | DL | 1,000 | 0 | 0 | 1,000 |
| 5/12/90 | BDL/ATL | DL | 1,000 | 0 | 0 | 1,000 |

310 - 1

# FIGURE 11.5e

2. *Travel department decision.* At companies in which travel reservations are made through an internal travel department, the company may exercise greater influence in the use of flight certificates. In this case, the travel department notes the receipt of a free travel award, monitors its expiration date, and applies the award certificate toward the traveler's next trip or a future trip, depending on anticipated travel plans. The use of the award may not be noticed by the traveler because the travel department handles the billing of travel and/or the application of flight certificates for company travel.

3. *Transfer of awards.* Another variation on the travel department's control over the award-redemption process involves transferring awards. Some airline frequent flyer award programs allow transfer of awards from one person to another. In such cases, award certificates are sent to the traveler whose account earned the free travel so that the traveler can sign off on the award for use on another employee's future trip. In this case, the company uses frequent flyer reports and an employee's travel history to maximize usage of company-owned awards.

Runzheimer comments, "The company that centralizes award usage through its travel department is better able to maximize award usage than a company that leaves award usage up to individual travelers. However, the clerical expenses associated with data entry, organization, and monitoring of award certificate expiration dates may not be cost-effective. Moreover, program rules constantly change and someone on staff must become a 'program expert' to ensure that the greatest value is gained and awards are used cost-effectively."

Runzheimer comments further that even if a company decides to do nothing, it should recognize and quantify the dollar value of award benefits enjoyed by its frequent flyers. When the bottom line gets squeezed and management seriously considers downsizing, or when management reacts to an eroding profit-sharing plan, top executives should be in a position to decide whether claiming awards makes sense. Capturing frequent flyer awards does, in fact, reduce and contain costs; that cannot be disputed. The dilemma is whether or not to confront the morale issue that comes with the decision to capture travelers' awards.

## CASE STUDY: WHIRLPOOL

Whirlpool Corporation, with its corporate headquarters in Benton Harbor, Michigan, is the world's largest manufacturer of major home appliances. Recently, Cary Marsh, director of the Whirlpool Business Travel Center and Judy Steinke, manager of commercial travel and NBTA member, began a frequent flyer program for their employees called Winning Choices. The purpose of this program is to get the frequent traveler to use some of his or her surplus miles for business flights.

The company's research showed that approximately 75 percent of frequent flyer miles are never redeemed. Some travelers never accumulate enough miles to redeem; some employees travel so much that they do not want to fly on their vacations; and others accumulate too many miles to ever use. Because many airlines are now putting expiration dates on their miles, a lot of free travel is at risk.

The objective of the Whirlpool program is to reduce corporate travel expense while offering employees flexibility and options. A six-month trial voluntary program that included 2,800 employees was put together. These employees may use frequent flyer certificates for business travel and can earn awards based on 50 percent of the lowest nonpenalty fare.

Whereas some corporate frequent flyer programs give the traveler cash, the Whirlpool program uses merchandise awards. The award program was suggested and put together by Maritz Motivation Corporation in St. Louis.

The mechanics of redemption are fairly straightforward and simple. The participant completes an expense report and a frequent flyer redemption authorization form and submits them to his or her supervisor. The supervisor approves and returns the authorization form and a copy of the itinerary to the employee. The traveler then submits this to the Maritz Travel Company, who handles the redemption. Maritz issues award credit vouchers on a monthly basis, which the traveler can use to select merchandise from the awards catalog. The awards voucher is returned with the order for merchandise.

Since the program is new, a communications plan was developed that included an announcement letter and an insert in a weekly company newsletter. This was followed by a letter to corporate officers, which was, in turn, followed by:

1. A reminder in the company newsletter two weeks after the initial communication.
2. Publication of the awards catalog and program rules.
3. Two-month and four-month mailers to respondents who requested the awards catalog and program rules.

## TRAVEL MANAGEMENT TIPS

- For the business traveler who passes airfare costs along to his or her employer, the quest for frequent flyer awards often takes precedence over shopping for the most economical airfares.
- The primary purpose common to all frequent flyer programs is to build customer loyalty by rewarding individual travelers who concentrate their travel with one airline.

## Chapter Twelve

# Managing Hotel Programs

H otels large and small face the never ending challenge of placing potential customers in rooms at prices acceptable to both customer and hotel. This is as much a marketing as a systems challenge, as the modern travel industry finds it impossible to separate purely management information systems (MISs) or accounting functions from revenue-producing or marketing functions. This is partly because of the whole industry's dependence upon automation and systems, and partly because the major CRSs have been positioned as distribution tools or systems, thereby inexorably linking their operating and systems characteristics to broader marketing concerns.

The hotel must effectively communicate its message to a large potential customer pool, where individual customers will want to deal through a variety of intermediaries:

1. Travel agents.
2. Telephone reservation centers.
3. Computerized on-line travel reservation services.
4. Airlines.
5. Tourist and convention bureaus.
6. Meeting planners.
7. Business travel departments.

Each intermediary has specific reservation-handling and information requirements that differ in complexity and composition. On-line travel reservation systems, for example, must be planned to accommodate novice users who are interested mainly in getting to price and availability quickly, while travel agents require much more descriptive detail on hotel property location and amenities.

Since the inception of automation in the hotel industry, various (often conflicting) systems solutions have been developed to handle differing reservation and information requirements. No single systems solution has been developed that effectively meets all user-group requirements (nor is one contemplated).

## HOTEL RESERVATIONS AND HOTEL MARKETING

Effective use of internal and external distribution systems is essential to any hotel, large or small, in today's marketplace. Since about 1984, most large hotel franchises and systems have actively sought to increase proportionate room-nights booked through existing, external distribution systems, notably CRSs. This is because these systems enjoy wide geographic point-of-sale placement throughout the retail (end customer-oriented) distribution system; in the case of CRSs, the systems largely define the distribution system. The logic here is that travel agencies identify with a CRS. The agency's work flow, compensation and cost structure, and marketing affiliations are each determined or at least highly influenced by what CRS is used by the agency.

This ongoing drive for greater product distribution received new emphasis in the early 1990s. The hotel industry had been financially practical because real estate prices for well-placed properties could be expected to appreciate year to year. Operating the physical facility was almost incidental to many properties.

With the general economic slowdown of the 1990s, and particularly with real estate prices failing to appreciate rapidly enough to support most hotels, financial support through operations became critical, which meant using whatever methods were available to reach as many customers as efficiently as possible. This situation was further complicated by significant overcapacity in many markets—another product of the 1980s hotel expansion.

Many hotel chains and systems came to regard third-party distribution as a cost-effective method of receiving reservations, a point disputed by major hotel chains where the central management facility's primary function is reservation acceptance and processing. As the cost of booking through a CRS continues to increase (approximately $3.00 to $4.00 per reservation), the implications of ever increasing CRS dependence come more into question—not to mention the negative strategic implications of dependence on CRS booking channels.

## IMPLICATIONS FOR THE FUTURE

Hotel system reservation and property management automation is undergoing transition, as the demands of the industry for more accurate and broader data force change into areas that previously were ignored or neglected. Several major hotel systems and independent service providers have extensive modernization programs underway that promise to move hotel automation into the next century.

Most hotel vendors will continue to use reservation and information management technology that is greatly inferior to that enjoyed by the travel industry's principal information suppliers—the CRSs. It is also questionable whether these systems will meet the hotel vendors' internal needs for increasingly more accurate and sophisticated reservation management, database control, and MIS.

System architectures and management techniques employed by the hotel industry must change rapidly if true marketing independence is to be enjoyed over the long term. Automation represents a serious point of competitive weakness, both in:

1. Competition between hotel chains and systems for customer stays.
2. Competition for customer access within the hotel industry and between the hotel industry as a whole and the airline CRS.

Data access and interpretation will be critical points of differentiation between vendors that will be able to address the marketing and product distribution challenges they now face and between those that will depend upon third parties for distribution systems of inventory management and who, therefore, relegated to following an undifferentiated course set by others.

## UNDERSTANDING HOTEL AUTOMATION

Although both hotel automation systems and airline CRSs manage reservations, and the travel industry is conditioned to think of reservations as if describing a condition or process that operates fundamentally the same throughout all product areas, airline system functionality and general system concepts differ significantly from those employed by most hotel reservation systems. These differences are important to an understanding of the hotel reservation process, its intrinsic limitations, and product-development courses in progress or likely to be pursued by major companies within the hotel industry.

## HOTEL RESERVATION CONCEPTS

Hotel inventory can be managed by a number of systems. Each imposes its peculiar set of functions and limitations on the reservation process and may also function in connection with other systems that likewise impose a different set of limitations. It is important to understand them in detail.

1. A central reservation processor operated by a hotel chain or system, or by a third-party reservation service, usually as part of a central reservation office (CRO).

Reservations management and operation are among the most important activities for any hotel. They are usually among the key services provided by a centrally managed hotel chain, group, or franchise system. The CRO consists of a reservations inventory environment, usually (but not always) a computerized database; the communications interfaces necessary to link that database with all reservation intermediary systems with which the hotel group desires to communicate; and the human operators necessary to staff telephones, open mail, read Telex messages and telegrams, and otherwise oversee the nonautomated interfaces with the reservation database.

In this sense, the term "interface" describes methods, both automated and manual, of interfacing with a computerized database in ways that are consistent with appropriate management and maintenance of that database and that also meet customer or user requirements. Users differ from customers in that reservation intermediaries, such as travel agents, are users but not ultimate customers.

The CRO is responsible for maintaining centralized database and reservation relationships with third-party reservation intermediaries, such as CRSs, on-line computer systems, and sometimes hotel representation services, on behalf of participating properties. These relationships are managed centrally because they are too complex and expensive for individual hotel properties to manage. The CRO also negotiates booking fees with these intermediaries on behalf of its hotels.

CRS traffic is usually routed to the CRO system through the special networks. These are packet-switched data communication systems developed to handle reservations and other communication traffic between airlines. Packet-switching involves electronically routing fixed format, addressed, data packets from one network user to another. Their advantage is that a packet occupies a network channel only for the duration of its transmission time, after which the channel is available for transmission of other data packets. Hotel reservation messages using these networks are encoded so as to carry information peculiar to hotels, such as room types, but they are very similar to airline reservation messages.

Some direct links between CRSs and the various CRO processors have been developed in recent years. These upgrade the speed, capacity, and integrity of hotel reservation messages flowing between a CRS and a CRO processor. While highly desirable and efficient, they are expensive and resource-intense to build for both CRS and CRO.

In some large hotel networks, the central system functions simply are a message switch to route reservation requests from customers or intermediaries to individual properties. In this sense the system serves as a reservation database, in that records of all reservation requests made through facilities that have access to the database are recorded, but it does not serve to control actual inventory.

Hotel inventory is maintained throughout the numerous properties comprising the physical hotel network rather than in one central database and is, therefore, subject to varying interpretation at each point.

2. Local or regional reservation centers that may be subservient to a central processing facility or that may operate independently.

Many hotel groups operate worldwide systems that are extremely difficult and expensive to control from a single central CRO, given the ever-present manual component of the reservation processing facility. Travelers in Europe, for example, would find it difficult and expensive to call the United States to make reservations for hotels within Europe. Even if the hotel group absorbed the telecommunications cost, the US-based CRO must staff for incoming European telephone calls during what are off-hours in the US. Language and cultural barriers would also be present.

Major international hotel groups find it more practical to operate reservation centers that directly support their major markets outside the US. While this answers the operational challenges just named, it still imposes other difficulties in that either all such local or regional centers must use the same database, which imposes significant telecommunications and database maintenance costs, or else a way must be developed to bring a number of databases into consistency.

For example, travelers originating in Germany for a US-based hotel group might require reservations for Seattle. If German travelers called a more accessible regional facility for reservations, that facility would advise a US facility that a room had been sold. This can be done in several ways:

A. The regional facility can maintain its own block or room allocation and sell against these rooms whenever its travelers require reservations. This is rarely done.

B. The regional facility can operate under a sell/no sell agreement. This means that it will sell rooms until it is told to stop. While a common practice, this procedure complicates the reservation process (some other database must be sending no-sell messages to any regional facilities constantly).

C. A central database can be maintained that has real-time links to all regional facilities, where a sell automatically decrements the same inventory database used by everyone worldwide who might want a room at any hotel belonging to the group. Although clearly the most efficient method, central databases with true decrementing inventory management are rare.

3. A local property management system (PMS) that controls reservations and other management functions at a specific hotel (may also be a manual process).

Hotel management tends to be very decentralized, even if a central chain or group affiliation exists. This is partly because the franchise system, which is used by most major hotel chains, encourages entrepreneurial spirit and independence. Further, hotel groups that technically do not franchise may be little more than cooperatives, wherein the members associate to receive the benefit of a common brand and pooled advertising, but few central support services.

This pervasive management looseness has database and reservation-management implications, as local hotel property managers often have reservation management goals that differ from those of a CRO. The property manager is responsible first and foremost for maintaining and boosting occupancy levels—the percentage of rooms occupied on any given night.

As a second priority, the manager must also maintain and boost per-room yield, but this is a much lower priority than occupancy because hotel operations have high fixed costs. For example, basic hotel pricing usually specifies a rack rate as a baseline—other commercial or promotional rates are discounts from the rack rate. A $100 rack rate at 60 percent occupancy generates less cash flow than a $90 discount rate at 75 percent occupancy. Short-term revenue-based thinking, therefore, says it is better to diminish yield to fill more rooms. In the property manager's mind, it is often better to sell rooms at almost any price than to let them go empty.

The CRO, on the other hand, is concerned with having its reservations honored by participating hotels and with the CRS relationships it administers. Its management wants as true a picture of individual property availability as possible, and is not particularly concerned with the rates any hotel is charging or with any other operational problems a hotel might have.

The property manager must try to reconcile these objectives with the necessity of dealing with less-than-perfect databases, data communications, and operational procedures—all while keeping customers happy. Among the worst things that can happen in a hotel is overselling—travelers arrive without any rooms available. The fear of having to turn good business away leads some property managers to hold back rooms for special situations, just in case they might be needed, as almost any hotel database gives less than a 100 percent accurate picture of true room availability. This is why it is sometimes possible to call a hotel directly and find a room available, when a CRS and even a call to a CRO indicates the property is full.

PMSs differ greatly both as to basic architecture and functionality, as there are over 400 competing vendors, and no single product dominates the market or significantly influences overall design. They typically provide:

A. A daily reservations management environment.
B. A billing and customer invoice generation system.
C. Other accounting and MIS features, depending upon the particular design employed, such as accounts payable, check writing, general ledger, payroll, and travel agency commission generation.

It is relatively rare to find a PMS interfaced or directly connected to the hotel system's central reservation processor, although in some large multinational hotel systems this is not uncommon and constitutes a design objective.

Not all hotels use a PMS; many operate entirely manually or use such a rudimentary PMS that no true reservation or accounting database exists.

4. A hotel reservation company that may manage part of a hotel's inventory and that services a typically limited customer group (usually travel agents).

Representation companies are essentially for-hire CROs, performing all the reservation-handling and database-maintenance functions of the CRO and charging fees for their services. Some representation services maintain CRS communications. Most do not accept calls from the general public, although they are configured as telephone reservation centers to handle agency bookings.

Most hotels contract with representation services directly, bypassing any central chain or CRS involvement. These services are essentially marketing tools that make reservations easier for the travel trade, while providing some marketing and promotion services. Since, by definition, most representatives serve a limited market and are primarily marketing and operational expediencies, they manage only a subset of hotel availability, typically operating from room blocks and reporting inventory sold on a daily basis.

## HOTEL RESERVATION HANDLING

Hotel reservation management faces several general challenges:

1. *Price.* The reservation process must be designed and managed so as to support the property's desire to sell rooms at the highest sustainable rate, while recognizing that a variety of discounts must be imposed in order to achieve optimal occupancy levels.

2. *Cost.* Regardless of the functionality of the reservation process, whether it is managed by a CRO or a PMS or booked through a CRS, bookings, charges, and cancellations must be delivered cost-effectively, through a process that provides cost escalation consistent with what the hotel can reasonably be expected to support over time.

3. *Certainty.* Reservations are not meaningful unless they will be honored as booked—respecting room availability and price. Trade confidence is severely undermined when either factor is not honored.

   CRS reservation agreements usually attempt to address both problems contractually. By the terms of their CRS agreements, hotels are not permitted to reject reservations made through the CRS, and must honor reservations at or below the price quoted in a CRS reservation. Most hotels return confirmation numbers, which are electronically generated transaction identifiers, to a CRS once a reservation has successfully reached the hotel's central database. Travelers and agents view these as verification that a valid reservation exists for a traveler's stay, but in practice, even this process is not infallible, as receipt of a confirmation number does not guarantee that the hotel's PMS actually received a valid reservation or that a room will be available upon the traveler's arrival.

   Contracts may reduce the number of electronic reject messages a travel agency receives through the CRS, but do nothing to address fundamental data-integrity and communication-reliability problems. Reservation certainty is among the most difficult data challenges facing the lodging industry.

4. *Follow-up.* This involves accurately identifying the source of a reservation so that an agency commission may be paid, if applicable, and researching irregularities and disputes. The ideal hotel system must have an accessible and flexible database to accommodate more than basic reservation confirmation.

When a customer desires a hotel reservation, either a travel agency or the vendor's telephone reservation center must be contacted, unless the traveler contacts the individual hotel directly. If a CRO is used, a reservationist responds to the customer's queries based upon information displayed on a computer terminal. Rooms available for sale usually comprise several categories, and seasonal rate periods are applicable to any given property.

The number of rooms may not be displayed if the central system operates on a sell/no-sell basis, a common practice in older hotel systems. All rooms are indicated as available for sale in the system and may be reserved until a predetermined cutoff point is reached. Thereafter, no-sell messages, applicable to specific room types and dates, are generated by the property and passed to the central system, thus closing available dates and rates from display when central availability requests are processed.

Under this system, which applies to many large hotel networks, availability is determined purely by the individual property, where it may be maintained using a PMS or held manually. When the property's reservation center establishes that no more space should be made available to the CRO, a decision which may be influenced by factors apart from the actual number of individual reservations held, a no-sell condition is created.

Many central reservation systems use large and relatively powerful computers because they must support hundreds of reservation terminals, each conceivably with concurrent transactions in progress, as well as numerous simultaneous communications links, not because they are managing a complex and resource-intense database application, as with a CRS.

## HOTEL INVENTORY SYSTEMS

In certain large hotel systems, central inventory management is practiced, and reservations deplete available rooms as they are processed. Even in these systems, however, variances between PMS-level inventory and the CRO system continue to exist, although the degree of variance is less than in systems where a central database does not exist.

This is because of the combinations of complex franchise, ownership, and property management relationships that most large hotel groups experience.

## RESERVATION PROCESSING

If a rate and a date show as available to sell in the central system, a reservation is processed, to which a computer-generated confirmation number is usually attached. Upon consummation of the reservation, a message is transmitted to the property in question with information that the local guest-information database should be updated.

These messages are communicated using almost every conceivable type of transmission technology, often varying within the same hotel network, depending upon the sophistication of the property's PMS, its physical distance from the central system, and the reliability of the communications media available to the property.

While a PMS may be linked using real-time, dedicated high-speed data communication circuits, most properties receive batch transmissions periodically. These may be transmitted using technology no more advanced than the teletype, or even by cablegram, necessitating manual reentry into the PMS upon receipt.

CRS-based reservation requests are similarly processed. Travel agency or other CRS-user queries are managed based upon availability information reflected by the CRS's hotel database. This represents yet another level of availability interpretation, as CRS hotel availability is maintained exclusively on a sell/no-sell basis separate and apart from any hotel system databases, and it usually requires positive action to be updated by the central system, which itself is often maintained by individual properties—all with varying degrees of accuracy.

CRS hotel displays also differ greatly as to depth and quality of information, reliability of data transmission, and ease of use. Whereas a CRS hotel database might display five rates and room-type categories, the hotel's own system may manage 15 or more, which means that some management decision must be made by the hotel vendor to determine which room rates will be displayed to the CRS user—which may or may not be compatible with the needs of the traveler. When a no-sell or closed situation exists at the central hotel reservation system, the CRS display for that property is updated so that the closed rate/room type is no longer displayed. If cancellations ensue and the rate again becomes available, the CRS display is rarely opened again. Further, where inventory is maintained and managed at the property level, it is doubtful that the central reservation system display will again be opened for the rate in question, as the hotel may prefer to accommodate local reservations or guests contacting the property directly instead.

The CRS generates a standard airline-type message to the central system, using principally the ARINC or SITA packet networks, wherein reservations typically drop to a single queue or a small group of queues, thereby minimizing the CRS's impact on conceivably hundreds of terminals generating simultaneous reservation requests. CRS-based bookings, therefore, are generally a less resource-intense process for the hotel vendor than are telephone queries.

After the CRS booking is received by the hotel reservation system, its processing may take any of several paths, based on its composition and the nature of the computerized systems involved on each side of the transaction. Although the hotel would ideally prefer to have all CRS bookings processed automatically as they reach the top of the CRS queue, in practice this is never the case. Agent errors, omission of required data, or basic incompatibility of the hotel system with the CRS create rejects which must be handled manually by agents at the hotel's reservation center.

A typical average reject rate for a large hotel system is 25 to 35 percent of all CRS bookings. Some CRS messages are wholly incompatible with certain hotel systems, creating a 100 percent reject rate, although rejects more typically occur because of incomplete or incorrect data provided by the CRS booking agent.

Compatibility varies greatly between CRSs and hotel reservation systems. Computer programs designed to be particularly sensitive to areas such as incorrectly formatted reservation guarantee information may cause high reject rates, but they also protect customers by catching computer difficulties before they result in incorrect or canceled reservations.

Compatibility problems also produce less-than-optimal booking choices for CRS users. If the CRO is not prepared to accept a high percentage of reject transmissions, specific properties may not be included in the CRS at all, or the number of bookable properties for the chain as a whole may be circumscribed to a manageable level.

## HOTEL SYSTEM CONFIGURATIONS

The lodging industry represents the most under-automated segment of the travel industry. Not only are many operations supported manually, but existing systems and processes represent inferior or outmoded technology. This is true for both hardware and software, as well as for communications and data transmission.

Large multinational hotel systems, which are almost exclusively based upon large-scale IBM mainframe central systems architecture, may employ hardware of comparatively recent vintage, such as IBM's 4300 processor series, which was introduced in the early 1980s. Software for these systems, by comparison, often originates with core programs that date back 15 or 20 years and can be considered primitive by current standards.

The management of hotel inventory, particularly the amount of control individual property managers have over all aspects of the process, has not changed materially since the origins of centralized hotel systems and usually does not reflect contemporary standards as to yield management and database control.

These limitations, together with communications and automated processing deficiencies, limit the ability of most hotel networks to leverage existing CRS-based travel agency distribution effectively. The positioning of current CRSs as principally airline distribution tools limits a hotel's ability to display the full range of its products and create marketing relationships with its distributors that benefit the hotel network. The uncertainties of hotel inventory management make it unclear what types of new and aggressive marketing relationships a hotel chain could actually deliver to its distributors.

Airline reservation systems trace their beginnings back 20 years, but they have evolved along significantly different lines than have most hotel systems. Most CRS software originated with PARS. PARS-type transactions are transaction-oriented, in that they employ conventions specifically designed to handle interactive reservation requests that involve frequent database queries, information entry, information retrieval, and information updating. The airline transaction system (TPF) operates in a multiprogramming environment so as to permit sharing of the same machine resources while making the individual programs available to the system more or less simultaneously. Airline systems also divide specific tasks, or sets of related tasks, across multiple processors that are coordinated in their actions and responses.

While airline reservations systems are comparatively difficult to maintain, and they impose some undesirable limitations upon programmers and developers, they succeed very well in meeting user needs for rapid availability of information, generally within a few seconds, from a database containing millions of individual records and information fields. PARS/TPF-type programming environments almost universally dictate a large, centrally managed, tightly controlled processor array, rather than true distributed processing techniques, whereby independently functional elements of the overall system are segmented to discrete processors, often at remote locations, that synchronize their actions and responses through peer-to-peer or master-slave communication relationships.

Hotel systems, although they involve numerous transactions, frequently employ less-robust and less-flexible technology than that in use by airlines. An example would be the Customer Information Control System (CICS), in use by some segments of the hotel industry, which is an interface method between a computer's general operating system and application programs developed principally by the user. CICS programs manage terminal interaction with a central processor database and permit efficient file management, but are not as dynamic at high transaction volumes as are TPF systems—although they do afford somewhat greater flexibility and generally employ more mainstream programming and development technologies. Some large hotel processors employ hybrids or variants of TPF-based protocols in an attempt to compensate for some of their undesirable characteristics.

## THE MYTH OF THE AVAILABLE ROOM

Few processes involving the delivery of customer commodities or services within the travel industry are as inexact as reserving a hotel room. Depending upon the method used to transmit the reservation request and the physical location of the person managing the transaction, as many as four interpretations of availability may affect a single room reservation, all of which may easily disagree as to the status of the property. This is why some travel agencies have adopted reservation procedures that call for reservation verification directly with the property for all or part of their customers. Usually this practice is confined to VIP accounts or special circumstances, such as last-minute booking or a situation in which a central reservations office cannot confirm space. Most agents have learned to check with the hotel anyway if a priority request is involved. Others compensate for the imagined or actual unreliability of most hotel booking systems by telephoning or telexing each hotel reservation direct to the property, irrespective of the circumstances surrounding the customer's request.

The reader should have a good knowledge of hotel automation and how this can affect the traveler. Few things are more frustrating to a tired business traveler than to go to a hotel and present a confirmation number, only to find that the hotel has no record of his or her reservation. It is important to know that some hotels are promising items such as "last room availability," which is simply not available. Information that can be used by the travel manager to negotiate better rates will now be presented.

## HOTEL YIELD MANAGEMENT

According to Jack Ferguson, national sales manager for Guest Quarters All Suites, "Yield management is a proven technique within the hotel industry to maximize revenues. It involves applying basic economic principles to pricing and controlling the hotel's room inventory—by adjusting rates in response to rooms booked for future arrival dates. If you can understand the concept of lowering prices to stimulate sales when demand is weak—then raising prices or limiting the number of lower-rated rooms in response to heavy demand should also be easy to understand."

Ferguson continues by stating that yield management is not a systematic approach to abusing customers, as many meeting-planning professionals believe. The practice simply attempts to bring hotel room pricing into alignment with actual market forces. Ferguson suggests that you think of it as a game in which all players can win. The harried business traveler finds a room on short notice for a peak busy night, the vacation traveler finds a time when deep discounts are available, and the hotel manager can achieve both higher occupancy and higher average rates.

The way hotel rooms have traditionally been priced considered just about everything except the customer's willingness to pay. At one time, the rule of thumb was to charge $1 for each $1,000 in construction costs. Other methods utilized to achieve a hotel's desired result include, return on investment, or break-even analysis plus a profit percentage. Those methods allow the hotel to back into price and occupancy goals.

The mechanics of yield management are approximately the same for hotels and airlines. Business bookings tend to be concentrated in the days immediately before a trip.

Jack Ferguson offers the following illustration to show the benefits to a hotel from using yield management:

Consider a 100-room hotel with the following typical market segments:

| | Number of Rooms | Average Daily Rate (ADR) |
|---|---|---|
| Transient | 20 | $100 |
| Government | 20 | $ 60 |
| Contract | 20 | $ 75 |
| Corporate | 20 | $ 80 |
| Group | 20 | $ 70 |
| TOTALS | 100 | $ 77 (ADR) |

If the manager knows in advance that there will be pressure in the marketplace because of a convention in town, he or she will change the room configuration in the following manner:

|  | Number of Rooms | Average Daily Rate (ADR) |
|---|---|---|
| Transient | 30 | $100 |
| Government | 0 | |
| Contract | 20 | $ 75 |
| Corporate | 40 | $ 80 |
| Group | 10 | $ 70 |
| TOTALS | 100 | $ 84 (ADR) |

When the lower rated rooms were closed out, the average daily rate rose by 9 percent. Ferguson comments, "Yield management is not a function of the need to produce profit but the basic economic premise of supply and demand." Ferguson offers the following example to illustrate what yield management can mean to a hotel property's bottom line:

For a conservative example, imagine a 250-room hotel with an average occupancy of 65 percent at $55 per night. Assume that the yield-management system increases their average occupancy by 1/4 percent and their average rate by only $2.40.

| | |
|---|---|
| Number of rooms | 250 |
| 365 days/year | × 365 |
| Potential rooms nights per year | 91,250 |
| Average occupancy percentage | × 65% |
| Average annual room nights | 59,313 |
| ADR-related increase | × $2.40 |
| Increased rate revenue | $142,351 |
| Average annual room nights | 59,313 |
| Occupancy-related increase | × 0.25% |
| Increases in annual room nights | 148 |
| Current ADR of $55.00 + $2.40 | × $57.40 |
| Increased occupancy revenue | $8,495 |
| TOTAL ANNUAL INCREASE IN YIELD | $150,846 |

## HOTEL SEGMENTATION

Generally, hotels can be classified into six categories:

1. Luxury.
2. Full service/upscale.
3. Moderately-priced.
4. No frills/economy.
5. Residential/extended-stay.
6. All-suite.

One of the better known hotel segmenters is Choice Hotels International. Choice has properties ranging from budget hotels to luxury hotels. Their brand names include:

1. Friendship Inns.
2. Econo Lodges.
3. Rodeway Inns.
4. Sleep Inns.
5. Comfort Inns.
6. Comfort Suites.
7. Quality Inns & Hotels.
8. Quality Suites.
9. Clarion Hotels and Resorts.
10. Clarion Carriage House Inns.
11. Clarion Suites.

## LUXURY HOTELS

Personalized service and attention to detail are the hallmarks of this hotel category. At a luxury hotel you will be provided with many guest services, such as terry-cloth robes, shoe shines, fruit baskets, and champagne or candy on arrival. Staying at a luxury hotel can be an important part of what makes up a business traveler's image. According to the Marriott Business Travel Institute, the traveler who stays at a luxury hotel can also expect the following:

1. *Serious dining.* Restaurants in luxury hotels may be among the best in the city, complete with fine china and crystal.

Of course, there is usually a more casual option, also serving high-quality food.

2. *In-room business centers.* Privacy is paramount at a certain level of doing business, and these hotels often provide fax machines, multiline phones, and other high-tech necessities in guest rooms.

3. *Personal guest files.* The guest's preferences are kept on file, from the type of pillow preferred to favorite beverages for the minibar, and these are delivered before the visit.

4. *24-hour valet and maid service.* A suit may be mended in the middle of the night. One-hour clothes pressing is available. Suitcases are unpacked.

5. *Health clubs.* An on-premises health club or temporary membership in a nearby club.

6. *Entertainment.* In-room VCR and movie-rental services.

The prices for luxury hotels can range from $145 to $365+ for a single occupancy per night.

## FULL-SERVICE/UPSCALE HOTELS

Most business travelers have experience with full-service/upscale hotels. According to a recent Marriott Business Travel Institute survey, these are among the most frequently recognized hotel types among business travelers. These hotels are used by a wide range of travelers, from vacationing families to conventioneers to business people. They are generally located in downtown, suburban, airport, and increasingly in resort locations.

The full-service hotel is known for offering:

1. Special corporate rates.
2. Frequent-stay programs.
3. Concierge floors.
4. Business centers.
5. Meeting space.
6. Exercise/health club facilities.
7. Guest services.
8. In-room business technology.

This category of hotel has rooms in the $95 to $200+ range for a single occupancy per night. The full-service hotel has everything a business traveler needs in terms of choice of restaurants, meeting space, accessible business centers, and concierge floors. If your meeting or seminar is being held in a full-service hotel, it may save commuting time and money to have attendees stay at that hotel despite higher room costs. The concierge floor is a special section of the hotel—usually one or more floors—set aside for the business traveler. Rooms run about $20 more per night than those on a standard floor. That buys such business services as fax machines, phones with teleconferencing, telexes, personal computers, multiline phones, speaker phones, secretarial services, and photocopiers. Extra services may include separate check-in and checkout, upgraded guest rooms with VIP amenities and appliances, and lounges offering complimentary breakfasts and late-day snacks and beverages. These floors offer a high level of privacy and are usually accessible only by a special elevator key.

## MID-PRICED HOTELS

For reasons of cost and convenience, these hotels are the most popular choices for business travelers. They are available in every city and are ideal for those on a budget or those who require only basic services.

According to the Marriott Business Traveler Institute, mid-priced hotels are difficult to pinpoint as far as amenities and services are concerned. Some of the mid-priced hotels are just a step up from their economy counterparts, others just a step down from full-service.

The mid-priced hotels usually offer a convenient location, food and beverage operations, video in-room, business centers, and meeting space. The prices for a mid-priced hotel range from $45 to $100+.

These hotels are excellent for short stays or when most of the time will be spent outside the room. This class of hotel is also good for budget watchers who need only basic services such as a clean room. The overall range of services offered by the mid-range hotels is very wide, and often it is best to call ahead of time.

## ECONOMY HOTELS

More and more corporations have looked to the use of economy and limited-service hotels to reduce travel budgets. Prices at these hotels run from about $25 a night for a bed, shower, and telephone to hotels that offer some of the amenities associated with full-service hotels.

These hotels appeal to business travelers on a per diem or to salespeople seeking to take advantage of a good price. This segment markets itself as the cost-conscious lodging alternative by combining consistent service and a clean room with exceptional value.

It is not wise to expect an economy hotel to have restaurants on the premises, although there are usually some nearby. Economy hotels also seldom have meeting rooms or fancy lobbies.

## RESIDENTIAL-STYLE/EXTENDED-STAY HOTELS

The extended-stay hotel is the newest segment of the hotel industry and is less familiar to many business travelers and planners. The key to their appeal is that they are designed for the business traveler who needs to stay in one place for a week or longer.

The typical guest stays more than 10 consecutive nights because he or she is being relocated to a new city, is on temporary assignment, or is attending a training meeting. Because guests may spend months at one of these properties, they strive to create a homelike environment. For example, the general manager might invite guests to a barbecue. As for the corporate budget, rates almost always decrease after five or six days and decrease again after longer periods of time.

Generally, extended-stay hotels offer the following services: complimentary continental breakfast and newspaper, separate living and sleeping areas, full-service kitchen, limited business services, health club, guest services, and homelike features.

For the business traveler who is faced with an extended stay away from home, the comforts of an extended-stay hotel may make the trip less stressful and more productive.

## ALL-SUITE HOTELS

The basic promise of all-suite hotels is "two rooms for the price of one." The secret is less public space such as ornate lobbies and meeting rooms.

This segment has changed over the years so that there are hybrids like full-service all-suites, but the appeal of these places remains constant: a separate room in which to work or hold small meetings. All-suite hotels can now be found in almost every price range, from economy to luxury.

A standard suite consists of a bedroom and a small living room. Room sizes and amenities vary widely from suite to suite and from chain to chain.

Along with handling a substantial amount of small meeting business, women have proven to be loyal all-suite customers for reasons of privacy and security.

An example of brand segmentation positioning is Choice Hotels. Choice markets hotel properties in the following segments:

1. Budget: ADR under $30: Friendship Inns.
2. Economy: ADR between $30 and $40: Econo Lodges, Rodeway Inns, and Sleep Inns.
3. Luxury Budget: ADR between $40 and $50: Comfort Inns.
4. Mid-Priced: ADR between $50 and $75: Comfort Suites, Quality Inns & Hotels, and Quality Suites.
5. Upscale: ADR between $75 and $100: Clarion Hotels and Resorts.
6. Luxury: ADR $100+: Clarion Carriage House Inns and Clarion Suites.

## CORPORATE-HOTEL RELATIONSHIPS

Roger Miersch, director of industry relations at Rosenbluth Travel in Philadelphia, Pennsylvania, gives the following four steps in forging a successful relationship with your hotel vendors:

1. Know thyself.
2. Setting goals.

3. Define strategy.
4. Implementation.

## Know Thyself

First of all, the corporation must define its price and service expectations regarding hotel accommodations in the following areas:

1. Stated policy.
2. Senior management.
3. Frequent traveler.
4. Travel arranger.
5. Travel manager.

Second, the corporate travel manager should define any travel stratification (i.e., executive level, government per diem limitations, etc.) that could create a caste system in approved accommodations. Miersch states that the third element in a corporation's knowing itself is to identify whether a consolidated hotel program will require control and enforcement. Will the travel manager be patient and allow divisions to buy into the program?

The fourth element is risk management. Has the travel manager taken the time to approve only those hotels that have safety features? The fifth element involves the travel manager's knowing the destinations the travelers visit in order to realistically access usable hotel locations.

According to Miersch, the sixth element is defining the data currently available on hotel-stay patterns, current discounts, average rate expenditures per city, etc. In defining your data requirements, Miersch reminds us that group and meeting travel should be included. With these elements in mind it is possible for the travel manager to arrive at realistic goals by balancing price and value.

## Setting Goals

For the travel manager, setting goals refers to targeting savings and service. Miersch points out that the greater the dollar-savings target, the greater the strain, change, and trauma on your company. Each company has a balance point. The further you attempt to go beyond that point, the greater the necessity for senior management support.

In setting your corporate goals, solicit input from frequent travelers. They will be more receptive if they are part of the process instead of the object.

Start out your goal-setting process by determining a base line, or starting point. While hotel savings often represent a moving target, there are some benchmarks to work from. First of all, what are your total hotel expenditures per quarter/per year? What is the total number of frequent travelers for the same period? Can your agency provide data on the company's total average daily rate (ADR), by city/market zone? Can you identify the 20 percent of your hotel markets that comprise 80 percent of your hotel expenditures? Can you define a minimal service standard for company hotel stays?

The next step depends on whether your goals are mandated from senior management ("reduce hotel expenditures by 20 percent") or established by your own analysis. Provide documentation as to what is required to attain those goals. Miersch provides two examples of how this can be done.

**Example 1.** Reducing hotel costs by 20 percent by negotiating preferred rates assumes that you can average a 20 percent reduction in the room rate at every hotel used by your travelers. Miersch states that this would be difficult for the following reasons:

1. Hotel room rates have increased on average from 4 to 8 percent per year.
2. You cannot negotiate with every hotel property used by your travelers.
3. Many of your travelers are already receiving discounted room rates through agency programs, promotional rates, frequent traveler benefits, "secretarial" programs, and company-negotiated programs.
4. If your company is growing, so too are the number of business trips resulting in hotel stays.
5. Travel patterns constantly shift, and new locations result in new and different accommodation needs.

**Example 2.** It may be possible, however, to achieve significant cost reductions by using some or all of the following approaches:

1. Issue a corporate mandate to enforce policy limitations.
2. Establish hotel per diems in major market areas.
3. Use the 80/20 rule—strong price negations in 10 to 15 high-volume markets.
4. Reduce the approved-hotel tier: move traffic from Hyatts to Holiday Inns as a matter of policy.
5. Match the travel need to the hotel product. For example, someone attending an all-day meeting, participating in a business dinner, and returning home the next morning does not need a full-service hotel at a premier price.

## Define Strategy

Miersch recommends that the corporate travel manager avoid the following pitfalls:

1. Negotiated rates in key markets can often create higher average daily rates. For example, your current ADR in Chicago is $98.00. You negotiate in key downtown and suburban locations for rates that reduce costs at four hotels that collectively receive 50 percent of your business. All four hotels are upscale properties with standard corporate rates ranging between $105 and $165. Your negotiated discounts average 25 percent and reflect an average of $101 at the four properties. These four hotels are defined as the approved selections in the Chicago area. Your current $98 ADR suggests that many travelers are staying in very moderately priced accommodations. Those price-conscious travelers are now effectively being told that it is OK to stay in four $100+ hotels. There is the possibility that many travelers will take the opportunity to upgrade their usual accommodations, since there is official authorization from the company.
2. Bells and whistles sound nice but can lead to problems. Upgrade commitments are easily made during a negotiation, but they often fuel expectations that can't be fulfilled at check-in. Each negotiated program enhancement creates

an "exception" policy for the hotel. Since most major hotel groups have special privilege cards for frequent-stay benefit packages, negotiate for free inclusion in any standard program offered by the hotel or chain. In this way you are not creating an unfulfilled expectation for which you or the company would be blamed.

3. Do not allow the hotel to impose "special" booking procedures. They will create problems (i.e., exceptions), raise costs, and undermine your agency's efficiency. Ensure that your agency can easily book your rates.

4. Do not promise more than you can deliver. Misrepresentation of data or of your ability to move market share will allow some short-term gains, but will undermine long-term credibility.

5. Do not flood each market with too many negotiated rates. Avoid the shotgun approach, which will diminish your leveraging ability.

6. Do not exclude your agency from the process if it has offered assistance. The best agencies can provide invaluable assistance and guidance. Solicit their expertise.

7. Do not work in a vacuum within your company. Ask for input before, during, and after the project. Compliance is difficult enough without the added antagonism of an imposed program.

8. Do not view chain-level programs as the ultimate answer. This is the easiest approach, but costs may increase if the selected chain generally provides upscale accommodations.

9. Do not commit to major savings unless senior management is willing to set policy and enforce it.

In negotiating with hotels, Miersch suggests the following approaches:

1. Concentrate first on 10 to 15 frequent destinations.

2. Rely on your agency program for all other secondary markets in the first year of the program.

3. Expand to other secondary markets in subsequent years only if significant additional savings can be realized.

4. Collect meaningful data from every available source. Refine that data into usable information which provides:

a. Total company room-night productivity per quarter/per year.
b. Room-night productivity per key market (10 to 15) per quarter/per year.
c. Total/key market average daily rate (ADR).
d. Major current hotel room-night usage and ADR.
e. Room-night productivity by market for each product tier, or price level, e.g., less than $50, $50–$75, $75–$100, $100–$125.
f. Use data from credit-card sources, expense reports, travel agencies, and key hotels. Be prepared to interpret and extrapolate, since none of the data sources are likely to match.

5. Meet with your agency experts to determine their involvement. A few agencies have dedicated strategists/negotiators for client-specific hotel programs.

6. Target currently used hotels from a variety of product tiers. Concentrate on price negotiations at the upscale properties, and service enhancements at the moderate and economy brands. If your goal is to reduce hotel costs, the most effective approach is to encourage or require the use of more moderately priced properties. If you can enhance service or benefits through negotiations with quality low-cost hotels, you will generate far stronger results than simply negotiating price concessions at hotels whose starting price is already high.

7. Know the current and projected market conditions for hotels in your key markets.

8. Concentrate chain-level programs at moderate or economy levels, but choose only those whose product is consistent. Do not look for major price concessions. Focus on service benefits, meal discounts at off-site restaurants, or program-specific incentives for weekend stays or office parties.

9. Give to get. Be prepared to support your preferred hotels by allowing them marketing opportunities in your company. Develop an awareness plan for company travelers.

10. Be clear on commissionable versus net-rate requirements to both your agency and selected hotels.

11. Ensure that negotiated rates can be booked by the approved agency(s), ideally through CRS automation.
12. All agreements should be in writing, based on a single RFP format developed to suit your needs.

### Implementation

After all agreements have been made, it is important to create a strategy to inform the corporate traveler and implement the program. Miersch suggests that there are three stages in the implementation process: Inform, monitor, and evaluate.

Use all company media vehicles to highlight the program and any expectations. Be sure to define procedures to travel planners and travelers. Emphasize single sourcing through the agency. Work with your agency to define point-of-sale wording, as well as program guidelines. Develop with your agency automated CRS displays that clearly outline the programmed hotel booking procedures. Develop an exception procedure that tracks reasons or excuses for declining preferred hotels.

## CASE STUDY: PEPSICO

Recently the PepsiCo Travel Management Council, with member representatives from the seven PepsiCo subsidiaries (PepsiCo, Pepsi-Cola, Frito-Lay, KFC, Pizza Hut, Taco Bell, and Pepsi Foods International), developed a negotiated hotel program. The following eight-step development process took approximately nine months to complete.

### Step One: Collecting Data—Establishing the Base Line

This initial step, which is perhaps most critical to program development and evaluation, involves (1) analyzing the present hotel selection and reservation process, and (2) building a database of the key destinations and properties used by all subsidiary office travelers for use as a base line for future program development and success measurement. It was found that roughly 50 percent of all domestic hotel activity was concentrated in 15 key cities. Travelers selected hotels based on individual needs, and reservations were made in a variety of ways—directly, through a travel agency, etc. Upwards of 30 different properties were used by PepsiCo subsidiaries in a given city, and often the rates charged at a given property would vary significantly from one PepsiCo subsidiary to another. Market-share stats and average room rate by market were developed for each key city.

### Step Two: Developing Selection Criteria

Addressing the cultural differences of the PepsiCo Travel Management Council member companies was essential in developing comprehensive selection criteria. Selection criteria are the key to the screening and ultimate selection of properties. Selection criteria address customer relationships, quality and service, proximity to offices, prior use, and competitive rates.

### Step Three: Screening Properties by City

A lengthy but necessary step required manual review and screening of properties against selection criteria by council members for final selection and rate-negotiation purposes. Input was solicited at the subsidiary-headquarters and field-office levels to ensure that key properties were not overlooked.

### Step Four: Rate Solicitation

Once properties in key markets had been identified, rate solicitation and negotiation followed.

### Step Five: Final Property Selection and Rate Acceptance

Following receipt of all proposals, the council reviewed and selected proposals. When needed, negotiations took place. Once final selection was made, confirmations were sent to each property selected. Confirmations are essential to ensure service and rate compliance.

### Step Six: Directory Design and Printing

Directory design and ease of use is the key to user acceptability. The directory states the program objectives and purpose. It not only lists recommended properties, rates, and the location of the nearest PepsiCo subsidiary office or airport, but it also outlines reservations procedures and follow-up for customer-service resolution.

### Step Seven: Directory Distribution and Marketing

Internal marketing of the directory and its distribution was tailored to meet the cultural differences of each subsidiary.

### Step Eight: Success Factors and Program Redevelopment

Cost control, consolidation of spending with key vendors, improvement in property usage, traveler feedback, and ease of use are our key measures. The ability to meet or exceed the expectations of both the traveler and the hotel business partner by the use of these measures will ultimately affect the success of the program. The development of a comprehensive hotel program is evolutionary, as experienced by the PepsiCo Travel Management Council. Council commitment to the initial project, in addition to annual program review and enhancement, is an essential ingredient to success.

## CASE STUDY: GUEST QUARTERS SUITES HOTELS

The following suggestions for negotiating are offered by Jack Ferguson, vice president of national sales at Guest Quarters Suites Hotels, located in Philadelphia. According to Ferguson, the three most important factors for a corporate travel manager to understand before beginning negotiations with a hotel are:

1. The economics of hotels.
2. Yield management.
3. The company's travel patterns.

Ferguson continues by stating that knowing the above three achieves the following: "It places the corporate travel manager in the 'driver's seat' with an existing hotel vendor or a possible new one as it emphasizes the manager has control of their company's business volume and its impact. Furthermore, the corporate travel manager will be able to direct business to a vendor in the form of volume room nights at an agreed-upon length for understood levels of service and accommodations as the customer and vendor have reached an agreement."

In the past, many corporate travel managers had the perception that hotels were not in the business of making a profit. With the tax laws introduced in the mid-1980s, hotels and their owners had to make sure everyone was focused on the fact that a hotel is a business investment. If it is not profitable, it will go out of business.

With this in mind, the corporate travel manager must have an appreciation for the economies of a hotel. Like any company, the hotel is striving to provide an excellent product at a fair price, but it must be capable of paying its bills and showing a profit after all costs of doing business are satisfied.

Hotel categories are: luxury, full service/upscale, moderately priced, economy, residential, or all suite. The category used by the traveler will be determined by market conditions and by the amenities and services provided within the category. It is up to the corporate travel manager to identify the needs of his or her travelers from the standpoint of what the company has determined as acceptable accommodations and service, and to pick out those hotels or hotel companies that provide such levels of service.

The corporate travel manager should identify his or her top ten most frequently traveled markets and negotiate according to the company's travel volume, inspecting specific hotels in that market. In this way, the corporate travel manager has the ability to significantly impact the economies of a hotel.

Yield management—the ability for a hotel to maximize its revenues—comes into the picture when a corporate travel manager who has significant room-night volume in the market obtains specific rate considerations for that volume of business. This business becomes "base business," which the hotel can rely on to create a demand for the hotel, from which it can control inventory.

Once the corporate travel manager has created base business for a particular hotel, this business cannot be taken for granted. The levels of accommodations and services agreed upon must be delivered every day to the valuable customer.

If a corporate travel manager finds that he or she does not have large volumes in a specific market, using a travel agency's buying power as an umbrella effect can provide significant cost savings.

## TRAVEL MANAGEMENT TIPS

- Placing customers in rooms at a reasonable price is as much a marketing as a systems challenge, as the modern travel industry finds it impossible to separate purely management information systems or accounting functions from revenue-producing or marketing functions.
- Effective use of internal and external distribution systems is essential to any hotel, large or small, in today's marketplace.
- Hotel inventory can be managed by a number of systems. Each imposes its peculiar set of functions and limitations on the reservation process and may also function in connection with other systems that likewise impose a different set of limitations. It is important to understand them in detail.
- Hotel management tends to be very centralized, even if a central chain or group affiliation exists. This is partly because the franchise system, which is used by most major hotel chains, encourages entrepreneurial spirit and independence.
- The hotel industry represents the most under-automated segment of the travel industry.
- The management of hotel inventory, particularly the amount of control individual property managers have over all aspects of the process, has not changed materially since the origins of centralized hotel systems and usually does not reflect contemporary standards as to yield management and database control.

## Chapter Thirteen

# Managing Meetings

M eeting planning is a relatively new field, which has emerged into a respected profession representing billions of dollars of revenue. Within the last ten years, there have been major strides in identifying the essential skills required to organize professional meetings.

The Convention Liaison Council, comprised of twenty organizations representing the convention, trade show, and exposition industry have identified 25 functions crucial to meeting planning as well as 17 independent conditions that affect meeting planning functions.

Meetings are constantly being held for a myriad of reasons. They can range from an informal meeting within an office environment to a congress of thousands. In this chapter we will explore the wide range of meetings and why they are held. The focus will be on who is planning the meeting and where the meeting is being held. Practical guidelines will be presented in the form of an extended case study.

## MEETING-PLANNING FUNCTIONS

1. Establishing meeting design and objectives.
2. Selecting site and facilities.
3. Negotiating with facilities.
4. Budgeting.
5. Handling reservations and housing.
6. Choosing among transportation options.
7. Planning the program.
8. Planning the guidebook/staging guide/documentation of specifications.

9. Establishing registration procedures.
10. Arranging for and using support services.
11. Coordinating with the convention center or hall.
12. Planning with convention services manager.
13. Briefing facilities staff—pre-meeting.
14. Shipping.
15. Planning function rooms setup.
16. Managing exhibits.
17. Managing food and beverage service.
18. Determining audiovisual requirements.
19. Selecting speakers.
20. Booking entertainment.
21. Scheduling promotion and publicity.
22. Developing guest and family programs.
23. Producing and printing meeting materials.
24. Distributing gratuities.
25. Evaluating—post-meeting.

## INDEPENDENT CONDITIONS THAT AFFECT MEETING PLANNING FUNCTIONS

1. Time of year/dates (seasonal/holiday/negotiations/ climate).
2. Labor conditions (union status of contract/nonunion/ availability).
3. Length of meeting.
4. Size of attendance.
5. Facility location (downtown; resort) and type (convention center; hotel).
6. Objective of meeting (education; incentive; exhibit; business sales; information).
7. Type of organization (association or society; corporation; religious group; governmental group).
8. Location/geography (city or resort; international or off-shore).
9. Budget (subsidized; break-even; profit; sponsorship).

10. Participant funding (attendee; organization; meeting support; restrictive per diem).
11. Management responsibility (staff; volunteer; contract service).
12. Space requirements (sleeping rooms; meeting rooms; banquet space; exhibit space).
13. Transportation variables (ground operator; airlines; accessibility).
14. Participant demographics (gender; age).
15. Social events (type; timing; availability).
16. Special requirements (meals/handicapped).
17. Weather.

## CASE STUDY: BONNIE WALLSH ASSOCIATES, LTD.

Bonnie Wallsh Associates, Ltd., located on Staten Island, New York, is one of the most respected meeting planning companies in the United States. Among other meetings, Bonnie Wallsh has been in charge of the "Focus on Automation," "Managing Business Travel," and "Managing Leisure Travel" meetings sponsored by *Travel Weekly* magazine. The material in this chapter will be taken from exhibits used in these meetings.

### Establishing Goals and Objectives

According to Wallsh, the first question that needs to be asked is, Why is a meeting being held? What do you want this meeting to accomplish? Wallsh states, "Too often meetings are planned without understanding their purpose. Perhaps it is one of those meetings that has always been held."

Often, people attending conferences have only a vague notion of what they were supposed to accomplish. Wallsh explains the reason for this: "If the person planning the meeting does not know why a meeting is being held, this same confusion will flow over to the attendees. The most crucial aspect in planning any meeting is to establish the goals and objectives. The goals may be educational, informational, sales, motivational, or social."

"Goals are broad and somewhat nebulous. Objectives, on the other hand, should be specific and measurable in a tangible way."

As an example of an objective for a meeting, consider the Republican or Democratic convention. These meetings bring together members of a political party every four years. The objective is to nominate a presidential and vice presidential candidate. A sales meeting is held to bring together a sales force for a pep rally and as a motivational forum for them to go out and sell. The specific objective might be to increase sales by a specific amount for each salesperson. The investment of both time and money expended should be able to be measured to determine the success of the meeting.

There are many different types of meetings that companies can hold. Wallsh offers the following as a partial list:

1. Association.
2. Board.
3. Incentive.
4. Product introduction.
5. Sales.
6. Stockholders.
7. Training.

### Planning Calendar

Once the goals and objectives have been established, the next step should be developing a time line or calendar of tasks to be accomplished, with the names of those responsible for each of the tasks (see Figure 13.1).

When the responsibilities are laid out, the planner is forced to develop an overview of the entire meeting. The planning list can be added to, and responsibilities should be checked off as they are accomplished. A weekly or biweekly calendar can augment the long-range calendar. At Bonnie Wallsh's company, the entire staff meets biweekly to lay out the responsibilities for the entire office staff. In addition, appointments and administrative responsibilities are included. This makes the staff aware of what responsibilities each of their colleagues are working on and helps them to cover for one another when someone is out of the office or

FIGURE 13.1

---

Travel Weekly's "Managing Business Travel '91"
May 19–22, 1990
Walt Disney World Dolphin
Lake Buena Vista, Florida
Abbreviations:

BWA   Bonnie Wallsh Associates, LTD.
TW    *Travel Weekly* magazine
MBT   "Managing Business Travel '91"
WDW   Walt Disney World

*Planning Calendar*

| Weeks Before | Task | Responsibility |
|---|---|---|
| **1990** | | |
| 24 (Dec. '90) | Develop budget | BWA |
| | Develop marketing plan | BWA |
| | Develop promotional calendar | BWA |
| | Follow-up with past exhibitors | BWA |
| | Send mailing to prospective exhibitors | BWA |
| | Develop list of prospective local exhibitors | BWA |
| | Send initial mailing offering $25.00 discounts to past nonexhibiting attendees | BWA |
| | Contact prospective sponsors | BWA |
| | Prepare sponsor chart | BWA |
| | Follow up with Stan Sudler regarding potential sponsors for golf/tennis tournament; local assistance | BWA |
| | Send out advisory board minutes to advisory board members | BWA |
| | Prepare workshop grid for programming workshops | BWA |
| | Begin contacting prospective speakers | BWA |
| | Follow up with Walt Disney World Seminar Productions for descriptive copy and name of presenter | BWA |
| | Contact Premier Cruise Lines for promotional copy for reduced-rate cruises | BWA |
| | Write preliminary press release to announce theme of TW's MBT '91 | BWA |
| | Prepare preliminary ad | BWA/TW |
| | Send out letters for reduced-rate transportation | BWA |

*Planning Calendar*

| Weeks Before | Task | Responsibility |
|---|---|---|
| | Contact Tom Bewley regarding revised program format (trade show 1 day only) Reduce room block to 500 rooms | BWA |
| | Determine in-house rates for Reed Travel Group exhibitors | BWA |
| 23 | Contact tape company | BWA |
| | Announce MBT '91 in TW | TW |
| 22 | Prepare initial brochure copy | BWA/TW |
| | Prepare ad schedule | BWA/TW |
| | Get approval from Premier Cruise Lines for their inclusion in ad | BWA/TW |
| | Determine ad schedule for CFOs/HRO | BWA/TW |
| | Firm up golf/tennis tournament | BWA/TW |
| | Establish cost and registration procedures | BWA/TW |
| | Arrange guest/children's program | BWA |
| **1991** | | |
| 20 (Jan. '91) | Send out 2nd exhibitor mailing | BWA |
| | Contract with mailing house | BWA/TW |
| | Preparation of mailing labels for corp/TA mailing | BWA |
| | Order ARC labels | BWA |
| | Proof brochure copy | BWA |
| | Contact associations, travel industry groups for promotion | BWA |
| | Speaker follow-through | BWA |
| | Review evaluation forms | BWA/TW |
| | Air concurrence follow-up | BWA |
| 18 | Send exhibitors discount tickets for promotional mailings | BWA |
| | Firm up sponsored functions | BWA |
| | Begin contacting airlines for speaker transportation | BWA |
| | Select on-site personnel | BWA |
| | Send initial list of exhibitors to exposition company | BWA |
| | Contact local suppliers—ground transport, printers, on-site staff, photographers | BWA/TW |
| 16 | First bulk-rate mailing of brochure to travel agents and corporate travel mgrs. | BWA |
| | Send press releases to business and consumer press | BWA |

*Planning Calendar*

| Weeks Before | Task | Responsibility |
| --- | --- | --- |
| 15 Feb. | Send preliminary hotel requirements to WDW Dolphin | BWA |
| | Prepare and mail exhibitor confirmation packages | BWA |
| | Prepare travel agent/corporate travel manager confirmation packages | BWA |
| 12 | Ongoing promotion | BWA |
| | Review all A/V requirements | BWA |
| | Review bios/outlines/handouts | BWA |
| | Begin mailing travel agent/corporate travel manager confirmation packages | BWA |
| 11 Mar. | Phone call follow-up with speakers | BWA |
| | Send pictures/bios/outlines to TW | BWA |
| | Draft program | BWA |
| | Prepare material for Focus edition | BWA |
| | Process applications for pre/post cruise | BWA |
| 7 April | Ongoing promotion | BWA/TW |
| | Process registrations for golf/tennis tournament | BWA |
| | Prepare signs | BWA |
| | Send updated hotel requirements to WDW Dolphin | BWA |
| | Prepare delegate registries | BWA |
| | Print program | BWA |
| 2 May | Reconfirm all speaker arrangements | BWA |
| | Reconfirm golf and tennis tournament arrangements | BWA |
| | Reconfirm pre/post cruise passengers | BWA |
| | Print evaluations | BWA |
| | Arrange limousines for Bill/Alan | BWA |
| | Print handouts | BWA |
| | Ship materials | BWA |
| | Prepare list of invitees for VIP reception | BWA/TW |
| 1 May | Pre-convention staff meeting | BWA |
| | Staff arrives on-site | BWA |
| | Review all arrangements on-site | |

(Reprinted with the permission of Bonnie Wallsh Associates, Ltd.)

unavailable. As tasks are completed, they are checked off. In meeting planning, there are a myriad of details to be considered.

Wallsh tells a number of stories about waking up during the middle of the night and remembering something else that has to be done. The purpose of the calendar is to give a planner peace of mind and to avoid any details falling through the cracks. It also helps to build a spirit among the staff, who can work together if someone is overburdened and needs assistance.

## Program Planning

The jobs of meeting planners vary from those who handle the logistics to those who are involved with every aspect of the meeting. The greater the involvement of the planner, the more status and importance the planner has within the company. Wallsh feels that one of the most important tasks in program planning is to sit in as the program is being developed.

Once the goal and objectives have been established, determine what the theme and the logo (if relevant) will be. After the theme has been developed, the program can be laid out. According to Wallsh, laying out the meeting involves these steps:

1. Sketching out the approximate time framework for general sessions, breakouts, and social functions. The meeting planner can develop the program by using an advisory board, which provides input by referring to evaluations from previous meetings, their own expertise and contacts.
2. Determine whether there will be exhibits and if so, whether they will be booths or tabletop. Only after this information is compiled can you begin selecting the location.
3. You will need to ascertain how many people will be attending the meeting. Will people be sharing rooms? Will suites be required? Will you require hospitality suites?

## Speakers

The meeting planner can provide an invaluable service by participating in the speaker selection process. Although the planner may not be familiar with the content or experts within the field, it is advisable to have the planner in on the discussions. This involvement will help the planner to interact better with the speakers. The planner can also make recommendations about scheduling or different formats that can be used (e.g., panels, workshops, brainstorming, meet the press). Influential individuals within a company who want to be on the program could be preceded and followed by stronger speakers to ensure that the program does not suffer for an extended period of time. You can recommend the use of audiovisual aids to liven up the presentation.

Once speakers are selected, the planner should be involved in the communication process. If a member of your company invites the speakers, the planner should participate in the correspondence. Figures 13.2 to 13.10 illustrate examples of forms used for speaker data.

An area should be set aside for speakers to sit and review their material or to meet with their fellow speakers. If the number of speakers warrants it, there should be a speakers' lounge. Arrange time for speakers to review their presentation and become comfortable with the room they will be presenting in. The planner or a member of the planner's staff should be available to assist them if material needs to be duplicated or distributed. A thank-you letter should be sent to the speaker following the presentation.

The planner may want to plan special amenities for certain speakers. The planner should take the time to call the speakers' secretaries to find out what specialties can be sent to their rooms. Instead of the customary fruit and cheese, find out if they are partial to chocolates, beer and pretzels, a certain brand of liquor, or cookies.

## Social Functions

Wallsh states that, "Social functions are an integral part of meetings. They offer participants an opportunity to meet together informally and to network. When planning social functions, the goals and objectives should be carefully determined. Social functions could include hospitality suites, receptions, theme parties, and sports events."

Wallsh recommends that when planning theme parties and sports events, the planner may want to call upon outside resources such

## FIGURE 13.2

---

### *MANAGING LEISURE TRAVEL*
### *CARNIVAL CRUISE LINES*
### *M/S FANTASY*
### *NOVEMBER 15–18, 1991*

#### SPEAKER DATA

NAME: _____ ID # _____

TITLE: _____ session #

COMPANY: _____

ADDRESS: _____
_____

PHONE: (_____) _____ FAX: (_____) _____

---

HOTEL:  ARRIVE: _____ TIME: _____ A.M. _____ P.M.

DEPART: _____ TIME: _____ A.M. _____ P.M.

COMPLIMENTARY ROOM NIGHT(S): (SINGLE/DOUBLE) _____
ADDITIONAL NIGHT(S): _____
NO ADDITIONAL NIGHT(S): _____

AIR (IF APPLICABLE): _____
_____
_____

---

SPEAKER INFORMATION FORM SENT: _____ RETURNED: _____

PUT ON BADGE LIST: _____

SPEAKER CONFIRMATION PACKAGE SENT: _____

---

SPEAKER MATERIALS SUBMITTED:

BROCHURE COPY: _____ BIOGRAPHY: _____ PHOTOGRAPH: _____

OUTLINE: _____ HANDOUTS: _____ # OF PAGES RECEIVED: _____

---

FOLLOW-UP PHONE CALLS MADE:
DATE: _____ COMMENTS: _____
DATE: _____ COMMENTS: _____

---

(Reprinted with the permission of Bonnie Wallsh Associates, Ltd.)

**FIGURE 13.3**

---

## FOCUS ON AUTOMATION
## ATLANTA HILTON & TOWERS
## SEPTEMBER 3–5, 1991

### SPEAKER REQUIREMENTS FORM

Name: _____ Title: _____

Company: _____

Address: _____

_____

Phone: (_____) _____ Fax: (_____) _____

Date of arrival: _____ Time: _____A.M. _____P.M.

Date of departure: _____ Time: _____A.M. _____P.M.

---

**Speaker Workshop Requirements:**

Session ID/Title: _____

Day/Date: _____ Time: _____

    We are unable to provide anything other than simple A/V setups. Please indicate by check mark which A/V you will require, as listed below. If you will not need any A/V, specify in the appropriate box.
    Choose One:
        ☐ 35 mm carousel slide projector/screen/remote (We cannot provide a projectionist, but each projector comes equipped with a remote control.)
        ☐ Flip chart & markers
        ☐ Overhead transparency projector/markers/screen
        ☐ Choose One Microphone: ___Lavaliere ___Podium ___Table
        ☐ Choose one ___6' Table or ___Podium
        ☐ I will not require any A/V

Handouts: ___Yes and the number of pages is_____.
Handouts are to be submitted no later than_____.
No handouts will be distributed without prior approval of BWA.
Maximum number of handouts allowed if four double-sided pages is

_____.

Enclosed: Biography_____ Photograph_____ Workshop outline_____

---

(Reprinted with the permission of Bonnie Wallsh Associates, Ltd.)

**FIGURE 13.4**

---

## TRAVEL WEEKLY'S FOCUS ON AUTOMATION
## ATLANTA HILTON & TOWERS    ATLANTA, GEORGIA
## SEPTEMBER 3–5, 1991

### GENERAL SESSION AUDIOVISUAL REQUIREMENTS

Name: _____ Title: _____

Company: _____

Address: _____

_____

Phone: (_____) _____ Fax: (_____) _____

Date of arrival: _____ Time: _____ A.M. _____ P.M.

Date of departure: _____ Time: _____ A.M. _____ P.M.

GENERAL SESSION REQUIREMENTS:

Session ID/Title: _____

Day/date: _____ Time _____

Your session will be set theater-style with a lectern off-center stage right. The moderator will determine the furniture and audiovisual requirements. If you have individual preferences, please contact the moderator. The moderator should contact us no later than June 28, 1991, with the following requests:

_____ 35 mm slide projector  _____ overhead projector
_____ microphone  _____ lectern
_____ 6' table (2 speakers per table)  _____ pointer
_____ armchair(s) with coffee table
_____ I will not require A/V

Special Requests: _____

Handouts:
    Will you have handouts? _____ Yes _____ No
Do you want BWA to reproduce them? _____ Yes _____ No
If yes, it will be the responsibility of BWA to photocopy the material, provided it is received by June 28, 1991, maximum number of handouts allowed is four double-sided pages. Otherwise you will be required to provide any handouts in quantities sufficient for distribution at your expense. In either case, prior approval of all handouts must be obtained from BWA before distribution to program participants.

---

(Reprinted with the permission of Bonnie Wallsh Associates, Ltd.)

## FIGURE 13.5

June 1990

To:       All speakers & workshop leaders

From:   Anne Schultz
          Speaker Coordinator

Re:      Focus on Automation
          September 4–6, 1990
          San Francisco Marriott
          San Francisco, California

We are pleased that you will be joining us at the San Francisco Marriott for what we are confident will be our best FOCUS ON AUTOMATION ever.

Enclosed is our FOCUS ON AUTOMATION promotional brochure.

If you have not already done so, please return your completed Speaker Information Form. It is extremely important that we are advised in advance of your audiovisual requirements. We appreciate your cooperation.

A room has been reserved for you at the San Francisco Marriott for the evening of _____. If you wish us to make reservations for additional nights at the rate of $119 (single/double) per night, complete and return the enclosed form BEFORE AUGUST 10. If the form is not returned by August 10, we will assume the reservation made by us is sufficient.

We look forward to welcoming you in San Francisco.

## FIGURE 13.6

---

### *TRAVEL WEEKLY'S*
### *FOCUS ON AUTOMATION*

YES, IN ADDITION TO THE RESERVATION MADE BY YOUR OFFICE, PLEASE MAKE A RESERVATION FOR THE EVENING(S) OF _____ AT THE RATE OF $119 (SINGLE/DOUBLE) PER NIGHT.

SINGLE_____ DOUBLE_____

NAME:_____

COMPANY:_____

THIS INFORMATION MUST BE RETURNED TO BONNIE WALLSH ASSOCIATES BEFORE AUGUST 10. IF YOU HAVE ANY QUESTIONS, PLEASE CALL NICK CALDAROLA AT (718) 979–1012.

IF THIS FORM IS NOT RETURNED BY AUGUST 10, WE WILL ASSUME THE RESERVATION MADE BY US IS SUFFICIENT.

---

(Reprinted with the permission of Bonnie Wallsh Associates, Ltd.)

**FIGURE 13.7**

---

### *TRAVEL WEEKLY'S*
### *FOCUS ON AUTOMATION*
### *SEPTEMBER 6–9, 1988*
### *CENTURY PLAZA HOTEL*
### *LOS ANGELES, CALIFORNIA*

RES SYSTEM INTERCHANGE WORKSHOP

SYSTEM:_____

CONTACT:_____ PHONE:_____

WORKSHOP ROOM:_____

A. FURNITURE REQUREMENTS:

_____
_____
_____


B. AUDIOVISUAL REQUREMENTS:

_____
_____
_____


C. TELEPHONE LINES:

_____
_____
_____


D. ELECTRICAL LINES FOR COMPUTER HOOK-UP:

_____
_____
_____


IMPORTANT: THE ABOVE INFORMATION MUST BE RETURNED TO
NICK CALDAROLA OF BONNIE WALLSH ASSOCIATES NO LATER
THAN AUGUST 5, 1988. YOUR COOPERATION IS APPRECIATED.

---

(Reprinted with the permission of Bonnie Wallsh Associates, Ltd.)

## FIGURE 13.8

---

*FOCUS ON AUTOMATION*
*SEPTEMBER 6–9, 1988*
*CENTURY PLAZA HOTEL*
*LOS ANGELES, CALIFORNIA*

HOTEL REQUIREMENTS

FRIDAY, SEPTEMBER 2, 1988

2:00 p.m.                    ARRIVAL
                             Bonnie Wallsh
                             Nick Caldarola

                             Bel Air Room to be set up for conference materials
                             Maximum of 6' tables to line perimeter of room
                             15 chairs
                             10 waste baskets
                             Electrical outlets for 3 typewriters
                             1 telephone with outside line
                             (must be modular for lap computer)
                             Pitchers of water, glasses, and ashtrays

                    NOTE: DO NOT DISPOSE OF ANY EMPTY CARTONS

3:00 p.m.                    Pre-conference meeting
                             Location to be advised by John Cushen

SATURDAY, SEPTEMBER 3, 1988

10:00 a.m.                   STAFF ARRIVAL

                             BEL AIR ROOM

                             Same setup as Friday, Sept. 2

                             Refreshen pitchers of water, glasses, ashtrays

SUNDAY, SEPTEMBER 4, 1988

8:00 a.m.                    STAFF WORKROOM

                             BEL AIR ROOM

                             Same setup as Saturday, Sept. 3
                             Refreshen pitchers of water, glasses

**FIGURE 13.8**   (concluded)

| | |
|---|---|
| 9:45–11:15 a.m. | WORKSHOP SESSION 1 |
| ID # 1–A | COVIA |
| | LOCATION: PACIFIC ROOM |
| | -speaker to be announced |
| | AV      T/B/A |
| | Audience: |
| | 100 theater |
| | Note: NO AUDIENCE MICROPHONE IN AISLE |
| | AV BILLING: SEE ATTACHED |
| ID # 1–B | USING YOUR OWN PC TO FACILITATE OFFICE MGMT. |
| | LOCATION: REDWOOD ROOM |
| | Davidoff |
| | Davidoff |
| | Head table for 2 |
| | 2 lavaliere microphones |
| | Flip chart |
| | Markers |
| | Overhead projector |
| | Screen |
| | AUDIENCE: |
| | 50 schoolroom |
| | NOTE: NO STANDING MICROPHONE IN AUDIENCE |

(Reprinted with the permission of Bonnie Wallsh Associates, Ltd.)

## FIGURE 13.9

---

### *STANDARD AV/FURNITURE FOR ALL BREAKOUT ROOMS*

1. EASEL FOR SIGN OUTSIDE ROOM

2. STANDING MICROPHONE IN CENTER AISLE EXCEPT WHERE
   OTHERWISE NOTED

3. WATER AND GLASSES IN REAR OF ROOM EXCEPT CLASSROOM
   STYLE, WHERE THEY WOULD BE ON TABLES

4. ASHTRAYS ON LEFT SIDE OF ROOM.

5. NO-SMOKING SIGN ON RIGHT SIDE OF ROOM

---

(Reprinted with the permission of Bonnie Wallsh Associates, Ltd.)

## FIGURE 13.10

---

### *MASTER ACCOUNT*
### *ROOM AND TAX ONLY*

| Name | D/A | D/D | Nites | Type |
|------|-----|-----|-------|------|
| Bales, Olga | 5/20 | 5/21 | 1 | suite |
| Bales, Virgil | 5/21 | 5/22 | 1 | single |
| Jabaay, Art | 5/21 | 5/22 | 1 | single |
| Jabaay, Hazel NOTE: 5/19, 5/20 - PBI; 5/21 - MA | 5/19 | 5/22 | 3 | single |
| Jenkins, Arlene NOTE: 5/22, 5/23 - PBI; 5/21 - MA | 5/21 | 5/24 | 3 | single |
| Kirby, Norma NOTE: 5/19, 5/29 - PBI; 5/21 - MA | 5/19 | 5/22 | 3 | double NON-SMOKING |
| Kirby, Wes | 5/21 | 5/22 | 1 | single |
| Wald, Margaret D. | 5/21 | 5/22 | 1 | single |
| Zigmund, Cynthia | 5/19 | 5/22 | 2 | single |

---

MA = MASTER ACCOUNT
PBI = PAYMENT BY INDIVIDUAL

as independent planners or destination marketing companies. The hotel property may be able to assist with decorations and menus for theme parties. To plan the appropriate event it is important to know who the participants are. It may be appropriate to plan programs for children and guests. If children's programs are planned, then the necessary insurance liability forms must be signed. Capable supervision is required. What were previously called spouse programs have become guest programs. Appropriate activities should be planned. Depending upon the type of attendee, you may find that the guest is a career person and, increasingly, a man. Makeup-applying sessions would hardly be appropriate.

## Budgets

As the meeting planning begins, a budget must be established. The budget will to a large extent control the selection of the property and meal planning and determine how much can be expended for speakers, amenities, and special events.

## Site Selection

The site selection process consists of data gathering, evaluation of potential sites, site inspection, and hotel negotiations. Wallsh recommends that the planner consider the following factors:

1. Proposed attendance.
2. Budget limitations.
3. Programming.
4. Legal restrictions.
5. Company policies.
6. Company politics.

Wallsh recommends the following sources for information on potential sites:

1. Other meeting planners.
2. Hotel associates.
3. Hotel and supplier correspondence files.
4. Business publications.

5. Convention and visitors' bureaus/tourist offices.
6. Hotel representatives (regional offices).
7. Hotel chains.
8. Airlines.
9. Evaluation reports from past meetings.

After considering these sources, the planner should narrow down the number of properties to be selected. Site inspections are time-consuming and expensive. There are varying opinions on whether properties should be advised in advance of inspection visits. Planners can make better use of their time by scheduling advance appointments. Wallsh advises that the planner should take the same mode of transportation that the attendees will use, even when the property tempts you with an offer of a limo. Wallsh also states, "The planner should walk around the property before scheduled appointments to get the feel of it. Check to see if employees are courteous and helpful. Walk through the space your group will be using. Find out who else will be in-house during your meeting. Also check to see if any construction is scheduled."

### Negotiations

When you negotiate with a hotel property, it is always important to know how they make their money. Guest rooms are the most profitable revenue source. Seventy-six cents of every dollar taken in by noncasino properties comes from rooms.

Wallsh recommends that the planner come prepared with the following information:

1. Previous history of the group.
2. How much potential income the group represents to the property.
3. How many people will be attending?
4. How long they will be staying?
5. What type of program is planned.
6. What the room occupancy pattern is (double or single occupancy).
7. Will people be on expense accounts?

The items that can usually be negotiated include:

1. Hotel rates.
2. Reception costs.
3. Gratuities.
4. Value discounts.
5. Recreation costs.
6. Group rates.
7. Miscellaneous costs.
8. Audiovisual equipment.
9. Security.
10. Coffee breaks.

One of the biggest problems in negotiating with a property is convincing them that your company will deliver what it says. The industry term is "shrinkage," and it refers to overinflated estimates of how many will attend. If a price is negotiated based on a volume that is not delivered, it is doubtful that property will give you much of a price break in the future. The meeting planner should never promise more than can be delivered.

### Hotel Requirements

A written document of specifications, called a staging guide, is essential in the management of a successful meeting. Wallsh emphasizes that everything must be in writing. Specifications should be reviewed with the planner's staff and key hotel representatives. The most important person in the hotel for the meeting planner to interface with is the convention service manager. He or she will serve as an extension of the meeting planner at the hotel. The range of the convention service manager's responsibilities varies greatly from property to property. The planner and the convention service manager are in close communication throughout the planning period. The planner should take nothing for granted. Every detail, no matter how small, should be written down.

The rooming list, including the master account, should be updated regularly and sent to the convention service manager. Notes indicating special requests should be included.

The meeting planner will schedule a preconference meeting, during which all aspects of the meeting will be reviewed with the key hotel staff. The preconference meeting is usually held at the hotel prior to the actual meeting taking place. Since the staff goes to preconference meetings on a regular basis, it is important for the meeting planner to focus on how this meeting will impact each person's department. Wallsh recommends that the following issues be discussed:

1. The group's arrival pattern, to assist staffing at the front desk.
2. Outline what use your group makes of the food outlets.
3. How much parking will be required?
4. Will there be heavy use of room service?
5. Will there be heavy use of telephones?

If the meeting lasts more than one day, arrange a time to sit down and review changes. After the meeting is completed, review the hotel bill carefully before you leave the property because it is easier to make changes on-site than afterwards.

## Food and Beverage Service

Wallsh feels that the three most important factors to be considered in arranging food and beverage are:

1. Budget.
2. Type of group.
3. Purpose of meal functions.

Generally, the meeting planner will work with a banquet manager, who will assist in menu selection. Some properties do not have prepared menus, but they will personalize a menu for you. The meeting planner should be aware of the latest trends in lighter foods. Men and women are both concerned with their cholesterol count and watching their diets. Breakfast cereals and fruit make a nice change of pace from eggs. Consider muffins or bagels instead of Danish pastry. Wallsh also recommends that a continental breakfast is more cost-effective than a full breakfast.

Yogurt, fruit, juices, and granola bars may be served at breaks. Attendees need an energy lift without empty calories. Lunch selections have shifted from beef to chicken. It is wise to rely on the creativity of the chef to come up with some interesting menu ideas. If your group is small, you may benefit by selecting the same menu other groups are using during your meeting to help bring the price down. Some creative meeting planners are surveying their groups in advance for their preferences.

There are a number of ways to save money on food for meetings. One way is to reduce the number of courses. Wallsh believes that the most important concept in food planning and budget considerations is to know your group.

## *Allied Services*

Outside vendors play an important part in any meeting. It is important for the meeting planner to develop relationships with vendors that can be used on a regular basis. There are at least ten types of vendors the meeting planner should be acquainted with:

1. Audiovisual services.
2. Exposition company.
3. Security.
4. Printing.
5. Staffing.
6. Destination management company.
7. Badges.
8. Office machines.
9. Signage.
10. On-site management.

**Audiovisual services.**  Hotels have in-house audiovisual companies who work with them. It is advantageous to have an office on-site, but your AV needs should be put out to bid. The bid process can call for a compromise between quality and price.

**Exposition company.**  If you are setting up a trade show with booths, you will need to hire an exposition company to work with you. They will create the floorplan, which must be approved by the fire marshall. Any variance must be approved. The fire marshall has absolute power in these situations and can close a show down if it does not meet fire regulations. The exposition company also prepares a package of services, which is sent directly to the exhibitor. These services include: electricity, flowers, upgraded furniture for the booths, etc. Telephone lines may have to be arranged through the hotel. It is the meeting planner's responsibility to assign booths and send the list to the exposition company. A representative from the exposition company will always be on-site to service the exhibitors.

**Security.** Some hotels may require security services. The meeting planner must check the hotel contract. Security personnel may need to be uniformed, or they could be in plain clothes. Security is needed for a variety of reasons, ranging from checking badges to protecting the group from intruders.

**Printing.** Although the meeting planner may use the company's regular printer for advance materials, it is wise to use a local printer for last-minute needs and to save on shipping costs. The convention service manager can make recommendations, or you can use the listings from convention and service bureaus.

**Staffing.** The meeting planner may bring in internal staff or hire temporary help.

**Destination management company.** If you want to arrange transfers or set up special trips, you may want to contract with a destination management company, which can make all the arrangements for you.

**Badges.** Most people want to know who they are talking to. Badges should be large enough to read and should include the person's name, company, city, and state.

**Office machines.** The meeting planner may want to rent typewriters or computers. The convention service manager or the convention and visitors' bureau can provide references.

**Signage.** Professional signs are a must. The meeting planners should put themselves in the position of one of the attendees entering the hotel: Can you find the registration desk? Signage should be on the hotel sign boards as well as on signs that you produce. Signs should be large enough to be easily seen. Signs should be placed outside each room where there are breakouts, with the topic, date, and time of the presentation. If there are two or more speakers, signs should be provided to enable attendees to identify the speakers.

**On-site management.** The meeting planner should always arrive one day early in anticipation that there may be problems. This also allows the meeting planner and the staff to get sufficient rest. The meeting planner's day will start very early, and it may be a good idea to schedule a staff breakfast at 6:00 A.M. to give everybody an opportunity to review the arrangements.

## Gratuities

There is no set rule for gratuities. However, the meeting planner may want to consider distributing some gratuities in advance to personalize your group with the hotel staff. Boxes of chocolates can be given to the front-desk manager and the telephone operators, who are not normally acknowledged. During the meeting, tipping money should be available to tip bellhops who bring in boxes from the shipping room or those who perform a similar function. The bulk of gratuities is placed on the master account so that money can be accounted for. A letter can be sent to the convention service manager or credit manager specifying who should receive what sum of money.

## Evaluations

Evaluations should be completed to enable you to determine whether the goals and objectives have been accomplished. Evaluations can be prepared for each of the attendees. In addition, a post-meeting session can be set up with the convention service manager and the food and banquet manager. It is also important for the meeting planner to internally review the entire meeting.

## MEETING MANAGEMENT RESOURCES

Publications: The following publications are free to qualified meeting planners.

*Corporate and Incentive Travel*
488 Madison Avenue
New York, NY 10022
(212) 888–1500
Dominick Gatto

*Corporate Meetings and Incentives*
747 Third Avenue
New York, NY 10017
(212) 418–4108
Connie Goldstein

*Meetings and Conventions*
500 Plaza Drive
Secaucus, NJ 07094
(201) 902–1700
Kate Rounds

*Meeting News*
1515 Broadway
New York, NY 10036
(212) 869–1300
Anthony Rutigliano

*Successful Meetings*
633 Third Avenue
New York, NY 10017
(212) 986–4800
Richard O'Connor

## ASSOCIATIONS

Convention Liaison Council
1575 I Street, N.W.
Washington, D.C. 20005
(202) 626–2764

Meeting Planners International
1950 Stemmons Freeway
Dallas, TX 75207
(214) 746–5222

Professional Convention Management Association
2027 First Avenue North
Birmingham, AL 35203

Society of Company Meeting Planners
2600 Garden Road
Suite 208
Monterey, CA 93940

## TRAVEL MANAGEMENT TIPS

- Meeting planning is a relatively new field, wh ch has become a respected profession representing billic ns of dollars of revenue.
- Too often, a meeting is planned without an understanding of its purpose.
- The most crucial aspect in planning any meeting is to establish goals and objectives.
- The next step should be developing a time line or calendar of tasks to be accomplished, with the names of those responsible for each of the tasks.
- The meeting planner can provide an invaluable service by participating in the speaker-selection process.
- Social functions are an integral part of meeting s. They offer participants an opportunity to meet together informally and to network.
- When you negotiate with a hotel property, it is always important to know how they make their money.
- A written document of specifications, called a sta ging guide, is essential in the management of a successful m eting.
- After the meeting is completed, review the hot l bill carefully before you leave the property because it is easier to make changes before you leave than afterwards.
- Outside vendors play an important part in any meeting.

## Chapter Fourteen

# Managing Car-Rental Programs

T he cornerstone of the car-rental industry in the United States is the business customer. To compete in the highly competitive corporate-account arena, car-rental companies must be able to offer certain specific benefits to their corporate clients in addition to competitive rates: a nationwide network of locations, a substantial fleet, a broad range of services, a sales force, corporate billing systems, and a computer network, among others.

Among the deciding factors for corporations choosing car-rental companies to service their accounts is the availability of sufficient locations nationwide to provide a network of rental offices and service. A corporate account with business offices or customers in cities around the country must ensure that its car-rental supplier will be available in those cities.

Further, it is important that the car-rental company have a sufficient fleet to serve the needs of that account as well as those of its other corporate clients. The business traveler flying into Owensboro, Kentucky, wants to know that the car-rental company operates in Owensboro and that a car will be waiting once he or she lands.

As important as the above two factors is the distribution of the locations between corporate and licensee ownership. Under corporate ownership, the car-rental company has control over the rates, services, and policies available to a corporate account. Consequently, the business traveler can be certain that the corporate rate quoted will apply at each of the company's corporate locations and that the services and policies will remain consistent.

The question of licensee versus corporate ownership is important to corporate accounts because of rate guarantees. The competition for corporate accounts focuses to a large degree on rates, and that competition is fierce. When renting from a supplier, a customer expects a corporate rate to apply. With no guarantee that a licensee will completely honor a corporate policy regarding corporate rates, the business renter may well find that with many smaller, primarily licensee-owned car-rental companies, the negotiated corporate rate is more chimera than reality.

All-inclusive rates are also an important factor for the corporate account. A corporate travel manager wants to ensure a simple, all-inclusive rate for the business renter that does not include extra costs, such as added-on airport fees, extra door charges, and others. In today's competitive corporate arena, corporate travel managers look for an all-inclusive rate rather than one with à la carte add-ons.

Beyond the tangibles necessary to serve corporate accounts—number and network of locations, fleet size, financial strength, reporting capability—lies the less tangible but no less critical issue of services and the standardization of those services. Frequent business renters want and expect consistency of service from suppliers.

## CAR RENTAL CHECK-IN AND CHECK-OUT

Car-rental companies do not have or need the settlement or accreditation process provided by the ARC to the airlines. Reservations can be made directly with the company or through a travel agency. The traveler does not need to provide a ticket to obtain their rental car, but rather goes through a check-in/check-out process. The check-in usually involves a search for the reservation and the presentation of a credit card and a driver's license by the person wishing to rent the automobile.

So that the reader will better understand the entire process in obtaining a rental car, the Hertz system will be examined closely. The Hertz reservation center, based in Oklahoma City, handles over 90,000 reservations daily. The Hertz system utilizes a Unisys 2200/644ES computer, which is capable of handling 57 million instructions per second and storing 1.5 million active reservations. The phone system processes in excess of 20 million calls annually, supports 700 agent positions, and accommodates half of the reservation volume. The remaining transactions are received through links with airline reservation systems.

With direct access, automated travel agents can communicate directly through their airline reservation system. This means that the agent is able to give the traveler the exact rates and information a Hertz reservation representative would give. The reservation system is part of a fully integrated on-line system that allows Hertz counter agents to access virtually any data from anywhere. The rental agent is able to obtain all the data required to process the rental agreement in a single operation.

Hertz has several methods of returning the rental car. One of these is the instant return system. The instant return system uses hand-held radio-frequency terminals to finalize the rental agreement as the customer returns the car, in many cases while the customer is still in the vehicle.

Using this system, the return procedure is as follows: The customer drives into the return lot and is approached by a representative. The customer gives his rental record to the representative, who enters the rental record into the hand-held terminal. The representative then enters the vehicle's current mileage and whether or not the customer has purchased fuel. If the customer has purchased fuel, the representative also enters the current fuel-tank level. Finally a receipt is printed out and the customer is underway, usually in less than two minutes.

The instant return system uses a Telxon PTC-750 hand-held radio-frequency terminal, into which the rental agreement number, vehicle mileage, and fuel information is entered. The hand-held terminal transmits the entered information via radio waves to a Telxon RFC-30 RF controller, which is attached to an IBM PS/2 model 50. The PS/2 receives information from several hand-held terminals from the RF controller and passes the information across the Hertz corporate network to a central group of mainframes located in Oklahoma City. A rental receipt is generated and sent back across the network to the PS/2. The PS/2 in turn passes the receipt information to the RF controller, which transmits it to the hand-held terminal. The hand-held terminal outputs the receipt to a portable printer.

Hertz has also introduced self-service return units at LaGuardia airport. The self-service return machines are manufactured by

Diebold Incorporated, which also manufactures automated-teller machines. The return machines are similar to the machines used at banks. They have a video screen that guides the customer through the process of entering the rental agreement number, odometer reading, whether gas was purchased and, if so, the fuel-gauge reading. Hertz' on-line computer then calculates the rental charges, and the self-service return unit prints out a receipt.

Hertz self-service return is tied directly into the Hertz system computer, linking Hertz rental locations and its mainframe computers in Oklahoma City. Rental information keyed into the Hertz self-service return unit by the customer is input directly into Hertz' customer records in Oklahoma City, just as if it were input by a Hertz representative at the counter.

Self-service return machines can be used by credit-card customers who need a receipt quickly for expense reports or record-keeping. In addition to the receipt provided by the self-service return machine, a copy of the completed rental agreement and an invoice will be sent to the customer separately.

## TIPS FOR SAVING MONEY ON CAR RENTALS

Kathy Passero in the October 1990 issue of *Corporate Travel* magazine gives fourteen tips for renting a car:

1. Find out about city and state sales taxes that will affect the rate, and ask for a breakdown of costs before you rent. Some firms will give renters a precalculated bill on request.
2. Never buy the rental agency's gas; it is often twice the standard market price.
3. Ask your travel agency to check on promotional rates and standard corporate rates that might be cheaper than your company's negotiated rate. Make sure these offer the same extras that your negotiated rate includes, such as free mileage.
4. Don't overlook local rental agencies. If your travelers visit a locale often, consider negotiating a rate with a local or regional rental firm. Caveat: Individual travelers should learn the details before signing any contract—some rent-

ers have opted for little-known local firms and discovered too late that the rock-bottom rates they were quoted only applied to cars without air-conditioning.

5. Ask about extra charges for late return, and find out how long the grace period is.

6. Decline the collision damage waiver (CDW). Most business travelers are already covered for damage under their company's insurance and/or their credit cards. Another problem with CDWs: they may not cover theft or certain types of damage.

7. Check the car carefully before you leave the parking lot. Some agencies have been known to charge customers who declined the CDW for scratches and dents that already existed.

8. Find out about hidden costs such as fuel charges, drop-off charges, fees to waive the CDW, and liability insurance charges before agreeing to any contract.

9. Estimate how far you will drive. If you won't need the car for long distances, you may be able to save by renting from a 100–150 mile-per-day category rather than unlimited mileage.

10. If you plan to carpool with other travelers, check on fees for extra drivers. Watch out for excessive charges tacked on for international drivers and for any driver under 25.

11. Compare the cost and convenience of renting a car versus using taxis and shuttles for each city. Figure in the costs likely for sales tax, parking, and valet service. If you're attending a meeting and aren't likely to make frequent trips, choose a hotel with free airport transportation and save the expense of car rental.

12. If you'll need the car for one day only, consider taking free airport transportation, renting the car the next day, and returning it at the airport to avoid two days of rental charges.

13. Reserve "least expensive" cars. Don't "buy" upgrades. If the agency offers an upgrade because it's out of the car you requested, make sure other charges such as insurance and gas won't increase.

14. Read the fine print to catch any problems before agreeing to the contract.

## CASE STUDY: NATIONAL CAR RENTAL

The following case was submitted by Gerald M. Dee, national contracts manager at National Car Rental, located in Minneapolis. Dee suggests as a strategy: "One method to determine which vendor is best suited to be awarded preferred status is the request for proposal (RFP) method. The RFP and the subsequent negotiating process will familiarize the travel manager with market price and service integrity within the car-rental industry, therefore providing the corporate travel manager the information to make an informed choice in awarding the business."

Dee identifies the following phases for the RFP process:

1. Research and investigative work.
2. Identify qualified suppliers.
3. Request for proposal.
4. Analyze return bids, first selection process.
5. Formal negotiation.
6. Awarding business.
7. Implementation.
8. Follow-up and measurement.

**Phase 1: Research and investigative work.** Dee states, "If you are expecting a car-rental company to develop a tailored bid which specifically addresses your pricing and service requirements, you need to do your homework. The more historical auto rental data you can provide the car-rental companies, the better your chances are of receiving bids which reflect a combination of the best pricing and service to meet your requirements." Historical auto rental data that is helpful to a car-rental company should include the following information about your company's travel:

1. Length of average rental days.
2. Average miles driven on each rental.
3. Number of one-way rentals.
4. Identify "paired cities," locations you travel between.
5. Top ten domestic rental locations your company travels to.
6. Top five international rental locations.
7. Format of payment used by your travelers to settle charges.

**Phase 2: Identify qualified suppliers.** The National Business Travelers Association (NBTA) annual conference, along with monthly meetings held by the NBTA affiliate groups, enables both the corporate travel manager and the car-rental companies to maintain close working relationships. To help corporate travel managers identify other car-rental companies that may meet their criteria, NBTA publishes a directory of all member car-rental companies' names and phone numbers. These companies would be glad to arrange, on a local basis, a meeting to discuss their interest in an opportunity to bid for the company's car-rental business.

**Phase 3: Request for proposal.** Dee states that the functions of the RFP are:

1. To ensure that the information on which the car-rental suppliers are bidding goes to all suppliers in exactly the same form.
2. To convey as much information in the RFP as possible about your company's travel pattern.

Dee states that the following information should be included in the RFP:

1. Historical auto rental data. All the research you completed in phase 1 to recapitulate past car-rental activity.
2. Bid instructions. Make clear all instructions for responding to the RFP, with due dates.
3. Subsidiaries.
4. Top rental locations. Provide a list of the top ten domestic locations and the top five international locations your company employees travel to.
5. Response format. Provide a format or pricing schedule you want the vendor to use to bid daily, weekly, and monthly prices. You may want to highlight your top rental locations.
6. Contract period. Make clear how long you intend to award business and find out how long the supplier will guarantee rates. Most contracts are guaranteed for one year. Beyond that, contracts can be reviewed and extended yearly, based on a mutually agreed index.
7. Annual volume. Make clear what portion of your business the supplier is bidding for. Will you be awarding an exclu-

sive, co-supplier, or primary with a secondary. Pricing is often based on volume commitment.

8. Pre-bid meeting. Some travel managers hold pre-bid interviews with suppliers to outline the requirements and to ask questions about the process.
9. Other information. The RFP should also include an understanding of such issues as:
   a. Scope of service.
   b. Conditions of agreement.
   c. Service capabilities.
   d. Car classes.
   e. Rental policy.
   f. Insurance coverage.
   g. Reports.
   h. Customer service.
   i. Termination clause.

**Phase 4: Analyze return bids, first selection process.** Those car-rental companies that conformed to bid criteria and responded with economic and service advantages should be invited to the formal negotiations.

**Phase 5. Formal negotiations.** Dee offers the following advice to corporate travel managers preparing to negotiate with car-rental suppliers:

1. The travel manager should be acquainted with the car-rental industry. The NBTA annual conference and trade show provides an excellent opportunity to meet and talk with top executives from each car-rental company.
2. The travel manager should be aware of the factors and forces that are at work in the marketplace. Networking opportunities within the NBTA and committee involvement will provide awareness in this area.
3. The travel manager should maintain a constant relationship with local sales representatives for information about the car-rental industry.
4. Gathering knowledge of service and pricing trends will be a time-consuming effort; however, the labor will prove most rewarding, as it enables the travel manager to pro-

ceed more intelligently with the negotiation phase in selecting the best car-rental company to service the corporation's needs.

5. After you determine which car-rental companies will be invited to the formal negotiations, they must be informed in writing of their selection and given further directions. In your communication, you must be very specific about which issues you wish to discuss in more detail. The suppliers should also be encouraged to take as much time to present anything they wish that would benefit the relationship if they are awarded the preferred status.

**Phase 6: Awarding business.** After the car-rental proposals are reduced to a comparable basis, as to the bidders' reliability and their ability to furnish exactly the service promised, the corporate travel manager must make the final decision.

Dee states that for those who were not successful, much can be learned from these exercises. Losses such as these can show what is needed to do better, so that they may be successful next time. The corporate travel manager, if called on, should be agreeable to meeting with the unsuccessful bidders to discuss the requirements that were not met. All can benefit from such information.

**Phase 7: Implementation.** A successful implementation process will increase awareness of the contractual relationship between the preferred supplier and the company. To say that a smooth implementation process is crucial to the corporate travel manager would not be an overstatement. Dee comments, "If this is the first time you are giving consideration to the implementation process, you already have a problem. The travel manager should request that the car-rental company present their action plan for implementation during the formal negotiation phase. A successful implementation will require a team effort on the part of the travel manager, car-rental contact, and the entire car-rental field sales team.

**Phase 8: Follow-up and measurement.** One worry that a corporate travel manager always has when a decision has been made to go with a new supplier is the level of follow-up on the part of the supplier. Since there is a greater probability of problems and misunderstandings during the first few months of a relationship, the degree of follow-up can make the difference between a good ongoing relationship or one filled with regrets and misgivings about the decision that was made.

The nature and extent of follow-up must be agreed upon by the corporate travel manager and the car-rental representative specifically responsible for the activity of the account.

The success of the follow-up depends largely upon the willingness of the car-rental representative to respond on a timely basis to the needs of the corporate travel manager. Follow-up must also include monthly updates of the results of the implementation.

Measurement makes the follow-up process continuous. It encourages the supplier to make enhancements that will benefit both the corporate travel manager and the supplier.

**Measurement.**  Dee identifies the following standards of measurement:

1. Monthly reports showing car-rental revenue generated by the new account.
2. Monthly reports showing usage of credit cards or loyalty cards to show the effects of implementation.
3. Surveys conducted by the company six months after the implementation to measure level of satisfaction with supplier.
4. Measurement of bookings by traveler to measure compliance with program.

## TRAVEL MANAGEMENT TIPS

- Never buy the rental agency's gas.
- Ask about promotional rates lower than the standard rates.
- Decline collision damage waiver.
- Check the car before leaving the parking lot.

# SECTION

# IV

This section of the book deals with internal ways of controlling travel. This involves accounting procedures, the use of a corporate credit card, and the proper use of information.

*Chapter Fifteen*

# Corporate Credit Cards

## BENEFITS OF CORPORATE CREDIT CARDS

Many corporate travel managers consider the corporate charge card (T & E card) the most important tool in business travel management, next to the travel policy.

Following airline deregulation, companies became aware of the opportunity to reduce airfare costs and initiated revisions to travel policies and processes. They also became aware of the magnitude of travel and entertainment costs at a time when interest rates (the cost of funds) was very high and the depth of good travel management information was very low. As companies with a high level of cash advances outstanding searched for a better solution, many started to view travel management in its entirety as a process that started with preliminary planning, trip authorization, and cash advances and proceeded through a series of related phases and ended after the expense voucher was filed and the data used to evaluate efficiency at each phase. They discovered corporate charge cards overlaid each phase of the process and offered significant benefits at all levels.

There is potential beyond the traditional applications and usage of corporate cards to become more than a payment instrument. For companies, the new ways to use corporate cards make management information and services more accessible. Consequently, in the 1990s, the utility, value, and service associated with corporate cards will be of more importance. Some of these benefits include:

1. For the corporation and the chief financial officer, the T & E card maximized cash retention by significantly reducing the corporate funds extended to travelers and thereby not available for company use. They discovered the T & E card

would limit corporate liability in travel related activity and also minimize the internal administrative costs that run at a rate of 6 percent to 9 percent or more of the travel budget to cover cash advance processing, expense report processing, and issuance of the reimbursement check.

2. For travel management and the travel manager, the T & E card provided easy access to vital management information that could be arranged in a variety of ways to satisfy a specific need. The comprehensive and accurate data could be summarized or broken down to departments for comparisons or displayed in several vendor analyses formats. All of this information, not before available, was provided at no additional cost to the corporation.

3. For the individual traveler, the T & E card provided the ability to reduce dependence on personal funds, assure coverage of large item travel expenses, make emergency services available, provide specific benefits such as additional insurance and reward points, and make settlement and reporting easier.

Corporate charge cards are important tools for the business travel manager to use in controlling expenses. Pamela Vance, travel manager at GTE Communications states that corporate credit cards offer travel managers several benefits:

1. A corporate credit-card program can provide the means for tracking spending patterns. The information gathered from credit cards can be used in vendor negotiations.

2. The issuance of corporate cards to traveling employees can lead to the elimination of cash advances, thereby increasing cash flow for the company. Selecting a card program with individual billing will encourage the prompt filing of expense reports by employees, as they become responsible for payments. Finally, eliminating centralized billings for travel and expense will streamline accounting procedures by eliminating the need for reconciliation.

3. A corporate card program can benefit traveling employees by providing increased insurance coverage, emergency services, an easy way to separate business from personal card charges, and the detailed monthly documentation necessary for the preparation of their expense reports.

Business cards are used by companies of all sizes to purchase and pay for airline tickets, business entertainment, fax machines, rental cars, computers, office supplies—anything related to business.

Corporate charge cards are not your usual credit or charge cards. They are financial management tools to help track and control all business expenses, including travel and entertainment.

What makes business cards management tools are MIS software packages that tell companies exactly how their money is being spent by category, individual, department, and geographic region.

According to a recent survey by the Visa Corporation, only 10 percent of the current 33 million US business travelers carry corporate cards, meaning that about 30 million Americans paid for business travel expenses through direct billing or with personal credit cards, traveler's checks, personal checks, or cash, with the resultant loss of management information.

## CORPORATE CARD FEATURES

Travel managers need a flexible product with services and benefits that can be structured to meet their needs with features such as:

1. Wide merchant acceptance and wide access to cash both domestically and internationally. It must open the doors to millions of hotels, restaurants, transportation, and other service and product providers, at a wide range of prices to fit every cardholder and company budget.

2. Management information system reports with report customization so that the company can select desired reports and report frequencies by company division or department levels, and select desired travel and entertainment or other spending categories to track information for monitoring and controlling expenses.

3. Travel assistance services which provide convenience and security for the traveling employee who needs emergency card replacement or cash delivery, legal, medical or other travel assistance services while away from the office. These services should be available toll-free from anywhere in the world.

4. Auto rental insurance which can save a company up to $13 per day when a corporate card is used to rent a car. This insurance automatically provides coverage against vehicle theft or damage during the rental period.

5. Corporate liability insurance which can protect a company from credit card misuse by employees.

Some of the more frequently used corporate charge cards include the following.

### Air Travel Card

The Air Travel Card is a limited use card. This means that it can only be used for charging airline tickets. It is used when companies want to have their airline tickets billed to a central account. A major benefit of the Air Travel Card is that there is no cost per card issued and there is no preset spending limit. The Air Travel Card provides a package of airline MIS reports and is able to reconcile agency transactions to credit card billing.

### American Express Card

The American Express Card is a full service corporate charge card with no preset spending limit. Cash advances can be obtained at selected automatic teller machines (ATM). American Express also offers emergency cash and card services. Both standard and customized MIS reports are available. It is also possible to negotiate various insurance packages. American Express also offers ticket reconciliation. Depending on your corporation's volume, the charge for each card varies from $5 to $55.

### Citicorp Diners Club

The Citicorp Diners Club card is a full service corporate charge card with no preset spending limit. Emergency card and cash services are available as well as optional insurance programs and ATM cash advances. The Citicorp Diners Club also offers a standard as well as a customized package of MIS reports. Diners Club also offers ticket reconciliation. The cost per card varies from $5 to $30.

### Master Card

The Master Card is a full service corporate charge card which sets the spending limit according to the company. Master Card offers emergency cash and card assistance, plus optional insurance programs and ATM service. The Master Card program comes with a standard set of MIS reports. The fees per card range from $35 to $45.

### Visa

The Visa card is a full service corporate card offering a varying spending limit. Visa offers a complete service of ATM, insurance, emergency card, and cash programs. Visa is also among those that offer both standard and custom MIS reports. Ticket reconciliation is also available through Visa. The cost per card varies from $0 to $45.

## THE MOVE TO CORPORATE CARDS

As American companies attempt to slash their travel budgets, the charge-card companies are contending with the prospect of shrinking revenues. In response, they are seeking to ensure their competitive position by enhancing their offerings. One card company is making travel industry headlines by openly offering rebates to corporations on their central-billed airline tickets by assisting these clients in seeking indirect rebates from vendors' charge-card sales and by waiving per-card fees. Another corporate vendor offers "one mile per dollar" on any airline, hotel, or car-rental purchase, to be redeemed in airline tickets on specific carriers.

New Internal Revenue Service rulings on cash advances are also impacting corporate decisions in selecting a card program. If an employee does not reimburse the company for a cash advance within 120 days, then the advance is considered taxable income to the employee. The company must report this advance on the employee's W-2 form and withhold the appropriate taxes.

## SELECTING A CORPORATE CHARGE CARD

The explosion of new market entrants has resulted in a myriad of opportunities, services, and dilemmas for travel managers as they try to compare not only the basic features of card programs such as acceptability, liability, and cost, but also the emergency services, reconciliation, frequent flyer benefits and particularly, reports customized to meet corporations' needs.

In selecting a charge-card program, whether or not you choose to use a formal RFP process, the more time you spend at the front end with preparation will save an enormous amount of time at the back end in the decision and implementation process. The size of your T & E budget and, to some extent, your corporate culture will help you determine whether you should undertake a formal RFP process or a less structured evaluation.

### *Define Your Goals and Objectives*

Define on paper your company's overall goals and objectives in selecting a charge card vendor or vendors. What is wrong with what you are doing today? Look at how you have been paying for travel all these years, how you have been doing cash advances, and how you have been reimbursing your travelers. What are you trying to accomplish through the evaluation process?

There are a number of reasons why companies go out and begin the process of evaluating and implementing a charge-card program. One may be a wish to improve traveler services or get out of a cash advance situation; the travelers may be complaining that their personal lines of credit are being impacted; they may want to improve insurance coverage, or have additional services that help travelers when they are on the road. There may also be financial considerations such as reduced card fees, improved float, or more favorable exchange rates. Companies may wish to streamline the overall T & E payment process: improve reports, combine travel expense with purchasing expenses, improve compliance to travel policy, collect actual usage data to leverage negotiating strength, and so on.

Determine your overall goals as you begin evaluating programs and keep those in mind as you determine which vendor(s) will best help you meet your goal.

As you evaluate programs it is important to clearly define your expectations and those of your company to potential suppliers.

## *Options*

There are a number of various options open to the travel manager such as:

1. Multipurpose.
2. Limited purpose.
3. A combination of limited and multi-purpose.
4. Centrally billed air with decentralized billing of nonair charges.
5. More than one supplier (one for centrally billed air; another for nonair).
6. Linking with a procurement card for small purchases.
7. Using the card in conjunction with a long distance phone company.

An example of a limited purpose card is the Air Travel Card which is issued by the airlines and used only for airline travel. Most of the other corporate cards used are multipurpose cards. Some travel managers like to use the Air Travel Card because it is easier to regulate travel only charges with central billing, resulting in greater data integrity, improved MIS, and compliance to policy.

## *Cards*

Determine who will get cards and what the manager's role is in controlling the process. Will there be a ghost card centrally billed for air or a central bill with credit card issued or decentralized billing? If the company uses a decentralized billing process, the bill is sent directly to the employee and the employee pays the bill with his/her own check. In a centralized billing, all of the expenses accrue to one credit card issued in the name of the company.

### Fees

With the exception of the Air Travel Card, generally there are per-card fees associated with the multipurpose card programs. They are determined largely by T & E volume and range from $5 to $60 per card. The travel manager should also be aware that there may be fees for late charges and MIS.

### Liability

In the case of employee misuse who is liable? Most times employee misuse occurs when the reimbursement check from the company to the employee is used to pay the employee's other bills leaving the corporate charge card unpaid. The company can be held liable for these charges or there can be negotiated a joint liability between the company and the traveler or the traveler may be fully liable.

### Cash Advances

The travel manager needs to decide if cash advances will be a part of the corporate card program. In many cases, the use of a corporate charge card for handling cash advances and emergency cash programs can reduce the cost and administrative burden of employee reimbursements.

### Spending Limits

As a travel manager, do you want to give all of your travelers unlimited credit? Identifying spending limits by travelers is an important part of the travel manager's job.

### MIS and Reporting Options

The travel manager needs to consider these in terms of specific goals and objectives. It is never a bad idea for the travel manager to consult with the MIS group within their own company. In many cases, the travel agency will have a MIS person who can give invaluable assistance.

### *Insurance and Other Card Benefits*

The travel manager should also consider these in terms of the overall objectives and look into potential redundancy with programs already offered to or used by your employees. Evaluate mileage and benefit programs offered by some card programs as a means to enhance compliance with travel policy.

## CORPORATE INFORMATION GATHERING

There are other issues that the travel manager needs to take into consideration. For example, the destinations frequented by the company's travelers may make a difference in which card is chosen. For example, some large manufacturing plants are located in small rural areas. Contrast this with a company that sends travelers only to areas such as New York and San Francisco. In addition to these, the travel manager should consider the type of merchants and establishments that they want their travelers to use. The domestic/international mix is also important in terms of understanding if vendor services meet your needs.

The travel manager needs to be aware of corporate and travel agency system capabilities. All charge card companies provide a lot of data and have a variety of programs which can help; however, they are useless if this data can not be incorporated within your current system capabilities. One of the most important parts of the travel manager's job will be information. It is information that puts the travel manager on the right side of the power curve.

The travel agency needs to be brought into the choice. Agencies have different relationships with the various card companies and these need to be known and understood.

As with any decision that the travel manager makes that will affect a large number of company employees, it is important to have the support and commitment of senior management, the travelers, and the departments the travelers represent. All of these people have their own expectations, agendas, and goals. It is critical to understand this because if these goals do not correspond with the program you select, you will have a very difficult experience regardless of the supplier you choose.

Travelers have their own agenda and specific concerns. They are the ones that will be using the charge-card program and faced with issues such as nonacceptance, frequent flyer mileage, and so on. It is important for the travel manager to understand what the travelers are looking for and talk with them in terms of how a charge card will benefit them through improvements in the total travel process.

The accounting department is going to have an agenda and specific concerns that have to be addressed. The travel manager needs to be aware of these concerns and be positive that the charge card chosen complements the existing accounting operation. The auditors are going to be very concerned about control. Many get scared when you start giving unlimited pieces of plastic to individuals. Their concerns will probably center around liability issues.

The finance department will be interested in float. It is helpful if the travel manager talks with the person in the company responsible for banking relationships. In some cases corporate charge card suppliers may be the same banks that the company already uses for other transactions. There is also the possibility there may be potential conflicts with banking relationships or agreements your company has in place. If the travel manager understands these before the process gets too far along, a lot of embarrassment can be avoided.

The legal department will be interested in the liability issue and will want to become involved in the contracts. If there are specific terms which must be in your contracts make sure you have identified them up front.

Senior management have their own priorities and objectives. Be sure that you understand these so that when the choice is made. The travel manager will ultimately be responsible for the success of the program. Make sure all involved parties have a voice in the selection process. Many times the choice made is a compromise between the manager's need to manage travel as efficiently and effectively as possible with the concerns and priorities of the other constituencies within your corporation. The more you think about this and identify all these issues the easier it will be when you start the evaluation and/or RFP process resulting in a program that will help your company better manage the business T & E environment.

## IMPLEMENTATION ISSUES

Once the corporate card program is chosen, then an implementation schedule must be established. The biggest hurdle in implementation will be employee acceptance and participation, especially in those companies in which centralized and/or direct billings have been the norm. Unqualified support and clear direction from senior management and the chief executive officer is critical to success. An announcement of the new card should be sent to all employees involved. Education as to how the card will benefit both the company and the traveler will allay fears and encourage compliance. Pamela Vance advises that travelers should be educated along these lines:

1. One card for all business-related expenses.
2. No tie-up of personal credit-card credit lines.
3. Increased insurance coverage.
4. Other card services such as emergency assistance, ATM capabilities, and check-cashing privileges.

Pamela continues her advice on implementing a credit-card program by stating, "Small companies may choose to hold orientation sessions to explain the program benefits and distribute applications. A timetable and coordination point should be determined in order for all applications to be returned to a specific person by a specific date. This will enable you to establish dates for advising the travel agency of card numbers to be used, to terminate any direct billing agreements, and to have the new travel and expense reporting and accounting procedures in place."

National implementation will require additional coordination and travel. Large companies may elect to distribute information through the finance department of the individual business units. A one-day meeting involving the card vendor, the representative from the company's corporate headquarters, and the designated card coordinators in the business units should allow sufficient time to explain the program, distribute materials, and establish target dates for completion.

Pamela Vance further states: "The keys to success of the corporate card program will be in senior management support and employee education. The company CEO, president, or CFO should announce the program and why it was selected. Employees need to be educated on the benefits of the corporate card to the company and to themselves. Time should be spent explaining the new travel and entertainment card reporting requirements. The corporate card perks must be emphasized to travelers as well as company policies concerning personal charges and prompt payments."

## TRAVEL MANAGEMENT TIPS

- Corporate charge cards are an important tool for the business travel manager to use in controlling expenses.
- Corporate charge cards are not your usual credit or charge cards. They are financial management tools to track and control all business expenses, including travel and entertainment.
- Once a corporate card program is chosen, then an implementation schedule must be established.
- Employees need to be educated in the benefits of the corporate card to the company and to themselves.

*Chapter Sixteen*

# Accounting for Travel and Entertainment Expenses

E xpense reporting and reconciliation offers management an important opportunity to control both direct and indirect expenses of travel and entertainment. According to Jeff Lang, director of consulting services at American Express Company, the following are the important concepts relating to travel and expense accounting:

1. The most important objectives of the expense-reporting process for the company.
2. Key issues in expense report processing.
3. The typical expense reporting work flow, in all of its complexity.
4. Key issues surrounding the auditing of expense reports.
5. What it costs companies to process an expense report.
6. The cycle of expense reporting, from the date the advance is taken until reimbursement is generated.

## KEY OBJECTIVES

The American Express Consulting Group lists the following five key objectives:

1. Some companies want to reduce the administrative time, effort, and expense it takes to process expense reports. This can take the form of head-count reduction, improvements in productivity, or streamlining and simplifying the work flow.

2. Other organizations want to be more effective in auditing expense reports. Do we choose to audit 100 percent of the reports that come in, or is it just as effective to choose a sample? What is the basis for our audit: simple math, blank field, and reasonableness of expenses; or do we also check for policy compliance, exact spending guidelines, and detailed documentation?

3. Still other companies are looking for more complete, useful information about their expenses; perhaps for budgeting and forecast purposes, or possibly for negotiating discounts with vendors.

4. Increasing float is the key issue for some firms. That is, the amount of time that an expense remains outstanding before the company has to pay for it, either through traveler reimbursement or payment of an invoice.

5. Finally, providing reimbursement to travelers within a reasonable period of time is a goal for most organizations. The need for the company to increase float as much as possible must be weighed against the need to avoid undue inconvenience to the traveler.

Because of the needs of the various parties involved (the company's desire to exert control in order to keep costs down, internal and external audit needs, new requirements posed by changes in the federal tax laws), the administrative burden associated with expense reporting will never go away. Since more employees are taking trips today, there are more expense reports to process. At the same time, companies are increasingly attempting to speed up the reimbursement cycle.

## ISSUES IN EXPENSE-REPORTING

The American Express Survey of Business Travel Management has been published every two years since 1982. According to the 1992 edition of the Survey, the burden of processing and auditing expense reports has not become any easier for American organizations. The 1600 survey participants identified some specific problem areas, discussed their policies regarding expense documentation, and provided insight about their experience with automating the steps of the expense-reporting process.

## EXPENSE-REPORTING PROBLEM AREAS

The expense-reporting process still presents problems for a majority of companies. Fully three-fourths of the survey respondents (and nearly 90 percent of companies with annual T&E volume of $1 million or more) consider late expense reports and incomplete documentation to be problems for their firms.

## DOCUMENTATION REQUIREMENTS

Receipt requirements are virtually unchanged over the past six years, with private sector companies almost evenly split between two approaches to documentation: requiring receipts for all expenses for which they can be obtained, and requiring receipts only for expenses over $25. Just under half of the surveyed companies require receipts only for expenses over $25, which provides them with the documentation they need to satisfy IRS requirements, while minimizing the burden on accounting personnel. Another 42 percent of the companies require receipts for all expenses for which they can be obtained.

## AUTOMATION OF EXPENSE-REPORT PROCESSING STEPS

In recent years, a growing number of companies have automated key steps in their T&E expense management processes, either obtaining services from outside vendors or developing their own software internally.

While only a small minority of firms overall have begun to automate their expense-management processes, the story is different among companies with the heaviest spending. Nearly half of the extra-high-volume survey participants have tried automated tracking of cash advances, and just over one-third of these heaviest spenders have tried automated reimbursement to travelers.

More than 60 percent of the private sector firms that have automated various parts of their T&E expense-management process report that the automation has been extremely effective or very effective. Across the board, automation steps are rated higher for effectiveness than they were two years ago, which raises the question of why more companies are not trying these techniques. Perhaps it is the complexity of the very process that they are trying to simplify that makes some companies hesitate.

## *Expense-Report Processing Work Flow*

The traveler returns from the trip and eventually prepares an expense report. The proper authorities approve that report, and it is sent to accounting. These three steps are notoriously the most time-consuming part of the process. The longer the delay in these areas, the longer the traveler must wait for reimbursement. The company is unable to book the expenses to the general ledger, and is also unable to bill out any expenses to be paid for by a contract client.

Once accounting receives the expense report, it is audited to some extent and entered into the books. The definition of "auditing" varies from company to company. Some organizations look at basic factors, such as correct math, approval signatures, and reasonableness of expenses, and see that receipts are attached. Other firms also check for policy compliance—staying within guidelines or per diem allowances, using preferred vendors, and traveling by the appropriate class of service. Obviously, the more manual effort involved in the auditing step, the greater the administrative time necessary before the expenses can be allocated.

Next, the accounting phase begins. Expense-report data is manually or systematically journalized. If the data is actually entered into a computer system, it could be very basic information, like accounting codes, subtotals of 100 percent and 80 percent deductible amounts, grand total expenses, and totals for the employee receivables system, including cash advances, centrally billed airline tickets, etc. Some companies also need more details: client billable versus nonbillable amounts, and company-specific job or client codes.

Finally, the employee receivables ledger is cleared by reconciling any cash advances or company-paid items. Reimbursement is generated for any amount due the employee, and expense reports are stored in some format.

## ISSUES IN EXPENSE-REPORT AUDITING

The respondents to the Survey of Business Travel Management also had something to tell us about how they audit expense reports, and two out of three consider the task to be a problem. One of the primary decisions they have to make is whether all expense reports are to be audited, or if a selected sample will suffice.

### Use of Spot Auditing

A majority of companies still audit all expense reports—a process that can be time-consuming and inaccurate if carried out manually. Remember that the meaning of "all reports are audited" depends on the company: "audit" may mean anything from a simple check of arithmetic to a line-by-line reconciliation against vendor or charge-card bills.

### Basis for Auditing Expense Reports

When expense reports are audited, more than 90 percent of companies in every volume category check for reasonableness of reported expenses, correctness of arithmetic, and proper documentation. The American Express survey indicates that these figures are up from 1988 virtually across the board, due largely to sizable increases among the lighter spenders. More firms check expense reports for policy compliance, and there has been a tremendous jump in those that check for the use of the designated travel agency.

## COST TO PROCESS EXPENSE REPORTS

Very few companies, even those with heavy travel and entertainment spending, have conducted studies to determine the cost of the administrative tasks associated with expense reporting and reconciliation. The American Express survey indicates that only one in seven private companies has ever attempted to calculate the cost of processing a temporary cash advance, and only one in ten has tried to estimate the cost associated with processing an expense report or issuing a reimbursement check.

In an attempt to get a handle on the cost of processing expense reports, American Express conducted a limited survey among some Fortune 500 companies. According to this report, the companies surveyed indicated that the cost of processing a report can vary from $2 to $25. These same companies also reported that it cost from $1 to $25 to issue a reimbursement check.

Estimates of the costs of carrying out the various administrative tasks involved in the expense-reporting process vary widely among the American Express survey participants—an indication that these tasks may be automated to a greater or lesser degree, depending on the company.

Another factor that varies dramatically from company to company is the amount of time necessary to complete the entire expense-report processing cycle.

## THE EXPENSE-REPORTING CYCLE

Studies conducted by the American Express Consulting Services have shown that it is not unusual for up to 25 percent of the expense reports received in accounting to be returned to the traveler or the initial approval authority for a variety of reasons, including incomplete documentation. These same studies have revealed that the average length of the expense-report processing cycle—that is, the period of time between the date a cash advance is drawn and the date reimbursement is made to settle the expense report—is 23 days.

According to Jeff Lang at American Express, the 23 days is to be considered a benchmark. Some organizations for which American Express has performed consulting services have had extremely long cycles.

Organizations need prompt reporting of expenses in order to settle balances due, clear advances, and allocate costs to the general ledger in a timely fashion. The key to monitoring the expense-report processing cycle is to have an audit trail of dates on the expense report to track all of these critical points. With all steps in the expense-reporting cycle dated, management can easily determine where in the process slowdowns are occurring.

## CASE STUDY: THE TRAVELMASTER
## AUTOMATED ACCOUNTING SYSTEM

A popular automated travel and expense management system is TRAVELMASTER from Coiva, located in Rosemont, Illinois.

TRAVELMASTER can feed travel accounting information to general-ledger or cost-accounting systems. The automated accounting systems can usually also establish sub-ledgers to track employee receivables, such as temporary advances, company-paid items, drafts, and more.

The automated system gathers information from various sources, such as advance reports, direct billing, expense reports, budget information, and travel reservations. After initial entry, information flows through the system without additional keying required. Once the data is collected, it can be edited against master files for validation and accuracy. This information is posted to user-defined sub-ledgers that track employee receivables. These transactions are also stored for hand-off to other accounting systems.

### Sources of Data

The TRAVELMASTER system can accept data from five main sources: advances, direct billing, expense reports, budgets, and travel reservations.

1. *Advances.* TRAVELMASTER can handle all forms of T&E advances as employee receivables, including multiple types of advances (temporary, education, relocation, as defined by the user). TRAVELMASTER can also accommodate multiple forms of disbursement, such as cash, check, traveler's check, electronic funds transfer, etc.

2. *Direct billing.* TRAVELMASTER can accept company-paid charges, either manually or on electronic media—tape or diskette—from vendors (credit card, travel agencies, vendors, etc.). Information provided on electronic media is used by TRAVELMASTER to automate the reconciliation of actual and approved expenses with company-paid charges. This process assures 100 percent audit capability.

3. *Expense reports*. Once the information is entered, TRAVEL-
   MASTER processes expense reports quickly and also has
   the ability to:
   a. automatically cross-check and balance expense reports.
   b. collect and retain detail on travel expenses for up to
      99 user-defined categories of expense.
   c. store expense distribution data without requiring addi-
      tional or further data entry into the general ledger or
      cost-accounting system.
   d. build and store information for the generation of ac-
      counting and management reports.
   e. accept expense-report information in foreign currencies
      for conversion to US dollars.
   f. present outstanding advance transaction detail for rec-
      onciliation at the time of expense-report processing.
   g. store vendor data for subsequent reporting and analysis.
   h. track taxable and nontaxable relocation expenses by cat-
      egory, and produce a worksheet for the preparation of
      IRS 4782 forms.
   i. track mileage and select costs for company-owned fleet
      vehicles. Also track personal use of fleet vehicles.
   j. calculate, display and schedule employee reimbursements.
4. *Budgets*. Information stored on TRAVELMASTER can be
   useful in the creation and subsequent analysis of T&E expense budgets. This allows the travel manager to compare
   actual expenses to established budgets as well as to historical spending levels.
5. *Travel reservations*. Travel reservation information can be electronically transferred and stored with TRAVELMASTER. This
   reduces data entry when processing expense reports or reconciling company-paid items. In addition, this data can be
   used to produce pre-trip expense reports, reminding travelers
   of approved reservations and company policies on rates and
   spending. This information can be stored and then retrieved
   for subsequent management analysis.

### Master Files

There are six master files in TRAVELMASTER: Travel Master,
Account Master, Organization Master, Employee Master, Company Policy, Government per Diems.

1. *Travel Master.* The Travel Master file allows the user to configure the system to accommodate unique requirements of the company. It defines the parameters of the system at the time of set-up, or they can be altered at a later time. Travel Master defines employee receivable sub-ledger accounts and defines the organization master structure. It also defines the expense categories and column titles to be included on the expense report screen. Also defined are disbursement or payment methods and codes (cash, manual check, electronic fund transfer, etc.).

2. *Account Master.* This file stores all valid account and project numbers for TRAVELMASTER. It also defines items in each account as direct/indirect, billable and/or subject to government contractor accounting requirements. Account Master supports on-line additions, deletions, and changes to account descriptions and status.

3. *Organization Master.* The Organization Master file defines your corporate organization within TRAVELMASTER. Multiple organization levels can be supported. The Organization Master file distributes employee expenses to the appropriate level and generates expense analysis reports according to defined levels.

4. *Employee Master.* The Employee Master file stores company traveler information such as name, address, and badge number.

5. *Company Policy.* TRAVELMASTER can monitor expenses according to established company guidelines, negotiated rates, and standard industry indexes.

6. *Government per Diems.* TRAVELMASTER gives the travel manager the ability to enter and allocate expenses by project and enables the company to comply with Public Law 99–234 by identifying those expenses that are unallowable, allowable, and in excess of government per diems. It also allows the proportionate assignment of allowable amounts to the appropriate accounts.

## System Processing

The system-processing abilities of TRAVELMASTER support three functions: edit and validation, subsidiary ledgers, and transaction storage.

1. *Edit and validation.* Upon input, transactions are edited for validation on-line. Included are edits for valid employees, account numbers, and cost centers.
2. *Subsidiary ledgers.* The system allows the travel manager to create user-defined subsidiary ledgers for employee receivable transactions. Subsidiary ledger information is available for management reports, individual employee statements, on-line reviews, and tracking:
   a. Ages and reports all open items.
   b. Makes data available for on-line inquiry.
   c. Provides for multiple sub-ledgers (temporary advances, company-paid charges, drafts, etc.).
3. *Transaction storage.* All TRAVELMASTER accounting transactions are stored for management reporting, hand-off to other accounting systems, vendor analysis, policy checking, etc.

### System Output

Besides reports, TRAVELMASTER produces an output file of journal entries to feed general-ledger/cost-accounting systems. It automates the process of system journal entries, eliminating the need for re-entering data. TRAVELMASTER can also generate checks or electronically transfer funds.

## CASE STUDY: MALLINCKRODT MEDICAL, INC.

Mallinckrodt Medical, Inc., located in St. Louis, is a billion-dollar-sales company in the field of medical supplies. The following is taken from their procedure memorandum:

1. PROPOSE
   To establish the procedure for reporting of employee business expenses.
2. APPLICABLE TO:
   All Mallinckrodt Medical Company personnel.
3. REFERENCE
   A. Policy Directives:
      01.01.005, "Corporate Travel Policy"

4. DEFINITION:

Employee business expenses are defined by the tax code as those "ordinary and necessary" in carrying on a business. They are generally limited to:

A. Travel and transportation expenses while an employee is away from home, which generally include such items as air, rail, bus, and taxi fares; automobile rentals and operating expenses; meals; lodging; gratuities; and telephone.

B. Automobile expenses, such as the use of an employee's personal automobile for business purposes, are reimbursable at a standard mileage rate as established by the Corporate Director of Financial Services. Parking fees and tolls are also allowable expenses.

C. Entertainment and recreation expenses that are directly business-related. The Company and the IRS do not permit any deduction for lavish or extravagant entertainment expenses.

D. Dues, education, and other expenses, which include such items as professional society dues, registration fees and business seminars.

5. GENERAL:

A. It is the intent of the Company to:

1. Comply fully with all IRS regulations on employee business expenses.

2. Pay or reimburse employees for all actual reasonable and necessary expenses incurred in the course of its business and which are properly accounted for and reported. The Company is not liable for payment of personal expenses incurred by an employee while in a travel status or otherwise.

B. Employees issued an American Express Corporate Card should utilize it whenever possible to pay for business expenses.

C. There will be no reimbursement for non-incurred expenses. Examples of this would be situations such as an employee charging mileage while riding with another employee, charging "equivalent motel charges" when an employee is staying with a friend or relative on a business trip, etc.

D. The Corporate Director of Financial Services has responsibility for interpretation of this Procedure; any questions regarding allowability of expenses should be referred to him or his designee.

E. Although it is the intent of this Procedure to establish guidelines relating to employee business expenses, it is recommended that certain situations requiring special consideration may occur from time to time. The fundamental procedures established by this directive must be administered by all divisions. Exceptions to any part of this procedure, which must be the result of unusual unique business conditions, must be approved in writing by the appropriate division head. Evidence of such written approval must be submitted with the related expense report.

6. GUIDELINES:
   A. All sites must use the same forms:
      1. Transportation Request—13567
      2. Expense Report—MK 14000
      3. Request for Check/Cash—MK 02643
   B. Transportation Request, Request for Check/Cash and Expense Report forms must be approved by an employee's superior who has been delegated this authority. There are two exceptions:
      1. A person at the level of Division Head or higher may approve his own request for travel advances and transportation.
      2. An employee in charge of a site located away from the base of his Division Head may approve his own travel and transportation advances up to a limit of $1,000.
      Note: Expense Report forms reporting travel advances and transportation advances mentioned above as well as any other Expense Report forms for persons noted in 1. and 2. must still be approved by that person's superior delegated this authority.

Any Expense Report with total expenditures exceeding $10,000 must be submitted to the President by the department responsible for Expense Report processing. Accordingly, this requirement does not preclude processing of the Expense Report or reimbursing balances due an employee who has incurred such business expenses, provided it is properly approved.

C. All requests for company-purchased air and rail tickets must be made on a Transportation Request form or other equivalent form and approved by the next higher level. Although an employee can decide upon his own travel arrangements, he should submit his Transportation Request to Accounts Payable to reconcile payment of central billing.

D. Company-purchased air and rail tickets and cash advances must be charged to employee accounts receivable advance accounts and reported on Expense Report forms.

E. Air travel arrangements are to be made in accordance with guidelines as established by Policy Directive 01.01.005.

F. A cash advance must be requested on a Request for Check/Cash form or other equivalent form and must be processed by the employee's site Cashier (or person designated to perform this function) and/or Accounts Payable department. It may be disbursed by another site when the employee alters his travel arrangements en route.

G. A cash advance must be used within a reasonable time period or returned by the employee to whom it is granted. Accordingly, permanent advances (cash advances which are held indefinitely for use on an "as needed" basis) are not allowed. In addition, cash advances are not transferable from one employee to another.

H. All employee business expenses must be substantiated by an Expense Report, with the following exceptions, which should be submitted on the appropriate form:
   1. Tuition refunds.
   2. Medical expenses.
   3. Moving expenses associated with the movement of household furnishings or other related expenses reimbursed through the employee's payroll department.

I. Expense Reports for local expenses, including business conferences, may be reported monthly. For out-of-town travel, an Expense Report should be prepared and submitted within seven calendar days after returning

from travel status. Payment for any balance due the
company must accompany the Expense Report unless:

1. The employee is to return to travel status within
   fourteen calendar days from the Expense Report's
   submission, or
2. The balance due is less than $100 and the employee
   is to incur additional expenses within fourteen days
   from the Report's submission.

Each employee is responsible for displaying a proper
accounting of business expenses on his Expense Report
and securing proper approval of it. In addition, each
employee is accountable for company-advanced funds
and company-purchased transportation through final
disposition. Such advances and/or transportation are
considered "due the company" until an Expense Report
has been properly prepared, approved, and processed.

J. Employees are reimbursed for the use of their personal
   automobiles at the standard mileage rate established by
   the Corporation. Local mileage qualifying for such
   reimbursement is that which is in excess of the
   round-trip mileage from an employee's residence and
   normal work site, provided such mileage is for
   business purposes and is incurred in one working day.

K. Meal expenses incurred by employees while in their
   home cities should be treated as personal expenses
   unless the meals are for necessary business purposes.
   In situations where the parties involved in
   reimbursable business meals have direct reporting
   relationships, the senior person present should pay the
   bill and request reimbursement on his own Expense
   Report. If a subordinate pays the bill and requests
   reimbursement on his Expense Report, approval must
   be obtained from the next highest level of authority
   above the senior person present.

L. In situations where exempt employees not eligible for
   overtime pay are required to work overtime, (1) reimbursement of reasonable amounts spent for meals is
   allowed, and (2) on nonscheduled workdays, mileage
   is reimbursable at the current standard mileage
   allowance.

M. Fees for employee's personal credit cards, not issued in
   the company's name, are not reimbursable charges.

N. Reporting expenses for other company personnel must be avoided whenever possible since this practice obscures and unduly inflates the expenses of the reporting employee.

O. Expenses for spouses (out-of-town travel, local expenses, etc.) are reimbursable only when the situation demands and, in addition to other approvals noted in this Policy, must be approved by the applicable Group Executive. Memberships for spouses are not reimbursable.

P. Expenses for child care are reimbursable for employees only if incurred as a result of approved out-of-town business travel by spouses.

Q. Dues for professional charges, provided that they are properly approved. Memberships in clubs and organizations (other than professional societies or travel clubs) for which dues are paid by the Company are reimbursable expenses, provided that the initial membership period is approved by the President.

R. The Company prefers that all expenses, regardless of amount, be supported by original receipts whenever possible. Original receipts must be submitted for hotel bills and all other individual expenses of $25 or more. The employee's copies of air and rail tickets and all American Express charge tickets, regardless of amount, must be submitted with Expense Reports.

## TRAVEL MANAGEMENT TIPS

- Expense reporting and reconciliation offers management an important opportunity to control both direct and indirect expenses of travel and entertainment.

- The expense-reporting process still presents problems for a majority of companies.

- A majority of companies still audit all expense reports. This is a process that can be time-consuming and inaccurate if carried out manually.

- When expense reports are audited, more than 90 percent of companies check for reasonableness of reported expenses, correctness of arithmetic, and proper documentation.

*Chapter Seventeen*

# Managing Travel Information

G iven the vast amount of data that is available, one of the main goals of travel managers should be to become more computer literate. This computer literacy involves basic knowledge about computers in general and the process by which information reports are generated. It is not enough to look at a report and read the numbers, the travel manager needs to become involved in the data-collection process and understand it fully.

Jeff Hoffman, president of Competitive Technologies, Inc., a computer software developer located in Houston, Texas, states, "Information management is the one area where the corporate travel manager can take control of his/her destiny. They need to know more than just how reservations are made. Travel managers need to have a computer on their desk and use it daily. Travel managers have been kept in the dark for too long by the vendors. The assumption on the part of the vendors was that the less the manager knew, the better. In a commission-based industry, the less the consumer knew, the more money the vendor could make. This is beginning to change as more and more travel managers are taking control of their lives and learning to manage information."

Hoffman continues, "Knowledge is power. We need to reverse the trend where the vendors held all of the power and give it back to the travel managers. After all, it is their money that is being spent here. As a consumer you would never go to a grocery store and hand somebody money and tell them to pick out your food for you and tell you what the best price is and what is good for you, yet this is exactly what is done every day in the travel industry."

The goal of this chapter is to show travel managers that the only time they have control of their job is when they have adequate information. This information is meaningful only when the manager understands how it was obtained.

## SYSTEMS CONCEPTS

The concept of a system underlies the field of information. Generally, a system is defined as a group of interrelated or interacting elements forming a unified whole. The planets form a solar system. Any living organism is a system. The entire travel industry is a system. When an airline raises its prices to a destination, there are fewer travelers, which leads to lower hotel occupancy and fewer car rentals.

The elements of the systems described above work together for a common goal. James O'Brien in his book *Introduction to Information Systems in Business Management* defines a system as a "group of interrelated components working together toward a common goal by accepting inputs and producing outputs in an organized transformation process." O'Brien explains that such a system has three basic functional components that interact:

1. *Input.* Input involves capturing and assembling elements that enter the system so they can be processed. Examples: raw materials, energy, data, and human effort must be secured and organized for processing.

2. *Processing.* Processing involves transformation processes that convert input into output. Examples: a manufacturing process, the human breathing process, data calculations.

3. *Output.* Output involves transferring elements that have been produced by the transformation process to their ultimate destination. Examples: finished products, human services, and management information must be transmitted to their human users.

O'Brien adds that the systems approach can be made more useful by including two additional components: feedback and control. A system with feedback and control components is sometimes called a cybernetic system, that is, a self-monitoring, self-regulating system. O'Brien defines the two additional components as follows:

1. *Feedback.* Feedback is data or information concerning the performance of a system.

2. *Control.* Control is a major system function that monitors and evaluates feedback to determine whether the system is moving toward the achievement of its goal. It then makes any necessary adjustments to the input and processing components of the system to ensure that proper output is produced.

There are other characteristics that are important to the understanding of systems. First of all, a system does not exist in a vacuum. O'Brien states that a system exists and functions in an environment consisting of other systems. If a system is one of the components of a larger system, it is called a subsystem, and the larger system is its environment. A system is separated from its environment and from other systems by its system boundary.

Other systems may also exist in the same environment. Some of these systems may be connected to each other by means of a shared boundary, or interface. A system that must interact with other systems in order to survive is called an open system. If a system is able to change itself or its environment in order to survive, it is known as an adaptive system.

## INFORMATION PROCESSING

O'Brien states that it is important to understand information systems in the context of their use in information processing, which is also called data processing. Generally, data or information processing is defined as the converting of data to make it more usable and meaningful. Data is normally not useful until it has been involved in a value-added process where:

1. it is organized.
2. its content is analyzed.
3. it is placed in a proper context for use (reports).

The common data elements used in information systems are a field, a record, a file, and a database. Each of these are defined by O'Brien in the following manner:

1. *Field.* A field is a grouping of characters that represent a characteristic of a person, place, thing, or event. For example, an employee's name field.
2. *Record.* A record is a collection of interrelated fields. For example, an employee's payroll record might consist of a name field, a social security number field, a department field, and a salary field.
3. *File.* A file is a collection of interrelated records. For example, a payroll file might consist of the payroll records of all employees of a firm.
4. *Database.* A database is an integrated collection of interrelated records or files. For example, the personnel database of a business might contain payroll, personnel action, and employee skills files.

## INFORMATION SYSTEMS CONCEPTS

An information system, according to O'Brien, is a set of people, procedures, and resources that collects, transforms, and disseminates information in an organization. O'Brien states that there are three major uses of information systems in an organization:

1. Support of business operations.
2. Support of management decision making.
3. Support of strategic organizational advantage.

In the 1980s, several new roles for information systems appeared. First, the rapid development of microcomputer processing power, application software packages, and telecommunications networks gave birth to the phenomenon of end-user computing. Now, end users can use their own computing resources to support their job requirements, instead of waiting for the indirect support of corporate information services departments. Next, it became evident that most top corporate executives did not directly use either the reports of information-reporting systems or the analytical modeling capabilities of decision-support systems, so the concept of executive information systems was developed. These information systems attempt to give top executives an easy way to get the critical information they want, when they want it, tailored to the formats they prefer.

Third, breakthroughs were made in the development and application of artificial-intelligence techniques to business information systems. Expert systems and other knowledge-based systems can now serve as consultants to end users by providing expert advice when needed to support specific job tasks.

Finally, an important new role for information systems appeared in the 1980s and is expected to continue into the 1990s. This is the concept of a strategic role for information systems, sometimes called strategic information systems. Now information systems are expected to play a direct role in helping a firm achieve its strategic objectives. This places a new responsibility on the information systems department of a business. No longer is it merely an information utility, a service group providing information-processing services to end users within the firm. Now it must become a producer of information-based products and services that earn profits for the firm and also give it a competitive advantage in the marketplace.

All these changes have increased the importance of the information-systems function to the success of the firm. However, they also present new managerial challenges to end users to effectively capitalize on the potential benefits of information systems.

## INFORMATION SYSTEMS FOR MANAGEMENT DECISION MAKING

The concept of management information systems (MIS) originated in the 1960s and became the basis of almost all attempts to relate computer technology and systems theory to data processing in organizations. During the early years of computing, it became evident that the computer was being applied to the solution of business problems in a piecemeal fashion, focusing almost entirely on the computerization of clerical and record-keeping tasks. The concept of management information systems was developed to counteract such inefficient development and ineffective use of computers by focusing instead on providing information needed for decision making by managers. Though tarnished by early failures, the MIS concept is still recognized as vital to efficient and effective information systems in organizations for two major reasons.

First of all, it emphasizes the management orientation of information processing in business. A major goal of computer-based information systems should be the support of management decision making, not merely the processing of data generated by business operations.

Second, MIS emphasizes that a systems framework should be used for organizing information systems applications. Business applications should be viewed as interrelated and integrated computer-based information systems and not as independent data processing jobs.

Management information systems support the decision-making needs of strategic (top) management, tactical (middle) management, and operating (supervisory) management. Operations information systems support the information-processing requirements of the day-to-day operations of a business, as well as some lower-level operational management functions.

Providing information and support for management decision making by all levels of management from top executives to middle managers to supervisors is a complex task. Conceptually, several major types of information systems are needed to support a variety of end-user managerial responsibilities.

## Information-Reporting Systems

Information-reporting systems provide managerial end-users with information products that support their day-to-day decision-making needs. Reports and displays produced by these systems provide information that managers have specified in advance as adequately meeting their information needs. Information-reporting systems access databases containing information about internal operations that has been previously processed by transaction processing systems. Data about the business environment is obtained from external sources.

Information products provided to managers include displays and reports that can be furnished on demand; or periodically, according to a predetermined schedule; or whenever exceptional conditions occur. For example, travel managers could receive visual displays at their workstations about hotel usage by department.

## Decision-Support Systems

Decision-support systems are a natural progression from information-reporting systems and transaction-processing systems. Decision-support systems are interactive, computer-based information systems that use a model base of decision models and specialized databases to assist the decision-making processes of managerial end-users. Thus, they are different from transaction-processing systems, which focus on processing the data generated by business transactions and operations. They also differ from information-reporting systems, which focus on providing managers with prespecified information (reports) that could be used to help them make more effective structured types of decisions.

Instead, decision-support systems provide managerial end-users with information in an interactive session on an ad hoc (as needed) basis. A decision-support system provides analytical modeling, data retrieval, and information presentation capabilities that allow managers to generate the information they need to make more-unstructured types of decisions in an interactive, computer-based process. For example, electronic spreadsheets and other decision-support software allow a managerial end-user to receive interactive responses to ad hoc requests for information, posed as a series of What if? questions. This differs from the prespecified responses of information-reporting systems. When using a decision-support system, managers are exploring alternative sets of assumptions. Thus managerial end-users do not have to specify their information needs in advance. Instead, the decision-support system interactively helps them find the information they need.

## Executive Information Systems

Executive information systems are management information systems tailored to the strategic information needs of top management. Top executives get the information they need from many sources, including letters, memos, periodicals, and reports produced manually as well as by computer systems. Other sources of executive information are meetings, telephone calls, and social activities. Thus, much of a top executive's information comes from noncomputer sources. Computer-generated information has not played a primary role in meeting many top executives' information needs.

The goal of computer-based executive information systems is to provide top management with immediate and easy access to selective information about key factors that are critical to accomplishing a firm's strategic objectives. Therefore, an executive information system is easy to understand and operate. Graphic displays are used extensively, and immediate access to internal and external databases is provided. Executive information systems provide information about the current status and projected trends for key factors selected by top executives.

## OTHER CLASSIFICATIONS OF INFORMATION SYSTEMS

Several major categories of information systems provide more specialized or broader classifications than those just examined. That is because these information systems can support operations, management, or strategic applications. For example:

1. Expert advice for operational or managerial decision making is provided by expert systems and other knowledge-based information systems.
2. Direct, hands-on support for both the operational and managerial applications of end-users is provided by end-user computing systems.
3. Operational and managerial applications in support of basic business functions are provided by business-function information systems.
4. Competitive products and services to help achieve strategic objectives are provided by strategic information systems.

### End-User Computing Systems

End-user computing systems are computer-based information systems that directly support both the operational and managerial applications of end-users. In end-user computing systems, end-users typically use microcomputer workstations and a variety of software packages and databases for personal productivity, information retrieval, decision support, and application development.

## Business Function Information Systems

Information systems directly support the business functions of accounting, finance, human resources management, marketing, and operations management.

## Integrated Information Systems

Most information systems are typically integrated combinations of the various types of information systems just described. That is because the conceptual classifications of information systems are designed to emphasize the many different roles of information systems.

In practice, these roles are integrated into composite or cross-functional information systems that provide a variety of functions. Thus, most information systems are designed to produce information and support decision making for various levels of management and business functions, as well as do record-keeping and transaction-processing chores.

## Expert Systems

The field of artificial intelligence (AI) deals with computers that have limited abilities to mimic human decision making. The goal of AI is to make machines smarter and to imitate people. HAL in the movie *2001* is an AI product. The whole area of AI is similar to yield management in terms of development, in that it was originally overpromoted to users, could not live up to its press, went through a period of disrepute, and has now found acceptable niches.

Despite the many uses AI systems could have in the travel industry, few have been developed. It is in this area that travel automation has lagged behind other industries. Part of the reason for this laggard behavior is that most of the automation talent in the industry is concentrated in developing and maintaining CRSs.

There is also a considerable dearth of AI expertise. Current AI travel uses range from travel planning to helping hotel managers price meeting and convention business.

Artificial intelligence technology represents a mind-set, a way of looking at solving problems from a particular point of view, that differs from the more traditional approaches. Much of this difference is traceable to the nature of the problems AI researchers tackle. Artificial intelligence research has concentrated on solving problems that are demonstrably solvable by human beings, but for which no currently well-formulated, feasible methodology exists. This class of problems includes:

1. How we learn.
2. How we play games.
3. How we communicate.
4. How we diagnose.
5. How we plan.
6. How we create.

The approaches to these problems can best be characterized as informal, symbolic, and conceptual rather than formal. Of course, where appropriate, formal approaches can be integrated into these more intuitive methods. The methods employed tend to be non-procedural, flexible, and adaptive. Knowledge can easily be added, deleted, or modified.

Although AI has much in common with other computer science disciplines, it differs from more conventional computer science areas in the following respects:

1. Viewpoint (plausible and logical reasoning, instead of quantitative calculation).
2. Subject matter very knowledge intensive.
3. Tolerance for errors and imprecise data.
4. Symbolic manipulation instead of numeric manipulation.
5. Inference and deduction capabilities.

Even though the field of artificial intelligence is only a few decades old, its foundations begin in the nineteenth century with the work of the logician George Boole (1815–1864). Boole gave us the formal logical definitions of "and," "or," and other terms that make up the vocabulary of artificial intelligence. In this century, artificial intelligence received its impetus from the work of Alan Turing (1912–1954). Turing was one of the first to put forth the idea that a machine could be programmed to exhibit intelligent behavior.

One of his ideas, the Turing Test, remains a landmark. Turing envisioned a test in which there is computer communication among three rooms. In one room, a person sits at the computer, and another room contains only the computer. Both claim to be a person, and someone in the third room has to decide which is the person and which is the computer. The person deciding can communicate with the others only through a computer screen. If after an hour the examiner cannot tell the difference between the person and the computer, then it could be said that the machine was intelligent.

One of the first persons who attempted the Turing Test was K. M. Colby, in the mid-1960s, who developed a program that simulated a conversation between a patient and a psychologist. Consider the following conversation, conducted via teletype:

**Therapist:**
How can I help you?
**Patient:**
I don't know.
**Therapist:**
Try to tell me something about it.
**Patient:**
No.
**Therapist:**
Can you elaborate?
**Patient:**
I am sick and tired today.
**Therapist:**
Do you have any idea why?
**Patient:**
Yes, I'm old.
**Therapist:**
Please go on.

**Patient:**

I seem to have lost interest in everything.

**Therapist:**

Tell me more about such feelings.

**Patient:**

I have some idea why I feel this way.

**Therapist:**

You have?

**Patient:**

It seems I miss having a family.

**Therapist:**

What makes you miss having a family?

**Patient:**

There is a challenge about it.

**Therapist:**

Why is that important to you?

This conversation may give you an eerie feeling that the computer has some understanding; in fact it has none, and is merely following some fairly simple rules. The fact remains that today we have advanced little closer to fulfilling the elements of the Turing Test than we were thirty years ago.

There are six main branches of AI: robotics, vision systems, natural language, sound recognition, knowledge systems, and neural networks. Robotics is the use of machines to perform tasks that were once done by humans. Most robotic applications are used by the military. Robotics is also used extensively in manufacturing. Vision systems are used to interpret two- and three-dimensional scenes from images obtained through artificial sensors. Natural language is the ability to talk to a computer by using only conventional language instead of computer languages. The fourth area of AI, sound recognition, deals with taking an audible sound and turning it into a readable language.

The fifth and sixth areas of AI, knowledge systems and neural networks, will be the main focus of this chapter. Knowledge systems are structured systems that concern a particular field of expertise. Knowledge systems combine human expert knowledge and informational databases. The CRS and other areas of travel automation involve collecting, organizing, and maintaining databases of information. Knowledge systems involve interpreting data and using it to make decisions. The main difference between AI and other computer areas is the way in which they process data. AI systems interpret the data and its relationships, whereas conventional computer techniques only manipulate data.

Neural networks attempt to model the human brain. Neural networks consist of layers, or arrays, of processing elements called elements: an input layer, an output layer, and one or more intermediate layers. In an analogy to the human brain, the processing units can be thought of as neurons and the connections as synapses. Each layer's processing units can be connected to any other unit, although they are most often just connected to units of neighboring layers. Typically, each unit is connected to a large number of input units, and it outputs to an equally large number of units. The processing elements combine their inputs nonlinearly.

## Knowledge Systems

The biggest impact that knowledge systems will have on the travel industry is in improving human productivity. The term "knowledge systems" is a very broad-based concept. A more commonly used term is "expert systems." Expert systems are knowledge systems used in a very limited subject area. An example of the difference between the two would be an expert system helping to diagnose heart problems, whereas a knowledge system would understand the workings of the entire body. Expert systems are the most widely used and practical AI area. The advantage of these systems is that they take knowledge from "experts" and program how the experts arrive at decisions. This allows a novice to have immediate access to years of experience in making a decision.

There is some disagreement as to all the areas covered by knowledge systems, but generally speaking they cover the following topics:

1. Classification models.
2. Diagnosis.
3. Hypothesis and test.
4. Collision model.
5. Design and configuration.
6. Planning and scheduling.

It is best to think of each of these areas in terms of models. A model is a representation or abstraction of something. As little kids we all made model airplanes (replicas of originals). Now as grown-ups we still make models, but thanks to modern computing power, the models are of complicated processes.

The first category, classification models, involves the process of sorting out the correct choice from among many alternatives. Classification models are fairly easy to develop because the goal is only to recognize a general pattern. A biologist who is confronted with the problem of cataloging a new species would find this type of model useful.

The next category, diagnosis, is more difficult to build than classification models because a specific cause is sought. In a diagnosis model, symptoms are used to arrive at causes. For example, a doctor might ask specific questions of a patient to determine what is wrong. In the movie *The Hunt for Red October*, the computer program used on the submarine to analyze the sounds made by different submarines was a diagnosis model.

The third category, hypothesis and test, is used to identify which course of action to choose from among many. This model is a combination of the first two. Using this method, you make initial hypotheses about possible courses of action to take. The program proceeds under the assumption that the direction you have picked is correct and plays out the scenario. The outcome shows how valid the initial assumptions are.

Under the collision model, patterns that are not desired are found and rejected. At first blush, this sounds a little funny, but there are numerous occasions when the unacceptable solutions are fewer and better defined than the acceptable ones. In this situation, it is more efficient to throw out these and accept what is left over.

The design and configuration approach consists of choosing a mixture of known components and using established rules to create new design patterns. The last model, planning and scheduling, entails a network of other models used to solve problems in timetable events such as airline schedules.

### Examples of Expert System Applications

- Text browsing and understanding.
- Monitoring the news.

- Human-directed interactive news or text browser.
- Intelligent front-end to multiple databases.
- Smart financial analyzer.
- Trader's dealing system uses natural language to read electronic messages and to build trade ticket.
- Natural language reading of money transfers.
- Business planning and forecasting.
- Sales advisor.
- Intelligent customer service assistance.
- Customizing customer catalogs and sales campaigns, with link to inventory management systems to identify slow movers, obsolete products, and nonstandard products..
- Sales and marketing prospecting and profiling for customized targeting.
- Custom investment advisor.
- Assessment of workers and department performance.
- Financial planner.
- Personal tax-planning advisor.
- Automated trading.
- Analysis of merger candidates.
- Corporate credit analyzer.
- Insurance underwriting advisor.
- Fraud detection.
- Gate scheduling for airlines.
- Automatic pilots.
- Automated order processing.
- Health claims adjustment.
- Records management.

## SAMPLE MANAGEMENT REPORTS

There are a variety of sample reports on the market:

1. Component Travel Management Summary Report.
2. Travel Detail Report.

3. Air Travel Detail Report.
4. Reason Code Summary Report.
5. Air Travel Exception Report.
6. Aging of Reservations Report.
7. Flight Class Summary Report.
8. Validating Airline Summary Report.
9. City Pairs by Carrier Report.
10. Voids and Refunds Report.
11. Hotel Detail Report.
12. Hotel Usage Report.
13. Car-Rental Detail Report.
14. Car-Rental Volume Report.
15. Car-Rental Size Report.
16. Aging Analysis of Reservations Report.
17. Airfare Cost Per Mile Analysis.
18. Potential Groups Analysis.

### Report 1: Component Travel Management Summary Report

The Component Travel Management Summary Report provides an overview analysis of airfare, lodging, and car-rental data. Current period and year-to-date data are presented by the organizational component, as designated by the client. This report provides the following benefits to the travel manager:

1. Provides a big-picture view of overall activity for the period and quick comparison to year-to-date benchmarks.
2. Highlights cost-containment successes and opportunities through vendor and class-of-service statistics, in addition to advance booking trends.
3. Allows comparison across divisions or departments when the report is run at different organizational levels.

### Report 2: Travel Detail Report

The Travel Detail Report provides a complete listing of all activity the travel management company processed during the reporting month. Air, hotel, and car-rental information is grouped by itinerary. This report provides the following:

1. Provides a single reliable reference of complete travel plans.
2. Identifies lost savings opportunities when air transactions are not accompanied by car reservations, and hotel bookings with overnight stays.

### Report 3: Air Travel Detail Report

The Air Travel Detail Report provides a complete listing of all air activity ticketed by the travel management company during the reporting month. The travel manager can use this information to:

1. Provide reliable reference for post-travel review of planned versus actual air expenditures.
2. Highlight compliance questions via review of travel time, class of travel, or reason code identified.

### Report 4: Reason Code Summary Report

The Reason Code Summary Report compiles the number of occurrences of each reason code for the month. The reason code identifies the reason why a traveler turned down a low-fare ticket. The financial implications associated with the reason code are also summarized. The travel manager can use this report to:

1. Highlight opportunities for air savings.
2. Identify overall trends toward or away from compliance with corporate travel policy.

### Report 5: Air Travel Exception Report

The Air Travel Exception Report provides a detailed listing of key air travel-related information. The report is sorted by reason code, and should be used in conjunction with report 4, Reason Code Summary, to identify why the lowest fare was or was not received.

The travel manager will use this report to provide an easy follow-up trail for reason-code issues identified on the Reason Code Summary, by detailing all occurrences by code, department, and traveler.

## Report 6: Aging of Reservations Report

The Aging of Reservations Report analyzes the timing of air-travel planning by reporting how far in advance tickets were purchased. The report can be for various levels of the organization and is divided into three sections:

1. Fares paid equal to regular fare—shows the number of tickets and the cost of tickets purchased at full fare. The totals are summarized by the number of days in advance in which the reservations were made.

2. Fares paid less than regular fare—shows the number of tickets and the cost of tickets purchased at a discounted fare. The totals are summarized by the number of days in advance in which the reservations were made.

3. Totals—shows a summarization of the two categories listed above.

## Report 7: Flight Class Summary Report

The Flight Class Summary Report totals the number of segments (flights) purchased on each airline carrier. In addition to grand totals by carrier, subtotals by flight class are also reported. This report provides the travel manager with negotiating leverage with carriers through documentation for more profitable airline negotiations.

## Report 8: Validating Airline Summary Report

The Validating Airline Summary Report totals dollars, tickets, and segments validated for individual airline carriers. Because the validating airline initially receives the total cost of the airline ticket and is responsible for reimbursing all other carriers involved, the validating airline benefits from the use of funds prior to reimbursing the other airlines.

This report is used to provide leverage through demonstration of the broader financial impact a company has on a specific carrier.

## Report 9: City Pairs by Carrier Report

The City Pairs by Carrier Report summarizes the company's travel between any two airports. Segments by carrier are summarized.

This report provides two main benefits to the travel manager:

1. Identifies market-specific negotiation opportunities.
2. Provides negotiating leverage, since information is verifiable and it is summarized to demonstrate market-share shift opportunities.

### Report 10: Voids and Refunds Report

The Voids and Refunds Report details all tickets voided or returned during the month. A ticket is considered void if the return is processed by the travel management company prior to reporting the ticket sale to the airlines.

This report documents ticket volume and flags travel management improvement opportunities if the return rate varies from history or from norms. It also supports returned ticket research.

### Report 11: Hotel Detail Report

The Hotel Detail Report provides a complete listing of all hotel reservations that were booked by the travel management company during the reporting month.

This report is used by the travel manager to highlight compliance questions via review of accommodation type, seemingly high room rates, or extended stays. It is also used to provide reliable reference for post-travel review of planned versus actual expenditures.

### Report 12: Hotel Usage Report

The Hotel Usage Report summarizes hotel reservation activity for the stated period. It can be sorted by location or hotel chain, and can also be produced for various organizational levels such as department or division. The final pages include domestic and international totals.

Travel managers use this report to:

1. Direct hotel negotiation strategy (e.g., the numbers indicate that you should pursue a national contract with hotel chain X, but conduct local negotiations in Los Angeles).

2. Provide leverage to secure negotiated rates from vendors, since the information is verifiable and it is summarized to demonstrate market-share shift opportunities.

3. Flag noncompliance issues by highlighting reservation activity at unapproved properties.

### Report 13: Car-Rental Detail Report

The Car Rental Detail Report provides a complete listing of all car-rental reservations that were booked by the travel management company during the reporting period. The travel manager benefits in two ways from this report:

1. It highlights compliance questions via review of vendor, car type, or extended rental periods.

2. It provides reliable reference for post-travel review of planned versus actual activity.

### Report 14: Car-Rental Volume Report

The Car Rental Volume Report summarizes car-rental activity by vendor and location for the stated period. The final pages include domestic and international totals by vendor. This report can be used in three ways by the travel manager:

1. To direct car negotiation strategy by identifying vendor activity by location.

2. To provide leverage to secure negotiated rates from vendors, since information is verifiable and it is summarized to demonstrate market-share shift opportunities.

3. To flag noncompliance issues by highlighting reservation activity with unapproved vendors.

### Report 15: Car-Rental Size Report

The Car Rental Size Report summarizes car-rental reservation activity by vendor and car type for the stated period. Domestic and international totals are also reported. There are three benefits to using this report:

1. It documents car usage by size for negotiation leverage, enabling the company to properly evaluate vendor contract proposals (e.g., is the offer to rent a luxury car for the price of a midsize meaningful?).
2. It flags a national contract opportunity if a large volume is split among multiple suppliers.
3. It flags compliance issues resulting from use of an unauthorized vendor or car type.

## Report 16: Aging Analysis of Reservations Report (Impact of Late Reservations)

The Aging Analysis of Reservations Report is a pro-forma report that answers the question, "What would the financial impact have been if I had ticketed all my travel on the A-B-A city pair one period earlier?" Number of tickets, fares, and discounts are identified by period. The total potential savings are also calculated.

## Report 17: Airfare Cost Per Mile Analysis

The Airfare Cost Per Mile (CPM) Analysis identifies, by city pair, the fares actually paid and the related cost per mile for the stated period. Detailing identified carriers and departure times helps explain fare or CPM variances noted within the city pair.

This report provides potential city-pair negotiation leverage through documented comparable activity and the ability to shift market share. It also flags noncompliance and/or productivity issues if mid-day travel is prevalent.

## Report 18: Potential Groups Analysis

The Potential Groups Analysis identifies, by destination city, negotiated group-fare opportunities that were not identified. Since the past is often a predictor of the future, this report flags travelers who can be contacted for coordination into future negotiated meeting-fare programs. It also provides a basis for evaluating if the meeting was necessary, and/or if all attendees were really required.

## BACK-OFFICE SYSTEMS

An area that is essential to understanding information in the travel industry is the back-office system. Back-office systems are important, because all information that goes to the travel manager comes through the back-office system.

The back-office system is essentially an accounting system. According to Nadine Godwin, special publications editor at *Travel Weekly* magazine, "The most sophisticated choice is an in-house computerized accounting system that involves placing a computer and all the necessary terminals in the agency office. . . . These systems have the ability to interface with an agency's automated reservation system. This arrangement allows information collected by the CRS in connection with a booking to be transferred immediately by connecting lines to the in-house computer.

## TRAVEL MANAGEMENT TIPS

- Given the vast amount of data that is available, one of the main goals of travel managers should be to become more computer literate.
- Data or information processing is defined as the converting of data to make it more usable and meaningful.
- Information reporting systems provide managerial end-users with information products that support their day-to-day decision-making needs.
- Decision-support systems are a natural progression from information-reporting systems and transaction-processing systems.
- Executive information systems are management information systems tailored to the strategic information needs of top management.
- The goal of computer-based executive information systems is to provide top management with immediate and easy access to selective information about key factors that are critical to accomplishing a firm's strategic objective.
- The biggest impact that knowledge systems will have on the travel industry is in improving human productivity.

# SECTION

# V

The last section of the book deals with some special topics that are important to the travel manager and could not be categorized in any of the other sections. We start out with official travel. There are very real differences in the way business people, government employees, and military personnel travel, and the travel manager needs to be aware of this.

The next chapter is on how the travel manager can use incentive travel programs to help motivate workers. This is an important chapter because these topics involve the travel manager more deeply in corporate strategies.

The last chapter of the book deals with relocation programs.

## Chapter Eighteen

# Managing Official Travel

G overnment travel is a significant market. The Society of Travel Agents in Government, located in Washington, D.C., estimates that the federal government is spending $6 billion per year on travel, while state and local governments spend $3.5 billion, and corporations under contract spend $5 billion. Bill Todd, marketing director at Choice Hotels, states, "Most people are not aware that the government is the travel industry's single largest client."

Todd continues that there are three main components to the reimbursement rates for government and military travelers.

1. Per diem.
2. Negotiated rates.
3. Cost-Reimbursable contractors.

## PER DIEM

A government per diem, according to Todd, is the "exact prescribed amount of money that a government employee will be reimbursed for expenses on travel each day." A per diem represents the total of two allowances; one amount allocated for lodging and another amount allocated for meals, tips, and incidentals. Per diems for domestic travel are set by the United States General Services Administration for every county in each state. They are printed in the *Federal Travel Directory* and the *Official Airline Traveler Guide*.

Travel outside the continental US is also restricted by per diems. These are set by both the State Department and the Department of Defense.

## NEGOTIATED RATES

Todd states, "Federal employees and the uniformed services must utilize a contracted travel agent when purchasing official air travel. Often leisure services are also provided, though these are very different standards and criteria. On the federal level, agencies that are dedicated to this market are called Federal Travel Management Centers, or FTMCs. Travel agencies are selected by bids on specified contracts either by department or geographic area."

The military also selects its agents by competitive bid and each branch has its own criteria. For example, the army awarded a contract to one of the mega-agencies for the entire Fifth Army, while the Air Force awards contracts simply by base.

## SATO

SATO stands for Scheduled Airline Traffic Offices. SATO is an airline industry-owned travel management corporation that specializes in the military and government traveler. It offers a complete range of official and leisure travel services. SATO's computer systems are customized to meet the distinctive needs of US military and government travel managers.

## NEGOTIATED RATES: AIR TRAVEL

The government puts all city pairs out to bid. The airline offering the best all-around package wins. Todd comments, "If all goes according to the plan, that airline should get most of the official traffic." Unavoidably, all competitors will drop their rates for government employees so, in a pinch, a government employee can fly a noncontracted airline. Government air fares carry different restrictions from those offered to the general flying public.

## NEGOTIATED RATES: HOTELS

As was stated earlier, each county has been assigned a specific limit on the amount of money a government traveler will be reimbursed for lodging. A hotel always has the option of offering a government rate, and if it does, the US government will gladly publish that rate in the *Federal Travel Directory*, published monthly by the GSA, and the *Official Airline Traveler Guide*. Not all hotels that have a government rate offer it year round, and often, the hotel's government rate applies only to a select number of rooms. For example, if there is a large convention in town, or the hotel is enjoying a high amount of corporate business during a specific week, it may opt not to offer the discounted government rate.

Bill Todd comments, "This creates confusion among government travelers and gives the impression that the government traveler is a second-class citizen. This problem is compounded for the travel agency making the reservation because many hotels will not pay a commission on a government rate."

## THE GOVERNMENT TRAVEL INDUSTRY

As explained by *Official Airline Traveler Guide's* Curt Reilly, general manager, government business, the government travel industry is broken down into three main groups.

1. *Travelers:* Employees of the federal government who are required to travel as part of their job on behalf of the agency that employs them. Also included are cost-reimbursable contractors (CRCs), who are employees of corporations under contract with the government who, when they travel, must travel under the same guidelines as government employees.

2. *Travel administrators:* Managers whose responsibility it is to manage the travel process, develop travel policies and guidelines, and select providers of travel services to their respective agencies.

3. *Travel service providers:* Companies who sell travel-related products and services (airlines, hotels, travel agencies).

According to Curt Reilly, "They all have different needs. The traveler wants to be able to accomplish travel as conveniently and comfortably as possible. The administrators, while they want to provide a quality service to their travelers, must also enforce their agency's travel policies. The travel service providers want to provide these services in a profitable manner.

"In order for each to be mutually successful in satisfing their respective needs and objectives, all the groups within the government travel industry must continue to improve the scope of the educational programs and interagency communications. The travel service providers must accelerate the technological advances of the products and services they offer to the government travel industry."

## Sources of Information

The *Federal Travel Directory* (FTD) is produced by Military Traffic Management Command (MTMC) and General Services Administration (GSA). This publication contains travel guidelines, contract flight information, and hotels/motels that offer government rates.

The OAG *Official Traveler* flight and travel guides offer the same information as the FTD, plus alternative flights within the 3300 CONUS contract city pairs and over 8000 noncontract city pairs. They also offer some 12,000 hotel/motels with government rates on easy-to-use maps of government and military facilities.

Some hotel chains and airlines offer guides that list their government locations. Travel agencies also have some government travel information in their reservation systems.

## CASE STUDY: BUSINESS TRAVEL MANAGEMENT—GOVERNMENT TRAVEL VERSUS THE PRIVATE SECTOR

The following article is taken from the August 1991 issue of *Business Travel Management*. This article was researched and written by Don Munro, a free-lance business travel writer based in Floral Park, New York, and is reprinted with his permission.

There is greener grass out there somewhere in the land of travel management, but where it grows is a matter of widespread disagreement.

Some think it is best being a travel manager on the government or government-contractor side. There, with the authority of federal per diem as a backup, they say enforcing travelers to use contracted hotels and car-rental firms can be a snap.

"I definitely think it's easier being a government contractor," says Mary Mahar, travel manager at Sanders Associates Inc., a Nashua, New Hampshire, electronics manufacturer with Department of Defense contracts. "Restrictive per diems are a tool to tell travelers, 'It's up to you to keep costs under control.' It makes enforcement easier, giving the travel policy some backup. It's not just me enforcing it, it's the government enforcing it."

Others tend to side with the private sector. There, they say, managers have the budgetary freedom to provide business travelers with the extra comforts of life—be they upscale hotels or luxury rental cars—that can make for happier, more productive employees. In addition, private-sector travel managers are not burdened with policing the extensive paperwork and documentation required by the government to substantiate travel expenses.

## UNAUTHORIZED CHARGES

"Certain perks are off-limits to government contractor travelers, such as alcohol expenses," says Judie Shyman, manager of travel administration at Hazeltine Corp., based in Greenlawn, New York, which also manufactures electronic equipment for the Department of Defense. "We reimburse our employees, but the government won't reimburse us for it in return."

Shyman says that government contractor travel managers, more so than private-sector managers, must "focus on accounting issues, such as sticking to approved methods of reporting expenses, in order to comply with government regulations. But at the same time, we have to do whatever we can for travelers to make them comfortable. We have to balance the two considerations."

Charles "Terry" Angelo, manager of travel and transportation at the US General Accounting Office, adds that "travel managers within government contractors are more focused on cost-accounting. That's not to say that they're not concerned with providing their travelers with good service. But corporate travel managers seem more focused on ensuring that their travelers don't suffer."

"It's harder being a government contractor travel manager in the sense that we need to set up systems to have people live within per diem guidelines, but at the same time keep up employee motivation," adds Robert Anderson, director of corporate travel at Unisys Corp., based in Blue Bell, Pennsylvania, which does a mix of commercial and government business. "Therefore, we have a greater compulsion to try to really work with (good) hotels, to get them to provide low rates."

Yet Anderson says that where policy enforcement is concerned, "government contractors have it much easier than commercial travel managers."

Judy Elliot, manager of meeting and travel services at Ralston Purina Co., based in St. Louis, says trying to get people to follow cost-saving methods is not a task peculiar to government and government contractor travel managers. "True, a good portion of my time is spent trying to make the traveler more and more cost conscious," she says, "but everybody today throughout the business world is being asked to do that, not just the government contractor firms."

But Mary Napoleone, travel manager at Duracell, Inc., a battery manufacturer based in Bethel, Connecticut, says enforcement is a bigger burden for travel managers in the private sector. "A big part of my job is getting people to use contracted hotels, airlines, and car rentals. We'll contract and then employees won't use them because the hotels or airlines aren't their favorites. All my negotiating has just gone out the window."

Napoleone, however, says per diems can also work against government contractors. "With the per diem set for their travelers, I would think that government contractor travel managers have a difficult time getting their travelers to live comfortably within those per diems. I mean the food costs alone in New York City would go above the set meal per diem. Those guidelines are just so far out of reach."

## MIXED BUSINESS

Some say that travel managers at corporations that do a mix of government and private business have it doubly tough, dealing with the reluctance of commercial travelers to use approved vendors and the added paperwork and other frustrations normal to government travel.

"If a company has a mix of business, there might not be black-and-white lines between government and commercial," says Mahar of Sanders Associates. "Travelers on commercial business might be able to spend whatever they want in travel, while government business travelers have limits. That creates employee morale problems, where they become aware of the differences in the two sides."

On an administrative level, "many companies that do a mix of business have to keep two sets of records and policies," adds Angelo of the GAO. "For employees who travel on both government and commercial business, it can be a confusing situation (as to who is allowed to do what). But the additional administrative burden to a company is also a hardship."

For example, extra record keeping is required when companies reimburse employees who travel on government business for reasonable and actual expenses, rather than just for the amount allowed under government guidelines, and then absorb the difference."

## PAPER TRAILS

Unisys picks up its travelers' costs that exceed what the government will reimburse, according to Anderson. But he says the rub is the amount of paperwork Unisys travelers must produce to substantiate government travel expenses.

"It seems like we're running a paper mill sometimes. There's just this enormous paper process," he says. "We have to have all the receipts that everybody else (nongovernment travelers) needs, but then, if necessary, we need other support, like statements from managers saying there was an extra need for an employee to go over a per diem."

Anderson notes that keeping track of commission share percentages from travel vendors and giving the government back its share is an added burden. "The government is supposed to be spending net cost," he explains, "so if the government buys from me certain kinds of things and I get credit from suppliers, I have to pass that credit back to the government."

Jay Butler, facility services manager at Fairchild Space Co., based in Germantown, Maryland, which makes satellites for the military and the private sector, says his biggest challenge is "keeping employees (both government business and commercial business travelers) straight. We don't get government rates on airlines. As a result, [Fairchild travelers are] always trying to outdo our corporate air travel policies, by doing things like flying on airlines whose frequent flyer programs they belong to."

As far as hotel rates are concerned, however, Butler says he does not have difficulties keeping track of which sector gets to stay in which hotel. The majority of Fairchild's business is government business, "so it's easier to keep track of things."

Kathy Hall, travel department supervisor at Moog, Inc., an aircraft parts manufacturer in East Aurora, New York, says she sometimes finds it confusing to deal with the special documentation that hotels require Moog government travelers to present when signing in. "That's the hardest part, really, discerning which hotel needs to see what kind of documentation."

But travel managers have developed ways to deal with the added burdens of record keeping and other challenges.


## EASING RESENTMENT

Jane Bruyer, travel manager at General Physics Corp. in Columbia, Maryland, a training and consulting company for power companies, says she has been successful in eliminating any resentment government travelers might have about the lodgings of commercial travelers. One tactic in that process has been to obtain similar rates at many properties for both groups of travelers, she says.

Bruyer also handles all travel arrangements in-house in order to ensure that the different hotel rates that do exist go to the right travelers. "Once, we tried to roll over extra travel requests to this department when we got busy. It didn't work," she says. "They gave the wrong rates to the wrong people."

Despite some of the inherent problems faced when dealing with government travel, where the use of per diems restricts the kinds of travel services an employee can use, many travel managers have come up with ways to deal with the drawbacks and added paperwork. In some ways, travel managers find government travel easier, due to its cut-and-dried approach, as opposed to private-sector travel, where a greater emphasis is placed on comfort.

## CASE STUDY: AN INTERVIEW WITH CHARLES (TERRY) ANGELO

Charles Angelo is director of the Travel and Transportation division of GSAs Federal Supply Service. The following interview is adapted from one that originally appeared in the April 1998 issue of Government Executive:

**Q:** Frequently, there are lower fares available than GSA contract fares. Must I still use the contract carrier?
**A:** The simple rule is that preference always goes to the contract carrier. However, if another carrier offers a lower fare which is available to the general public but not matched by the contract carrier, it may be used. (Note that so-called government "matching fares" offered by noncontract carriers are not available to the general public and thus may not be used to substantiate a cost comparison.)

When it comes to airline fares, what sounds like a bargain often may not be. It is important to look at all costs associated with some lower fares, such as penalty fees up to 100 percent for changing or canceling reservations, and week-end-stay requirements that could involve up to two additional days of lodging and meal expenses in order to qualify for the lower-priced ticket. The average discount for a contract fare is 50 percent below coach, generally with none of the restrictions associated with advertised discounts.

**Q:** With so many different fares, how can I keep them all straight without wasting a lot of productive time in the process?
**A:** The vast majority of federal and military travelers arrange their travel through a commercial travel agency or Scheduled Airlines Traffic Office (SATO) under an arrangement with GSA, the Defense Department, or NASA. Through the use of automated reservations, these trained agents are responsible for assuring that travelers are booked at the lowest available fares consistent with government and agency policies.

**Q:** Why, when there are airlines that offer nonstop transcontinental service, does GSA sometimes contract with carriers whose flights require a change of planes en route? Isn't that a tremendous waste of time and money?

**A:** This is a good example of the delicate balance between cost and service. There are some who argue that GSA should focus its attention on price alone, even if that means always having to make connections en route. Others say no price is too high for the convenience of nonstop travel. Both positions are extreme, and it falls to GSA to seek a common middle ground.

In its air and rail contracts, GSA does specify a minimum level of service, i.e., nonstop, direct or connecting, as well as a minimum number of flights per day for each route for which bids are requested. Both of these criteria generally must be satisfied before fares offered by competing carriers are evaluated and contracts are awarded.

**Q:** What about frequent flyer programs? Can I join them and what can I keep for my own personal use?
**A:** Federal employees are free to join frequent flyer programs or for that matter, any of the other frequent traveler programs offered by hotel, car-rental, or other travel vendors. Based on Comptroller General decisions, however, anything earned at government expense belongs to the government. Generally, this means that any up-grades—such as from coach to first class—for which accumulated miles are redeemed, and any free tickets earned, must be used for official travel only. This rule applies even when some of the accumulated miles are earned at personal rather than government expense. Consequently, those who travel frequently other than for the government might want to consider separate frequent flyer memberships in order to avoid commingling their earnings.

Travelers may retain for their own use such benefits as free first-class upgrades purchased at their own expense, or similar benefits considered to have no intrinsic value to the government. At the same time, frequent travelers can help to reduce their agency's travel costs by claiming and using free tickets for official travel, thereby stretching often tight travel budgets.

**Q:** My agency issued a travel charge card to me to use for official travel, but says GSA will not allow the card to be used for any personal expenses. Why not?
**A:** Under the terms of its current contract with Citicorp Diners Club, charge cards are to be issued to employees of participating

agencies for official use only. There are several reasons for this restriction, which is also a common, though not universal, practice among private companies.

First, the government-issued Diners Club card is the only form of payment airlines and Amtrak will accept for government fares in lieu of a Government Transportation Request. By restricting the use of the card, carriers are better assured that employees who present the card for government discounts are on official, not personal, travel. Second, a number of important concessions have been offered by the card contractor to the government, not the least of which is an agreement to issue cards to designated employees without prior credit checks, as well as waivers of all annual membership fees and interest charges, free accident and baggage insurance, and free overseas currency conversions. In other words, the card is like a calculator, computer, or any other tool provided to employees to help them do their jobs. It is intended to be used on the job only.

Finally, to combine personal with business expenses would dilute the value of management reports provided to GSA and participating agencies to help control travel costs and conduct more-informed vendor negotiations.

**Q:** Why does GSA restrict travel advances for employees who are issued these cards?
**A:** Actually, GSA does not set specific travel advance policies in conjunction with the use of charge cards. That decision is left to each participating agency. Current practices vary widely, but efforts on the part of the Office of Management and Budget to develop more-uniform policies are underway. One of the primary benefits of using a corporate-style card program, however, is to reduce the amount of cash that agencies must maintain in imprest funds, thereby contributing to more-efficient cash management practices within government.

**Q:** Should I purchase the collision damage waiver offered by car-rental companies? Is that a reimbursable expense?
**A:** Under the terms of car-rental discounts negotiated by MTMC, government travelers on official business who provide a copy of their travel orders receive free collision coverage as part of the daily rental fee. This policy has been in effect since 1986.

Most of the larger major car-rental companies and many local firms participate in the MTMC program at locations around the country. While they are not a mandatory source of supply like air and rail contractors, they should be considered the first, or preferred, source of supply for government travelers.

Travelers who use nonparticipating companies are reminded that the cost of the optional collision insurance is not a reimbursable expense.

**Q:** On a recent business trip, I made a reservation at a hotel that offers a government discount. Upon checking in, however, I was informed that there were no rooms available at the government rates and was charged almost double that amount. What can be done to prevent such situations in the future?

**A:** For 1988, almost 10,000 hotels worldwide are participating in GSAs hotel and motel discount program. For many hotels in the low-to-moderate price range, government travelers make up a large percentage of the clientele. Such hotels often offer an "unrestricted" government rate—one which is always available as long as the hotel has a vacant single room, where government discounts can be as much as 50 percent or more below their normal room rates. The number of rooms available at those rates frequently is limited.

It is not enough simply to call, make a reservation, and assume that by identifying yourself as a government traveler, you will be given the government rate. You should confirm the rate at the time reservations are made and ask for a confirmation number in case there is any question when you check in.

**Q:** How does one find out about all of these discounts?

**A:** Where available, the travel agent or SATO supporting your agency is a primary source of such information. GSA, in cooperation with MTMC, also publishes the monthly *Federal Travel Directory*, a compact listing of all contract air and rail routes, including fares and carrier schedules, hotel and car-rental discounts by county, state, and city, and other travel information, such as per diem rates, noncontract rail and bus discounts, and ground transportation information for major cities. Check first with your agency's travel or publications office, since most agencies order copies. Annual subscriptions are also available through the Government Printing Office.

# CASE STUDY: GOVERNMENT CONTRACTOR AIR FARES—NBTA'S POSITION

The following material was contributed by Norman Sherlock, executive director of NBTA. This material relates to congressional interest in reimbursing airfare for domestic contractors. The positions represented in this case were those put forth by the NBTA, which ultimately prevailed. This represented a major victory for NBTA members and the industry because the Defense Department in the end did not refuse to pay air reimbursements to defense contractors above the government rate, saving corporations millions of dollars. Sherlock comments, "This was a clear indication of the evolving strength of NBTA and corporate travel managers. It is an outgrowth of defining the basic interest of the members, organizing, speaking in a collective voice, and lobbying hard—a good formula for success."

Congressional sources are pressing the Department of Defense to disallow reimbursement of air fares for contractors that exceed the rates negotiated for government employees. A savings of $63 million was dictated. Separately, a GSA-proposed ruling is still pending that would disallow reimbursement above government rates unless contractors show on a trip-by-trip basis that the rates are not available to them.

It will not be hard for contractors to substantiate that they can't get government rates, since the airlines refused to extend them to contractors in the negotiations on rates for 1992. Only Hawaiian Airlines, on a few inter-island routes, agreed to offer anything. Despite that, the outlook is for continued trouble with Congress on this issue because of staff's embedded belief that contractors are receiving excessive reimbursement.

Defense Department officials meeting with NBTA in late 1991 reiterated their view that the congressional directive in the final appropriations bill set a goal that is not feasible. They indicated that contractors would not be denied legitimate reimbursement. Congressional staff people, however, continue to be adamant and are pressing hard. Whether or not DOD is forced to yield now, the issue will have to be faced again during the appropriations process in some fashion. The Senate Appropriations Committee indicated in 1992 that it would move to disallow reimbursement by a statutory requirement if the agency did not achieve it by administrative action.

## FACT SHEET

### *DOD and Contractors' Reimbursement*

The Senate committee report puts the Defense Department "on notice that it will consider imposing a statutory ban on reimbursement of contractor air travel costs in excess of government fares, if the Pentagon does not impose such a ban administratively."

NBTA supports the committee's objectives to achieve savings for the taxpayer. NBTA also supports efforts to negotiate savings both for the government and its contractors. Our members will use the rates equivalent to government employees' air fares, if the airlines grant them.

However, NBTA rejects the implication that contractors have avoided the use of available government discounts. Government discount airfares are different from other available discounts such as advance-purchase or volume discounting. They are available only on the basis of specific negotiations and contracts between the government and each carrier. They are not generally available through most travel agencies or computer reservation systems.

NBTA believes that the Senate committee's report reflects a fundamental misunderstanding of the basis of negotiated discount airfare contracts and completely ignores government efforts to extend such discounts to contractors. The report also shows confusion and a lack of reliable information concerning the current amounts of government travel and the division of travel between government employees and contractors.

Finally, the report ignores the fact of regulations which are currently under review by both the GSA and the DOD. These regulations, which are set forth in FAR Case 91–36 (56 Fed. Reg. 33822, July 23, 1991), would impose a substantial administrative burden on contractors to certify the unavailability of government discount fares.

### *Government Efforts to Extend Contract Airfares*

FAR Case 91–36 responds to the Department of Defense Authorization Act for Fiscal Year 1989 (P. L. 100–456, 833), which required GSA to "enter into negotiations with commercial air carriers" in order to extend the availability of discount airfares to government contract employees. Since 1988, GSA and DOD have responded to the directive and attempted to negotiate such extensions of government discounts.

Such efforts have resulted in total failure. By the summer of 1991, only four relatively small regional carriers—Midway, Southwest, Hawaiian, and America West—were extending such discounts to government contractors. Since then, Midway has gone bankrupt, Southwest has announced that they will no longer extend such discounts to contractors after January 1, 1992, and America West is currently operating under Chapter 11. America West and Hawaiian represent only a tiny percentage of capacity for government and contractor travelers.

The major carriers have declined to extend such discounts because of the negative revenue impact. In light of recent substantial losses by the major carriers, it is highly unlikely that carriers will change their position on this issue.

NBTA filed comments in opposition to the proposed GSA regulation. NBTA's opposition was based on the following factors, which are equally applicable to the Appropriations Committee report:

1. The proposals will not increase the availability of government discounts to contractors. The government does not have the power to unilaterally extend such agreements, and the airlines have adamantly refused to extend such discounts.

2. An increased administrative burden created by proposed certification requirements ultimately results in higher, not lower, costs to the government.

3. The proposals reflect a fundamental misunderstanding of the relationship between contractors, airlines, and the government, as well as of the specific nature of government contract discounts. Government discounts cannot be extended absent an agreement with the airlines, which the government has not been able to obtain.

4. The proposals imply that the failure of contractors to use discounts shows a lack of concern for cost. Contractors and the NBTA fully support the goal of lowering overall travel costs. However, such savings must be based on a

realistic approach and not on a requirement to use fares that are not legally available.

5. FAR Case 91–36 could create inexorable pressure for improper use of such fares in violation of existing agreements with the airlines.

## RECOMMENDATIONS

NBTA supports the savings objectives reflected by both the Appropriations Committee report and the GSA/DOD regulations. However, a more realistic approach must be taken to achieve such savings, based on accurate understanding of government and contractor air travel and the existing contract discount structure. NBTA recommends the following steps:

1. Authorize a study to accurately determine total airfare expenditures by the government, DOD, and the government contractors. Only with accurate data can the government and Congress make a realistic determination of the true situation regarding reimbursement of government contractors and any potential government savings.

2. NBTA proposes to meet with and discuss the current status and availability of government discounts with all government representatives. NBTA suggests a meeting of representatives of the Appropriations Committee, the Department of Defense, the GSA, NBTA, representatives of major contractors, and the airlines.

## TRAVEL MANAGEMENT TIPS

- The government is the travel industry's single largest client.
- A government per diem is the prescribed amount of money that a government employee will be reimbursed for travel expenses for each day.
- A per diem represents the total of two allowances—one amount allocated for lodging and another amount for meals, tips, and incidentals.

- Federal employees and the uniformed services must utilize a contracted travel agent when purchasing official air travel.
- SATO stands for Scheduled Airline Traffic Offices. SATO is an airline industry-owned travel management corporation that specializes in the military and government traveler.
- The government puts all city pairs it travels out to bid.

*Chapter Nineteen*

# Managing Travel Incentive Programs

I n the area of incentive travel, the travel manager has the chance to get into corporate strategy, since incentive programs relate to company sales and revenues.

Bob Swearingen, president of Maritz Travel, located in St. Louis, states, "America has the highest-paid employees, salespeople, and executives in the world. Still, these individuals are dissatisfied, and our rate of productivity increase is lower than many of the countries with which we compete. Obviously, monetary income alone does not encourage improved performance in the majority of job situations. Something else is needed, something called "psychic income." Psychic income, when translated, means income of the mind, or memorable and tangible rewards for having shared in the achievement of company goals. Research has demonstrated psychic income can be far more motivating than monetary income because psychic income is that something extra individuals desire as recognition for extra effort, improved performance, and a job well done."

This chapter will introduce you to the power of psychic income and how it can help to achieve corporate objectives.

## WHAT IS AN INCENTIVE PROGRAM?

An incentive program is any structured activity designed to motivate participants to attain a pre-established set of objectives. It is a plan of action that motivates employees to do what needs to be done.

A lot of incentive programs are used to increase sales or employee productivity. Swearingen states, "The majority of users apply incentives to the task of increasing sales or improving productivity. Others want to increase market share or penetrate new markets. An increasing number look to incentives as a way to positively impact quality, one of the buzz words of the 90s. The fact is, incentives have proven effective whenever human performance can be motivated."

## WHY INCENTIVES?

The main reason for incentives, according to Swearingen, is that few people are motivated to work up to their full potential. Most employees work until they find a comfort level that puts bread on the table and houses their family. Even commission or bonus plans generally fail to push us beyond a certain level of performance.

Incentives can sometimes take over where cash fails. In addition to providing psychic income, incentive awards provide direction in the form of goals. A well-designed incentive program tells the participants that if they do this, they will earn that. In the busy world of business, few people take the time to match their individual goals to those of a corporation. Incentives ensure that process.

Incentives do one thing regular compensation cannot. They provide a tangible means for a company to honor and recognize performance beyond the comfort level. Swearingen argues, "Most people would consider it bad form to brag about a raise or bonus, but these same individuals can tell the world they earned a trip for two to Paris. In many ways, the 'winning' is as important as the trip because winning elevates self-esteem and gives individuals a forum to boast of their accomplishment. When you think about it, what other activity gives the average person an opportunity to become a superstar?"

## TYPES OF AWARDS—WHICH ONE IS THE BEST?

There are four major motivators used in incentive programs:

1. Merchandise.
2. Honor.

3. Recognition.

4. Travel.

Although cash is still used, it is not a psychic motivator. All-cash incentive programs are easy to administer and offer a medium everybody understands; however, cash awards don't have trophy value. Furthermore, cash awards can be confused with normal compensation, and in fact can come to be considered a part of an individual's compensation package.

According to a survey conducted by the American Productivity & Quality Center, all three of the non-cash incentives produce more measurable results than cash. The most commonly used incentive—merchandise—remains a powerful motivator. Unlike cash, merchandise awards are highly promotable and are not confused with regular compensation. One of the big benefits of merchandise is its ability to serve as a trophy for performance beyond the ordinary. Merchandise awards also act as a catalyst to get an entire family involved in an incentive program because merchandise awards, once earned, are generally shared by members of a family.

Unfortunately, the use of merchandise presents a number of negatives. Generally, programs that employ merchandise as a motivator require more-detailed administration than cash-only programs. For example, the sponsoring company must work out in advance matters such as how to handle ordering, shipping, and returns. Every step must be taken to avoid disappointing individuals who have extended themselves to earn awards.

Honor and recognition rewards are a second type of non-cash motivator. Honor and recognition awards can take many forms; for example, a plaque to recognize top performers or a jacket to signify membership in the President's Club. Normally, honor and recognition awards are not the major awards; instead they are used to supplement an incentive program and recognize top-level performances. Swearingen recommends that honor and recognition awards be included in all programs.

Swearingen asserts that travel awards, the third type of non-cash incentive, are effective because a travel award is glamorous, exciting, alluring, and highly appealing to just about everybody. Everybody dreams of an exotic trip to a place they have never been. According to Swearingen, "Cash pays the bills. Travel excites and motivates."

Potential winners in group programs know that if they earn the travel award, they will have all of the details worked out for them. There is no worrying about ticketing, connections, hotel reservations, tours, etc. They also know that they will be with their peers. Chances are, winners will broaden their knowledge through exposure to a new destination and through idea sharing with other winners.

Sponsoring companies know that group travel incentive programs provide them with an opportunity that they cannot get using other motivators. Management has the chance to mix with the company's top performers or its best customers in an atmosphere that is conducive to building loyalty and teamwork.

The group travel business is in the process of going through an evolution as sponsoring companies look for new ways to motivate prospective participants. A recent trend is toward what are called "lifestyle programs," programs that offer participants a variety of destinations and activities that match individual preferences.

## IS GROUP TRAVEL RIGHT FOR EVERYONE?

Group travel is not necessarily right for everyone. For example, if one of the guidelines of a program is to have everybody who contributes earn something, travel may not be for them. Because group travel programs can be costly, most sponsoring companies do not have the budget to make it possible for everybody to win. In addition, group programs can be an administrative nightmare for a travel planner because of the myriad details associated with setting up and running a successful program operation.

Individual travel can be an answer to a number of the concerns associated with group travel. The major difference between the two forms is that individual travel awards allow the winners to select from an extensive offering of travel opportunities and enjoy their selection when they wish to go. Maritz Travel Company, for example, offers an individual travel product called "Exclusively Yours." Using Exclusively Yours checks—available in denominations of $10 and $50—participants can design and set up their own travel experience. To help in the process, Maritz produces a four-color Exclusively Yours Book of Awards, which features a selection of award opportunities ranging from hotels to cruises, tours to hunting and fishing adventures, airlines to hot-air balloon rides.

Individual travel awards such as Exclusively Yours checks give companies a low-cost alternative to group travel. This option can be used for a variety of reasons. It might serve as the award in sport campaigns or as an adjunct to merchandise award offerings. A number of incentive companies, including Maritz Travel, also offer a full line-up of creative materials, in addition to a colorful book of awards, to enhance and promote the program.

There is at least one negative side to individual travel: Unlike group travel programs, individual travel awards do not allow the sponsoring companies to enjoy the benefits that come from gathering all winners at one destination, a process that builds loyalty and encourages idea sharing.

## PUTTING INCENTIVES TO WORK

There are three steps that the corporate travel manager should follow in setting up an incentive program:

1. Establish program objectives—what is it you want to accomplish?
2. Develop rules—how should your program be structured to maximize results?
3. Develop a budget—how much do you have to spend to fund the incentive program?

### Establish Program Objectives

The first question that must be asked is, What do you want to accomplish? The answer you come up with can spell the difference between a highly successful incentive program and one that produces marginal results. You should begin by looking at what needs to be done in your organization. For example, have sales plateaued? Is the quality of your product suspect? Are your distributors purchasing from other suppliers? Is your customer base declining?

Chances are you will develop a fairly comprehensive list of problem areas that can be addressed through the introduction of an incentive program, especially if you examine needs in sales, distribution (dealers, distributors, brokers, etc.), and production.

Once the list is developed, you will want to refine it to one or two challenges that, if met, will produce the most significant results. As you go through this process, make sure you come to grips with the various ramifications. For example, if you are losing market share, you will want to examine the reasons. Are there problems with your product? For example, has the quality declined? Or does the problem have something to do with your sales force or distributors? If they are not delivering the results you want, you should take the time to determine the reasons. When you have come up with the answers, you are ready to translate your need into an objective for your incentive program.

It is important to make the objective precisely worded, easily understood, measurable, and attainable. Make certain you have reduced the objective to a few carefully selected words (e.g., increase sales of the product by 10 percent during the next 12 months) so that it can be accomplished within the time frame you have defined, and that you have the means to measure results. If you can answer yes to all of these parameters, you are ready to proceed to the next step.

### Develop Rules

Swearingen states, "The core of a sound incentive program is the rules structure. The perfect rules structure is 'do this . . . get that.' Unfortunately, the business world is complex and the tendency is to encumber a program with a complex structure."

Swearingen continues, "Chances are that competition may be a key ingredient to your award structure. This competition can take any number of forms. For example, salespeople or distributors can compete against previous performances, against quotas established by you, against other salespeople or distributors or against teams composed of other salespeople or distributors. The competition can be company-wide or consist of competition within districts, regions, or even among distributors or brokers."

Another key element in the development of a successful rules structure is to include all of the individuals who can contribute to the attainment of your objectives. In some cases, you may want to offer a top award for those who are in a position to make the most significant contribution, and then motivate the balance with awards of lesser value. For example, merchandise awards or individual travel awards are ideal tools to reward those whose contributions are limited; group travel is the ideal motivator for those who make the greatest contribution.

Unfortunately for the travel manager, there is no magic formula for setting up the rules of an incentive program. However, it is in this area that the travel manager can become invaluable to the corporation by contributing to corporate strategies. Every rules structure must be customized to the objectives and participants and must be consistent with the sponsoring company's culture.

## *The Incentive Program Budget*

Bob Swearingen maintains that a company does not have to spend anything if they have done a good job structuring the program. "What you have to be willing to do is to invest money to make or save money." At the same time, the company must realize that it has to spend money up-front, on administration, promotion, award deposits, etc., to get the program started.

How much of the total budget is allocated to each of the various incentive elements depends on a number of factors. Maritz Performance Improvement Company suggests the following as guidelines:

1. Administration .................................................... 10%
2. Promotion ......................................................... 15%
3. Program awards .................................................. 75%

At some point in the process, the manager must determine if it is desirable to control award costs or if he or she is willing to exchange additional money for increased levels of performance. Most companies choose the latter programs, which are termed "open-ended."

Because most incentive programs are funded out of incremental increases in sales or improvements in productivity, these programs are particularly good investments.

Close-ended programs, on the other hand, limit the motivation appeal of an incentive program because they limit the number of winners, in many cases to the very top performers. Sponsoring companies, however, have the comfort of knowing their total award exposure at the outset of the program.

If you decide to base the budget on incremental sales, Maritz Performance Improvement Company believes you should allocate 8 to 10 percent of the increment as a reliable guide. In other words, you are exchanging a dime for every new dollar in sales revenue. A 1 percent allocation is the recommended figure when the budget is predicated on total anticipated sales during the program period.

## IMPLEMENTING AN INCENTIVE AWARD

Once the objectives of the incentive program have been defined, the rules structure is determined, and a budget is set, the next step is the actual program implementation.

One important step in that process is selecting the right motivator. As previously mentioned, the four choices are: cash, merchandise, honor and recognition, and travel (individual and group). For the purpose of this chapter, we are going to assume you have selected the most popular incentive as well as the one that is most difficult for travel planners to use effectively: group travel.

According to Bob Swearingen, there are seven steps travel planners and incentive travel companies must tackle to set up and manage a group travel program. These seven steps are:

1. Qualification of participants.
2. Selection of the "right" group travel award.
3. Negotiation and purchase of program ingredients.
4. Promotion of the program.
5. Administration of the program.
6. Management of the operation.
7. Auditing of the program.

## Qualifying the Participants

The fourth annual incentive travel survey conducted by *Successful Meetings* magazine shows that the third most common failure of an incentive program is the failure of the trip to motivate the target audience. When you qualify the participants, you are putting your finger on the collective pulse of the participants. Incentive travel involves motivation, and to motivate successfully, you have to know what the participants' dreams are. When this is well done, an incentive program has an excellent chance of succeeding. When it isn't, you are inviting failure.

Knowing the dreams of the participants is not a trivial matter, considering the diversity of most groups. Do men and women employees react to the same destinations? How important is age? Is the choice of program activities as important as the selection of the destination?

Some companies try to figure out what makes their participants tick through one-on-one contact, but if the group is large, that may not be practical. Others survey participants, asking them to list their favorite types of program activities and destinations. It is a good idea to survey participants after a program on various matters including an evaluation of the importance of the various components of a travel program (destination, hotel, food, activities, etc.). It is also a good idea to ask the participants to list the top three choices for future travel destinations. The results of the surveys can be shared with others to help fine-tune future operations.

## Selecting the Right Travel Award

Using information you have gathered through the qualification process should give you a head start in your efforts to select the right travel award for your company employees. But even this step has been clouded in recent years as a result of an explosion in the forms of group travel.

For purposes of illustration, let's assume you have determined that your target audience is fairly evenly split between a holiday in Hawaii and one in Great Britain. In addition, you determine that your potential participants are an active group who have ex-pressed interest in golf, hunting, fishing, and something Bob

Swearingen refers to as "self-enhancement." You also ask your participants the importance of including family members in the program operation, and you get a favorable response. Now what should you do?

Swearingen believes that if you are like an increasing number of decision makers, you will consider a lifestyle-type program in lieu of the traditional one-destination, everybody does the same thing program. Lifestyle programs cater to the individual dreams of participants. For example, in a lifestyle program, the target audience might be offered the opportunity to partake in a five-night program on Maui that concentrates on golf, a hunting and fishing adventure in Wales, a self-enhancement holiday in Scotland, and a family fun program in London, providing something individual and special for everybody who hits the required performance level.

## Negotiating and Purchasing Program Ingredients

Once the right psychic motivator has been identified for your participants, you are ready to negotiate and ultimately purchase the various elements that make up a group travel operation, including air transportation, ground arrangements, and hotel or cruise accommodations.

Bob Swearingen recommends the following guidelines to travel managers when negotiating with ground suppliers and hotels:

### Ground-supplier negotiations

1. What are the savings if I buy transportation differently?
   a. By the bus versus per person?
   b. Buses by the hour or by the day?
2. Will you provide complimentary (or low-cost) signage?
3. Will you provide luggage transfers at no additional charge?
4. Do we know all inclusions/exclusions with price quoted?
5. What new activities/tours are available?
6. What is a minimum group size for a tour/activity? (Will you waive that minimum for this group?)
7. Do we know all inclusions for an off-property theme evening? Can we reduce or avoid venue rental fee?

8. Are there any cost savings for advance payments?
9. Can you guarantee the exchange rate for this group?
10. Can you provide complimentary welcome packets?

### Hotel negotiations

1. How can I get a better rate from you? (What amenities can you include at no extra cost?)
2. How can we buy staff rooms better?
   a. Can we get complimentary over and above the normal complimentary policy?
   b. No limit on the number of staff?
3. Can we negotiate early check-in/late check-out at no additional charge?
4. Can we upgrade accommodations and maintain the same rate?
5. Will you provide a complimentary function with purchase of similar?
6. Any cost savings for advance payments?
7. Will you guarantee the foreign currency rate at the time of sale?
8. What complimentary amenities would you throw in to get this group?
9. Will you confirm this year's pricing for next year's program?

## Promoting the Program

Program promotion is easier for most travel planners than negotiating the lowest possible program cost. Still, effective promotion and communications requires a certain expertise if results are to match expectations.

Meaningful, personalized, positive communications translate corporate goals into individual objectives, then serve to focus and maintain attention on those objectives. The first step in that process is the development of a theme—an urge to action that is descriptive and memorable. What you want is a catchy set of words that tell participants "to do this in order to get that." Look for an active verb as the first word of your theme. For example, *go, grow, make, win, move, plan, discover,* and so on. Try to make certain your theme promises a benefit and strongly conveys the award you are offering.

When you have made your selection, have it converted into a graphic treatment. What you decide on will be reproduced on all of your program materials, so make sure it is not too complicated. Return it to the designer until you are satisfied that it conveys the excitement you want your participants to feel for the program.

The promotion budget is usually spent on a kick-off meeting, a program announcement, and regular follow-up mailers.

The kick-off meeting is a great opportunity to gather all participants and announce the program in person. In a session of this nature, you not only have an opportunity to motivate, but you may also be able to provide training to help participants reach the level of performance desired.

Unfortunately, many companies have operations and offices that span the country, which makes it expensive to gather everyone in one place at one time. When this is the case, you may want to sponsor a series of individual kick-offs in cities located close to participants. Another option is sending a video that provides a personalized message designed to inform and motivate.

In addition to a kick-off, announcements and follow-up mailers are good tools to promote the incentive program. The announcement is an all-purpose tool. In it, you must state the objectives of the program, communicate all aspects of the rules, and create enthusiasm for the rewards. If spouses are eligible to participate in the travel award, which is the case in almost all successful incentive travel programs, copy should be written to appeal to them as well.

Bob Swearingen recommends the following guidelines when developing program materials:

1. Travel lends itself to four-color, so try to budget enough to print in full color.

2. Convey quality to avoid confusing your participants. If your announcement does not say "quality," your participants may believe your travel award is not worth winning.

3. Be creative. Take the time to design your announcement and develop copy that catches the attention of your prospective participants.

The follow-up mailers should be prepared with the same guide-lines in mind, especially creativity. Consider incorporating desti-nation and hotel brochures, posters (if your budget allows), and dimensionals (tangible items such as bags of sand for sand and fun destinations or a flag of the destination). Swearingen recommends that you include standing reports to keep participants aware of where they stand versus goals. Mailers should be sent out every two to four weeks, depending on how long the promotion lasts.

### Administering the Program

Bob Swearingen has identified over 100 individual chronological steps that must be taken to make sure all of the details of the administration of the travel program are handled. The following are a few of the tasks:

1. Confirmation of land and air arrangements.
2. Monitoring air "block space" deadlines to control financial exposure and ensure the most convenient routing of your participants.
3. Monitoring deposit and cancellation policies with hotels or cruise lines and ground suppliers to eliminate possible penalties.
4. Enrollment of participants.
5. Booking participants' flights, making sure seat assignments are matched to participant specifications.
6. Issuance of tickets, seat assignments, and boarding passes.
7. Handling individual requests for land and/or air arrange-ments schedules before or after the group program.
8. Preparation and forwarding of detailed trip-operating materials.
9. Generation of lists required by hotels, airlines, immigration agencies, etc., as well as those required for internal purposes.

### Managing the Operation

To this point, every step taken, from the establishment of the objectives through the development of the rules to the promotion of the awards, has been directed toward one objective: a successful, totally memorable program operation that matches winners' expectations. This objective will not be realized unless the operation is professionally managed from the moment winners step aboard their flights to their return home several days later.

As you consider this aspect of the program, remember what was stated earlier regarding the description of the travel awards: "Winners in group programs know that if they earn the travel award, they will have every last detail worked out for them. There is no worrying about ticketing, connections, hotel reservations, tours, etc."

Ideally this calls for the services of an experienced travel staff capable of providing all of these services:

1. Participation in a pre-program briefing at which all details of the pending program are discussed.
2. Advancing the destination and the hotel or ship to make certain all arrangements have been made and will be fulfilled.
3. Greeting and directing winners upon arrival.
4. Coordination of all on-site arrangements.
5. Assisting with luggage handling, transfers, and room or cabin assignments.
6. Responding to participant questions in an informed and friendly manner.
7. Staffing the hospitality desk.
8. Assisting guests with departure.
9. Remaining on-site following the operation to verify all supplier charges, to protect your financial interests.

Managing the operation also requires attention to the winners' personal needs from the moment they depart their home cities to their return. In many instances this requires setting up an operations control center, which serves as a single point of control throughout operations to handle any unexpected irregularities such as airline strikes, flight delays, or personal emergencies. The control center should be accessible 24 hours a day, seven days a week, a fact that gives winners peace of mind, one of the key things they expect when they exert the extra effort required to qualify for a travel award.

## *Auditing the Program*

Once the program is over and the winners have returned home safely, all that is left is the post-trip auditing, a step that must be taken to verify how your incentive investment was managed.

Bob Swearingen lists the following as steps in this process:

1. Auditing all program expenditures to ensure an accurate final billing that matches your program specifications, a procedure that should include negotiations with suppliers to ensure return of deposits, if applicable.

2. Preparation of comprehensive reports to provide totals by participants and summaries of services provided by various suppliers during the program.

3. Preparation of a variety of tax-reporting services to satisfy government agencies.

## TRAVEL MANAGEMENT TIPS

- An incentive program is any structured activity designed to motivate participants to attain a pre-established set of objectives. It is a plan of action that motivates employees to do what needs to be done.

- Travel awards are effective because a travel award is glamorous, exciting, alluring, and highly appealing to just about everybody. Everybody dreams of an exotic trip to a place they have never been.

- Cash pays the bills, but travel excites and motivates.

- Once the objectives of the incentive program have been defined, the rules structure is determined, and a budget is set, the next step is the actual program implementation.

*Chapter Twenty*

# Managing Relocation Programs

A ccording to the Employee Relocation Council, a trade association located in Washington, DC, there is a growing trend among large corporations to consolidate relocation matters under one department. However, in many smaller and medium-sized companies, the travel manager is often called upon to handle relocation. Even if relocation is managed under a different department, the travel manager should be in constant contact with the relocation people to ensure that they are aware of relocation fares and other cost-saving opportunities that are available.

A major resource available to the travel manager who is assigned relocation matters is the Employee Relocation Council (ERC), located at 1720 N St. NW, Washington, DC 20036.

The ERC offers a number of publications for the novice as well as materials aimed at the experienced. The ERC publishes a book entitled *A Guide to Employee Relocation and Relocation Policy Development*. This book should be required reading for the travel manager who has job responsibilities relating to relocation.

## TRANSPORTATION OF HOUSEHOLD GOODS

According to the ERC, the procedures for obtaining the moving service must involve minimal effort for the transferee. Ideally, the personnel manager or coordinator (the person hiring or transferring the employee) would provide the moving administrator with a form indicating the transferee's name, address, and phone numbers. The form should indicate the number of rooms of furniture, and any bulky articles such as pianos, automobiles or boats. It should state if the transferee will receive the complete household-goods moving program or only a portion (normally for nonexperienced new hires, i.e., recent college graduates). This information is necessary so that the moving administrator will know exactly what the transferee is authorized to move. Most corporations offer the same type of service for new hires as for transferees.

An important aspect of transporting household goods is the corporate policy. The ERC recommends the following:

> *The policy must be clear and concise to let the transferee know what to expect. This means stating or listing what is allowed and not allowed to be moved at company expense. If your company differentiates between a regular employee, new hire with experience, or a new hire without experience (recent college graduate), the policy must specify what services will be offered for the move.*
>
> *By defining what is or is not allowed and leaving some flexibility for exceptions, the transferee will be more productive at the new location.*
>
> *Normally, packing and unpacking services and appliance service at the origin and destination cities are allowed to regular employees and new hires with experience.*
>
> *Normally, carriers will not be held responsible for any perishable articles (food or plants) included in a shipment. They may agree to transport plants, for example, but will advise the transferee that they will not accept any liability. Transferees should be advised to use, sell, or give away all frozen foods in advance of the move. The same often is true with plants since some corporations do not permit their inclusion in shipment. Most household goods carriers have brochures advising how to safely transport house plants.*

A policy for new hires without experience normally would allow the moving (packing, unpacking) of their personal goods from their present location to the city of employment. The rationale is that students normally have books, a TV, a stereo, and clothing, and they will establish residence in a furnished apartment or will acquire furnishings after the move to the new location.

The ERC recommends that the general relocation policy also include items that are not covered (excluded items), such as heavy or bulky items. Many companies refuse to include these items in relocation because of the expense. Another very sensitive area, according to the ERC, is the transportation of pets.

By regulation, household-goods carriers cannot transport animals. The most common method of transporting animals is by automobile or airplane, or through private companies that specialize in transporting animals. The ERC recommends that your policy should include:

1. Whether or not you will pay for transportation of pets.
2. The number of pets covered.
3. The kinds of pets covered.
4. Whether or not temporary boarding expenses are covered.

Another important policy area is storage-in-transit. Storage-in-transit allows a transferee's goods to be temporarily stored, at origin or destination, until the transferee moves into a new residence. The normal time period for storage-in-transit is 60 days.

### Estimates and Authorization

ERC advises that estimates for the approximate cost of the move be obtained. In most cases, the estimated or approximate cost is never the final cost. ERC states: "The difference is due to a transferee deciding at the last minute to take or leave articles previously inventoried. The trend is for a company to request a premove survey by the carrier, resulting in an estimate of the cost. The premove survey is useful to your company and the carrier in determining the services and equipment that will be required to provide a trouble-free move for your transferee. Additional costs such as crating, long carries, and bulky items are determined during the survey. Inform your transferee to notify you or your department, and the carrier's agent who made the estimate or survey, of last-minute changes. This information is important in scheduling equipment and labor for packing the move."

There are various ways to communicate with a carrier or carrier's agent to initiate a household goods move, and your policy should state what method will be used. The most common methods are a purchase order or a form letter. One of the most efficient methods is to phone the information to the agent in order to provide the agent with an opportunity to answer any questions. This conversation would then be followed up with the purchase order or letter.

The ERC advises that your policy should be specific about what will and will not be covered at company expense. Depending on the status of the transferee, your policy should allow optimum productivity at the new location. Recent ERC surveys indicate that more than 90 percent of companies provide full reimbursement of moving expenses, including shipping, packing, storage (when necessary), insurance, and unpacking.

## Selection of Carriers

The ERC suggests that the minimum investigations to be carried out in selecting a carrier are:

1. Contact companies similar to yours and discuss why they use certain carriers' agents at origin and destination cities.
2. Check the financial stability of both carrier and agent through Dun & Bradstreet, credit bureaus, or other financial reference sources.
3. Request a copy of their Interstate Commerce Commission (ICC) certificate to verify their authority.
4. Investigate programs to prepare the transferee and family for moving.
5. Check into the experience of an agent's packers and drivers as well as the training programs provided for these critical personnel.
6. Investigate the agent's quality-control program to verify proper packing and unpacking and appliance servicing.
7. Visit their warehouse and observe its organization, general appearance, and the age of vans and tractors.
8. Visit the agent's office and observe how orders are processed and billed and how claims are handled.
9. Review the communications systems established for the driver and the dispatching system.
10. Investigate rates, ancillary service charges, guaranteed delivery dates, contract rates, and volume discounts on the total charges of the move.
11. Ask to visit a home where the agent's employees are packing or unpacking household goods. By observing, you can determine the agent's employees' experience and personal interaction with the owners of the household goods.

### Insurance Coverage

Damage and/or loss of household goods does occur. Any claim at all is an unpleasant experience involving cherished belongings, sometimes with irreplaceable sentimental value. Therefore, insurance coverage is important.

The ERC lists the following different types of insurance available from all major carriers:

1. *Released value.* Under tariff regulation, this is the least amount of liability a mover can assume when transporting your goods. This option should be considered only by self-insured companies who prefer to handle settlement of claims in-house, or by companies that have purchased policies from outside insurance companies to cover any additional costs of repairs or replacement. Be sure that your transferee understands that he or she must refile through his or her corporation for full and final settlement after settling with the carrier. The corporation will be responsible for payment of the bulk of the claim costs.

To obtain this minimal protection, the shipper must sign a specific statement on the bill of lading agreeing to it. Remember that unless you sign such an agreement, the mover is liable for $1.25 per pound and can charge you for it.

2. *Declared value ($1.25 times the weight of the shipment in pounds).* The mover is required to assume liability for the entire shipment at an amount equal to $1.25 per pound. For example, if your shipment weighs 4,000 pounds, the mover will be liable to you for loss or damage up to $5,000. Liability is limited to current replacement cost less depreciation. However, total liability is not to exceed the actual value declared on the shipment for any one item or all items tendered to the carrier.

3. *Declared value (lump-sum value).* If the value of your shipment exceeds $1.25 per pound, you may obtain additional liability protection by declaring a specific dollar value for your shipment. If you ship articles that are high in value, such as antiques or artwork, be sure to declare their full value in the declaration of a specific amount. Settlement on this protection amounts to the cost of repairs of transit damage, or the depreciated value of the current replacement cost, whichever is less.

4. *Full-value coverage (no deductible).* Liability covers the full cost of repairs, or the full replacement cost at today's prices without depreciation. If a lost or broken item is part of a set that cannot be matched, the carrier will pay to replace the entire set. This protection usually is given on shipments with a declared value of $3.50 per pound or greater.

5. *Full-value coverage (with a $250, $500, or $1,000 deductible).* Limits of liability are current replacement cost of items, less deductible. The shipper will assume the first $250 ($500 or $1,000) of any claim whether items are repaired or replaced.

6. *Valuation for national accounts under contract.* Insurance coverage can be a negotiated item when you enter into a contract carriage agreement. You can contract for additional coverage (beyond $0.60/lb.) to be at no additional cost to your company. Many van lines are offering full replacement insurance at no cost for a relatively small volume commitment under contract. This is an excellent option for companies with a small administrative staff that lack the personnel necessary to evaluate and settle claims.


## HOME-PURCHASE PROGRAMS

Appraisers are used extensively in relocation to establish the "most probable sales price" for a relocated employee's home, assuming an arms-length transaction. The ERC states, "Once established, the most probable sales price can be used either as an offer to purchase an employee's home or as a guarantee to protect an employee against loss in selling the home immediately. In most instances, two or three appraisals are ordered for each home, with a pre-established variance allowed between values before additional appraisals are ordered."

The relocation policies of most companies apply clear guidelines as to which properties are eligible for their home-purchase programs. Those homes usually included in a company's policy are single-family dwellings that are on land of customary lot size and that are the primary residences of employees at the time of transfer (includes condominiums and townhouses).

Other properties may be included in a home-purchase program, but usually they are treated as exceptions. Among these kinds of properties are duplexes, mobile homes, cooperative housing, and properties with excess acreage. Income or investment property and vacation property are generally excluded by a relocation policy.

The ERC gives the following advice as to eligibility: "A standard methodology has been established for calculating the market value based on independently obtained appraisals. The procedure is to obtain two written appraisals for the specified property, the reports to be received within approximately 10 days of the order. These appraisals are reviewed for thoroughness, accuracy, similarities, and differences. Appraisers may employ slightly different methods for arriving at the appraised value, but are nonetheless expected to conform to standard appraising principles and practices. The appraisals will be used to determine the market value, provided they are within a specific percent variance of one another. The average of the appraisals becomes the market value offer extended to the homeowner. In those cases where the variance between appraisals is greater than the allowed tolerance, a third appraisal is usually ordered. Market value then may be based on an average of all three appraisals, on the two closest appraisals, or on some other configuration specified in the individual company's relocation policy."

Appraisals serve a dual purpose. They are indicators of the eventual expense the company will incur in the purchase and disposition of the home, and they are evidence, to most employees, of the degree of concern and fairness shown to them during their transfer.

As a basis for a company's relocation expense, appraisals offer the first indication of the value of the home, the market conditions under which it must be sold, and the condition of the home and its environs. An accurate appraisal allows a company to obtain a working idea of the eventual expense of handling the employee's home. At best, even the most accurate appraisal can provide only an estimate of the home disposition costs, but accuracy is nonetheless essential because an accurate appraisal report with accompanying recommendations and analysis will allow a company to formulate an effective marketing strategy.

No appraiser can be 100 percent accurate. Each kind of mistake in an appraisal has its own consequences. An appraisal that overestimates the value of a property will result in a windfall to the employee, which translates into a loss to the company when the house is sold. Conversely, low appraisals will greatly upset the transferring employee. Relocation assistance is intended as an employee benefit, and all parties agree that every reasonable effort should be made to provide the transferred employee with an equitable offer for the home. The offer based on below-market-value appraisals is likely to be refused. The employee then markets the home through a local broker, secures a buyer who is willing to pay a higher price, and either assigns the sale to the relocation management firm for closing or sells the home independently and submits to the company for reimbursement.

Accurate appraisals are good indicators of the success of a relocation program. Each appraisal, individually, is an estimate and appreciation. What really matters is the aggregate accuracy of appraisals over time. The ERC gives the following advice on what appraisals should reflect:

1. Minimized variance with respect to appraisals of individual properties.
2. Minimal (3 to 5 percent) variance between appraised value and sales price, for regular, assigned sale, and amended value transactions.
3. A reasonable percentage (approximately 35 percent) of all offers bettered by employees, taking into consideration the quality of the market and the average amount by which the employee betters the offer.

## REAL ESTATE SALES ASSISTANCE

Over the past twenty years four major types of real estate sales assistance programs have evolved. The ERC describes them as follows:

1. *Third-party purchase.* The company employs an outside service company to purchase and sell the employee's home.
2. *In-house purchase program.* The company actually purchases the relocated employee's home at market value, and then resells the home.

3. *Guaranteed-against-loss plan.* This program does not involve an offer to purchase the residence. The company guarantees a value, based upon appraisals, that the transferee can depend upon to net from the sale, less the outstanding mortgage that may exist. The company usually pays the selling expenses.

4. *Direct reimbursement plan.* This plan does not provide for home purchase or a guaranteed value. The employee is responsible for the sale and the company reimburses some or all of the selling expenses.

## ASSISTANCE FOR RENTERS

Until now the discussion has revolved around homeowners; however, renters also face relocation problems that need assistance. These problems include breaking leases, choosing the new apartment, paying security deposits, signing leases, paying finder's fees, and sometimes higher rent.

The ERC comments that in the past, it was accepted practice to insert a transfer clause in a lease to avoid a lease-breaking penalty. Today, with the high demand for apartment rentals and limited availability in some parts of the country, leasing agreements exclude this clause and a lease-breaking penalty for the full term of the agreement may be incurred. Standard reimbursement for the majority of companies generally does not exceed three months' rent. Payment for exceptions beyond three months may require negotiation among the company, the employee, and the rental agency or owner.

## HOUSE-HUNTING, TRAVEL, TEMPORARY LIVING, AND RETURN VISITATION TRIPS

Prior to the house-hunting trip, the employee should be contacted by a home-finding specialist (either an independent or a relocation director of a local broker) to discuss housing needs and concerns. Issues to be discussed should include: required home size; affordability based on equity and current interest rates;

maximum acceptable commuting time to and from the office; educational concerns (both traditional and special); and any other concerns. By focusing on wants, needs, hopes, and finances, the employee will be more prepared for the house-hunting trip, and the home-finding specialist will be able to focus on these needs in planning area tours and in helping the employee in the home selection process.

In order to facilitate this process, the ERC has accumulated a directory that is of invaluable assistance to the travel manager who helps coordinate these activities.

It is in this area that the travel manager should work closely with the relocation specialist, making sure the employee books relocation fares and stays in hotels that are more suited to long-term stays. Temporary living arrangements are important for a number of reasons. According to the ERC, there are generally four reasons for a gap between the employee's starting date on the job and the family's arrival date for the move into the new house.

The most common reason for the delay is that the new residence is not ready for occupancy. In most parts of the country, there is a 30- to 60-day gap between the offer to purchase the home and the settlement or escrow date.

Other reasons relate to management's need for the employee to start the job as soon as possible; an employed spouse who has a contract commitment in the old location; and the parents' decision to delay the move until the end of the school year.

## DESTINATION SERVICES

The ERC states, "In recent years, more emphasis has been placed on the relocation services offered at the transferee's new location. This type of assistance, often referred to as destination services, includes: prepurchase appraisals, job placement assistance, area counseling, and mortgage counseling."

The concept of destination services is an outgrowth of the home-finding assistance programs of the 1970s. These programs, while helpful, often placed too much emphasis on the referral aspect rather than providing a real service. The concern of major employers that their relocating employees were buying blind prompted the development of a variety of services to take away many of the uncertainties of buying for the employee and assuring a better move in the future for the company.

## NEW HIRES

The ERC maintains, "A new hire can be subjected to a greater level of stress than a transferred employee. He or she really does not know the company, supervisor or peers, and may have some apprehensions about whether the right decision was made in joining the firm. In addition to these job-related concerns, the new employee usually experiences some apprehension about the new location and how the family will react to the relocation and the new community."

Relocation coverage typically provided to new hires historically has lagged behind that which is offered to transferred employees. This philosophy is not surprising as corporations feel a greater obligation to existing employees being asked to relocate at the company's convenience.

This is changing as competition and other forces are causing corporations to offer new hires relocation coverage equivalent to that of existing employees.

The ERC states, "As a result, the bare-bones coverage prevalent in the past has given way to more complete coverage approaching, if not equal to, that provided to existing employees. There is, of course, significant variation among programs offered; certainly company size and geographic location, along with management philosophy pertaining to benefit programs, influence variations in coverage."

## GROUP MOVES

A group move is the relocation of a significant number of employees, as a group, on a planned and scheduled basis. The ERC maintains that managing group moves is vastly different from managing individual moves. Four reasons are given for this belief:

1. Group moves nearly always involve relocating with one's old job, or at least to a similar job at the same level, while individual relocations typically are promotions.

2. Group moves frequently raise serious questions of job security—you either move or you look for another job.

3. Group moves often jar an entire community and the real estate market at both the departure and destination points.

4. Group moves are characterized by a kind of group dynamic in which employee fears and concerns can be magnified by a process of increasing reverberation within the group.

## TRAVEL MANAGEMENT TIPS

- There is a growing trend among large corporations to consolidate relocation matters under one department. However, in many smaller and medium-sized companies, the travel manager is often called upon to handle relocation.

- Relocation policy must be clear and concise to let the transferee know what to expect. This means stating or listing what is allowed and not allowed to be moved at company expense.

- The trend is for a company to request a pre-move survey by the carrier, resulting in an estimate of the cost.

- Appraisers are used extensively in relocation to establish the "most probable sales price" for a relocated employee's home.

- Once established, the most probable sales price can be used as a guarantee to protect an employee against loss in selling the home immediately.

- Renters face relocation problems that need assistance. These problems include breaking leases, choosing the new apartment, paying security deposits, signing leases, paying finder's fees, and sometimes higher rent.

- Prior to the house-hunting trip, the employee should be contacted by a home-finding specialist.

# Index

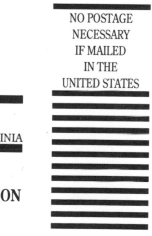

## DISCOVER THE NATIONAL BUSINESS TRAVEL ASSOCIATION

for the Industry Advantage

- ✓ Annual Convention & Exposition
- ✓ Chapter Affiliation
- ✓ Legislative Affairs

- ✓ Professional Certification
- ✓ Mailing Lists
- ✓ and much more!

❏ Please send me information about NBTA.

Name _____

Title _____

Company _____

Address _____

City _____ State/Province _____

Zip/Postal Code _____ County _____